Y0-BZI-235

Dear NFT User:

What you are holding in your hot little hands is a comprehensive user's guide to the City of Brotherly Love. Known all over the world as the birthplace of America, Philly has many historic guidebooks, but none as unique as this one. Containing thousands of listings, hundreds of descriptions, and dozens of maps, it's designed so you, the loyal denizens of the city, can benefit from all this nutty town has to offer—and get the straight dope besides.

To natives, Philly feels like the best-kept secret of the Northeast. Here, you have all the expected benefits of a huge metropolitan center (at last check, the fifth largest in the country) -- including amazing museums, a world class orchestra, theater and film possibilities galore and several major universities -- while still offering relatively affordable housing and a wealth of fascinating, integrated neighborhoods. And the food? Fuggeddaboutit. You could eat out every day and night for a year and still not experience all of the culinary delights the city has to offer.

In order to maximize its usefulness, this book has been pressure cooked into a dynamite little package, small enough to take with you in a purse or backpack, yet big enough to hold an amazing amount of info. But don't just take our word for it—take it for a test spin and see for yourself.

In any event, this is our first edition of NFT Philly, which means if we're missing anything, we encourage you to tell us about it. As always, we're interested in your favorite haunts as well as more of Philly's weird and notable landmarks. Any additions or comments can be emailed to us through our website: www.notfortourists.com.

Yo, enjoy.

Piers, Rob, Diana & Jane

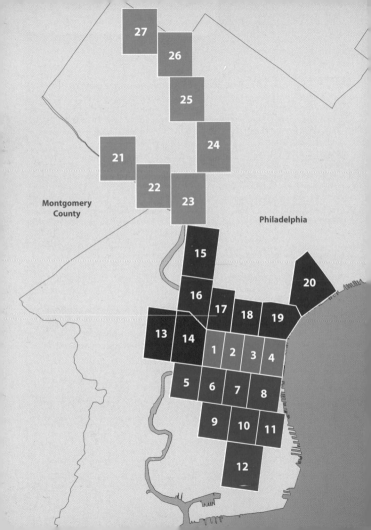

Not For Tourists Guide to **PHILADELPHIA**

Not For Tourists, Inc

2005-2006

published and designed by:
Not For Tourists, Inc
NFT~TM~**—Not For Tourists**~TM~ **Guide to Philadelphia 2005-2006**
www.notfortourists.com

Publisher & Editor
Jane Pirone

Information Design
Jane Pirone
Rob Tallia
Scot Covey
Diana Pizzari

Managing Editors
Rob Tallia
Diana Pizzari

City Editor
Piers Marchant

Writing and Editing
Ozzilyn Bean
Cathleen Cueto
Joseph Ferraro
Piers Marchant
Diana Pizzari
Rob Tallia

Research
Ben Bray
Erin Kreindler

Editorial Interns
Amanda Fortier
Annie Karni
Tim O'Keefe
Jennifer Spelkoman

Research Interns
Bri Kapellas
Orsiola Mehmeti

Database Design
Scot Covey

**Graphic Design/
Production**
Scot Covey
Ran Lee
Christopher Salyers

Graphic Design Interns
Ola Kapusto
Mike Ross
Danielle Young

Contributors
Erik Brooks
Alli Hirschman
Annie Holt
Paul Mazurek
Iya C. Perry

Printed in China
ISBN# 0-9758664-2-7 $14.95

Every effort has been made to ensure that the information in this book is as up-to-date as possible at press time. However, many details are liable to change—as we have learned. The publishers cannot accept responsibility for any consequences arising from use of this book.

Not For Tourists does not solicit individuals, organizations, or businesses for listings inclusion in our guides, nor do we accept payment for inclusion into the editorial portion of our book; the advertising sections, however, are exempt from this policy. We always welcome communications from anyone regarding ANYTHING having to do with our books; please visit us on our website at www.notfortourists.com for appropriate contact information.

Table of Contents

Map 1 · **Center City West**

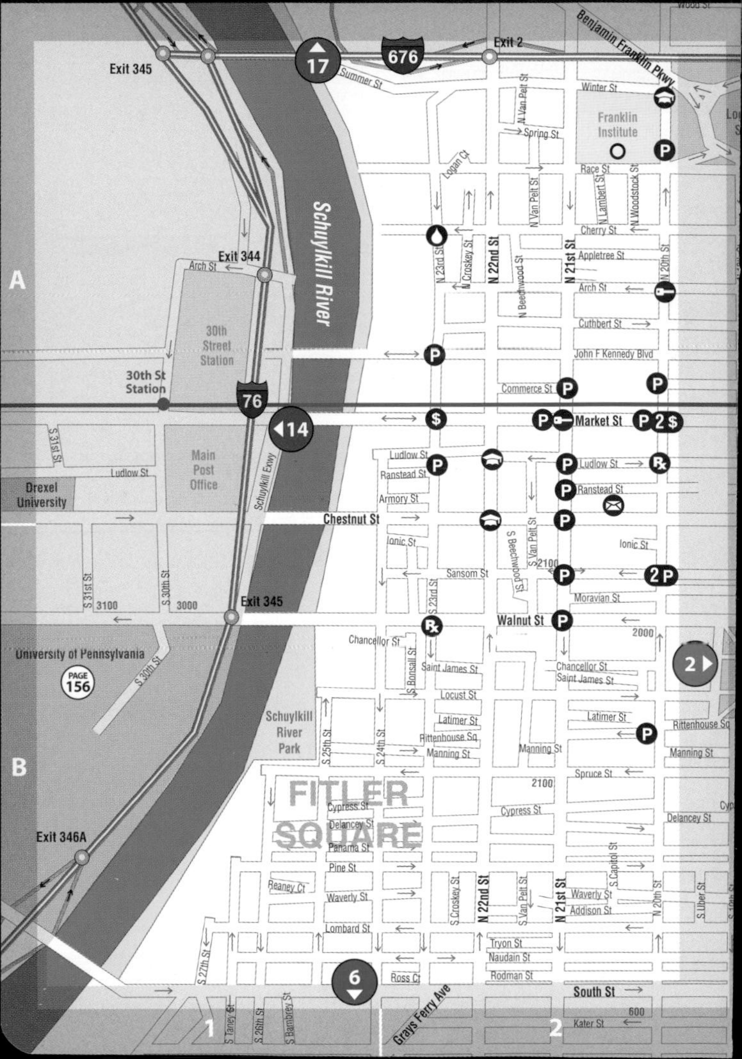

N

Benjamin Franklin Pkwy

Wood St

Exit 345

676

Exit 2

17

Summer St

Winter St

Franklin Institute

Logan Ct

N Van Pelt St

Spring St

Race St

W Lambert St

N Woodstock St

P

Exit 344

Arch St

Schuylkill River

Cherry St

Appletree St

Crosley St

N 23rd St

N 22nd St

N 21st St

N 20th St

A

Arch St

30th Street Station

N Beechwood St

Cuthbert St

John F Kennedy Blvd

30th St Station

76

Commerce St

P

P

14

S 31st St

Market St

P

2

$

$

Drexel University

Main Post Office

Ludlow St

Ludlow St

Rx

S 33rd St

Ludlow St

Ranstead St

P

Ranstead St

Armory St

P

Chestnut St

Ionic St

S Beechwood St

P

Ionic St

S 31st St

3100

S 30th St

3000

Sansom St

S 22nd St

2100

P

2

P

Exit 345

Moravian St

Chancellor St

Rx

Walnut St

P

2000

University of Pennsylvania

PAGE 156

S 30th St

Bonsall St

Saint James St

S 25th St

Chancellor St

Saint James St

2

B

Locust St

Rittenhouse Sq

Schuylkill River Park

Latimer St

Manning St

S 24th St

Rittenhouse Sq

Latimer St

P

Manning St

Manning St

Spruce St

Exit 346A

FITLER SQUARE

Cypress St

2100

Cypress St

Delancey St

Panama St

Pine St

Reaney Ct

S 22nd St

Waverly St

N Crosley St

N Van Pelt St

N 22nd St

Waverly St

Addison St

N 20th St

S Colville St

Lombard St

Tryon St

Naudain St

S 28th St

S 26th St

S Bambrey St

Ross Ct

Rodman St

6

South St

600

1

Grays Ferry Ave

2

Kater St

A cozy neighborhood with Penn students commingling with successful professionals and other blue bloods. The River Park is an under-utilized gem with a great dog park and plenty of other recreational opportunities. Fitler Square remains the crown jewel of the area, but there are plenty of other luxurious haunts if you have the portfolio.

$ Banks

· **Citizens Bank** · 2001 Market St
· **First Penn Bank** · 2301 Market St
· **Sovereign Bank** · 2000 Market St

Car Rental

· **Avis** · 2000 Arch St
· **Budget** · 2101 Market St

Car Washes

· **Executive Auto Care** · 117 N 23rd St

O Landmarks

· **The Franklin Institute** · 222 N 20th St

P Parking

Rx Pharmacies

· **Doctor's Pharmacy** · 17 S 20th St
· **Rite-Aid** (24 hrs) · 2301 Walnut St

Post Offices

· **Middle City Station** · 2037 Chestnut St

Schools

· **The College of Physicians of Philadelphia** ·
  19 S 22nd St
· **Greenfield** · 2200 Chestnut St
· **Moore College of Art & Design** ·
  20th St & Benjamin Franklin Pkwy

Map 1 • **Center City West**

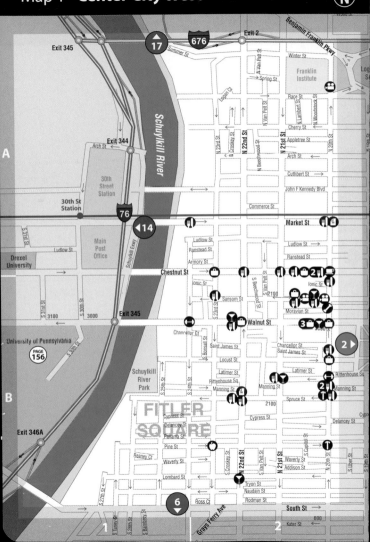

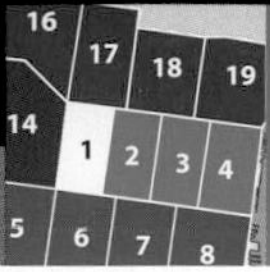

Sundries / Entertainment

Home of Doobie's, one of the best dive bars in CC, the area is also flush with great chow (Audrey Claire, Friday Saturday Sunday, Bistro St. Tropez, to name a few) and rollicking night life. The Roxy is good place to catch a limited-release flick, as long as you can stand the super-uncomfortable seats. IMAX rules.

Map 1

Coffee
· **Dunkin' Donuts** · 2001 Chestnut St

Copy Shops
· **FedEx Kinko's** (24 hrs) · 2001 Market St
· **Ridgeway's** · 261 S 22nd St

Farmer's Markets
· **Fitler Square** · S 23rd St & Pine St

Gyms
· **Rittenhouse Square Fitness Club** ·
  2002 Rittenhouse Sq
· **Sweat** · 200 S 24th St

Hardware Stores
· **Lee's Hardware** · 266 S 20th St
· **Rittenhouse Hardware** · 2001 Pine St

Movie Theaters
· **Adonis Theater** · 2026 Sansom St
· **Roxy Theatre Philadelphia** · 2023 Sansom St
· **Tuttleman IMAX Theater Franklin Institute** ·
  222 N 20th St

Nightlife
· **Cibucan** · 2025 Sansom St
· **Doobie's** · 2201 Lombard St
· **Irish Pub** · 2007 Walnut St
· **Roosevelt Pub** · 2222 Walnut St
· **Tank Bar** · 261 S 21st St

Pet Shops
· **Rittenhouse Square Pet Supplies** · 135 S 20th St

Restaurants
· **Amara Café** · 105 S 22nd St
· **Audrey Claire** · 276 S 20th St
· **Bistro St Tropez** · 2400 Market St, 4th Fl
· **Cibucan** · 2025 Sansom St
· **Erawan Thai Cuisine** · 123 S 23rd St
· **Friday Saturday Sunday** · 261 S 21st St
· **Fuji Mountain** · 2030 Chestnut St
· **Mama Palma's** · 2229 Spruce St
· **Marathon Grill** · 2001 Market St
· **Melograno** · 2201 Spruce St
· **Midtown IV** · 2013 Chestnut St
· **Porcini** · 2048 Sansom St
· **Primo Hoagies** · 2043 Chestnut St
· **Roosevelt Pub** · 2222 Walnut St
· **Salt** · 253 S 20th St
· **Sushi on the Square** · 255 S 20th St
· **Tampopo** · 104 S 21st St
· **Twenty Manning** · 261 S 20th St
· **XO Kitchen** · 106 S 20th St

Shopping
· **Bilt Well Furniture Showroom** · 2317 Chestnut St
· **Body Klinic** · 2012 Walnut St
· **Chaos Hair Studio** · 2032 Chestnut St
· **Classical Guitar Store** · 2038 Sansom St
· **Dahlia** · 2003 Walnut St
· **Julius Scissor** · 2045 Locust St
· **Pleasure Chest** · 2039 Walnut St
· **Springboard Media** · 2212 Walnut St
· **Wonderland** · 2037 Walnut St

Map 2 · **Rittenhouse / Logan Circle**

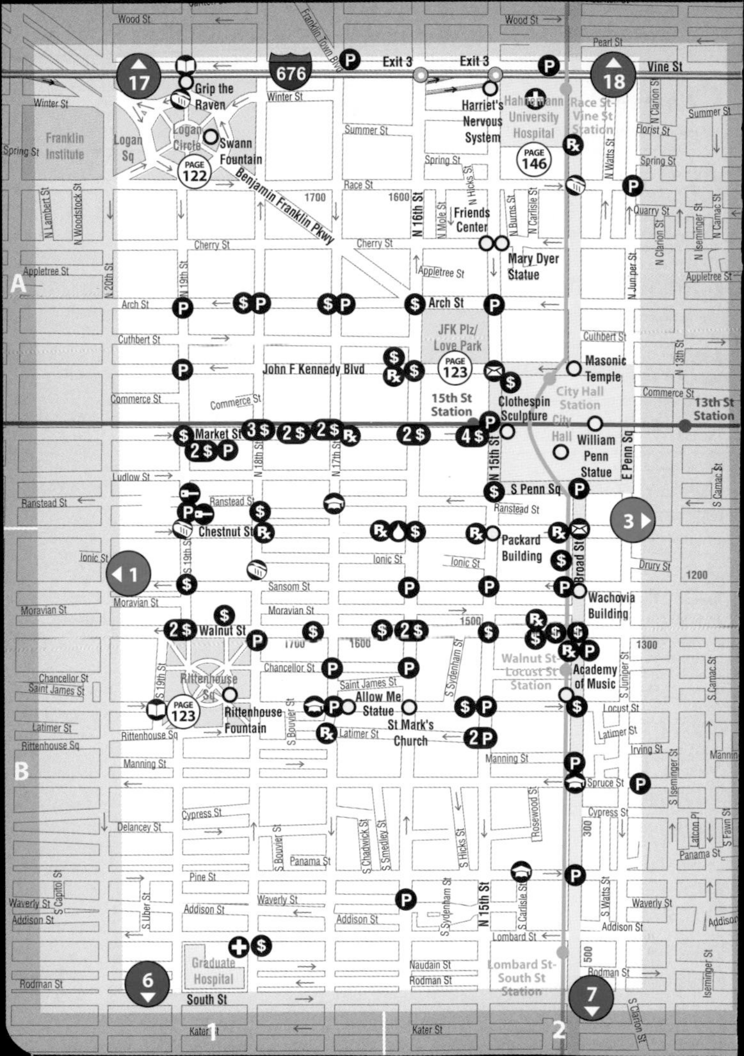

N

Wood St

Wood St

Pearl St

17

Vine St

18

Winter St

676

Exit 3

Exit 3

Vine St

Franklin Institute

Winter St

Grip the Raven

Summer St

Harriet's Nervous System

Hahnemann University Hospital

Race St–Vine St Station

Summer St

Florist St

Logan Sq

Logan Circle

PAGE 122

Swann Fountain

Spring St

Spring St

Rx

Spring St

Spring St

Benjamin Franklin Pkwy

1700

1600

Race St

Friends Center

N Carlisle St

N Juniper St

Quarry St

N 15th St

N 16th St

N Mole St

N Burns St

N Clarion St

N Camac St

Cherry St

Cherry St

Mary Dyer Statue

Appletree St

Appletree St

Appletree St

A

Arch St

$

P

$

P

$

Arch St

P

JFK Plz/ Love Park

PAGE 123

Masonic Temple

Cuthbert St

Cuthbert St

Commerce St

13th St Station

John F Kennedy Blvd

$

Rx

15th St Station

$

City Hall Station

N 20th St

N 19th St

N 18th St

N 17th St

Clothespin Sculpture

City Hall

Commerce St

Commerce St

Market St

$

$ 3

2 $

2 $

Rx

2 $

4 $

N 15th St

William Penn Statue

E Penn Sq

13th St Station

2 $

P

Ludlow St

Ranstead St

S Penn Sq

E Camac St

Ranstead St

S 19th St

S 18th St

S 17th St

P

Chestnut St

Rx

Ranstead St

Packard Building

Broad St

Drury St

1200

Ionic St

Rx

Ionic St

Ionic St

Wachovia Building

3

Moravian St

1

Moravian St

Sansom St

1700

1600

1500

Walnut St–Locust St Station

Walnut St

2 $

Walnut St

P

$

2 $

Rx

$

Academy of Music

S Juniper St

S Camac St

1300

Chancellor St

Chancellor St

Saint James St

S Sydenham St

$

Locust St

Saint James St

Chancellor St

Rittenhouse Sq

PAGE 123

Allow Me Statue

Locust St

B

Latimer St

Saint James St

Rittenhouse Fountain

Rx

St Mark's Church

2 P

Irving St

Rittenhouse Sq

S Bouvier St

Latimer St

Latimer St

Rittenhouse St

Manning St

Manning St

Spruce St

P

Delancey St

Cypress St

Cypress St

S Clarion St

S Camac St

S Perth St

Panama St

Pine St

S Chadwick St

S Smedley St

S Hicks St

Rosewood St

300

Panama St

Waverly St

Addison St

Waverly St

Addison St

S Sydenham St

N 15th St

S Carlisle St

S Watts St

Waverly St

Addison St

Addison St

6

Graduate Hospital

$

Naudain St

Rodman St

Lombard St– South St Station

500

Rodman St

7

South St

Kater St

Kater St

2

Philly's answer to 90210 is filled to brimming with uber-professionals, other Type A's ,and B's galore. It also happens to be one of the more telegenic areas—housing the eponymous Rittenhouse Square (easily the most beautiful of the four in CC), as well as numerous restaurants, clubs, and super-swank hotels.

$ Banks

- **Beneficial Savings** · 1600 Chestnut St
- **Citizens Bank** · 1417 Walnut St
- **Citizens Bank** · 1515 Market St
- **Citizens Bank** · 1735 Market St
- **Commerce Bank** · 121 S Broad St
- **Commerce Bank** · 15th St & John F Kennedy Blvd
- **Commerce Bank** · 1726 Walnut St
- **Commerce Bank** · 1900 Market St
- **First Penn Bank** · 11 Penn Ctr
- **First Penn Bank** · 1632 Walnut St
- **First Penn Bank** · 1835 Market St
- **Firstrust** · 1515 Market St
- **Firstrust** · 1901 Walnut St
- **Fleet** · 1428 Walnut St
- **Fleet** · 1600 John F Kennedy Blvd
- **Fleet** · 1818 Market St
- **Hudson United** · 1607 Walnut St
- **Hudson United** · 1845 Walnut St
- **Hudson United** · 31 S 18th St
- **Hudson United** · N 18th St & Arch St
- **Mellon** · 1735 Market St
- **National Penn Bank** · 161 / John F Kennedy Blvd
- **NOVA Savings** · 1535 Locust St
- **NOVA Savings** · 200 S Broad St
- **Philadelphia Federal Credit Union** · 1600 Arch St
- **PNC** · 1511 Walnut St
- **PNC** · 1600 Market St
- **PNC** · 1001 Market St
- **PNC** · 19th St & Walnut St
- **PNC** · 230 S Broad St
- **Prudential Savings** · 112 S 19th St
- **Republic First** · 1601 Market St
- **Republic First** · 1601 Walnut St
- **Republic First** · 1800 Lombard St
- **Royal Bank** · 30 S 15th St
- **Sovereign Bank** · 1500 Market St
- **Sovereign Bank** · 1717 Arch St
- **Sun Federal** · 1801 Market St
- **Sun National** · 1701 Market St
- **Wachovia** · 1500 Market St
- **Wachovia** · 1700 Market St

Car Rental

- **Hertz** · 31 S 19th St
- **National** · 36 S 19th St

Car Washes

- **Preston's Auto Handwash & Detail** · 1625 Chestnut St

Cheesesteaks

- **Dolce Carlini** · 1929 Chestnut St
- **Jake's Pizza** · 201 N Broad St
- **Swann Lounge at Four Seasons** · 1 Logan Sq
- **Tony Luke Jr's Old Philly Style Sandwiches** · 118 S 18th St

+ Hospitals

- **Graduate** · 1800 Lombard St
- **Hahnemann** · Broad St & Vine St

O Landmarks

- **Academy of Music** · Broad & Locust Sts
- **Allow Me Statue** · 17th & Locust Sts
- **City Hall** · Broad St & Market St
- **Clothespin Sculpture** · 15th & Market Sts
- **Friends Center** · 15th & Cherry Sts
- **Grip the Raven** · 1901 Vine St
- **Harriet's Nervous System** · 15th & Vine Sts
- **Love Park** · 15th St & JFK Blvd
- **Mary Dyer Statue** · 15th & Cherry Sts
- **The Masonic Temple** · 1 N Broad St
- **Packard Building** · 15th & Chestnut Sts
- **Rittenhouse Fountain** · b/w 18th & 19th and Locust & Walnut Sts
- **St Mark's Church** · 1625 Locust St
- **Swann Fountain** · Logan Circle
- **Wachovia Building** · Broad & Sansom Sts
- **William Penn Statue (City Hall)** · Broad St & Market St

Libraries

- **Central Library** · 1901 Vine St
- **Philadelphia City Institute** · 1905 Locust St

P Parking

Pharmacies

- **CVS** · 1424 Chestnut St
- **CVS (24 hrs)** · 1826 Chestnut St
- **Eckerd** · 1426 Walnut St
- **Familymeds Pharmacy** · 245 N Broad St
- **Medical Tower Pharmacy** · 255 S 17th St
- **Pickwick Pharmacy** · 1700 Market St
- **Rite-Aid** · 1535 Chestnut St
- **Rite-Aid** · 1628 Chestnut St
- **Rite-Aid** · 215 S Broad St
- **Walgreens** · 1617 John F Kennedy Blvd

Post Offices

- **Land Title Bldg Station** · 100 S Broad St
- **Penn Center Station** · 1500 John F Kennedy Blvd

Schools

- **Peirce College** · 1420 Pine St
- **The Curtis Institute of Music** · 1726 Locust St
- **University of Phoenix - Center City Campus** · 30 S 17th St
- **University of the Arts** · 320 S Broad St

Map 2 · **Rittenhouse / Logan Circle**

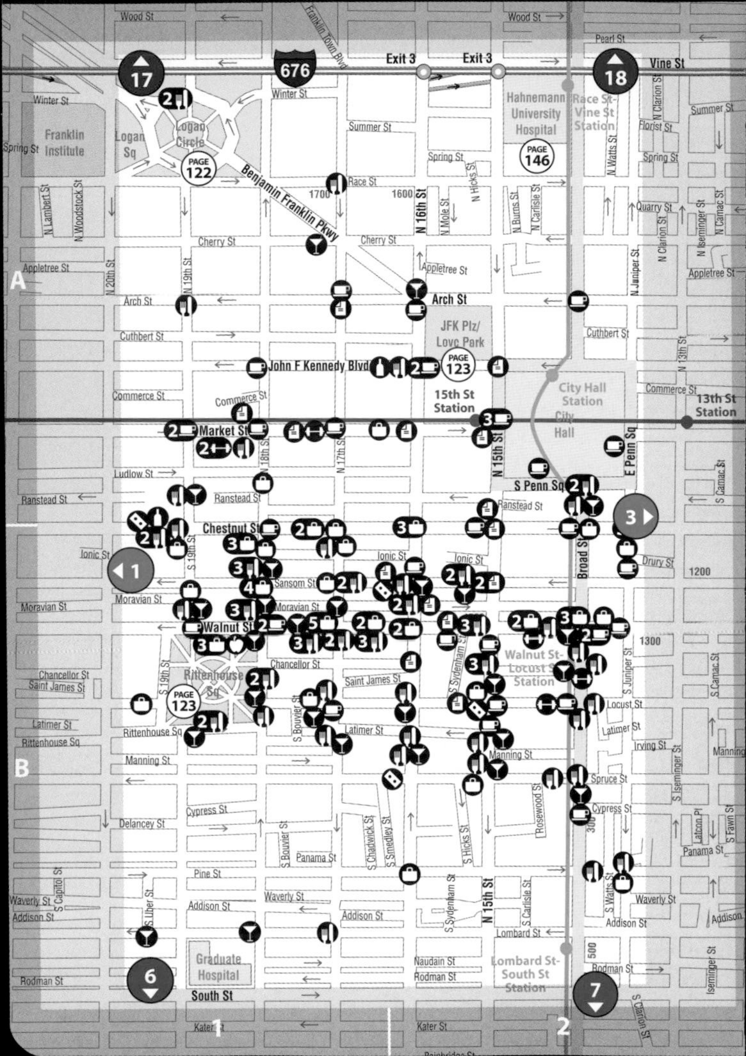

N

Wood St

Wood St

Pearl St

Franklin Town Blvd

676

Exit 3   Exit 3

Vine St

17

18

2

Winter St

Winter St

Hahnemann
University
Hospital

PAGE
146

Race St-
Vine St
Station

Summer St

Spring St

Logan
Sq

Logan
Circle

Summer St

Florist St

Spring St

Spring St

N Clarion St

N Juniper St

N Watts St

Quarry St

N Reminger St

N Camac St

Franklin
Institute

PAGE
122

Benjamin Franklin Pkwy

1700

Race St

1600

N 16th St

N Mole St

N Burns St

N Hicks St

N Carlisle St

Cherry St

Cherry St

Cherry St

N Clarion St

Appletree St

N Lambert St

N Woodstock St

N 20th St

N 19th St

Arch St

Arch St

Arch St

N 13th St

A

Cuthbert St

Cuthbert St

JFK Plz/
Love Park

Cuthbert St

PAGE
123

City Hall
Station
City
Hall

13th St
Station

John F Kennedy Blvd

2

15th St
Station

Commerce St

Commerce St

Commerce St

N 17th St

E Penn Sq

N Camac St

2

Market St

2

N 15th St

3

S Penn Sq

3

3

Ludlow St

Ludlow St

Ranstead St

N 13th St

Ranstead St

Ranstead St

Broad St

Drury St

1200

Ionic St

1

8

Chestnut St

2

3

Ionic St

Ionic St

3

3

2

2

Moravian St

Sansom St

2

1

Moravian St

2

3

2

2

1300

Walnut St

3

3

2

2

2

Walnut St
Locust St
Station

Chancellor St

Chancellor St

Saint James St

Saint James St

S Juniper St

S Camac St

Rittenhouse
St

PAGE
123

2

S 18th St

S Bouvier St

Latimer St

Latimer St

Locust St

S Sydenham St

Irving St

Latimer St

Chancellor St
Saint James St

2

Rittenhouse Sq

Manning St

Spruce St

S Iseminger St

S Camac St

Manning

B

Manning St

Delancey St

Cypress St

8

Cypress St

Cypress St

S Watts St

Panama St

Panama St

S 19th St

S Chadwick St

S Smedley St

S Hicks St

Thisewood St

S Carlisle St

Waverly St

Pine St

Pine St

Waverly St

Addison St

Addison St

Addison St

Waverly St

Addison

S Capitol St

S Iseminger St

Waverly St
Addison St

S 19th St

S Sydenham St

500

6

Graduate
Hospital

Naudain St

Rodman St

Lombard St-
South St
Station

Rodman St

7

Rodman St

South St

Kater St

Kater St

2

Map 2

Famed restaurant row on Walnut offers some of Philly's finest culinary experiences, including posh French (Le Bec-Fin), stylish pan-Asian (Susanna Foo), and absolutely top-notch pizza (Joe's). There are also a fine selection of shopping boutiques (Ann Taylor, Halloween), classy bars (Bar Noir, Happy Rooster), and more decent coffee joints than you could name.

Coffee

- Amazon Café • 1500 Market St
- Amazon Café • 1800 Chestnut St
- Amazon Café • 1900 Market St
- Amazon Café • 200 S Broad St
- Capriccio's Café • 1701 Locust St
- Cool Beans • 121 S Juniper St
- Cosi • 140 S 11th St
- Cosi • 201 S 18th St
- Cosi • 235 S 15th St
- Dunkin' Donuts • 1 E Penn Sq
- Dunkin' Donuts • 100 N 17th St
- Dunkin' Donuts • 101 N Broad St
- Dunkin' Donuts • 117 S 16th St
- Dunkin' Donuts • 1324 Walnut St
- Dunkin' Donuts • 1500 Market St
- Dunkin' Donuts • 1507 Chestnut St
- Hausbrandt • 207 S 15th St
- La Colombe Panini • 130 S 19th St
- Metro Café • 100 S Broad St
- Mums & Pops Café • 1 S Penn Sq
- Passero Gourmet Coffee • 1401 Locust St
- Passero's Gourmet Coffee • 1601 John F Kennedy Blvd
- Passero's Gourmet Coffee • 1601 John F Kennedy Blvd, Suburban Station Concourse
- Passero's Gourmet Coffee • 1800 John F Kennedy Blvd
- Starbucks • 1500 Market St
- Starbucks • 1528 Walnut St
- Starbucks • 1600 Arch St
- Starbucks • 1801 Market St
- Starbucks • 1900 Market St
- Starbucks • 200 S Broad St
- Starbucks • 254 S 15th St
- Starbucks • 337 S Broad St
- Yann's Pastries & Café • 122 S 18th St

Copy Shops

- A-C Reproduction & Copy Center • 1510 Sansom St
- Can Do Service Center • 1530 Locust St
- Conant • 425 15th St, 9th Fl
- Copy Cat Printers • 1506 Sansom St
- FedEx Kinko's • 216 S 16th St
- IKON Document Services • 1760 Market St
- Kelly & Partners • 1500 Market St
- Liberty Quish Print • 2 Penn Centre
- Medical Copy Services • 1601 Market St
- The Printer's Place • 126 S 16th St
- Quality Copy • 100 N 17th St, 2nd Fl
- Reliablecopy Services • 1818 Market St
- Sir Speedy • 1630 Sansom St
- Staples • 1500 Chestnut St
- Taws (24 hrs) • 1527 Walnut St

Farmer's Markets

- Rittenhouse • Walnut St, west of S 18th St

Gyms

- Bally's • 1435 Walnut St
- Philadelphia Sports Club • 1735 Market St
- Shapes • 1420 Locust St
- The Sporting Club at the Bellvue • 220 S Broad St
- West End Athletic Club • 1835 Market St
- Weston Fitness • 1835 Market St

Liquor Stores

- State Liquor Store • 1628 John F Kennedy Blvd
- State Liquor Store • 1913 Chestnut St

Nightlife

- Bar Noir • 112 S 18th St
- The Black Sheep • 247 S 17th St
- Bleu • 227 S 18th St
- Boathouse Row Bar • 210 W Rittenhouse Sq
- Cadence • 300 S Broad St
- Chaucer's Tabard Inn • 1946 Lombard St
- Copa Too • 263 S 15th St
- Denim Lounge • 1712 Walnut St
- Good Dog • 224 S 15th St
- Happy Rooster • 118 S 16th St
- Library Lounge at the Bellevue • 1415 Chancellor Ct
- Loie • 128 S 19th St
- Mace's Crossing • 1714 Cherry St
- McGlinchey's • 259 S 15th St
- Monk's Café • 264 S 16th St
- Nodding Head Brewery and Restaurant • 1516 Sansom St
- Paris Bar • 10 Ave of the Arts
- Potcheen • 1735 Locust St
- Redhead Lounge • 135 S 17th St
- Ritz-Carlton Rotunda • 10 S Broad St
- Rouge • 205 S 18th St
- Tangier Café • 1801 Lombard St
- Tequila's Bar • 1602 Locust St
- Tir Na Nog • 1600 Arch St
- Tragos • 40 S 19th St
- Tria • 123 S 18th St
- Zanzibar Blue • 200 S Broad St

Restaurants

- Alma de Cuba • 1623 Walnut St
- Astral Plane • 1708 Lombard St
- Black Sheep Pub • 247 S 17th St
- Bleu • 227 S 18th St
- Brasserie Perrier • 1619 Walnut St
- Buca di Beppo • 258 S 15th St
- Cadence • 300 S Broad St
- Capital Grille • 1338 Chestnut St
- Copa Too • 263 S 15th St
- Davio's • 111 S 17th St
- Denim Lounge • 1717 Walnut St
- Devon Seafood Grill • 225 S 18th St
- Dolce Carini • 1929 Chestnut St
- Fountain Restaurant • 1 Logan Sq
- Genji • 1720 Sansom St
- Good Dog • 224 S 15th St
- The Grill • 10 S Broad St
- Il Portico • 1519 Walnut St
- Joe's Pizza • 122 S 16th St
- La Creperie • 1722 Sansom St
- La Viola • 253 S 16th St
- Lacroix at the Rittenhouse • 210 Rittenhouse Sq
- Le Bec-Fin • 1523 Walnut St
- Le Castagne • 1920 Chestnut St
- Le Cigale • 113 S 18th St
- Lil' Spot • 103 S Juniper St
- Little Pete's • 1904 Chestnut St
- Little Pete's • 219 S 17th St
- Loie • 128 S 19th St
- Lombardi's • 132 S 18th St
- Los Catrines • 1602 Locust St
- Marathon Grill • 121 S 16th St
- Marathon Grill • 1339 Chestnut St
- Marathon Grill • 1617 John F Kennedy Blvd
- Marathon Grill • 1818 Market St
- Matyson • 37 S 19th St
- McCormick & Schmick's • 1 S Broad St
- Miel Patisserie • 204 S 17th St
- Monk's Café • 264 S 16th St
- Morton's • 1411 Walnut St
- Moshi Moshi • 108 S 18th St
- Nodding Head Brewery & Restaurant • 1516 Sansom St, 2nd Fl
- Oasis • 1709 Walnut St
- Paolo's Pizza • 1334 Pine St
- Parkway Diner • 1939 Arch St
- Pasion! • 211 S 15th St
- Pietro's Coal Oven Pizzeria • 1714 Walnut St
- Prime Rib • 1701 Locust St
- Rouge • 205 S 18th St
- Roy's • 124 S 15th St
- Ruth's Chris Steak House • 260 S Broad St
- Sansom Street Oyster House • 1516 Sansom St
- Shiroi Hana • 222 S 15th St
- Shula's Steak House • 201 N 17th St
- Smith & Wollensky • 210 W Rittenhouse Sq
- Sotto Varalli • 231 S Broad St
- Susanna Foo • 1512 Walnut St
- Sushi on the Avenue • 1431 Spruce St
- Swann Lounge • 1 Logan Sq
- Upstares at Varalli • 1345 Locust St
- Valentino • 1328 Pine St
- Wok • 1613 Walnut St
- Yann • 122 S 18th St
- Zanzibar Blue • 200 S Broad St

Shopping

- Adresse • 1600 Pine St
- AIA Bookstore & Design Center • 117 S 17th St
- Ann Taylor • 1713 Walnut St
- Anthropologie • 1801 Walnut St
- Barnes & Noble • 1805 Walnut St
- Benjamin Lovell Shoes • 119 S 18th St
- Benton Method Electrolysis • 1601 Walnut St
- Bon Voyage • 1625 Chestnut St
- Boyd's • 1818 Chestnut St
- Bundy • 1809 Chestnut St
- Burberry's Limited • 1705 Walnut St
- Center City Business Systems • 100 S Juniper St
- City Sports • 1608 Walnut St
- Daffy's • 1700 Chestnut St
- Danielle Scott LTD • 1718 Walnut St
- David Michie Violins • 1714 Locust St
- Estetica • 1736 Chestnut St
- Francis Jerome • 124 S 19th St
- Frankinstein Bike Worx • 1529 Spruce St
- Gentleman's Retreat • 20 S 18th St
- Giovanni & Maggi • 1701 Walnut St
- Halloween • 1329 Pine St
- Hangers • 1953 Locust St
- Hope Chest • 200 S Broad St
- Jacob's Music Pianos • 1718 Chestnut St
- Joseph A Bank Clothiers • 1650 Market St
- Joseph Fox Bookshop • 1724 Sansom St
- Kenneth Cole • 1422 Walnut St
- Knit Wit • 1721 Walnut St
- Lucky Jeans • 1634 Walnut St
- Maron Chocolates • 107 S 18th St
- Motherhood Maternity • 1625 Chestnut St
- Nicole Miller • 200 S Broad St
- Pearl of the East • 1615 Walnut St
- Rittenhouse Camera • 135 S 18th St
- Ritz Camera • 1330 Walnut St
- Robin's Book Store • 1837 Chestnut St
- Sophisticated Seconds • 116 S 18th St
- Stiletto • 124 S 18th St
- TLA • 1520 Locust St
- Tower Records • 100 S Broad St
- Tweeter • 1429 Walnut St
- Urban Outfitters • 1809 Walnut St
- Vigant • 200 S Broad St

Video Rental

- Flick's Video To Go • 1635 Spruce St
- Hollywood Video • 1930 Chestnut St
- TLA Video • 1520 Locust St
- Video Liquidators • 1632 Sansom St

Map 3 • **Center City East**

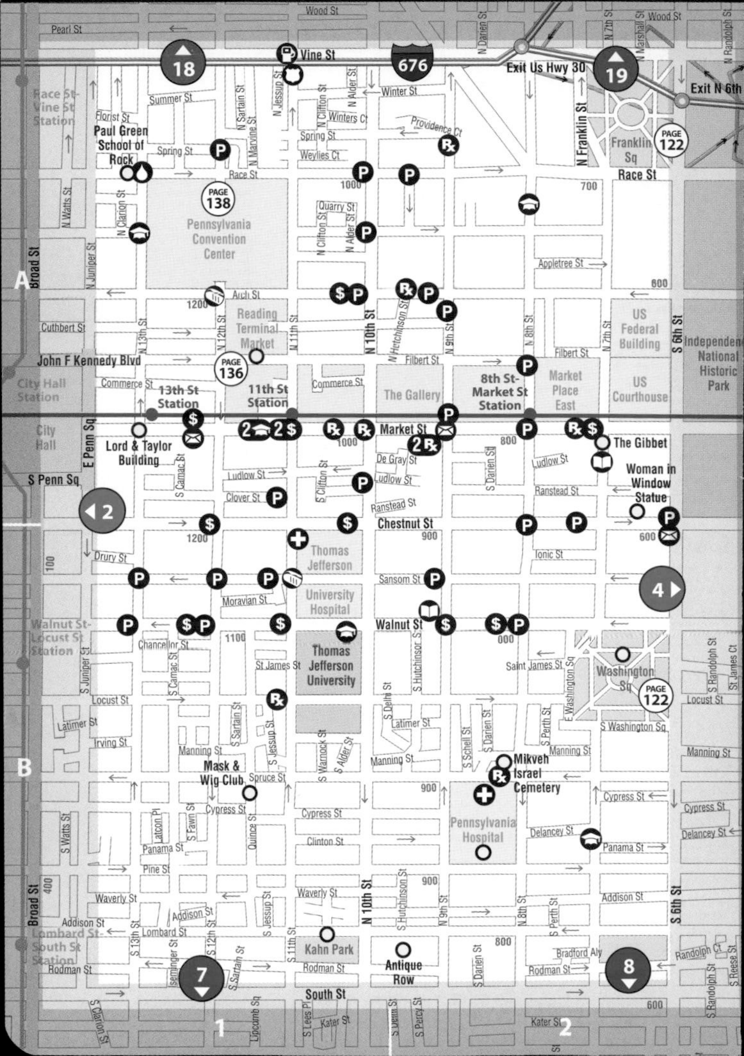

N

Wood St

Pearl St

Vine St
18
676
Exit Us Hwy 30
Exit N 6th
19

N Randolph St
N 2nd St
Wood St

Race-Vine St Station

Summer St
N Jessup St
N Clifton St
Winter St
N Alder St
Providence Ct
N Franklin St
Franklin Sq
PAGE 122

Florist St
Paul Green School of Rock
Spring St
N Clarion St
N Marvine St
Spring Garden
Weylies Ct
Rx
Race St
700

N Watts St
N Juniper St
Quarry St
1000

Broad St

PAGE 138
Pennsylvania Convention Center
N Clifton St
N Alder St
Appletree →

A

Arch St
N 11th St
N 10th St
N Hutchinson St
N 8th St
N 9th St
600

Cuthbert St
$
Rx
US Federal Building
S 6th St

Reading Terminal Market
Filbert St
Filbert St

John F Kennedy Blvd
PAGE 136

City Hall Station
Commerce
13th St Station
11th St Station
Commerce St
The Gallery
8th St-Market St Station
Market Place East
US Courthouse
Independent National Historic Park

City Hall
E Penn Sq
$
Lord & Taylor Building
2 $
Rx
1000
Market St
2 Rx
800
Rx $
The Gibbet

S Penn Sq
S Camac St
De Gray St
Woman in Window Statue

2
Ludlow St
S Clifton St
Ludlow St
Ranstead St
Ranstead St
600

1200
Clover St
Ranstead St
Chestnut St
900
Ionic St
4

$
$
Drury St
Thomas Jefferson University Hospital
Sansom St

P
Moravian St
Walnut St
Walnut St
$ P
000

Walnut St-Locust St Station
S Juniper St
S Camac St
Chancellor St
1100
S James St
Thomas Jefferson University
Saint James St
S Hutchinson St
S Darien St
S Perth St
S Washington Sq
Washington Sq
PAGE 122
Locust St

Latimer St
Irving St
Latimer St
Manning St
S Washington Sq
Manning St

Rx
Manning St
S Warnock St
S Alder St
S Schell St
S Darien St
S Perth St

B

Mask & Wig Club
Spruce St
Mikveh Israel Cemetery
Cypress St →
Cypress St

S Watts St
Cypress St
Latton Pl
S Fawn St
Quince St
900
Pennsylvania Hospital
Delancey St
Panama St →
Panama St

S Juniper St
Panama St
Clinton St

Broad St
400
Waverly St
Waverly St
N 10th St
N 9th St
N 8th St
S 7th St
900
Addison St
Addison St

Lombard St-South St Station
Addison St
Lombard St
S 13th St
S 12th St
S Juniper St
Kahn Park
Antique Row
800
Bradford Aly
Rodman St
S 8th St
S Randolph St

Pine St
Rodman St
7
South St
1
8
Kater St
2
600

Here is the low-key answer to the splash and flash across Broad Street. CC's most prominent gayborhood resides here (roughly from 9th to 13th Streets, between Sansom and Pine Streets), as well as Thomas Jefferson Hospital and its subsidiary schools, centers, and branches. The convention center also looms across Market Street, beckoning marketeers.

$ Banks

- **Citizens Bank** · 1234 Market St
- **Citizens Bank** · 701 Market St
- **Citizens Bank** · 830 Walnut St
- **HSBC** · 1027 Arch St
- **Hudson United** · 1100 Walnut St
- **Philadelphia Federal Credit Union** · 1206 Chestnut St
- **PNC** · 1111 Market St
- **PNC** · 9th & Walnut St
- **Royal Bank** · 1230 Walnut St
- **Sovereign Bank** · 1101 Market St
- **Wachovia** · 1032 Chestnut St

Car Washes

- **Center City Car Wash** · 1308 Race St

Cheesesteaks

- **Philly Style Pizza** · 126 S 11th St
- **Rick's Philly Steaks** · 1136 Arch St

Gas Stations

- **Sunoco** · 1135 Vine St

Hospitals

- **Jefferson** · 111 S 11th St
- **Pennsylvania** · S 8th St & Spruce St

O Landmarks

- **Antique Row** · Pine St b/w 12th & 9th Sts
- **The Gibbet** · 15 S 7th St
- **Kahn Park** · Pine St & 11th St
- **Lord & Taylor Building** · 13th St & Market St
- **Mask & Wig Club** · 310 S Quince St
- **Mikveh Israel Cemetery** · Spruce St b/w 8th & 9th Sts
- **Paul Green School of Rock** · 1320 Race St
- **Pennsylvania Hospital** · 800 Spruce St
- **Reading Terminal Market** · 12th & Arch Sts
- **Washington Square Park** · Walnut St b/w 6th & 7th Sts
- **Woman in Window Statue** · Chestnut St b/w 6th & 7th Sts

Libraries

- **Independence Branch** · 18 S 7th St
- **Library for Blind and Handicapped** · 919 Walnut St

P Parking

Rx Pharmacies

- **Arch Pharmacy** · 933 Arch St
- **CVS** · 1046 Market St
- **Franklin Drug Center** · 829 Spruce St
- **K-Mart** · 901 Market St
- **Neff Surgical Pharmacy** · 222 N 9th St
- **Rite-Aid** · 1000 Market St
- **Rite-Aid** · 730 Market St
- **Statscript Pharmacy** · 1117 Locust St
- **Walgreens** · 901 Market St

Police

- **6th Police District** · 235 N 11th St

Post Offices

- **Continental** · 615 Chestnut St
- **John Wanamaker Station** · 1234 Market St
- **William Penn Annex** · 900 Market St

Schools

- **Hussian School of Art** · 1118 Market St
- **McCall** · 325 S 7th St
- **Pennsylvania Academy of the Fine Arts** · 1301 Cherry St
- **Phila High** · 1118 Market St
- **Temple University School of Podiatric Medicine** · N 8th St b/w Race St & Cherry St
- **Thomas Jefferson University** · 1020 Walnut St

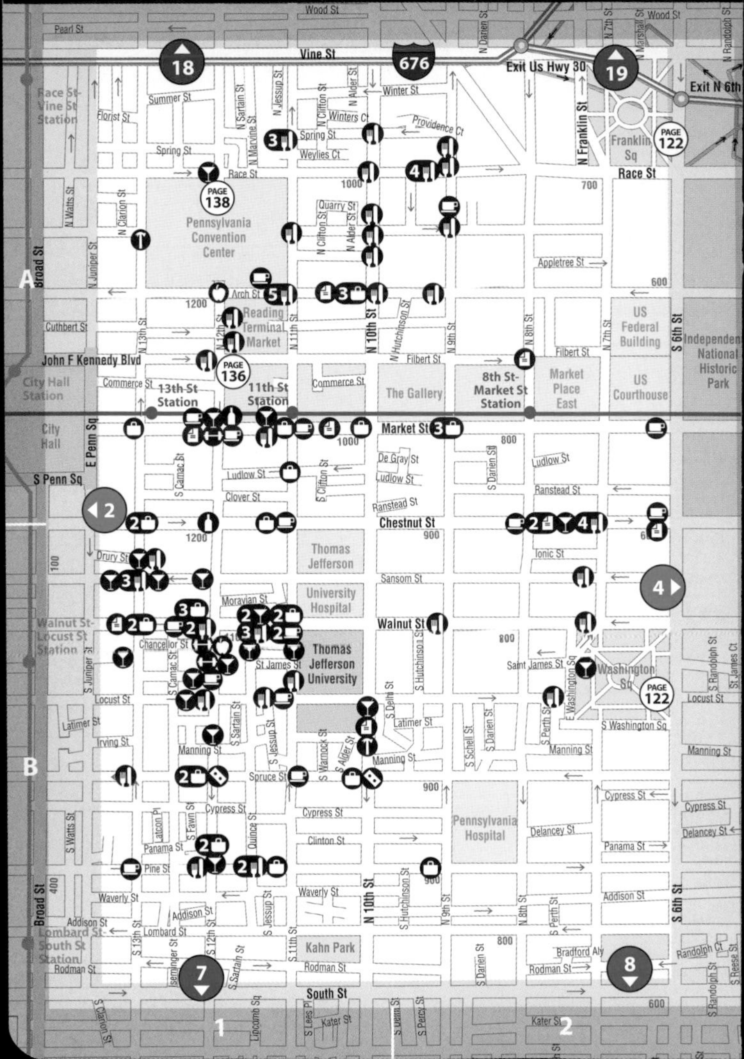

Map 3 · **Center City East**

(N)

Pearl St

Wood St

Vine St

18

676

Exit US Hwy 30

19

Exit N 6th

N Randolph St

N 7th St

N 8th St

N 9th St

Wood St

Florist St

Summer St

N Clarion St

N Juniper St

N 13th St

N Marvine St

N Sartain St

N Jessup St

N Clifton St

N Alder St

Winter St

Spring St

Providence Ct

N Franklin St

Franklin
Sq

PAGE
122

Race St

US
Federal
Building

US
Courthouse

Independence
National
Historic
Park

S 6th St

S 7th St

Spring St

Race St

3

N Watts St

Weylies Ct

4

Quarry St

1000

700

600

Broad St

PAGE
138

Pennsylvania
Convention
Center

Appletree St

Cuthbert St

Arch St

5

3

Reading
Terminal
Market

PAGE
136

Filbert St

8th St-
Market St
Station

Filbert St

Market
Place
East

A

John F Kennedy Blvd

Commerce St

Commerce St

The Gallery

City Hall
Station

13th St
Station

11th St
Station

Market St

3

800

De Gray St

1000

Ludlow St

Ludlow St

Ranstead St

Ranstead St

S Darien St

City
Hall

◀ 2

Ludlow St

Clover St

Chestnut St

900

2 4

Ionic St

6

S Penn Sq

E Penn Sq

100

Drury St

3

1200

Camac St

Clifton St

Thomas
Jefferson
University
Hospital

Sansom St

Walnut St

Saint James St

Washington
Sq

4 ▶

Walnut St-
Locust St
Station

2

Chancellor St

3

3

Moravian St

Thomas
Jefferson
University

S Darien St

S Hutchinson St

S Washington Sq

PAGE
122

Locust St

B

Locust St

S 13th St

Camac St

St James St

S Sartain St

S Jessup St

Irving St

Latimer St

Latimer St

Manning St

Manning St

2

2

Spruce St

Manning St

900

Manning St

S Watts St

Cypress St

Cypress St

Pennsylvania
Hospital

Cypress St

Cypress St

Quince St

Clinton St

Panama St

Panama St

2

Panama Pl

S Juniper St

S 13th St

S 12th St

Pine St

Waverly St

2

Waverly St

N 10th St

N 9th St

S 8th St

Delancey St

Delancey St

Addison St

Addison St

Broad St

400

Lombard St
South St
Station

Addison St

Lombard St

Kahn Park

800

Bradford Aly

Rodman St

S 11th St

Rodman St

S Darien St

S Perth St

Randolph St

7

South St

8

600

Isminger St

Lipincott St

S 13th St

S Juniper St

S 12th St

S 11th St

Kater St

S Darien St

S Perth St

Kater St

1

2

An area with much to recommend itself, including fab restaurants ranging from contemporary classics like Joseph Poon and Morimoto to the all-you-can-eat vegetarian Indian buffet at Samosa. There's also the drab-but-necessary Gallery Mall, the ever-popular Redding Terminal Market for Amish chow, and a growing club scene, especially for the LGBT community.

Coffee

- **Amazon Café** · 11th St & Market St
- **Amazon Café** · 1207 Walnut St
- **Amazon Café** · 615 Chestnut St
- **Cosi** · 1128 Walnut St
- **Dunkin' Donuts** · 1105 Chestnut St
- **Dunkin' Donuts** · 12th St & Market St
- **Dunkin' Donuts** · 634 Market St
- **Dunkin' Donuts** · 808 Chestnut St
- **Joe's Coffee Bar** · 1101 Walnut St
- **Last Drop Coffee House** · 1300 Pine St
- **Mean Bean** · 1112 Locust St
- **Millennium Coffee** · 212 S 12th St
- **Old City Coffee** · 1136 Arch St
- **Ray's Café & Tea House** · 141 N 9th St
- **Starbucks** · 1201 Market St
- **Stellar Coffee** · 11th St & Spruce St

Copy Shops

- **Centennial Philadelphia Blueprint** · 725 Chestnut St
- **Copies Now** · 725 Chestnut St
- **Copy Center** · 615 Chestnut St
- **Creative Characters** · 237 S 10th St
- **FedEx Kinko's (24 hrs)** · 1201 Market St
- **Jack Hathaway Photographer** · 1025 Arch St
- **The Printer's Place** · 1410 Walnut St
- **Sir Speedy** · 47 N 8th St
- **Staples** · 1044 Market St

Farmer's Markets

- **12th & St James Streets** · S 12th St b/w Walnut St & Locust St
- **Reading Terminal Market** · 12th St & Arch St

Gyms

- **12th Street Gym** · 204 S 12th St
- **Balance Spa & Fitness (Lowes Hotel)** · 1200 Market St
- **Club Body Center II** · 1220 Chancellor St

Hardware Stores

- **Buck's Hardware** · 122 N 13th St
- **Washington Square Paint & Hardware** · 257 S 10th St

Liquor Stores

- **State Liquor Store** · 1210 Chestnut St
- **State Liquor Store** · 5 N 12th St

Nightlife

- **12th Air Command** · 254 S 12th St
- **2-4 Club** · 1221 St James St
- **Bike Stop** · 206 S Quince St
- **Bump** · 1234 Locust St
- **Dirty Frank's** · 347 S 13th St
- **Doc Watson's Pub** · 216 S 11th St
- **El Vez** · 121 S 13th St
- **Fergie's Pub** · 1214 Sansom St
- **Hard Rock Cafe** · 1113 Market St
- **The Irish Pub** · 1123 Walnut St
- **Las Vegas Lounge** · 704 Chestnut St
- **Locust Bar** · 235 S 10th St
- **Ludwig's Garten** · 1315 Sansom St
- **McGillan's Old Ale House** · 1310 Drury St
- **Moriarty's Restaurant** · 1116 Walnut St
- **Polly Esther's** · 1201 Race St
- **Pure** · 1221 St James St
- **Sisters** · 1320 Chancellor St
- **Tellers' Bar at PSFS** · 1200 Market St
- **Washington Square** · 210 W Washington Sq
- **Woody's** · 202 S 13th St

Restaurants

- **Angelina** · 706 Chestnut St
- **Aoi** · 1210 Walnut St
- **Basic Four Vegetarian** · 1136 Arch St
- **Bassett's Ice Cream** · 1136 Arch St
- **Blue in Green** · 719 Samsom St
- **Capogiro Gelateria** · 119 S 13th St
- **Caribou Café** · 1126 Walnut St
- **Charles Plaza** · 234 N 10th St
- **Delilah's Southern Café** · 1136 Arch St
- **Deux Cheminees** · 1221 Locust St
- **Down Home Diner** · 51 N 12th St
- **Effie's** · 1127 Pine St
- **El Azteca II** · 714 Chestnut St
- **El Fuego** · 723 Walnut St
- **El Vez** · 121 S 13th St
- **Hard Rock Cafe** · 1113 Market St
- **Harmony Vegetarian** · 135 N 9th St
- **House of Chen** · 932 Race St
- **Imperial Inn** · 146 N 10th St
- **Jones** · 700 Chestnut St
- **Joseph Poon** · 1002 Arch St
- **Kingdom of Vegatarians** · 129 N 11th St
- **La Buca** · 711 Locust St
- **Lakeside Chinese Deli** · 207 N 9th St
- **Lee How Fook** · 219 N 11th St
- **Lolita** · 106 S 13th St
- **Maggiano's Little Italy** · 1201 Filbert St
- **More Than Just Ice Cream** · 1119 Locust St
- **Moriarty's** · 1116 Walnut St
- **Morimoto** · 723 Chestnut St
- **Nan Zhou** · 927 Race St
- **Penang** · 117 N 10th St
- **Pho Xe Lua** · 907 Race St
- **Pine Street Pizza** · 1138 Pine St

- **Pompeii Cucina D'Italia** · 1113 Walnut St
- **Rick's Steaks** · 1136 Arch St
- **Salumeria** · 45 N 12th St
- **Samosa** · 1214 Walnut St
- **Sang Kee Peking Duck House** · 238 N 9th St
- **Santa Fe Burrito Company** · 212 S 11th St
- **Shiao Lan Kung** · 930 Race St
- **Siam Cuisine** · 925 Arch St
- **Singapore Kosher Vegetarian** · 1006 Race St
- **Taco House** · 1218 Pine St
- **Tai Lake** · 134 N 10th St
- **Taste of Thai Garden** · 101 N 11th St
- **Vetri** · 1312 Spruce St
- **Vietnam** · 221 N 11th St
- **Vietnam Palace** · 222 N 11th St
- **Yogi's Eatery** · 929 Walnut St

Shopping

- **After Hours Formalwear** · 1201 Walnut St
- **Aldo Shoes** · 901 Market St
- **Armand Records** · 1100 Chestnut St
- **Beaux Arts Video** · 1000 Spruce St
- **Bike Line** · 1028 Arch St
- **Buffalo Exchange** · 1109 Walnut St
- **Burlington Coat Factory** · 1001 Market St
- **Children's Place** · 901 Market St
- **Claire's Boutique** · 901 Market St
- **Comet Camera Repair** · 1209 Walnut St
- **De Carlo Salon** · 1211 Walnut St
- **Eighth Street Music Center** · 1023 1/2 Arch St
- **Funk O Mart** · 1106 Market St
- **Giovanni's Room** · 345 S 12th St
- **Hibberds Books** · 1306 Walnut St
- **I Goldburg** · 1300 Chestnut St
- **Lord & Taylor** · 1300 Market St
- **Lunacy Antiques** · 1118 Pine St
- **M Finkel & Daughter** · 936 Pine St
- **Mid-City Camera** · 1316 Walnut St
- **Mitchell & Ness** · 1318 Chestnut St
- **Quaker Photo** · 1025 Arch St
- **Rustic Music** · 333 S 13th St
- **School of Hard Knox Barber** · 1105 Walnut St
- **Sound of Market Street** · 15 S 11th St
- **Spruce Street Video** · 1201 Walnut St
- **Uhuru** · 1220 Spruce St

Video Rental

- **Beaux Arts Video** · 1000 Spruce St
- **Spruce Street Video** · 1201 Spruce St

Map 4 • **Old City / Society Hill**

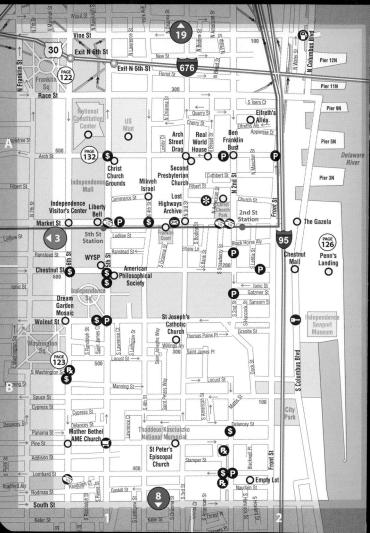

Once you get past the inevitable congestion of South Street-graduate clubbers, wanna-be scenesters, and well-to-do urban pros, the area is rich with history. Home to the burgeoning Independence Mall site, the US Mint, and B-Frank's own museum, the area is also rife with nightlife, baby, hitting you in droves with groovy clubs and yummy eats.

$ Banks

- **Beneficial Savings** · 530 Walnut St
- **Commerce Bank** · 200 Lombard St
- **Firstrust** · 111 S Independence Mall E
- **Hudson United** · 5 5th St & Chestnut St
- **PNC** · 400 Market St
- **PNC** · 602 Washington Sq S
- **Wachovia** · 101 N Independence Mall E
- **Wachovia** · 340 S 2nd St
- **Wachovia** · 601 Chestnut St

Car Rental

- **Avis** · 201 S Columbus Blvd

Cheesesteaks

- **Campo's Deli** · 214 Market St
- **Gianna's Grille** · 507 S 6th St
- **Grande Olde Cheesesteak** · 21 S 5th St
- **Sonny's Famous Steaks** · 216 Market St

Community Gardens

Gas Stations

- **Gulf** · 2 Vine St

Landmarks

- **American Philosophical Society** · 104 S 5th St
- **Arch Street Drag** · Arch & 3rd Sts
- **Ben Franklin Bust** · Arch & 2nd Sts
- **Chestnut Mall** · Chestnut St & Columbus Blvd
- **Christ Church Grounds** · 5th & Arch Sts
- **Christ Church Park** · 2nd & Market Sts
- **Dream Garden Mosaic** · 601-45 Walnut St
- **Elfreth's Alley** · b/w Front & 2nd Sts and Arch & Race Sts
- **Empty Lot** · b/w Front & Second Sts and South & Lombard Sts
- **Franklin Court** · Market St b/w 3rd & 4th Sts
- **The Gazela** · Columbus Blvd & Market St
- **Independence Visitor's Center** · 6th & Market Sts
- **Liberty Bell** · Market St b/w 5th St & 6th St

- **Lost Highways Archive** · 307 Market St
- **Mikveh Israel** · 44 N 4th St
- **Mother Bethel AME Church** · 6th & Pine Sts
- **National Constitution Center** · 525 Arch St
- **Penn's Landing Marina** · Penn's Landing & Columbus Blvd
- **Real World House** · 249-251 Arch St
- **Second Presbyterian Church** · 3rd & Arch Sts
- **St Joseph's Catholic Church** · 321 Willings Aly
- **St Peter's Episcopal Church** · 313 Pine St
- **US Mint** · 151 N Independence Mall East
- **WYSP** · 101 S Independence Mall E

P Parking

Rx Pharmacies

- **CVS** · 421 S 2nd St
- **Eckerd** · 522 S 2nd St
- **Washington Square Pharmacy** · 241 S 6th St

Post Offices

- **B Free Franklin** · 316 Market St

Supermarkets

- **Super Fresh** · 5th St & Pine St

Map 4 • **Old City / Society Hill**

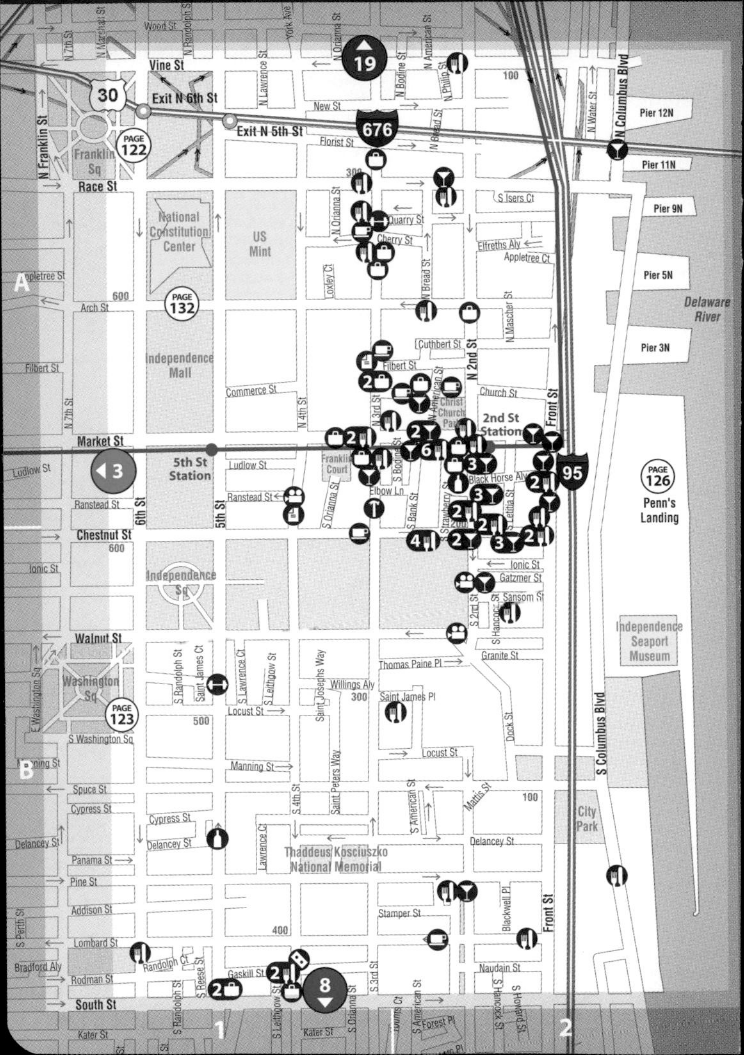

N

Wood St
N Randolph St
N 7th St
N Marshall St
York Ave
N Orianna St
N Bodine St
N American St
N Philip St
N Water St
N Columbus Blvd

Vine St
Exit N 6th St
New St
Pier 12N

30

Exit N 5th St
676
Pier 11N

PAGE 122
Florist St
S Isers Ct
Pier 9N

N Franklin St
Race St
300
N Orianna St
Quarry St
Cherry St
S Mascher St
Elfreths Aly
Appletree Ct
Pier 5N

National Constitution Center
US Mint
Loxley Ct
N Broad St
Delaware River

Appletree St
600
PAGE 132
Arch St
Cuthbert St
Pier 3N

Filbert St
Independence Mall
Commerce St
Filbert St
Christ Church
Church St
N 2nd St
2nd St Station
Front St

Market St
5th St Station
Ludlow St
N 4th St
Franklin Court
N Bodine St
Black Horse Aly
95

Ludlow St
3
Ranstead St
N Orianna St
Elbow Ln
N Bank St
N Strawberry St
S 2nd St
PAGE 126
Penn's Landing

Chestnut St
6th St
5th St
600
4

Ionic St
Independence Square
Ionic St
Gatzmer St
Sansom St
S 3rd St
S Hancock St
Independence Seaport Museum

Walnut St
Washington Square
PAGE 123
S Randolph St
Saint James Ct
S Lawrence Ct
S Leithgow St
Thomas Paine Pl
Saint James Pl
Granite St
Dock St

S Washington Sq
500
Locust St
Saint Josephs Way
Willings Aly
300
Locust St

S Washington Sq
Manning St
S 4th St
Saint Peters Way
S American St
Mattis St
100
City Park

Spruce St
Cypress St
Cypress St
Delancey St
Lawrence Ct
Delancey St
Delancey St

Delancey St
Panama St
Pine St
Thaddeus Kosciuszko National Memorial
Front St

Addison St
Stamper St
Blackwell Pl

Lombard St
400
S 3rd St
S 4th St
S American St
Front St

Bradford Aly
Rodman St
Randolph St
Gaskill St
8
Naudain St
S Howard St

South St
S Perth St
S Reese St
S Leithgow St
S Orianna St
Kater St
Kater St
S American St
Forest St

1
2

19

As long as you like your scenes loud and your booze pricey, you've got it all here. Home of perhaps more whipped-up-to-frothing bars/clubs per capita than any other area of the city, you can sample fine Asian fusion at Anjou, hit The Continental for a signature martini, and devour a chocolate-banana cookie from Petit 4.

Coffee

- Bucks County Coffee • 240 Locust St
- Café Au Lait • 147 N 3rd St
- Cosi • 215 Lombard St
- Cosi • 325 Chestnut St
- Old City Coffee • 221 Church St
- Starbucks • 57 N 3rd St

Copy Shops

- Goodway Copy Center • 49 S 4th St
- The UPS Store • 51 N 3rd St

Gyms

- Old City Iron Works II • 141 N 3rd St
- Philadelphia Sports Club • 720 S 5th St

Hardware Stores

- Olde City Hardware • 41 S 3rd St

Liquor Stores

- State Liquor Store • 32 S 2nd St
- State Liquor Store • 326 S 5th St

Movie Theaters

- Ritz 5 • 214 Walnut St
- Ritz at the Bourse • 400 Ranstead St
- Ritz East • 125 S 2nd St

Nightlife

- 32 Degrees • 16 S 2nd St
- Bleu Martini • 22 S 2nd St
- Buffalo Billiards • 118 Chestnut St
- The Continental • 138 Market St
- Cuba Libre • 10 S 2nd St
- Dark Horse • 421 S 2nd St
- Eulogy Belgian Tavern • 136 Chestnut St
- Five Spot • 1 S Bank St
- Glam • 52 S 2nd St
- Khyber Pass • 56 S 2nd St
- LoungeOneTwoFive • 125 S 2nd St
- Paradigm • 239 Chestnut St
- The Plough and the Stars • 123 Chestnut St
- Race Street Café • 208 Race St
- Red Sky • 224 Market St
- Rock Lobster • 221 N Columbus Blvd
- Rotten Ralph's • 201 Chestnut St
- Sassafras • 48 S 2nd St
- SoMa • 33 S 3rd St
- Sugar Mom's • 225 Church St
- Swanky Bubbles • 10 S Front St
- Tangerine • 232 Market St
- Warmdaddy's • 4 S Front St

Restaurants

- Adriatica • 217 Chestnut St
- Anjou • 206-08 Market St
- Billy Wong's • 50 S 2nd St
- Bistro Romano • 120 Lombard St
- Bluezette • 246 Market St
- Campo's Deli • 214 Market St
- Chloe • 232 Arch St
- Cuba Libre • 10 S 2nd St
- Dark Horse • 421 S 2nd St
- DiNardo's Famous Seafood • 312 Race St
- Django • 526 S 4th St
- Dolce • 242 Chestnut St
- Eulogy Belgian Tavern • 136 Chestnut St
- Fork • 306 Market St
- Gianfranco Pizza Rustica • 6 N 3rd St
- Gianna's Grill • 507 S 6th St
- Karma • 114 Chestnut St
- Konak • 228 Vine St
- La Famiglia • 8 S Front St
- La Locanda del Ghiottone • 130 N 3rd St
- Marmont Steakhouse • 222 Market St
- Marrakesh • 517 S Leithgow St
- Mexican Post • 104 Chestnut St
- Moshulu • 401 S Columbus Blvd
- Novelty • 15 S 3rd St
- Pagoda Noodle Café • 125 Sansom St

- Paradigm • 239 Chestnut St
- Patou • 312 Market St
- Petit 4 Pastry Studio • 160 N 3rd St
- Philadelphia Fish & Co • 207 Chestnut St
- Pizzicato • 248 Market St
- The Plough and the Stars • 123 Chestnut St
- Race Street Café • 208 Race St
- Ristorante Panorama • 14 N Front St
- Sassafras International Cafe • 48 S 2nd St
- Sfizzio • 237 St James Pl
- Sonny's Famous Steaks • 216 Market St
- Spasso • 34 S Front St
- Swanky Bubbles • 10 S Front St
- Tangerine • 232 Market St

Shopping

- Big Jar Books • 55 N 2nd St
- Cappelli Hobbies • 313 Market St
- Charles Porter Boutique • 212 Market St
- Coach • 38 N 3rd St
- Digital Ferret • 526 S 5th St
- Foster's Urban Homeware • 124 N 3rd St
- Friedman Umbrellas • 14 S 3rd St
- Kamikaze Kids • 527 S 4th St
- Lele • 30 S 2nd St
- Pierre's Costumes • 211 N 3rd St
- Red Red Red Hair Salon • 222 Church St
- Rescue 138 • 138 N 3rd St
- Subzero • 520 S 5th St
- Vagabond • 37 N 3rd St

Video Rental

- TLA Video • 517 S 4th St

21

Map 5 · **Gray's Ferry West**

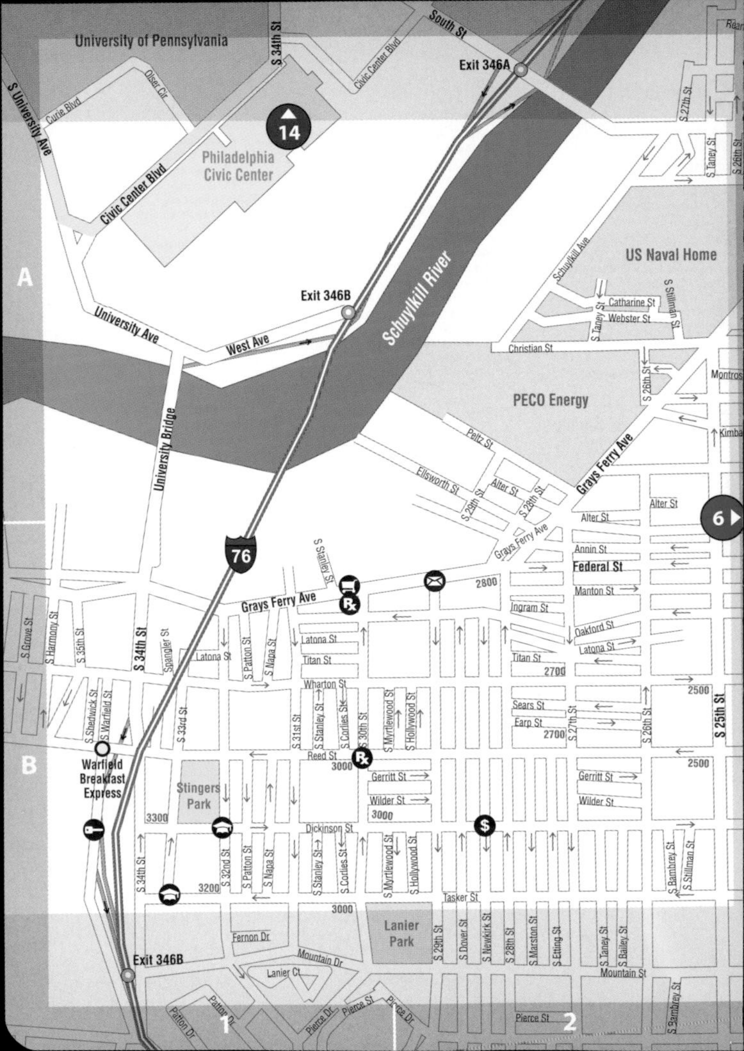

N

University of Pennsylvania

South St

S 34th St

Exit 346A

S 22nd St

Cutie Blvd

Osler Dr

Civic Center Blvd

14

Philadelphia
Civic Center

Civic Center Blvd

S University Ave

Schuylkill River

Exit 346B

US Naval Home

Schuylkill Ave

S Taney St

Catharine St

Webster St

A

University Ave

West Ave

Christian St

PECO Energy

S 26th St

S 27th St

Montros

Kimbal

University Bridge

Peltz St

Ellsworth St

Alter St

S 28th St

S 29th St

Grays Ferry Ave

Alter St

6

76

S Stanley St

Rx

Grays Ferry Ave

2800

Annin St

Federal St

Manton St

Grays Ferry Ave

Ingram St

2500

S 33rd St

Spangler St

Latona St

S Patton St

S Napa St

Latona St

Titan St

Oakford St

Latona St

S 31st St

S 26th St

S 27th St

S 25th St

Titan St

2700

Wharton St

Sears St

2500

S 32nd St

S Stanley St

S Corlies St

S 30th St

S Myrtlewood St

S Hollywood St

Earp St

2700

S 28th St

S 34th St

Reed St

3000

Rx

B

S Grove St

S Harmony St

S 35th St

S Sheldrick St

S Warfield St

Warfield
Breakfast
Express

Gerritt St

Wilder St
3000

Gerritt St

Wilder St

S Banbury St

S Silliman St

**Stingers
Park**

$

3300

Dickinson St

3200

S 34th St

S 32nd St

S Patton St

S Napa St

S Stanley St

S Corlies St

S Myrtlewood St

S Hollywood St

Tasker St

3000

Fernon Dr

**Lanier
Park**

S 29th St

S Dover St

S Newkirk St

S 28th St

S Marston St

S Etting St

S Taney St

S Bailey St

Mountain St

Exit 346B

Lanier Ct

Mountain Dr

Lanier Dr

Pierce Dr

Pierce St

Pierce St

S Stanley St

1

Patten Dr

2

A somewhat forgotten and neglected area, especially considering how close it is to both Rittenhouse and West Philly, Gray's Ferry is yet another up-and-comer. Students are discovering its relative affordability, and with students comes much in the way of basic commerce. Expect many more pizzerias, bars, and coffee joints in the next few years.

$ Banks
· **First Penn Bank** · 1501 S Newkirk St

Car Rental
· **Ryder** · 1450 S Warfield St

O Landmarks
· **Warfield Breakfast Express** · Warfield & Reed Sts

Rx Pharmacies
· **Pathmark** (24 hrs) · 3021 Grays Ferry Ave
· **Rite-Aid** · 3000 Reed St

Post Offices
· **Schuylkill Station** · 2900 Grays Ferry Ave

Schools
· **Audenreid Senior High** · 3301 Tasker St
· **James Alcorn** · 3200 Dickinson St

Supermarkets
· **Pathmark** (24 hrs) · 3021 Grays Ferry Ave

Map 5 · **Gray's Ferry West**

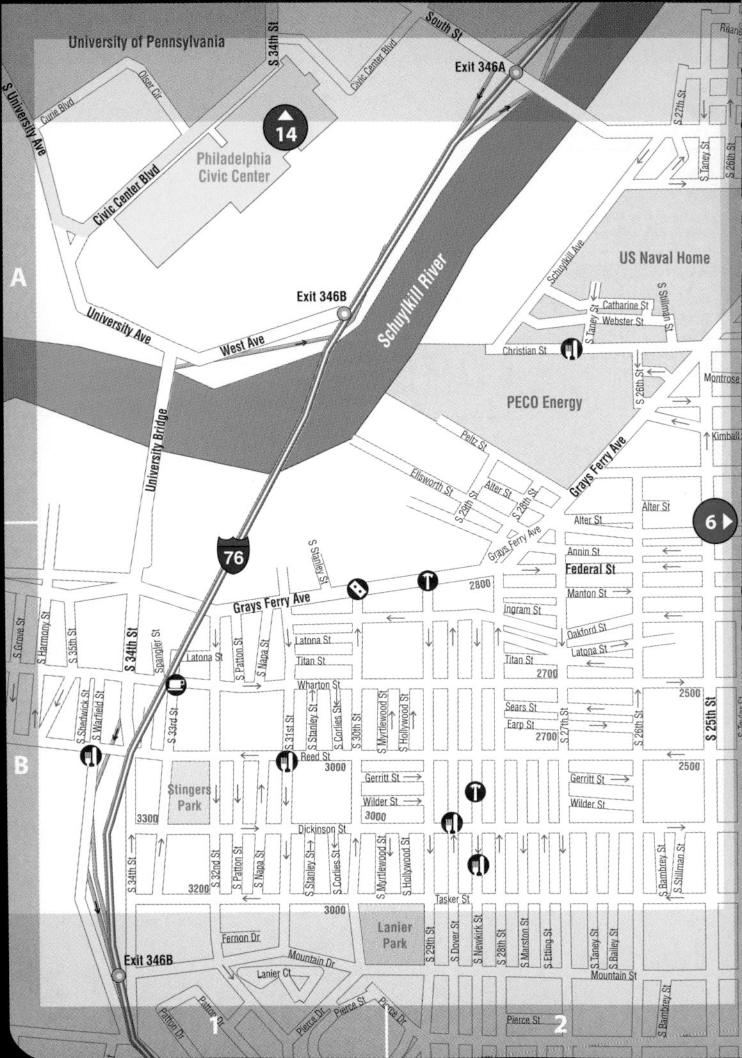

Map 5 · Gray's Ferry West

University of Pennsylvania

South St

Exit 346A

S 34th St

Civic Center Blvd

Curie Cut

Dixie Cut

Curie Blvd

Philadelphia
Civic Center

14

Civic Center Blvd

S University Ave

Exit 346B

West Ave

University Ave

Schuylkill River

West Ave

University Bridge

US Naval Home

Schuylkill Ave

Catharine St
Webster St

S Taney St

S Bonsall St

Christian St

Montrose

PECO Energy

Kimball

Petr St

Ellsworth St

Alter St

S 28th St

S 27th St

Grays Ferry Ave

Alter St

Alter St

6

S Stanley St

Grays Ferry Ave

Annin St

Federal St

Manton St

2800

Grays Ferry Ave

Ingram St

I-76

Oakford St

Titan St

Latona St

2700

S 34th St

S 35th St

S Grove St

S Harmony St

Spangler St

S 33rd St

Latona St

S Patton St

S Napa St

Latona St

Titan St

Wharton St

S 31st St

S Stanley St

S Corlies St

S 30th St

S Myrtlewood St

S Hollywood St

Sears St

2700

Earp St

2500

S 25th St

S Sheldrick St

S Warfield St

Reed St

3000

Gerritt St

Wilder St

Gerritt St

Wilder St

2500

Stingers
Park

3300

S 34th St

S 32nd St

S Patton St

S Napa St

Dickinson St

S Stanley St

S Corlies St

S Myrtlewood St

S Hollywood St

Wilder St

3000

3200

Tasker St

S 29th St

S Dover St

S Newkirk St

S 28th St

S Marston St

S Etting St

S Taney St

S Bambrey St

S Stillman St

3000

Lanier
Park

Fernon Dr

Mountain Dr

Exit 346B

Lanier Ct

Pierce Dr

Pierce Dr

Patton Dr

Pierce St

Mountain St

S Bambrey St

1

2

You shouldn't miss the infamous breakfast pizza at La Rosa, if you can stand to put that many carbs in your gullet at one time. For cheap Mob thrills, you can always check out the Warfield Breakfast Express, where La Costa Nostra member Joe Ciancaglini was rubbed out back in 1993.

Coffee

· **Dunkin' Donuts** · 3313 Wharton St

Hardware Stores

· **Diamond Tool** · 29th St & Grays Ferry Ave
· **Newkirk Hardware & Locks** · 1454 S Newkirk St

Restaurants

· **B&B Restaurant** · 2629 Christian St
· **Bridgit's Deli** · 1500 S Dover St
· **D'ambrosio's Bakery** · 1401 S 31st St
· **Kelly's Deli** · 1555 S Newkirk St
· **La Rosa Café** · 1300 S Warfield St

Video Rental

· **Blockbuster** · 3008 Grays Ferry Ave

Map 6 • Gray's Ferry East / Graduate Hospital

Essentials

Perhaps the very definition of an on-the-rise neighborhood, a few scant years ago the area was known more for urban decay than much else. Since then, however, things have definitely turned around. South Street has gotten much-needed new blood and, just about everywhere you look, new construction is in progress.

$ Banks
· **Firstrust** · 1332 Point Breeze Ave

Cheesesteaks
· **Old Town** · 2301 Grays Ferry Ave

Community Gardens

Libraries
· **Queen Memorial Library** · 1201 S 23rd St

Rx Pharmacies
· **Christian Street Pharmacy** · 1947 Christian St

Police
· **17th Police District** · 20th St & Federal St

Schools
· **Chester A Arthur** · 2000 Catharine St
· **Peirce Middle** · 2400 Christian St
· **Smith** · 1900 Wharton St

(27)

Map 6 • Gray's Ferry East / Graduate Hospital

Most of the action remains on South Street, including the influential Ten Stone and L2 bars, the cornerstones of the neighborhood. For cyclists, there's also the single best bike shop in CC, Bicycle Therapy, whose friendly owners are all too willing to impart you their knowledge of rocking trails nearby.

Hardware Stores

· **AS Hardware & Home Center** ·
   1229 Point Breeze Ave
· **Center City Home Center & Millwork** ·
   1931 Washington Ave
· **PAEK Hongki Home Center** ·
   1320 Point Breeze Ave
· **South Square Hardware** · 2235 Grays Ferry Ave

Liquor Stores

· **State Liquor Store** · 1446 Point Breeze Ave

Nightlife

· **L2** · 2201 South St
· **Ten Stone Bar & Restaurant** · 2063 South St

Restaurants

· **L2** · 2201 South St
· **My Thai** · 2200 South St
· **Phoebe's Bar-B-Q** · 2214 South St
· **Ten Stone Bar & Restaurant** · 2063 South St

Shopping

· **Bicycle Therapy** · 2211 South St
· **Sweetwater Swimwear** · 715 S 18th St #B

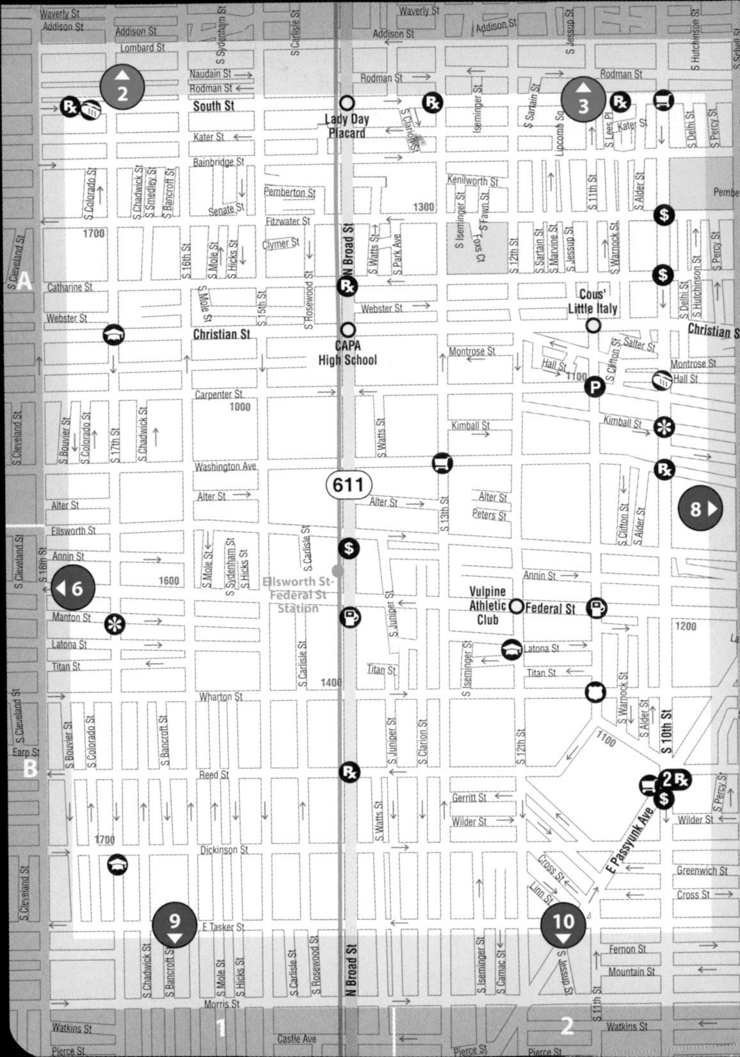

Map 7 · **Southwark West**

Waverly St
Addison St
Lombard St
Waverly St
Addison St
Jessup St
Hutchinson St

Naudain St →
Rodman St →
Rodman St →
Rodman St

South St
Lady Day Placard

Kater St
S Carlisle St
S Sydenham St
S Percy St
S 11th St
S Alder St
S Delhi St

Bainbridge St
Kater St
S Lees St

S Colorado St
S Chadwick St
S Smedley St
S Bancroft St

Pemberton St
Kenilworth St
1300

Senate St
Fitzwater St
S 11th St
S Alder St
S Percy St

1700
Clymer St
S Watts St
S Park Ave
S 12th St
S Sartain St
S Marvine St
S Jessup St
S Warnock St
S Delhi St
S Hutchinson St
S Percy St

Catharine St

Webster St
N Broad St
Webster St

Pembe

A
S Cleveland St

S Bouvier St
S Colorado St
17th St
S Chadwick St
S 16th St
S Mole St
S Hicks St

Christian St

Carpenter St
1000
CAPA High School

Cous' Little Italy

Christian S

Washington Ave
Alter St
611
Alter St

Hall St
S Clifton St
S Alter St
Montrose St
Hall St

Kimball St
Kimball St

Alter St
S Watts St
S 13th St
Peters St

S Clifton St
S Alder St

8 ▶

Ellsworth St
S 18th St

Annin St
S Mole St
S Sydenham St
S Carlisle St

Ellsworth St-Federal St Station

Annin St
S Warnock St
S 10th St
1200

6 ◀
1600

Manton St
Latona St
S Juniper St
Vulpine Athletic Club
Federal St

Latona St
S Isemniger St
La

Titan St
S Carlisle St
1400
Titan St

S Cleveland St
S Bouvier St
S Colorado St
S Bancroft St

Wharton St
S Juniper St
S Clarion St
S 12th St
1100

B
Earp St

Reed St
S Watts St

1700
Dickinson St
Gerritt St
Wilder St

E Passyunk Ave
2
Wilder St
S Percy St

9 ▼
E Tasker St
Cross St
Lim St
10 ▼
Greenwich St
Cross St

Morris St
S Chadwick St
S Bancroft St
S Mole St
S Hicks St
S Carlisle St
S Rosewood St
N Broad St
S Isemniger St
S Camac St
S Juniper St
Fernon St
Mountain St

Watkins St
Castle Ave
Pierce St
Pierce St
Watkins St

1
2

Pierce St

Another up-and-comer, the area is home to a growing Latino and Asian community, who seem to get on perfectly well with the old hard-line South Phillians. Broad Street is as vibrant here as it is closer to Market Streets and there remains a good deal of nearly-affordable housing available.

$ Banks

- **First Penn Bank** · 10th St & Catherine St
- **United Savings Bank** · 732 S 10th St
- **Wachovia** · 1165 S Broad St
- **Wachovia** · 1400 E Passyunk Ave

Cheesesteaks

- **Lazaro's** · 1743 South St
- **Shank's & Evelyn's Luncheonette** · 932 S 10th St

Community Gardens

Gas Stations

- **Mobil** · 1201 S 11th St
- **Mobil** · 1243 S Broad St

O Landmarks

- **CAPA High School** · 901 S Broad St
- **Cous' Little Italy** · 901 S 11th St
- **Lady Day Placard** · Broad & South Sts
- **Vulpine Athletic Club** · 12th & Federal Sts

P Parking

Rx Pharmacies

- **Acme** · 1400 E Passyunk Ave
- **Broad Street Pharmacy** · 1412 S Broad St
- **CVS** · 1001 Washington Ave
- **CVS** · 1051 South St
- **CVS (24 hrs)** · 1405 S 10th St
- **Lombard Apothecary** · 1745 South St
- **Rite-Aid** · 810 S Broad St
- **Young's Drugs** · 1306 South St

Police

- **4th Police District** · 11th St & Wharton St

Schools

- **Childs** · 1541 S 17th St
- **Jackson** · 1213 S 12th St
- **Stanton** · 1700 Christian St

Supermarkets

- **Acme** · 1400 E Passyunk Ave
- **Save-A-Lot** · 1300 Washington Ave
- **Super Fresh** · 10th St & South St

Map 7 · **Southwark West**

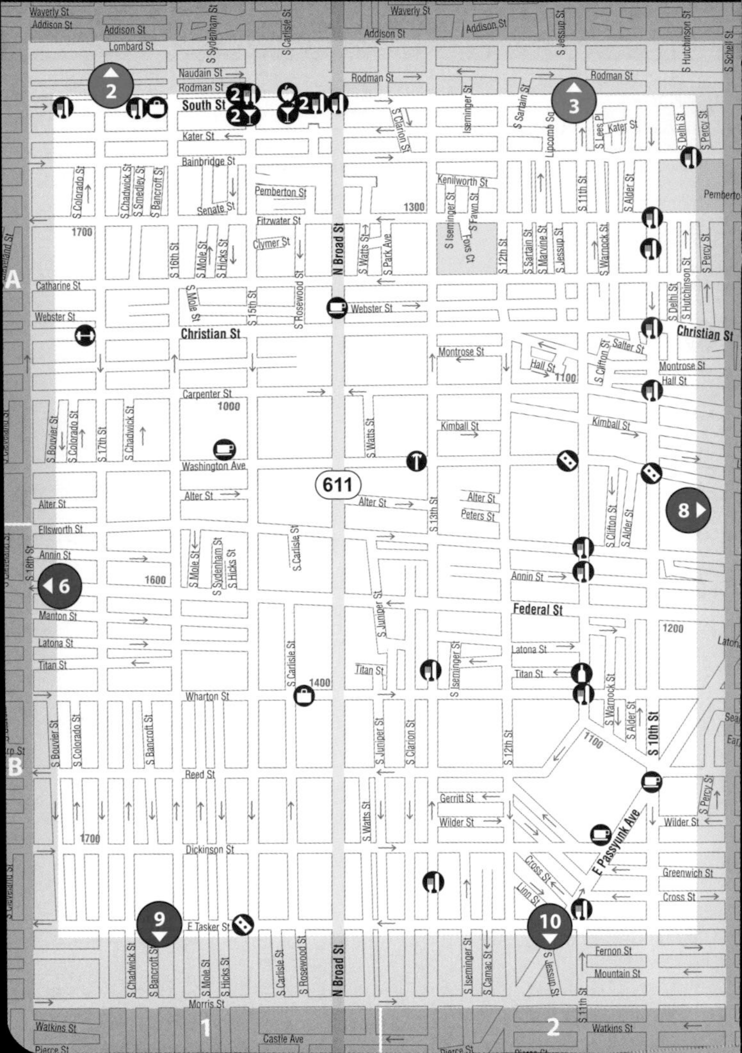

N

2

3

Waverly St
Addison St
Addison St
Lombard St
Waverly St
Addison St
Addison St
Rodman St
Rodman St

Naudain St
Rodman St
South St
Kater St
Bainbridge St
Pemberton St
Fitzwater St
Senate St
Clymer St
Webster St

Kenilworth St

1300

1700

Catharine St
Webster St

A

Christian St
Christian St

Carpenter St
1000
Montrose St
Montrose St

Washington Ave
Hall St
Hall St

611
Kimball St
Kimball St

Alter St
Alter St
Alter St
Peters St

Eltsworth St
Annin St

6
Annin St

1600
Manton St
Latona St
Titan St
Federal St
Latona St
Titan St
Titan St

8

1200

Wharton St
1100

1400

B

Reed St

1700
Gerritt St
Wilder St
Wilder St

Dickinson St
Cross St
Greenwich St
Cross St

Cross St
Lum St

9
E Tasker St
10
Fernon St

Mountain St

Morris St
Watkins St
Watkins St
Castle Ave

1
2

S Colorado St
S Chadwick St
S Smedley St
S Bancroft St
S 16th St
S Mole St
S Hicks St
S 15th St
S Rosewood St
N Broad St
S Watts St
S Park Ave

S Clarion St
S Iseminger St
S Sartain St
S Juniper St
S 12th St
S Sartain St
S Marvine St
S Warnock St
S Jessup St
S 11th St
S Lees Pl
S Delhi St
S Hutchinson St
S Percy St

S Bouvier St
S Colorado St
S 17th St
S Chadwick St
S Sydenham St
S Hicks St
S Carlisle St
S Watts St
S 13th St

S Clifton St
S Salter St
S Alder St
S Delhi St
S Hutchinson St

S Juniper St
S Iseminger St
S Clarion St
S Watts St

S Clifton St
S Alder St
S 10th St
S Percy St

E Passyunk Ave

S Warnock St
S Alder St
S 10th St

S Camac St
S 11th St

Asian and Latino markets and restaurants dot Washington Avenue with hard-to-find items for would-be chefs while Shank's & Evelyn's Luncheonette remains a beacon for more traditional cheesesteak lovers. If you can stand the wait, Morning Glory is a viable brunch hotspot and, for those with a sweet tooth, Isgro Pastries is a classic.

 ## Coffee

- **Café O Sole Mio** · 1500 E Passyunk Ave
- **Dunkin' Donuts** · 1401 S 10th St
- **Dunkin' Donuts** · 1551 Washington Ave
- **Dunkin' Donuts** · 809 S Broad St

 ## Farmer's Markets

- **South Street West at the Jamaican Jerk Hut** · 1436 South St

 ## Gyms

- **YMCA-Christian Street** · 1724 Christian St

 ## Hardware Stores

- **C&R Building Supply** · 1322 Washington Ave

 ## Liquor Stores

- **State Liquor Store** · 1237 S 11th St

 ## Nightlife

- **Bob & Barbara's Lounge** · 1509 South St
- **Fiso Lounge** · 1437 South St
- **Tritone** · 1508 South St

Restaurants

- **August** · 1247 S 13th St
- **Bitar's** · 947 Federal St
- **Carman's Country Kitchen** · 1301 S 11th St
- **Dante & Luigi's** · 762 S 10th St
- **Felicia's** · 1148 S 11th St
- **Fiso Lounge** · 1437 South St
- **Franco's & Luigi's** · 1549 S 13th St
- **Govinda's** · 1408 South St
- **Isgro Pastries** · 1009 Christian St
- **Jamaican Jerk Hut** · 1436 South St
- **Lazzaro's Pizza House** · 1743 South St
- **Morning Glory Diner** · 735 S 10th St
- **Pico de Gallo** · 1501 South St
- **Ricci Bros** · 1165 S 11th St
- **Ron's Ribs** · 1627 South St
- **Shank's & Evelyn's Luncheonette** · 932 S 10th St
- **Tre Scalini** · 1533 S 11th St
- **Tritone** · 1508 South St

 ## Shopping

- **Awa's Hair Braiding** · 1608 South St
- **Sistah's Consignment Shop** · 1442 Wharton St

 ## Video Rental

- **Danny New Video Store** · 1514 Tasker St
- **Hollywood Video** · 1001 Washington Ave
- **Jacky Video & Music** · 1120 Washington Ave

Map 8 · **Bella Vista / Queen Village**

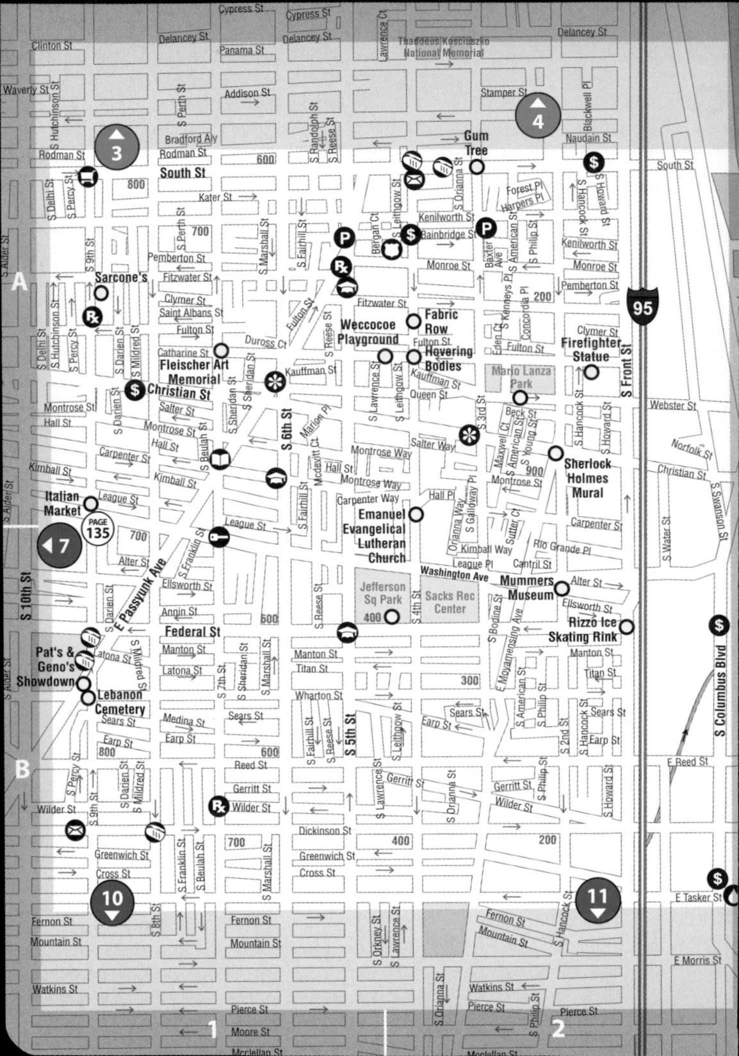

N

Cypress St
Cypress St
Clinton St
Delancey St
Panama St
Delancey St
Thaddeus Kosciuszko
National Memorial
Delancey St

Waverly St
Addison St
Stamper St

Rodman St
Bradford Aly
Rodman St
600
Gum
Tree
4

800
South St
South St

Kater St
Forest Pl
Harpers Pl

S Perth St
Pemberton St
Kenilworth St

Sarcone's
Fitzwater St
Bainbridge St
Monroe St
Pemberton St

A
Clymer St
Saint Albans St
Fulton St
Fitzwater St

Catharine St
Duross Ct
Weccacoe
Playground
Fabric
Row
Fulton St
Hovering
Bodies
Clymer St
Firefighter
Statue
95

Fleischer Art
Memorial
Kauffman St
Kauffman St
Mario Lanza
Park
Webster St

Christian St
Salter St
Queen St

Montrose St
Hall St
Montrose St
Salter Way
Norfolk St

Kimball St
Carpenter St
McDevitt St
Hall St
Montrose Way
900
Sherlock
Holmes
Mural
Christian St

Kimball St
Carpenter Way
Carpenter St

Italian
Market
7
PAGE
135
League St
Hall Pl
Emanuel
Evangelical
Lutheran
Church
Rio Grande Pl

Ellsworth St
League St
Washington Ave
Mummers
Museum
Alter St

Angin St
600
Jefferson
Sq Park
Sacks Rec
Center
Ellsworth St

Federal St
Manton St
Manton St
Rizzo Ice
Skating Rink

Pat's &
Geno's
Showdown
Latona St
Latona St
300
Titan St

Lebanon
Cemetery
Medina St
Sears St
Wharton St
Sears St

B
Earp St
800
Sears St
600
Earp St

Wilder St
Reed St
Gerritt St

Gerritt St
Wilder St
Wilder St

Greenwich St
Dickinson St
400
200

10
Greenwich St
Cross St
11

Fernon St
Fernon St
Fernon St
E Tasker St

Mountain St
Mountain St
Mountain St
E Morris St

Watkins St
Pierce St
Pierce St
Pierce St

Moore St

McClellan St
McClellan St

1
2

An aspiring-to-be neighborhood with a growing legion of devotees, convinced they've found themselves the perfect combo of downtown living, convenient accessibility, and reasonable cost. The truth, as always, lies somewhere between that optimism and a more negative outlook, but the area is chock-full of young homeowners looking to finally settle down.

$ Banks

- **Hudson United** · 1100 S Columbus Blvd
- **Hudson United** · 135 South St
- **PNC** · 801 Christian St
- **Sharon Savings** · 420 Bainbridge St

Car Rental

- **Penske Truck** · 709 Washington Ave

Car Washes

- **Southport Plaza Car Wash** · 1600 Columbus Blvd

Cheesesteaks

- **Cosmi's Deli** · 1501 S 8th St
- **Geno's Steaks** · 1219 S 9th St
- **Ishkabibbles Eatery** · 337 South St
- **Jim's Steaks** · 400 South St
- **Pat's King of Steaks** · 1237 E Passyunk Ave

Community Gardens

O Landmarks

- **Emanuel Evangelical Lutheran Church** · 1001 S 4th St
- **Fabric Row** · 4th St b/w Bainbridge & Catharine Sts
- **Firefighter Statue** · Queen St b/w Front & 2nd Sts
- **Fleischer Art Memorial** · 719 Catharine St
- **Gum Tree** · 3rd & South Sts
- **Hovering Bodies** · corner of 4th & Catharine Sts
- **Italian Market** · 9th St b/w Bainbridge St & Washington Ave
- **Jefferson Square Park/Sacks Rec Center** · Washington Ave b/w 4th & 5th Sts
- **Lebanon Cemetery** · 9th & Passyunk Sts
- **Mario Lanza Park** · Queen St b/w 2nd & 3rd Sts
- **Mummers Museum** · 1100 S 2nd St
- **Pat's & Geno's Showdown** · 9th St & Passyunk Ave
- **Rizzo Ice Skating Rink** · 1101 S Front St
- **Sarcone's** · 758 S 9th St
- **Sherlock Holmes Mural** · 2nd St b/w Christian & Moyamensing Sts
- **Weccocoe Playground** · Catharine St b/w 4th & 5th Sts

Libraries

- **Charles Santore Branch** · 932 S 7th St

P Parking

Rx Pharmacies

- **Rite-Aid** · 1443 S 7th St
- **Rite-Aid** · 704 E Passyunk Ave
- **Rite-Aid** · 801 S 9th St
- **Wal-Mart** · 1601 S Columbus Blvd

Police

- **South Street Detail (3rd District)** · 420 Bainbridge St

Post Offices

- **Penn's Landing Retail** · 622 S 4th St
- **Southwark Station** · 925 Dickinson St

Schools

- **Meredith** · 725 S 5th St
- **Nebinger** · 601 Carpenter St
- **Washington** · 1190 S 5th St

Supermarkets

- **Whole Foods** · 929 South St

Map 8 · Bella Vista / Queen Village

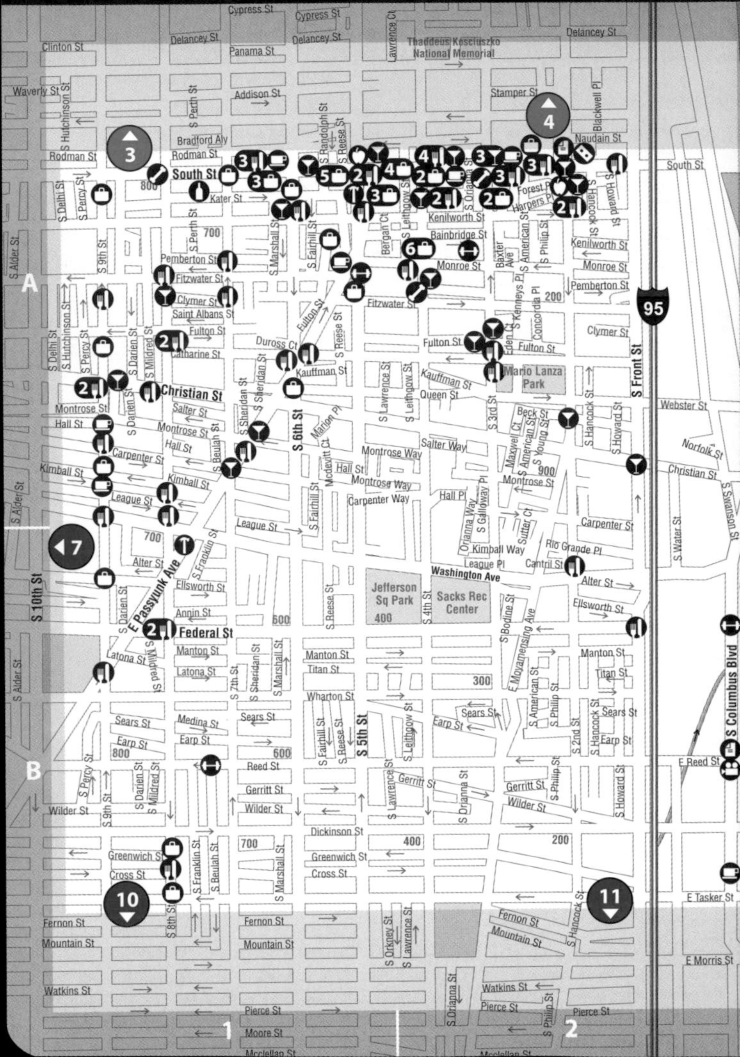

N

Cypress St
Cypress St
Clinton St
Delancey St
Panama St
Delancey St
Delancey St
Lawrence Ct
Thaddeus Kosciuszko
National Memorial
Waverly St
Addison St
Stamper St
Blackberry Pl
S Perth St
Bradford Aly
Naudain St
4
Rodman St
Rodman St
3
South St
800
Kater St
Naudain St
South St
Howard St
3
Forest St
Harpers Pl
700
Kater St
Pemberton St
Bergen St
Bainbridge St
Baxter St
Kenilworth St
6
Kenilworth St
Fitzwater St
Monroe St
Monroe St
Pemberton St
A
Clymer St
Saint Albans St
Fitzwater St
S 3rd St
Concordia St
200
Clymer St
Fulton St
Fulton St
Catharine St
Duross Ct
Mario Lanza
Park
Christian St
Kauffman St
Kauffman St
Queen St
Beck St
Salter St
Lethgow St
Montrose St
Montrose St
Lawrence Ct
Salter Way
Hall St
Hall St
Montrose Way
Young St
900
Kimball St
Beulah St
Montrose Way
Carpenter St
Carpenter Way
Hall Pl
Carpenter St
S Water St
League St
League Pl
Kimball Way
Rio Grande Pl
7
Alter St
Franklin St
League St
Washington Ave
Cantril St
Alter St
Ellsworth St
Jefferson
Sq Park
400
Sacks Rec
Center
Ellsworth St
Annin St
S 10th St
2
Federal St
Manton St
300
Manton St
Latona St
Titan St
Titan St
Latona St
Wharton St
Sears St
Sears St
Sears St
Earp St
Earp St
800
Medina St
600
Reed St
Earp St
B
Reed St
Gerritt St
Gerritt St
Wilder St
Wilder St
Wilder St
Dickinson St
400
200
Greenwich St
Cross St
Greenwich St
Cross St
10
E Tasker St
11
Fernon St
Fernon St
Fernon St
E Reed St
Mountain St
Mountain St
Mountain St
E Morris St
Watkins St
Pierce St
Pierce St
Pierce St
Moore St
McClellan St

95
S Front St
S Columbus Blvd

1   2

Here, you have so bloody many restaurants, cafes, and bars, you'll never run dry. Among other faves, Dmitri's remains near the top, as well as Mezza Luna and Pat's/Geno's. For nightlife, the New Wave Café is always a good bet, along with Saloon, as long as you've got your good suit back from the cleaners.

Coffee

- Alhambra · 607 S 3rd St
- Anthony's Italian Coffee · 919 S 9th St
- Bean Café · 615 South St
- Dunkin' Donuts · 1580 Columbus Blvd
- J&F Italian Market Café · 1024 S 9th St
- Java at the Gym · 700 E Passyunk Ave
- Starbucks · 347 South St

Copy Shops

- Staples · 1300 S Columbus Blvd
- The UPS Store · 211 South St

Farmer's Markets

- 2nd & South Streets ·
  S 2nd St & South St
- South & Passyunk · South St b/w
  S 5th St & E Passyunk Ave

Gyms

- Curves · 1100 S Columbus Blvd
- Fitness World Philadelphia ·
  714 Reed St
- Pennsport Athletic Club (24 hrs) ·
  325 Bainbridge St
- Sweat · 700 Passyunk Ave

Hardware Stores

- Cohen & Co Hardware & Home Goods
  · 615 E Passyunk Ave
- Wilensky's Hardware & Locks ·
  1113 E Passyunk Ave

Liquor Stores

- State Liquor Store · 724 South St

Movie Theaters

- United Artists Riverview Stadium 17 ·
  1400 S Columbus Blvd

Nightlife

- 12 Steps Down · 9th & Christian Sts
- Bridget Foy's · 200 South St
- Cheers to You · 430 South St
- Fluid · 613 S 4th St
- For Pete's Sake · 900 S Front St
- Jon's Bar & Grill · 606 S 3rd St
- L'Etage · 624 S 6th St
- Low · 947 E Passyunk Ave
- Lyon's Den · 848 S 2nd St
- New Wave Café · 784 S 3rd St
- O'Neal's · 611 S 3rd St
- Player's Pub · 615 S 2nd St
- Royal Tavern · 937 S Passyunk Ave
- Saloon · 750 S 7th St
- Southwark · 701 S 4th St
- Tattooed Mom's · 530 South St
- TLA · 334 South St
- Vesuvio · 736 S 8th St

Pet Shops

- Accent on Animals · 804 South St
- Aquarium City Center · 740 S 4th St
- Chic Petique · 616 3rd St

Restaurants

- Azafran · 617 S 3rd St
- Beau Monde · 624 S 6th St
- Bridget Foy's · 200 South St
- Café Huong Lan · 1037 S 8th St
- Café Nhuy · 802 Christian St
- Café Sud · 801 E. Passyunk Ave
- Copabanana · 344 South St
- Cucina Forte · 768 S 8th St
- Dmitri's · 795 S 3rd St
- El Rey Del Sol · 819 South St
- Famous 4th Street Deli · 700 S 4th St
- Fitzwater Café · 728 S 7th St
- Geno's Steaks · 1219 S 9th St
- Gnocchi · 613 E Passyunk Ave
- Golden Empress Garden · 610 S 5th St
- Hikaru · 607 S 2nd St
- Hosteria Da Elio · 615 S 3rd St
- Ishkabibble's Eatery · 337 South St
- Jim's Steaks · 400 South St
- Johnny Rockets · 443 South St
- Judy's Café · 627 S 3rd St
- La Fourno Trattoria · 636 South St
- La Lupe · 1201 S 9th St
- La Vigna · 1100 S Front St
- Latest Dish · 613 S 4th St
- Little Fish · 600 Catharine St
- Lorenzo Pizza · 900 Christian St
- Lorenzo & Son Pizza · 305 South St
- Lovash · 236 South St
- Mezza Luna · 763 S 8th St
- Mustard Greens · 622 E 2nd St
- Napoli Pizzeria · 944 E Passyunk Ave
- New Wave Café · 784 S 3rd St
- Next · 223 South St
- Pat's King of Steaks ·
  1237 E Passyunk Ave
- Pif · 1009 S 8th St
- Pink Rose Pastry Shop · 630 S 4th St
- Ralph's · 760 S 9th St
- Sabrina's Cafe · 910 Christian St
- Saloon · 750 S 7th St
- Salsolito Café · 602 South St
- Snockey's · 1020 S 2nd St
- Tamarind · 117 South St
- Taqueria La Veracruzana ·
  908 Washington Ave
- Termini Brothers Bakery ·
  1523 S 8th St
- Vesuvio · 736 S 8th St
- Villa di Roma · 932 S 9th St

Shopping

- 611 Records · 611 S 4th St
- Antiquarium's Delight · 615 S 6th St
- Bella Boutique · 624 S 3rd St
- Cohen Hardware · 615 E Passyunk Ave
- Cue Records · 617 S 4th St
- Essene · 719 S 4th St
- Fante's · 1006 S 9th St
- Game Gallery · 505 South St
- Garland of Letters · 527 South St
- Goldstein's Roy's & Men's Wear ·
  811 S 6th St
- Greene Street · 700 South St
- Guacamole · 422 South St
- Hand Impressions · 759 S 4th St
- Hats in the Belfry · 245 South St
- House of Tea · 720 S 4th St
- Kroungold's Better Furniture ·
  710 S 5th St
- Le Bomb Chele · 1134 S 9th St
- Maxie's Daughter · 721 S 4th St
- Mood · 531 South St
- Mostly Books · 529 Bainbridge St
- Nocturnal Skateshop · 610 S 3rd St
- Pearl Art Supply · 417 South St
- Pearl of Africa · 624 South St
- Philadelphia Bar & Restaurant Supply
  · 629 E Passyunk Ave
- Philadelphia Record Exchange ·
  618 S 5th St
- Retrospect · 534 South St
- Revelations · 711 S 4th St
- Rode'o Kidz · 721 S 4th St
- Showcase Comics · 640 South St
- South Street Vintage · 329 South St
- Spaceboy Music · 409 South St
- State of the Art Records · 638 South St
- Termini Brothers Bakery ·
  1523 S 8th St
- Triple Play Sporting Goods ·
  827 S 9th St
- Via Bicycle · 606 S 9th St
- Zipperhead · 407 South St

Video Rental

- Blockbuster · 201 South St

Map 9 • **Point Breeze / West Passyunk**

It doesn't get much more South Philly than this, with lots of maddeningly similar looking row homes, bizarre double-parking maneuvers, and lots of great eating everywhere you look. Girard Park offers a bit of rare greenery in what is otherwise a pretty consistently concrete-seeming façade.

$ Banks
- **First Penn Bank** · 21st St & Passyunk Ave
- **Prudential Savings** · 1834 Oregon Ave
- **Wachovia** · 2300 Snyder Ave

Car Washes
- **Car's** · 1927 W Passyunk Ave
- **Classic Car Cleaners** · 1937 S 17th St

Cheesesteaks
- **Primo Hoagies** · 1528 W Ritner St

Gas Stations
- **Amoco** · 2101 W Passyunk Ave
- **Getty** · 2101 W Oregon Ave
- **Sunoco** · 2700 S 15th St

Landmarks
- **Melrose Diner Parking Lot** · 1501 Snyder Ave

Libraries
- **Thomas F Donatucci Sr Branch** · 1935 Shunk St

Pharmacies
- **CVS (24 hrs)** · 1901 W Oregon Ave
- **Medicine Shoppe** · 1951 W Passyunk Ave
- **Pharmacy DUR** · 1419 Oregon Ave

Post Offices
- **Point Breeze Postal Store** · 2437 S 23 St

Schools
- **Girard** · 1800 Snyder Ave
- **McDaniel** · 2100 Moore St

Supermarkets
- **Save-A-Lot** · 2120 S 23rd St

Map 9 • **Point Breeze / West Passyunk**

Lots of nooks and crannies holding nifty one-of-a-kind bars and restaurants, including the sublime L'Angolo for regional Italian and the ever-popular (and busy) Melrose Diner, whose fame—and pancakes—are well known throughout the city. For the puckheads, DeNic's is a bastion of Flyer-friendliness.

Coffee

- **Caffe Italia** · 1424 Snyder Ave
- **Cousins Coffee Shop** · 2340 S Hemberger St
- **Dunkin' Donuts** · 2308 W Passyunk Ave
- **Dunkin' Donuts** · 2654 S 18th St

Gyms

- **Bally's** · 2500 S 24th St, 2nd Fl
- **Body World** · 1622 W Passyunk Ave
- **Curves** · 2115 Oregon Ave
- **RMC Health & Fitness** · 2317 S 23rd St

Hardware Stores

- **Albert's Supply** · 1814 S 20th St
- **Barlow's Stores** · 2216 Snyder Ave
- **Ritner Hardware Store** · 1641 W Ritner St

Nightlife

- **DeNic's Tavern** · 1520 Snyder Ave

Restaurants

- **Barrel's** · 1725 Wolf St
- **Buon Appetito** · 1540 Ritner St
- **L'Angolo** · 1415 Porter St
- **La Stanza** · 2001 Oregon Ave
- **Matteo Cucina** · 1900 W Passyunk Ave
- **Melrose Diner** · 1501 Snyder Ave
- **Mio Sogno** · 2650 S 15th St
- **Royal Villa Café** · 1700 Jackson St

Map 10 · **Moyamensing / East Passyunk** N

Gerritt St
Wilder St
Dickinson St
Gerritt St
Wilder St

S Watts St
Cross St
S Juniper St

Greenwich St
Cross St

S Percy St
S Franklin St
S Beulah St

S Marshall St

Greenwich St
Cross St

Tasker St
7
8

S Iseminger St
S Camac St
S Jessup St

Fernon St
Mountain St
Morris St
Watkins St

Fernon St
Mountain St

700

Tasker St · Morris St Station

Castle Ave

Pierce St
Pierce St

S Alder St

Pierce St
Moore St
McClellan St

S Broad St

McClellan St
Sigel St
McClellan St
Sigel St

800

Mifflin St

S Watts St

S Iseminger St
S Camac St
S Jessup St
S 11th St
S Warnock St
S Alder St

1100

Hoffman St
900

Hoffman St
Dudley St
McKean St

S Hutchinson St
S Percy St
S Darien St
S Mildred St

Rx

Emily St
Mercy St
Snyder Ave

Emily St
Mercy St

S 6th St

Cantrell St
Winton St

600

Rx

9
Snyder Ave Station

S Iseminger St

Tree St
Daly St

S 11th St
S 10th St
S 9th St
S Darien St
S Mildred St

Tree St
Daly St

Jackson St
S 7th St

S Reese St

11

Durfor St
Fitzgerald St

S Watts St
S Juniper St
S Clarion St
S 13th St

Durfor St
Fitzgerald St

W Moyamensing Ave
900

Wolf St

S 5th St

LA 2300

Mifflin Sq

S Broad St

Rx

W Porter St

S Watts St
S Juniper St
S Clarion St
S 12th St
S Iseminger St
S Camac St
S Sartain St
S Jessup St

S Warnock St
S Alder St

W Ritner St

800
700
S Darien St
S Mildred St
S Franklin St
S Beulah St
S Sheridan St
S Marshall St
600

500

S Reese St

500

Voll

700

W Shunk St

S Watts St
S Juniper St
S Clarion St
S Carlisle St

S Iseminger St
S Camac St
S Sartain St
S Jessup St

1300
1200

S Warnock St
S Alder St

Rx

S Fairhill St

St Michael

12

W Oregon Ave
1000

Oregon Ave Station

Marconi Plaza

Mollbore Ter

S Iseminger St
S 13th St
S 12th St
S Marvine St
S 11th St
S Warnock St
S Alder St

Johnston St

S Hutchinson St
S Darien St
S Mildred St

S Franklin St

Mollbore Ter

S Sheridan St
S Marshall St
600
S Fairhill St

2

A busy (and somewhat congested) section of South Philly that features lots of residential living space stacked not-so-neatly on top of itself. S. Broad takes on the appearance of a blocked artery during peak rush hours, and the curious parking regulations, wholly unique to the area, don't really help matters.

Banks

- **Beneficial Savings** · 2037 S Broad St
- **Citizens Bank** · 2001 S Broad St
- **Commerce Bank** · 2201 S Broad St
- **Commerce Bank** · 2653 S 5th St
- **First Penn Bank** · 1833 E Passyunk Ave
- **First Penn Bank** · Broad St & Porter St
- **Prudential Savings** · 1722 S Broad St
- **Sovereign Bank** · 2701 S 10th St
- **St Edmond's Federal Savings** · 1901 E Passyunk Ave
- **United Savings Bank** · Broad St & Passyunk Ave
- **Wachovia** · 1931 S Broad St
- **Wachovia** · 2039 S 10th St
- **Wachovia** · 2532 S 13th St

Hospitals

- **Methodist** · 2301 S Broad St

Libraries

- **Fumo Family Branch** · 2437 S Broad St
- **South Philadelphia Branch** · 1700 S Broad St

Pharmacies

- **Broad Street Pharmacy** · 2426 S Broad St
- **Center Apothecary** · 2110 S 7th St
- **Familymeds Pharmacy** · 2655 S 10th St
- **Passyunk Pharmacy** · 1804 E Passyunk Ave
- **Rite-Aid** (24 hrs) · 2017 S Broad St
- **Walgreens** (24 hrs) · 2014 S Broad St
- **Zevin's Pharmacy** · 800 McKean St

Post Offices

- **Castle** · 1713 S Broad St

Schools

- **Jenks** · 2501 S 13th St
- **Key** · 2230 S 8th St
- **South Philadelphia High** · 2101 S Broad St
- **Southwark** · 1835 S 9th St
- **Vare** · 621 E Moyamensing Ave

Map 10 · **Moyamensing / East Passyunk** (N)

Gerritt St
Wilder St
Dickinson St
Cross St
Linn St

Greenwich St
Cross St

Gerritt St
Wilder St

Greenwich St
Cross St

S Watts St

S Franklin St
S Beulah St

S Marshall St

S Lawrence St

S Pickney St

7

Tasker St
Morris St Station

Tasker St

S Iseminger St
S Camac St

S Juniper St

S Darien St
S Mildred St

Fernon St
Mountain St
Morris St
Watkins St

8

Fernon St
Mountain St

700

S Franklin St

(T)

Castle Ave

Pierce St

E Passyunk Ave

Pierce St

Pierce St
Moore St
McClellan St
Sigel St

A

S Broad St

S Camac St
S Rosewood St

McClellan St
Sigel St

S Iseminger St
S Camac St

McClellan St
Sigel St

S Alder St

800

Mifflin St

Sigel St

S 6th St

S Sartain St
S Jessup St

1100

S 11th St
S Warnock St
S Alder St

Hoffman St
900

Hoffman St
Dudley St
McKean St

S Watts St

Emily St
Mercy St

Emily St

S Hutchinson St

S Percy St
S Darien St
S Mildred St

Emily St
Mercy St

Snyder Ave Station

Snyder Ave

600

9

S Watts St
S Juniper St
S Clarion St

S 13th

Cantrell St
Winton St

B

Jackson St

S 6th St

11

S Rosewood St

Tree St

S 11th St

S 10th St

S 9th St
S Darien St
S Mildred St

Tree St

S 7th St

Daly St

Daly St

S 5th St

Wolf St

S Reese St

Mifflin Sq
2300

S Broad St

Durfor St
Fitzgerald St

S Warnock St
S Alder St

S Hutchinson St

S Percy St

Durfor St
Fitzgerald St

Mifflin St

W Moyamensing Ave

W Ritner St

S 5th St

S Reese St

900

800

700

500

S Okray St

B

S Iseminger St
S Juniper St
S Clarion St

S 12th St
S Sartain St
S Jessup St

W Porter St

S Warnock St
S Alder St
S Percy St

S Darien St
S Mildred St
S Franklin St
S Beulah St

S Sheridan St
S Marshall St
600

S Fairhill St

Vollmer

B

W Shunk St

700

S 5th

St Michael Dr

St Lawrence St

B

Oregon Ave Station

Marconi Plaza

S Watts St
S Juniper St
1300

S Iseminger St
S Camac St
1200

S Sartain St
S Jessup St

W Oregon Ave

12

S Warnock St
S Alder St
1000

S Hutchinson St

S 9th St
S Mildred St

Mollbore Ter

Johnston St

S Darien St
S Franklin St

Mollbore Ter

S Sheridan St
S Marshall St
S Fairhill St

2

S Sterling St

S 12th St
S Marvine St

For an unpretentiously romantic evening, Mr. Martino's BYOB is always a fine bet; the husband-and-wife team never disappoint. For more laissez-faire fare, Marra's remains a cornerstone of Philly cuisine, offering fine pizzas. You will never want for pasta around these parts.

Coffee

- **Caffe Chicco** · 2532 S Broad St
- **Dunkin' Donuts** · 2025 S Broad St
- **Starbucks** · 2201 S Broad St

Gyms

- **Lady Fitness Center** · 2439 S Broad St

Hardware Stores

- **Albert Hardware** · 1609 S 7th St
- **Bruskin Hardware & Lock** · 2451 S 5th St
- **Jam's Hardware** · 2323 S 9th St

Restaurants

- **Criniti Pizza & Restaurant** · 2601 S Broad St
- **Cucina Pazzo** · 1000 Wolf St
- **Johnnie's** · 1400 S 17th St
- **Mamma Maria** · 1637 E Passyunk Ave
- **Marra's** · 1734 E Passyunk Ave
- **Mr Martino's Trattoria** · 1646 E Passyunk Ave
- **Scannicchio's** · 2500 S Broad St

Shopping

- **Fabulous Finds** · 1146 McKean St
- **Interior Concepts** · 1701 E Passyunk Ave

Video Rental

- **Blockbuster** · 1001 Synder Ave
- **South Phila Video** · 2654 S 11th St

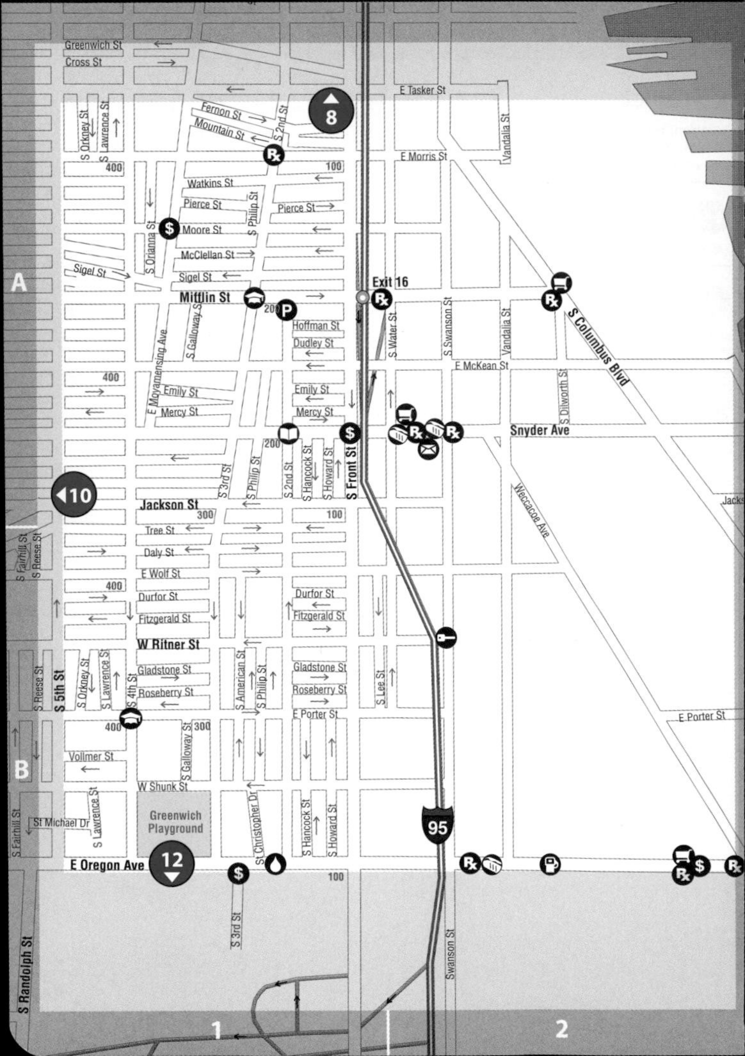

Map 11 · **South Philly East**

N

Greenwich St
Cross St

E Tasker St

Fernon St
Mountain St

8

S Orkney St
S Lawrence St
S 2nd St
S Philip St

400

100

E Morris St

Vandalia St

Watkins St
Pierce St
Pierce St
Moore St

McClellan St

Sigel St
Sigel St

Mittlin St

200

Exit 16

S Water St
S Swanson St
Vandalia St
S Columbus Blvd

A

Hoffman St
Dudley St

E McKean St

S Dilworth St

Snyder Ave

Emily St
Mercy St
Emily St
Mercy St

S Marvdfertising Ave
S Galloway St

400

200

S 3rd St
S Philip St
S 2nd St
S Hancock St
S Howard St
S Front St

Jackson St

300

100

10

Tree St
Daly St
E Wolf St

S Fairhill St
S Reese St

Durfor St
Fitzgerald St
Durfor St
Fitzgerald St

W Ritner St

Gladstone St
Roseberry St

S American St
S Philip St

Gladstone St
Roseberry St
E Porter St

S Lee St

400

S 5th St
S Orkney St
S Lawrence St
S 4th St
S Galloway St

300

Vollmer St

W Shunk St

E Porter St

B

St Michael Dr
S Lawrence St

S Fairhill St

Greenwich
Playground

S Christopher Dr
S Hancock St
S Howard St

E Oregon Ave

12

100

Swanson St

95

S Randolph St

S 3rd St

1   2

For all intents and purposes, the area is connected to the stadiums, if for no other reason than its proximity to both 95 and to Columbus—the two main conduits to the sports complex. It is also land of the Mummers, with "Two Street" being their main thoroughfare.

$ Banks

- **Citizens Bank** · 330 E Oregon Ave
- **Prudential Savings** · Moyamensing Ave & Moore St
- **Wachovia** · 2710 S 3rd St

Car Rental

- **U-Haul** · 2401 S Swanson St

Car Washes

- **Ritz Car Wash & Detail Center** · 234 W Oregon Ave

Cheesesteaks

- **John's Roast Pork** · 14 Snyder Ave
- **Slack's Hoagie Shack** · 41 Snyder Ave
- **Tony Luke Jr's Old Philly Style Sandwiches** · 39 E Oregon Ave

Gas Stations

- **Exxon** · 80 E Oregon Ave

Libraries

- **Whitman Branch** · 200 Snyder Ave

P Parking

Rx Pharmacies

- **K-Mart** · 424 E Oregon Ave
- **Linsky Pharmacy** · 1701 S 2nd St
- **Pathmark (24 hrs)** · 330 E Oregon Ave
- **Rite-Aid** · 10 Snyder Ave
- **Rosica Pharmacy** · 21 Snyder Ave
- **Super Fresh** · 1851 S Columbus Blvd
- **Target** · 1 Mifflin St
- **Vitale Apothecary** · 10 E Oregon Ave

Post Offices

- **Snyder Avenue Station** · 58 Snyder Ave

Schools

- **Furness High** · 1900 S 3rd St
- **Taggart** · 400 W Porter St

Supermarkets

- **Pathmark (24 hrs)** · 330 E Oregon Ave
- **Save-A-Lot** · 48 Snyder Ave
- **ShopRite** · Front Ave & Snyder Ave
- **Super Fresh** · 1851 S Columbus Blvd

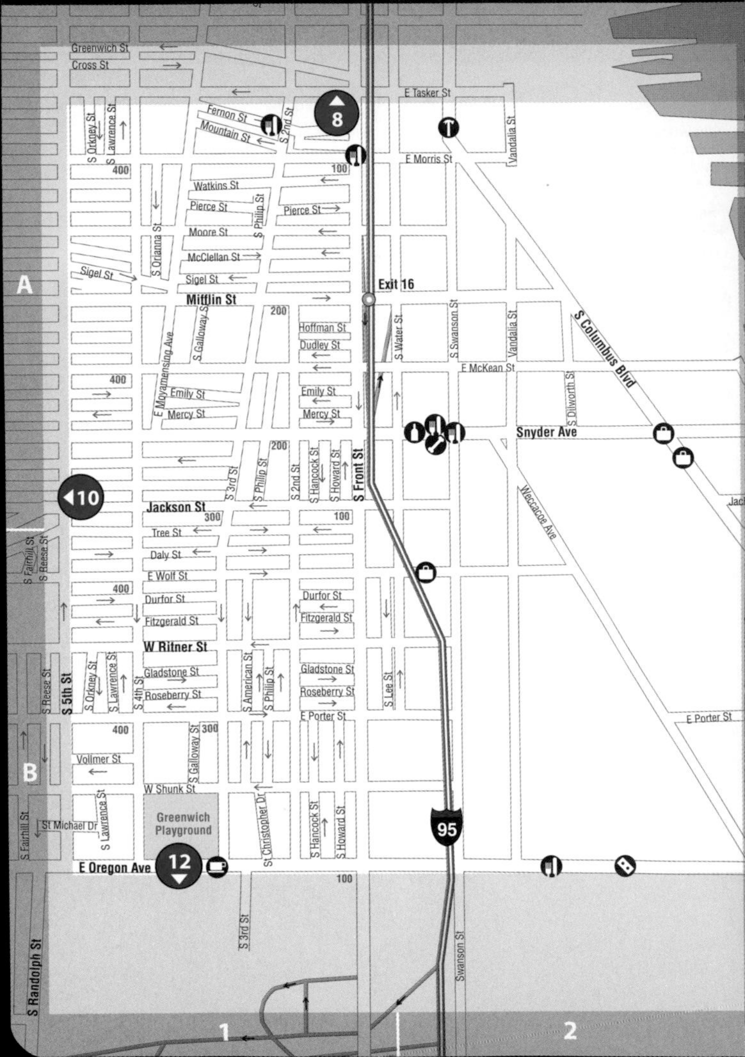

Map 11 · **South Philly East**

N

Greenwich St
Cross St

Fernon St
Mountain St

E Tasker St

E Morris St

▲ 8

S Orkney St
Lawrence St

S 2nd St

S Philip St

Vandalia St

400

100

Watkins St
Pierce St
Moore St
McClellan St

Pierce St

S Oriana St

Sigel St

Sigel St

Mifflin St

Exit 16

S Water St

S Swanson St

Vandalia St

S Columbus Blvd

200

Hoffman St
Dudley St

E McKean St

S Dilworth St

S Galloway Ave

400

Emily St
Mercy St

Emily St
Mercy St

Snyder Ave

S Moyamensing Ave

200

◀ 10

S 3rd St

S Philip St

S 2nd St

S Hancock St

S Howard St

S Front St

Jackson St

300

Jackson St

S Fairhill St

S Reese St

Tree St
Daly St
E Wolf St

100

Wescacoe Ave

S 5th St

Durfor St
Fitzgerald St

Durfor St
Fitzgerald St

W Ritner St

S Orkney St

S Lawrence St

S 4th St

S American St

S Philip St

Gladstone St
Roseberry St

Gladstone St
Roseberry St

E Porter St

S Lee St

E Porter St

400

S Fairhill St

St Michael Dr

Vollmer St

S Lawrence St

S Galloway St

S 300 St

W Shunk St

S Christopher Dr

S Hancock St

S Howard St

Greenwich Playground

95

E Oregon Ave

▼ 12

100

S 3rd St

Swanson St

S Randolph St

1

2

B

A sampling of South Philly in all its glory: lots of Italian joints, with a growing faction of Asian and Latino restaurants emerging. You also have a Tony Luke's for your hoagie-craving needs and a pretty close proximity to the growing shopping region on South Columbus, especially with the arrival of Ikea and Lowe's.

Coffee

· **Dunkin' Donuts** · 330 W Oregon Ave

Hardware Stores

· **The Home Depot** · 1651 S Columbus Blvd

Liquor Stores

· **State Liquor Store** · 35 Snyder Ave

Pet Shops

· **Monster Pets** · 27 Snyder Ave

Restaurants

· **China House** · 49 Snyder Ave
· **Chuck E Cheese's** · 9 Snyder Ave
· **Langostino** · 100 Morris St
· **Tony Luke Jr's Old Philly Style Sandwiches** · 39 E Oregon Ave
· **Two Street Pizza** · 1616 S 2nd St

Shopping

· **Forman Mills** · 22 Wolf St
· **Ikea** · 2206 S Columbus Blvd
· **Lowe's** · 2106 S Columbus Blvd

Video Rental

· **Blockbuster** · 200 Oregon Ave

Map 12 · **Stadiums**

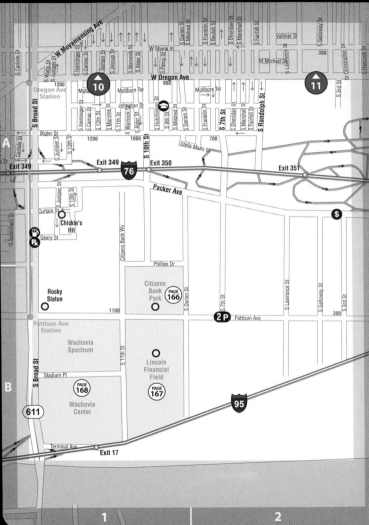

Oh to live in the shadow of the goalposts and foul poles! Of course, for this extreme proximity to Philly's fabled stadia, you must pay a heavy price in daily aggravation, from extreme noise pollution (lots of booing, which carries surprisingly far) to always-jammed streets, to drunken louts peeing on your zinnias.

Banks

• **PNC** • 330 Packer Ave

Gas Stations

• **Citgo** • 3000 S Broad St

O Landmarks

• **Chickie's Hit** • Curtain & Juniper Sts
• **Citizen's Bank Park** • 1 Citizens Bank Way
• **Lincoln Financial Field** • 1020 Pattison Ave
• **Rocky Statue** • 3601 S Broad St

Parking

Pharmacies

CVS • 3000 S Broad St

Schools

• **Thomas** • 927 Johnston St

Map 12 · **Stadiums**

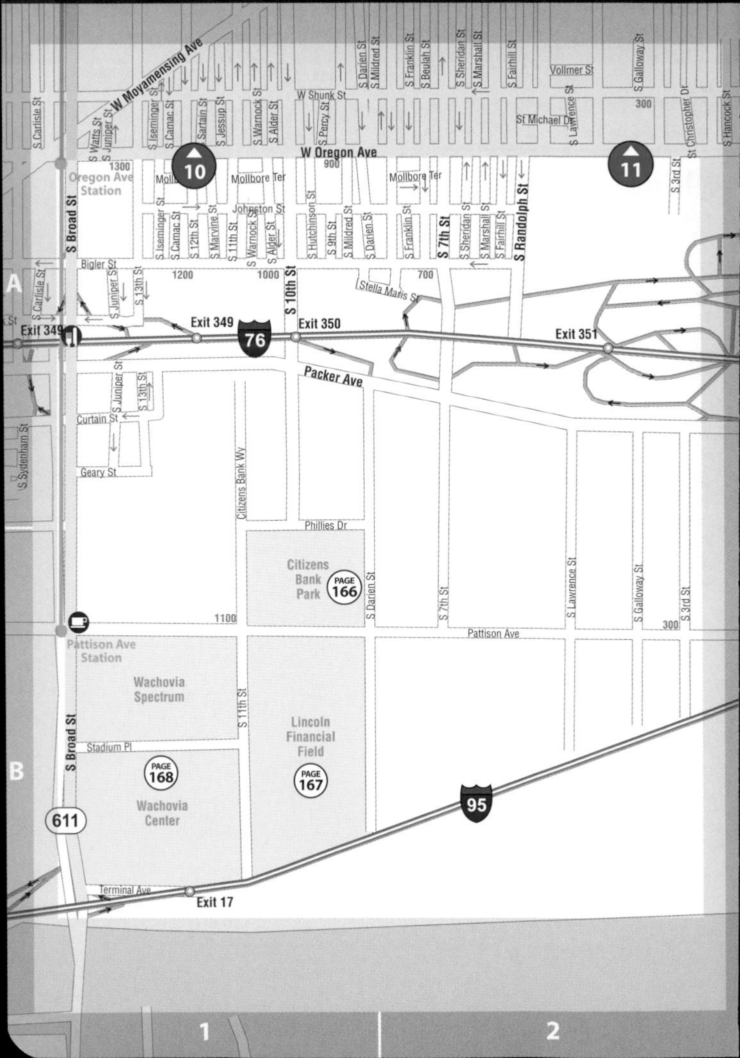

N

S Carlisle St
S Watts St
S Juniper St
W Moyamensing Ave
S Iseminger St
S Camac St
S Sartain St
S Jessup St
S Warnock St
S Alder St
W Shunk St
S Percy St
S Darien St
S Mildred St
S Franklin St
S Beulah St
S Sheridan St
S Marshall St
S Fairhill St
Vollmer St
S Galloway St
S Hancock St
S 3rd St
Christopher Dr

W Oregon Ave
900
St Michael St
S Lawrence St
300

1300
Oregon Ave Station
Moll
Mollbore Ter
Mollbore Ter

10
11

S Iseminger St
S 12th St
S Marvine St
S 11th St
S Warnock St
S Alder St
Johnston St
S Hutchinson St
S 9th St
S Mildred St
S Darien St
S Franklin St
S 7th St
Sheridan St
S Marshall St
S Fairhill St
S Randolph St

Bigler St
1200
1000
700

S 13th St
S Juniper St
S 10th St
Stella Maris St

A

S Carlisle St

Exit 349
Exit 349
Exit 350
Exit 351
76

S Juniper St
S 13th St

Packer Ave

Curtain St
Citizens Bank Wy

Geary St

S Sydenham St

Phillies Dr

Citizens Bank Park
PAGE **166**

S Darien St
S 7th St
S Lawrence St
S Galloway St
S 3rd St
300

1100
Pattison Ave
Pattison Ave Station

S 11th St

Wachovia Spectrum

Lincoln Financial Field
PAGE **167**

B

S Broad St

Stadium Pl
PAGE **168**

Wachovia Center

611
95

Terminal Ave
Exit 17

1
2

Pretty much everything revolves around the stadium complex here, from nightlife to dining and entertainment. Two Street Pizza (Map 11) has a bit of a following, as do a fair number of other similarly themed eateries and bars, but it's all about the teams down here.

Coffee

• **Dunkin' Donuts** • 3601 S Broad St

Restaurants

• **Talk of the Town** • 3020 S Broad St

Map 13 · **West Philly**

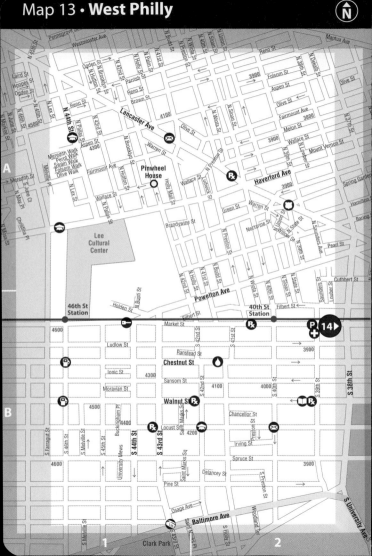

Gorgeous, giant houses dominate the neighborhoods—Victorian monoliths almost too extraordinary to be real. For many years, this was a severely undervalued area, as many of the homes were in various stages of disrepair, but no more. Thanks to Penn's proximity, affluent students have been snapping the houses up and treating them to much-needed refurbishing.

Car Rental

· **Hertz** · 4422 Market St

Car Washes

· **High Tech Brushless** · 4131 Chestnut St

Cheesesteaks

· **Wurst House** · 4301 Baltimore Ave

Gas Stations

· **Amoco** · 4600 Chestnut St
· **Sunoco** · 4601 Walnut St

Hospitals

· **Presbyterian Medical Center** · 39th St & Market St

O Landmarks

· **Pinwheel House** · 42nd & Wallace Sts

Libraries

· **Walnut Street Branch** · 3927 Walnut St

Parking

R Pharmacies

· **Bell Apothecary** · 4014 Lancaster Ave
· **CVS** · 3923 Walnut St
· **CVS** · 4314 Locust St
· **Eckerd** · 4055 Market St
· **Rite-Aid** · 4237 Walnut St

Police

· **16th Police District** · 39th St & Lancaster St

Post Offices

· **Lancaster Avenue Station** · 4123 Lancaster Ave
· **University City** · 228 S 40th St

Schools

· **Locke** · 4550 Haverford Ave
· **Martha Washington** · 766 N 44th St
· **Penn Assisted** · 42nd St & Locust St

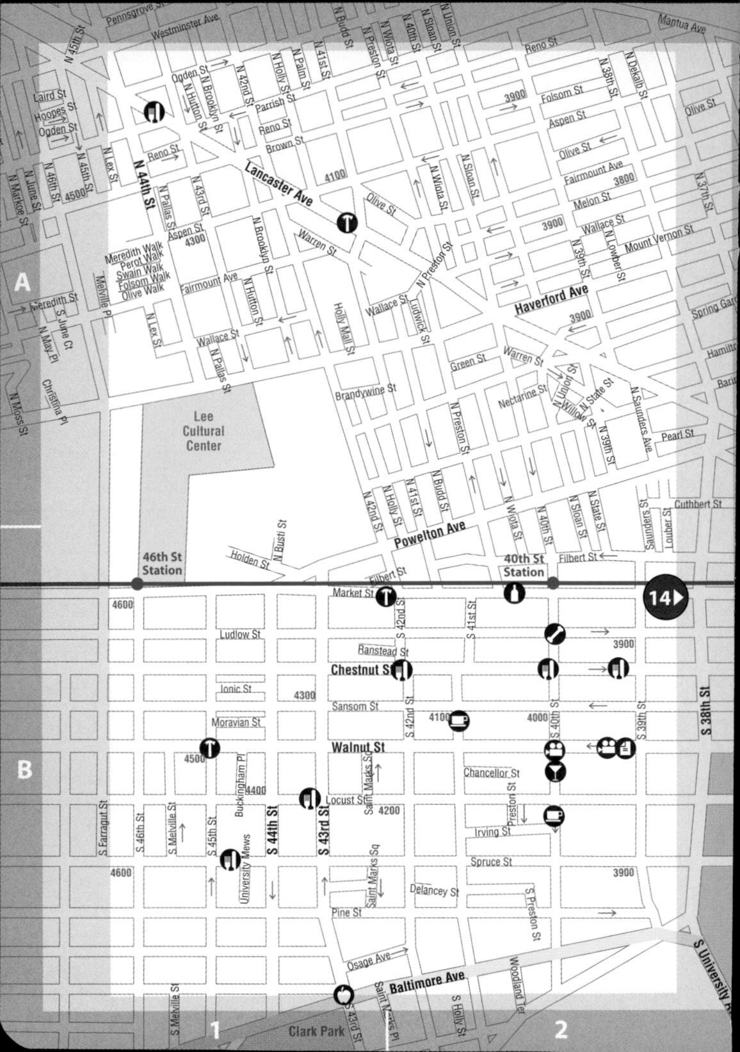

Map 13 • **West Philly**

N

A

Pennsgrove St
Westminster Ave
Mantua Ave

N 48th St
N 47th St
Ogden St
Hoodes St
Laird St
Ogden St
N 46th St
N Ruby St
N 45th St
4500
N Market St

N 44th St
N Pallas St
Reno St

Ogden St
N Brooklyn St
N Preston St
N Palm St
N Wiota St
Parrish St
Reno St
Brown St

Reno St
N Sloan St
N Union St
N 40th St
N Desaix St
N 38th St

3900
Folsom St
Aspen St
Olive St
Olive St

Fairmount Ave
3800
Melon St
Wallace St
Mount Vernon St

N 37th St

Lancaster Ave
4100
Olive St
Warren St

4300
Meredith Walk
Perot Walk
Swain Walk
Folsom Walk
Olive Walk
Meredith Pl
N Alder Pl
N Max Pl
N Christina Pl
N Moss Pl

Aspen St
Fairmount Ave
N Hutton St
Wallace St

Holly Mall St
Wallace St
N Preston St
N Wiota St
N Sloan St
Haverford Ave
3900
Spring Gar
Hamin

Green St
Warren St
N State St
N Saunders Ave
Bart

Brandywine St
N 42nd St
N Budd St
N Preston St
Nectarine St
N Wiota St
N Willow St
N 39th St
Pearl St

Lee Cultural Center

N 41st St
N Budd St
Powelton Ave
N Wiota St
N State St
N 38th St
Saunders St
Louber St
Cuthbert St

S Bust St
Holden St
Filbert St

46th St Station
40th St Station
Filbert St

Market St
Ranstead St
N 42nd St
N 41st St
3900
Market St

14▶

B

4600
Ludlow St
Ionic St
4300
Moravian St
4500

Chestnut St
Sansom St
4100
Walnut St
Chancellor St
Irving St
Spruce St
Delancey St
Pine St

Ranstead St
Chestnut St
S 42nd St
S 41st St
S 40th St
S 39th St
3900
4000
Chancellor St
S Preston St
Irving St
3900
S 38th St

S Farragut St
S 46th St
S Melville St
S 45th St
Buckingham Pl
University Mews
S 44th St
S 43rd St
Saint Marks St
4200
4400
Locust St
4600
Pine St
Osage Ave

Baltimore Ave
Clark Park
S Melville St
S 43rd St
Saint Georges St
S Hicks St
Woodland Ter
S University A

1
2

International cuisine rules the day in West Philly, from Jewish (Koch's) to Thai (Thai Singha House), to Pakistani (Kabobeesh), to the down-home (Dwight's Southern Bar-B-Q), with much in-between. If you ever get your face away from the plate, Smokey Joe's is a Penn staple for quaffing brews.

Coffee

- **Bucks County Coffee** · 240 S 40th St
- **Paris Café 41** · 124 S 41st St

Copy Shops

- **FedEx Kinko's** · 3923 Walnut St

Farmer's Markets

- **Clark Park** · S 43rd St & Baltimore Ave

Hardware Stores

- **CI Presser** · 4224 Market St
- **Mike's Hardware** · 4118 Lancaster Ave
- **Monarch Hardware** · 4502 Walnut St

Liquor Stores

- **State Liquor Store** · 4049 Market St

Movie Theaters

- **Cinemagic 3 at Penn** · 3925 Walnut St
- **The Bridge: cinema de lux** · 40th St & Walnut St

Nightlife

- **Smokey Joe's** · 210 S 40th St

Pet Shops

- **Trade Winds** · 29 S 40th St

Restaurants

- **Dwight's Southern Bar-B-Q** · 4345 Lancaster Ave
- **Kabobeesh** · 4201 Chestnut St
- **Koch's Deli** · 4309 Locust St
- **Pattaya Grill** · 4006 Chestnut St
- **Rx** · 4443 Spruce St
- **Thai Singha House** · 3939 Chestnut St

Map 14 · **University City**

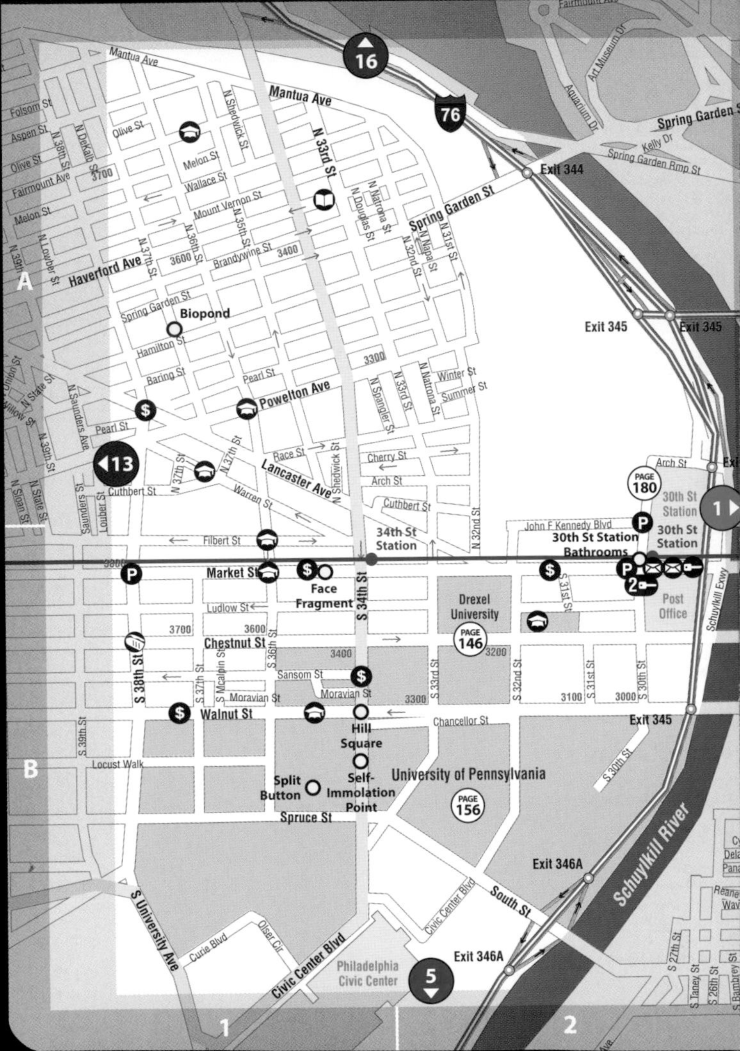

N

Mantua Ave

Mantua Ave

N 33rd St

76

Exit 344

Spring Garden St

Spring Garden St

Fairmount Ave

Kelly Dr

Spring Garden Rmp St

Folsom St

Aspen St

Olive St

Olive St

Fairmount Ave

Melon St

N Dekalb St

N Sheridan St

Melon St

Wallace St

Mount Vernon St

3700

Brandywine St

3600

3400

N Newkirk St

N Natrona St

N 34th St

N Douglas St

Exit 345

Exit 345

Haverford Ave

N Lambert St

Spring Garden St

3300

Biopond

Hamilton St

Baring St

Pearl St

Powelton Ave

N Saunders St

N 40th St

N 39th St

N 38th St

N 37th St

N 36th St

N 35th St

N 34th St

N Natrona St

N Spangler St

Winter St

Summer St

Arch St

Exit

13

Pearl St

$

Cuthbert St

N Saunders St

N Sloan St

N Stanley St

N 41st St

Race St

Lancaster Ave

Cherry St

Arch St

Cuthbert St

N 32nd St

PAGE
180

30th St
Station

$

Warren St

Filbert St

34th
Station

John F Kennedy Blvd

P

30th St Station
Bathrooms

1

P

$

Market St

P

$

Face
Fragment

S 34th St

Drexel
University

$

P

Post
Office

Schuylkill Expwy

Ludlow St

3700

3600

Chestnut St

S McAlpin St

S 37th St

3400

Sansom St

3300

PAGE
146

3200

S 33rd St

S 32nd St

S 31st St

S 30th St

Exit 345

3100

3000

S 38th St

$

Walnut St

Moravian St

Moravian St

Chancellor St

Hill
Square

Locust Walk

Split
Button

Self-
Immolation
Point

University of Pennsylvania

PAGE
156

S 38th St

Exit 346A

Schuylkill River

S University Ave

Curie Blvd

Osler Dr

Spruce St

Exit 346A

Civic Center Blvd

Philadelphia
Civic Center

5

S 26th St

S Taney St

A

B

1

2

With the proximity to Penn and Drexel, there is a definite collegiate vibe to the environs here. Lots of students, protests, progressive stores, cheap restaurants—and keggers. Despite the high level of education, there is still a somewhat festive atmosphere to the proceedings. And by festive, we of course mean beer.

$ Banks

- **Citizens Bank** · 134 S 34th St
- **Commerce Bank** · 3735 Walnut St
- **PNC** · 3535 Market St
- **Sovereign Bank** · 3131 Market St
- **United Bank of Philadelphia** · 38th St & Lancaster Ave

Car Rental

- **Budget** · 30th Street Train Station
- **Hertz** · 2951 Market St
- **National** · 30th Street Train Station

Cheesesteaks

- **Abner's Cheesesteaks** · 3801 Chestnut St

O Landmarks

- **30th St Station Bathrooms** · Market & 30th Sts
- **Biopond** · 3740 Hamilton Wk
- **Face Fragment** · 35th & Market Sts
- **Hill Square** · 34th & Walnut Sts
- **Self-Immolation Point** · 34th & Locust Sts
- **Split Button** · Dtwn 31 & 36 Sts & Locust & Spruce Sts

Libraries

- **Charles L Durham Branch** · 3320 Haverford Ave

P Parking

Post Offices

- **30th Street Train Station** · 2955 Market St
- **Philadelphia Main Office** · 2970 Market St

Schools

- **The Cittone Institute** · 3600 Market St
- **Drew** · 3724 Warren St
- **Drexel University** · 3141 Chestnut St
- **McMichael** · 3543 Fairmount Ave
- **Powel** · 301 N 36th St
- **University City High** · 3601 Filbert St
- **University of Pennsylvania** · 3451 Walnut St

Map 14 · **University City**

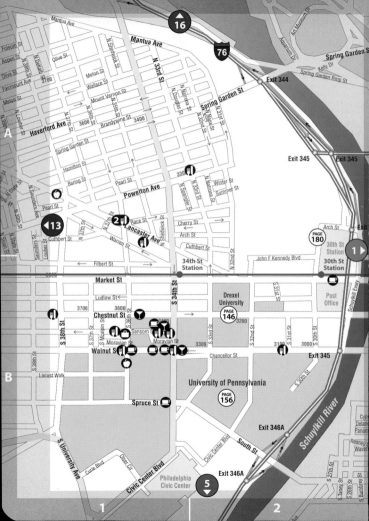

Haven for college students. Rocking bars (New Deck Tavern is especially popular) and assorted eateries, from the cheap (Mad 4 Mex) to the pricey (Zocalo), to the ultra-futuristic (Pod). There's plenty of action to choose from if you want to put the book down and get away from the library for a while.

Coffee

- **Amazon Cafe** • 3417 Spruce St
- **Bucks County Coffee** • 2951 Market St
- **Bucks County Coffee** • 3430 Sansom St
- **Cosi** • 140 S 36th St
- **Dunkin' Donuts** • 3437 Walnut St
- **Starbucks** • 3401 Walnut St

Farmer's Markets

- **Penn Campus** • S 36th St b/w
  Walnut St & Sansom St
- **Powelton** • Lancaster Ave b/w
  N 38th St & Powelton Ave

Nightlife

- **Mad 4 Mex** • 3401 Walnut St
- **New Deck Tavern** • 3408 Sansom St
- **Top Dog Sports Grille** • 3549 Chestnut St

Restaurants

- **Abner's of University City** • 3813 Chestnut St
- **Lemon Grass Thai** • 3626 Lancaster Ave
- **Lou's Retaurante** • 305 N 33rd St
- **Mad 4 Mex** • 3401 Walnut St
- **New Deck Tavern** • 3408 Sansom St
- **Penne** • 3611 Walnut St
- **Picnic** • 3131 Walnut St
- **Pod** • 3636 Sansom St
- **Rana/Ed's** • 3513 Lancaster Ave
- **White Dog Cafe** • 3420 Sansom St
- **Zocalo** • 3600 Lancaster Ave

Shopping

- **EMS** • 130 S 36th St

Map 15 · **Fairmount**

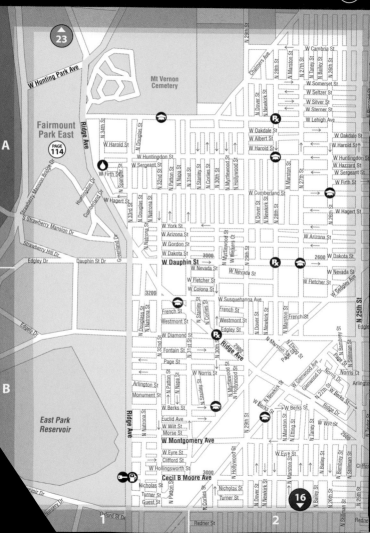

Just north of the Art Museum area and within walking distance of Fairmount Park, the area is coming up big time in Philly's revival. Always bustling Ridge Avenue is crowded with shops and eateries, and for even more green space, the Mt. Vernon Cemetery beckons.

Car Rental

- **U-Haul** · 1701 N 33rd St

Car Washes

- **Clarence Soft Glove Car Wash** · 2533 N 34th St

Gas Stations

- **Getty** · 1701 N 43rd St

Pharmacies

- **Mansion Pharmacy** · 3031 W Diamond St
- **Rite-Aid** · 2801 W Dauphin St
- **Samuel J Robinson Pharmacy** · 2848 W Lehigh Ave

Schools

- **Blaine** · 3001 W Berks St
- **Dr Ethel Allen** · 3200 W Lehigh Ave
- **Fitzsimons Middle** · 2601 W Cumberland St
- **Gideon** · 2817 W Glenwood Ave
- **Strawberry Mansion High** · 3133 Ridge Ave
- **Walton** · 2601 N 28th St
- **Wright** · 2700 W Dauphin St

Map 15 · **Fairmount**

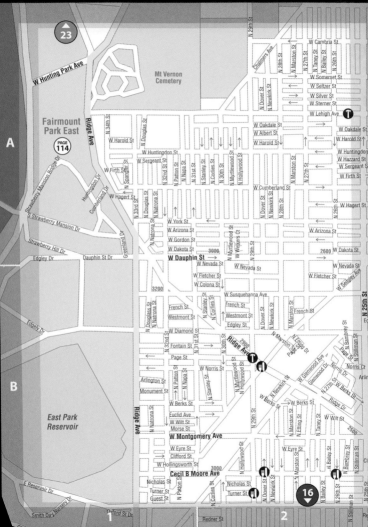

Map 15

Ridge and Cecil B. Moore Avenues are two main arteries of the area. Both are laden with moderate-to-lower-end restaurants, though Dominic's Fish Market has long established a name for itself. Otherwise, you're looking at a pretty standard mix of pizza joints, Chinese restaurants, and plenty of cheesesteak options.

Hardware Stores

- **Bob's Hardware** · 2548 W Lehigh Ave
- **Ridge True Value Hardware** · 2915 Ridge Ave

Restaurants

- **Dominic's Fish Market** · 2842 Cecil B Moore Ave
- **H&J Pizza Delite** · 2832 Ridge Ave
- **Norma's Steak & Hoagie Shop** ·
  2604 Cecil B Moore Ave
- **Yuri Deli** · 1618 N 29th St

Map 16 · **Art Museum West**

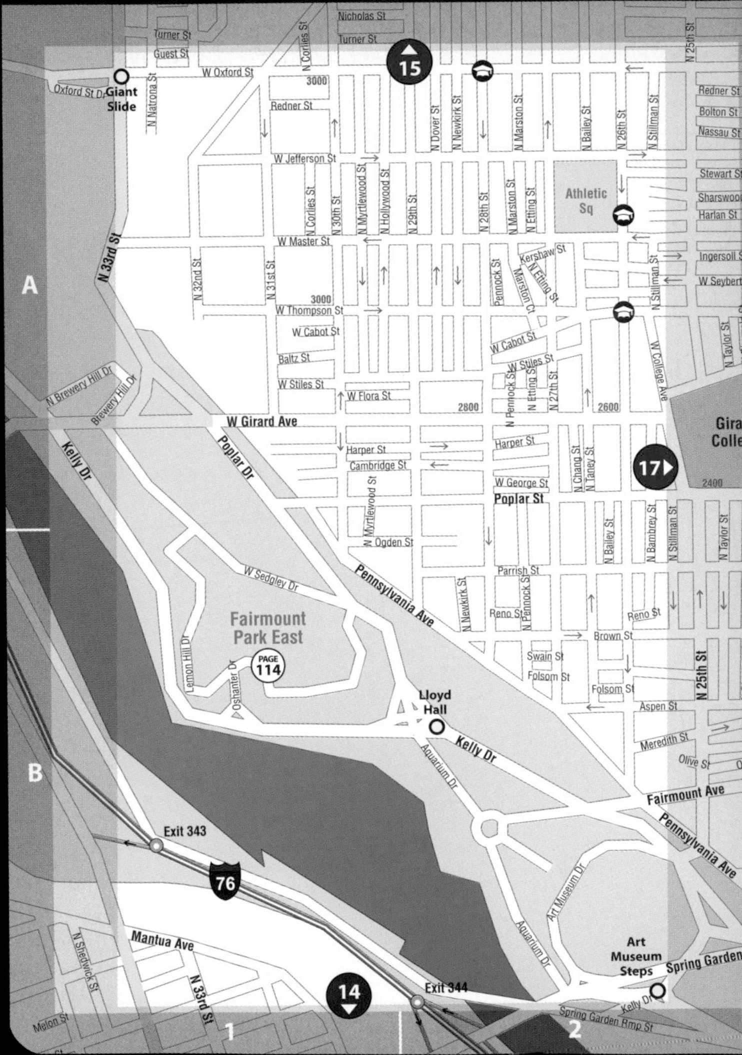

N

Turner St
Guest St
Nicholas St
Turner St
W Oxford St

15

Redner St
Bolton St
Nassau St

Oxford St Dr
Giant Slide
Redner St
W Jefferson St

Stewart St
Sharswood
Harlan St

W Master St

Athletic Sq

Ingersoll S
W Seybert

3000
W Thompson St
W Cabot St

Baltz St
W Cabot St
W Styles St

W Stiles St
W Flora St

W College Ave

2800

A

N 33rd St
N Natrona St
N Corlies St
S 32nd St
N 31st St
N 30th St
N Myrtlewood St
N Hollywood St
N 29th St
N 28th St
N Marston St
N Etting St
Pennock St
Kershaw St
Marston Ct
N Etting St
N Pennock St
N Etting St
N 27th St
N Stillman St
N Taylor St

2600

W Girard Ave

Harper St
Cambridge St

Harper St
W George St
Poplar St

Girard College

N Brewery Hill Dr
Brewery Hill Dr
Kelly Dr
Poplar Dr

N Myrtlewood St
N Ogden St

W Sedgley Dr
Pennsylvania Ave

Parrish St
Reno St
N Chang St
N Taney St
N Bailey St
N Bambrey St
N Stillman St
N Taylor St

Reno St

17

2400

Fairmount Park East
PAGE **114**

Lemon Hill Dr
Ogontier Dr

Brown St

Swain St
Folsom St

Swain St
Folsom St

N 25th St

Lloyd Hall

Kelly Dr

Aspen St

Meredith St

Olive St

B

Aquarium Dr

Fairmount Ave
Pennsylvania Ave

Exit 343

76

N Sheffield St
N 33rd St

Mantua Ave

Art Museum Dr

Aquarium Dr

Art Museum Steps
Spring Garden

Spring Garden Rmp St

Kelly Dr

14

Exit 344

Spring Garden

1   **2**

There is tremendous range in this area, from cold-cash professionals looking to start families to college students ganging together for beer bashes, to families trying to make ends meet. Its proximity to both I-76 and the infamous Loop down Kelly Drive makes it hugely desirable for just about everyone.

O Landmarks

- **Art Museum Steps** • 26th & Benjamin Franklin Pkwy
- **Giant Slide** • 33rd & Oxford Sts
- **Lloyd Hall** • Boathouse Row

Schools

- **Boone** • 1435 N 26th St
- **Kelley** • 1601 N 28th St
- **Morris** • 2600 W Thompson St

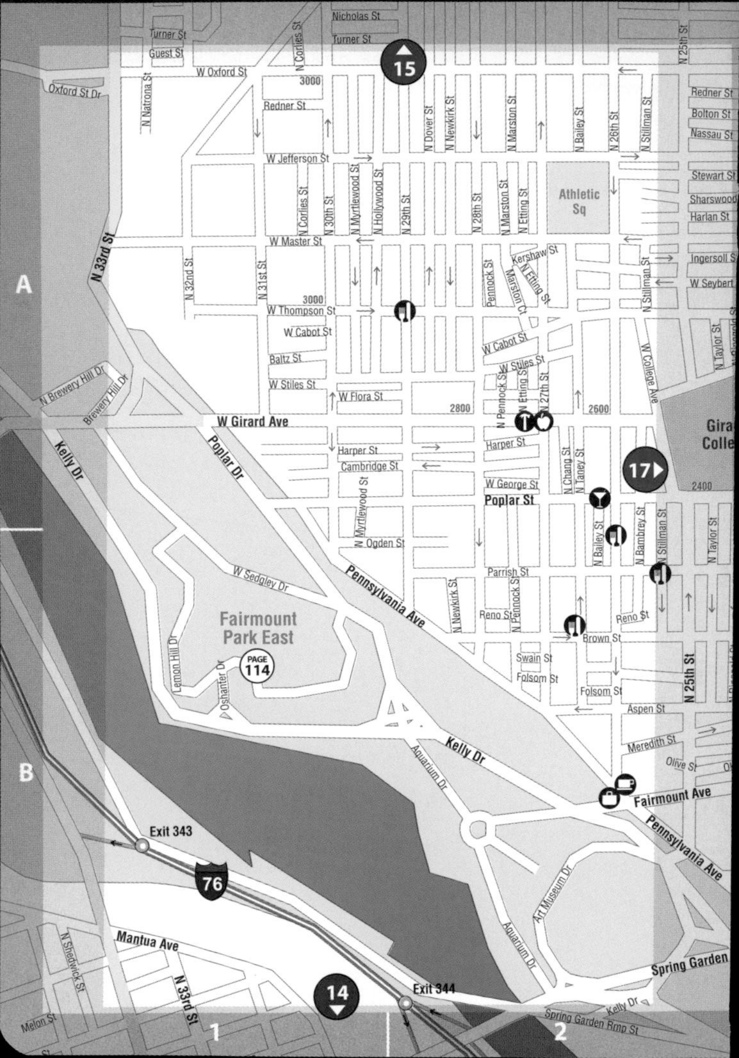

Map 16 · **Art Museum West**

N

Turner St
Guest St
W Oxford St
Nicholas St
Turner St

15

Oxford St Dr
3000
Redner St

N Natrona St
N Corlies St
N Dover St
N Newkirk St
N Marston St
N Bailey St
N 28th St
N Stillman St

W Jefferson St

Redner St
Bolton St
Nassau St

N 33rd St

W Master St

N 32nd St
N 31st St
N 30th St
N Myrtlewood St
N Hollywood St
N 29th St
N 28th St
N Marston St
N Marston St
N Etting St

Athletic
Sq

Stewart St
Sharswood St
Harlan St

A

3000
W Thompson St
W Cabot St
Baltz St
W Stiles St

Kershaw St
Marston St
N Etting St

Ingersoll St
W Seybert St

N College Ave

N Taylor St

W Cabot St

W Flora St

2800

W Stiles St
N Pennock St
N Etting St
27th St

2600

W Girard Ave

N Brewery Hill Dr
Brewery Hill Dr

Poplar Dr

Harper St
Cambridge St

Harper St

N Chang St
N Taney St

Gira
Colle

Kelly Dr

N Myrtlewood St

W George St
Poplar St

N Bailey St
N Bambrey St
N Stillman St

17▶

2400

N Ogden St

N Taylor St

W Sedgley Dr

Pennsylvania Ave

Parrish St

Reno St
N Newkirk St
N Pennock St

**Fairmount
Park East**
PAGE
114

Osheaffer Dr
Lemon Hill Dr

Reno St
Brown St

N 25th St

Swain St
Folsom St

Folsom St

B

Aspen St

Meredith St
Olive St

Fairmount Ave

Aquarium Dr

Kelly Dr

Pennsylvania Ave

Exit 343

76

Aquarium Dr
Art Museum Dr

N Shields St
N 33rd St

Mantua Ave

14

Exit 344

Spring Garden

Melon St

Spring Garden Rmp St
Kelly Dr

1
2

Map 16

For music-lovers, the North Star Bar is one of the premier venues for off-beat tunes and indie rock. Nearby Kelly Drive is a great place to skate or run and meet/pick up similar-minded folk.

Coffee
· **Coffee Room** · 2601 Pennsylvania Ave

Farmer's Markets
· **Girard & 27th** · W Girard Ave & N 27th St

Hardware Stores
· **Nagelberg Hardware** · 2721 W Girard Ave

Nightlife
· **North Star Bar** · 2639 Poplar St

Restaurants
· **China Lotus** · 1301 N 29th St
· **Eg Zolt Soul Food** · 2624 Brown St
· **Regional Pizza** · 873 N 26th St
· **Rose's Deli** · 847 N Stillman St

Shopping
· **Drive Sports** · 2601 Pennsylvania Ave

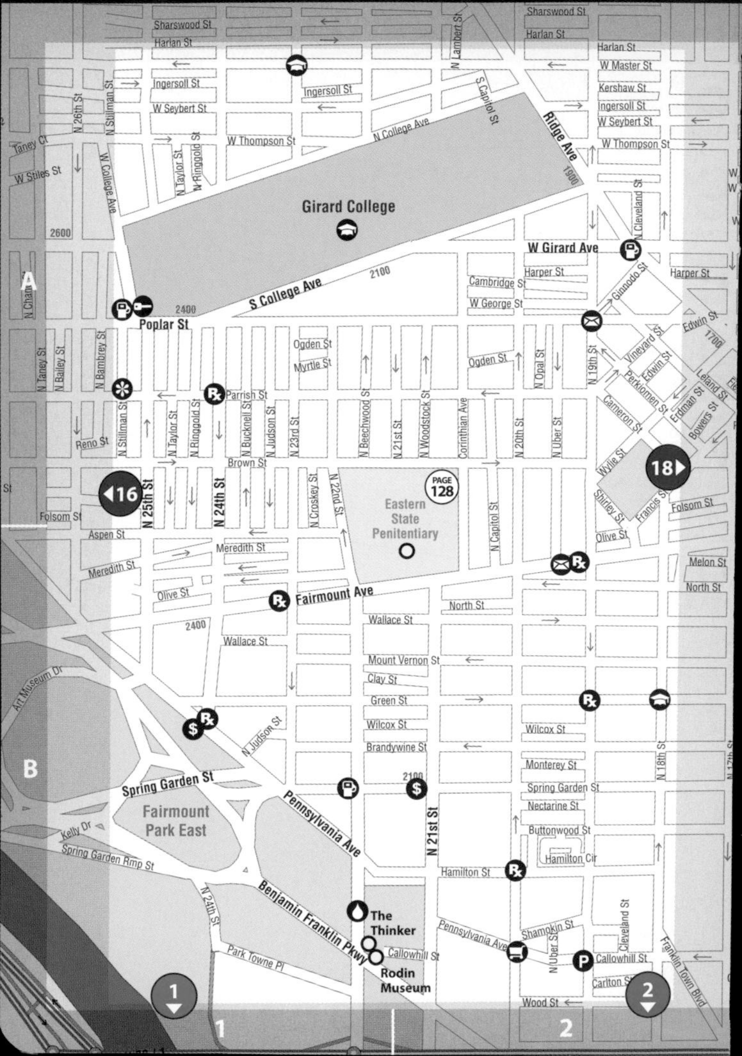

Map 17 · **Art Museum East**

Sharswood St
Harlan St
Sharswood St
Harlan St

Ingersoll St
W Seybert St
W Thompson St
Ingersoll St

Harlan St
W Master St
Kershaw St
Ingersoll St
W Seybert St
W Thompson St

Taney Ct
W Stiles St

N 26th St
W Seybert St

N College Ave
W Taylor St
N Ringgold St

N College Ave
W Thompson St

Girard College

Ridge Ave

W Girard Ave

N Chad

A

2600

S College Ave
2100

Cambridge St
Harper St
W George St

Gunnado St
Cleveland St

Harper St

Edwin Trn

Poplar St
2400

N Taney St
N Bailey St
N Bambrey St

Ogden St
Myrtle St

Ogden St

N 19th St
Vineyard St
Edwin St
Parchment St

Leland St
Erdman St
Bonsall St

Parrish St

Reno St
N Stillman St
N Taylor St
N Ringgold St
N Bucknell St
N Judson St
N 23rd St
N Beechwood St
N 21st St
N Woodstock St
Corinthian Ave
N 20th St
N Uber St

Cameron St
Wylie St

Brown St

◀**16**
N 25th St
N 24th St
N Croskey St

Eastern State Penitentiary
PAGE 128

N Capitol St

Sidney St
Francis St

Folsom St

18▶

Folsom St

Aspen St
Meredith St

Meredith St
Olive St

Olive St

Melon St

Fairmount Ave
2400
Wallace St

Wallace St
Mount Vernon St
Clay St
Green St
Wilcox St
Brandywine St

North St

North St

Wilcox St

N 18th St

B

Fairmount Park East

N Judson St

Spring Garden St

Pennsylvania Ave

2100
N 21st St

Monterey St
Spring Garden St
Nectarine St
Buttonwood St
Hamilton Cir

Kelly Dr
Spring Garden Rmp St

Hamilton St

Benjamin Franklin Pkwy

N 24th St

The Thinker

Callowhill St

Pennsylvania Ave
Shamokin St

N Uber St
Cleveland St
Callowhill St
Carlton St

Franklin Town Blvd

Rodin Museum

Park Towne Pl

Wood St

1

2

Lots of families, students, and young couples—living in sin and duplexes. The area is close to both Fairmount Avenue and 676, which makes it convenient to many places (other than Center City). On the positive side, Eastern State Penitentiary is now open only as a museum and rocking Halloween haunted house.

$ Banks

- **Polonia Bank** · 2133 Spring Garden St
- **Wachovia** · 2401 Pennsylvania Ave

Car Rental

- **U-Haul** · 900 W College Ave

Car Washes

- **Executive Auto Salon of Center City** · 22nd St & Ben Franklin Pkwy

Community Gardens

Gas Stations

- **Amoco** · Ridge Ave & Girard Ave
- **Gulf** · 2201 Spring Garden St
- **Sunoco** · 900 W College Ave

O Landmarks

- **Eastern State Penitentiary** · 22nd St & Fairmount Ave
- **Rodin Museum** · N 22nd St & Benjamin Franklin Pkwy
- **The Thinker** · N 22nd St & Benjamin Franklin Pkwy

P Parking

Rx Pharmacies

- **CVS** · 2320 Fairmount Ave
- **Eckerd** · 2000 Hamilton St
- **Fairmount Pharmacy** · 1900 Green St
- **Henneberry Pharmacy** · 838 N 24th St
- **Philadelphian Pharmacy** · 2401 Pennsylvania Ave
- **Rite-Aid** · 1924 Fairmount Ave

Post Offices

- **Fairmount** · 1939 Fairmount Ave
- **Fairmount Station** · 900 N 19th St

Schools

- **Girard College** · 2101 S College Ave
- **Vaux Middle** · 2300 W Master St
- **Waring** · 1801 Green St

Supermarkets

- **Whole Foods** · 2001 Pennsylvania Ave

Map 17 · **Art Museum East**

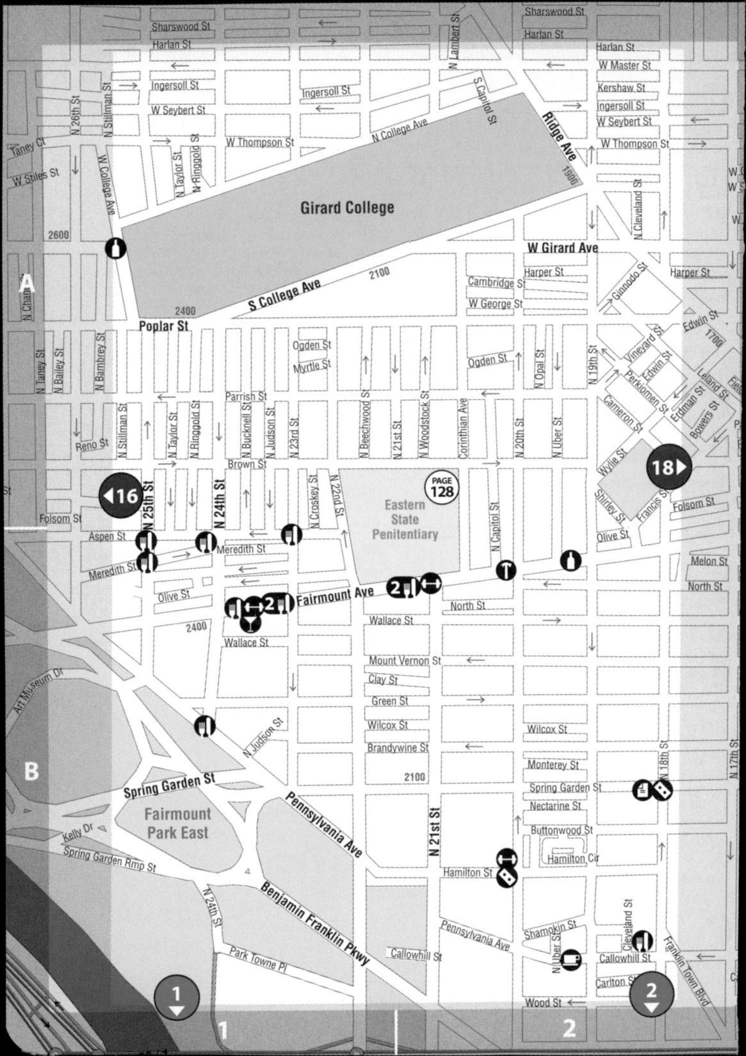

N

Sharswood St
Harlan St
Sharswood St
Harlan St

Ingersoll St
W Seybert St
W Thompson St

W Master St
Kershaw St
Ingersoll St
W Seybert St
W Thompson St

N College Ave

S Capitol St

Ridge Ave

N 26th St
Taney Ct
N College Ave
N Taylor St
N Ringgold St

W Stiles St
W Seybert St
W Thompson St

Girard College

2600

A

N Char

2400

S College Ave

Poplar St

2100

W Girard Ave

Cambridge St
W George St

Harper St

N 19th St

N Cleveland St

Harper St

Edwin St

2400

Poplar St

N Taney St
N Bailey St
N Bambrey St
N Stillman St
N Taylor St
N Ringgold St
N Bucknell St
N Judson St
N 23rd St
N Beechwood St
N 21st St
N Woodstock St
Corinthian Ave
N 20th St
N Uber St

Reno St

Ogden St
Myrtle St

Parrish St

Brown St

Ogden St

N 19th St
Ormond St
Bowers St
Eldman St
Leland St

Cameron St

Parkmonte St

N 18th St

◄16

N 25th St
N 24th St
N Croskey St
N pizza St

Wylie St

Shamoka St
Francis St

18►

Folsom St

Aspen St

Meredith St

Olive St

Eastern State
Penitentiary

PAGE
128

N Capitol St

Olive St

Melon St

North St

Meredith St

2

Fairmount Ave

2

Folsom St

Melon St
North St

Olive St

2

Fairmount Ave

2400

Wallace St

Wallace St

North St

Art Museum Dr

N Judson St

Mount Vernon St
Clay St
Green St
Wilcox St
Brandywine St

Wilcox St

Monterey St
Spring Garden St
Nectarine St

N 18th St

Spring Garden St

B

Fairmount
Park East

Spring Garden St

Pennsylvania Ave

2100

N 21st St

Buttonwood St

Hamilton Cir

Kelly Dr

Spring Garden Rmp St

Benjamin Franklin Pkwy

Hamilton St

N 21st St

Pennsylvania Ave

Callowhill St

Shamokin St

N Uber St

Cleveland St

Callowhill St
Carlton St

Franklin Town Blvd

Park Towne Pl

Wood St

1

1

2

2

Everybody loves Bridgid's, a casual bar/restaurant that is typical of the atmosphere in the area. The Bishop's Collar is a formidable drinking hole, offering many different beers and lots of exciting, cool people with which to hang. For cheap, late-night munchies, Little Pete's is always there for you.

Coffee

• **Starbucks** • 1945 Callowhill St

Copy Shops

• **FedEx Kinko's** • 1816 Spring Garden St

Gyms

• **Curves** • 2333 Fairmount Ave
• **Life Sport Fitness Resource Center** •
  2112 Fairmount Ave
• **Philadelphia Sports Club** • 2000 Hamilton St

Hardware Stores

• **Farimont Hardware** • 2011 Fairmount Ave

Liquor Stores

• **State Liquor Store** • 1935 Fairmount Ave
• **State Liquor Store** • 2511 W Girard Ave

Nightlife

• **The Bishop's Collar** • 2349 Fairmount Ave

Restaurants

• **Aspen** • 747 N 25th St
• **The Bishop's Collar** • 2349 Fairmount Ave
• **Bridgid's** • 726 N 24th St
• **Figs** • 2501 Meredith St
• **Gloria's Gourmet** • 2120 Fairmount Ave
• **Illuminare** • 2321 Fairmount Ave
• **Jack's Firehouse** • 2130 Fairmount Ave
• **Little Pete's** • 2401 Pennsylvania Ave
• **London Grill** • 2301 Fairmount Ave
• **Rembrandt's** • 741 N 23rd St
• **Rose Tattoo Cafe** • 1847 Callowhill St

Video Rental

• **Hollywood Video** • 2000 Hamilton St
• **TLA Video** • 1808 Spring Garden St

Map 18 · **Lower North Philly**

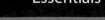

Essentials

Map 18

The area is dominated by the Community College of Philadelphia, a sprawling affair that has actually turned out to be an absolute boon to the area. There are also a number of high schools nearby, so it is not uncommon to see the streets teeming with students of various ages.

$ Banks
- **Citizens Bank** · 1201 Spring Garden St
- **PNC** · 702 N Broad St

Car Rental
- **U-Haul** · 1200 Spring Garden St
- **U-Haul** · 314 N 13th St

Community Gardens

Gas Stations
- **Gulf** · 11th St & Spring Garden St

O Landmarks
- **Metropolitan Opera House** · Broad St & Fairmount Ave

P Parking

Pharmacies
- **CVS** · 922 N Broad St
- **Rite-Aid** · 1201 W Girard Ave

Post Offices
- **Girard Avenue Station** · 905 N Broad St

Schools
- **Community College of Philadelphia** · 1700 Spring Garden St
- **Eastern University-Campolo School for Social Change** · 990 Buttonwood St
- **Franklin High** · 550 N Broad St
- **Masterman** · 1699 Spring Garden St
- **Spring Garden** · 1130 Melon St
- **Stoddart-Fleisher Middle** · 540 N 13th St

Map 18 • **Lower North Philly**

N

W Seybert St
W Thompson St
W Cabot St
W Stiles St
W Flora St

W Flora St
N Burns St

Patrick Henry Pl
Curtis Pl
N Jessup St
Valley Forge Pl
Lafayette Pl
W Stiles St
N Percy St
W Stiles St

1500
Girard Ave Station
1400
1300
W Girard Ave
1100
W Flora St
N Danien St

Harper St

Vineyard St
Edwin St
1100
Green Hills St
Cambridge St
Cambridge St
W Harper St
N 12th St

Harmer St
W George St
Poplar St
George Pl
N Percy St
N Hutchinson Pl

A
Ogden St
Parrish St
Ogden St
Myrtle Pl
N Camac St
N Budd St
Sartain Pl
Jessup Pl
N Budd St
Parrish Dr
N Hutchinson Pl
Oden Pl
Percy Pl
N Percy St

Leland St
Field St
Reno St
Parrish St
Noddels Ct
N Burns St
S Broad St
Howard St

Bowers St
Brown St
Reno St
N Camac St
Reno St
Brown St

Francis St
Edgemont St
Chadwick St
Swain St
Olive St
Brown St

Folsom St
Ridge St
Fairmount Ave Station
Fairmount Ave
N Sydenham St
W Potts St
Potts St
1200
Fairmount Ave
N Danien St

◀17
Fairmount Ave
Melon St
Melon St
Melon St
Melon St
19▶
Melon St
N Park Ave

North St
Lemon St
North St
Warnock St
Aldet St
Melon St

Wallace St
N Watts St
Lemon St
Lemon St
Mount Vernon St
Clay St
Green St
Brandywine St
N Percy St

Spring Garden St Station
Ridge St
Spring Garden 1100

Spring Garden St
N 16th St
N 12th St
Nectarine St
Nectarine St
Buttonwood St
Hamilton St

B
Buttonwood St
Community College of Philadelphia
Hamilton St
Hamilton St
Noble St
Shamokin St
N 12th St
N Percy St
N 9th St

Fairmount Town Blvd
Callowhill St
Carlton St
Carlton St
Wood St
Pearl St
Wood St
Exit US Hwy 3

N 15th St
N Clarion St
Vine St
676
Exit 3
2
Exit 3
3

Winter St
Summer St
Summer St
Spring St
N Watts St
N Clarion St
Florist St
Summer St
N Sartain St
N Marvine St
N 11th St
N Clifton St
N Jessup St
Spring St
Winters Ct
Spring St
Winter St
Providence Ln

2
N Alder St

Race St

Sundries / Entertainment

For quick-and-dirty chow, you could do much worse than hitting up the ubiquitous food trucks tucked around the CCP campus. Otherwise, the cabbage-filled scent emanating from the Warsaw Café attracts those of Eastern European descent with its high-carb siren song.

Coffee

- **Café Nine Ninty** · 990 Spring Garden St
- **Dunkin' Donuts** · 839 N Broad St
- **Dunkin' Donuts** · 917 W Girard Ave

Copy Shops

- **Docucare Copy Service** · 900 N Broad St

Farmer's Markets

- **Girard & 13th** · W Girard Ave & N 13th St

Restaurants

- **City View Pizza** · 1547 Spring Garden St
- **Siam Lotus** · 931 Spring Garden St
- **Warsaw Cafe** · 306 S 16th St
- **Westy's Tavern & Restaurant** · 1440 Callowhill St

Shopping

- **Diving Bell Scuba Shop** · 681 N Broad St

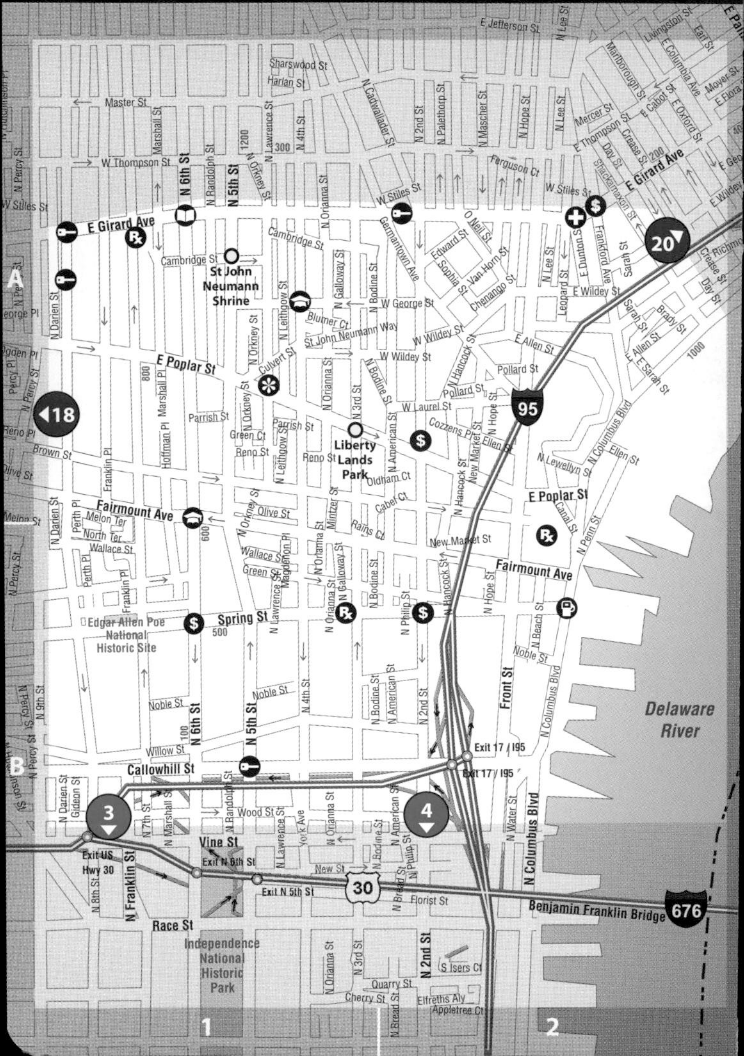

Map 19 · **Northern Liberties**

Master St
Harlan St
Sharswood St
E Jefferson St
W Thompson St
N 6th St
N Randolph St
N 5th St
1200
300
N Orkney St
W Lawrence St
W Montgomery Ave
N 2nd St
W Palethorp St
N Mascher St
W Hope St
N Lee St
E Columbia Ave
E Thompson St Crease St
Day St
E Oxford St
E Girard Ave
E Girard Ave

Cambridge St
Cambridge St
W Stiles St
O Neil St
Edward St
Sophia St
Van Horn St
N Lee St
E Dunton St
Leopard St
W Wildey St
Shackamaxon St
Frankford Ave
20

St John
Neumann
Shrine
N Dickey St
N Lethgow St
N Galloway St
N Bodine St
W George St
St John Neumann Way
Blumer Ct
Chenango St
E Allen St
E Allen St
1000

E Poplar St
N Orkney St
N Calvert St
N 3rd St
N Orianna St
W Wildey St
W Hancock St
Polliad St
Polliad St
E Allen St

Parrish St
Green Ct
Reno St
N Lethgow St
Parrish St
N 3rd St
W Laurel St
Cozzens St
W Hope St
New Market St
New Market St
Ellen St
95

Liberty
Lands
Park
Oldham Ct
Cabot St
N Hancock St
N Lewellyn St
N Columbus Blvd
Ellen St

Fairmount Ave
600
Melon Ter
North St
Wallace St
N Orkney St
Olive St
Mintzer St
N Orianna St
Rains Ct
Cabot Ct
New Market St
N Beach St
N Penn St
Fairmount Ave

Edgar Allen Poe
National
Historic Site
Spring St
500
Wallace St
Green St
Napoleon St
N Lawrence St
N Orianna St
N Galloway St
N Bodine St
N Philip St
Front St
N Beach St
N Columbus Blvd

Noble St
Noble St
N 4th St
N Bodine St
N American St
N 2nd St
N Hope St

Delaware
River

Willow St
Callowhill St
N 6th St
N 5th St
Exit 17 / I95
Exit 17 / I95

3
Wood St
N Randolph St
Marshall St
York Ave
N Orianna St
N American St
4

Vine St
Exit US Hwy 30
Exit N 8th St
Exit N 5th St
New St
N Bread St
N Bodine St
N Philip St
N Beach St
Florist St
N Water St
N Columbus Blvd
676

30
Benjamin Franklin Bridge

Race St
Independence
National
Historic Park
N Orianna St
N 3rd St
N 2nd St
S Isers Ct

Quarry St
Cherry St
N Beach St
Elfreths Aly
Appletree Ct

18
A
B

1
2

For ten years, people have been talking about this neighborhood taking off—and those predictions are finally coming true. Despite not having any convenient supermarkets or other necessities, the area is booming with artists, hipsters, and hippies, all grooving on the multitudes of refurbished lofts and smooth urban vibe.

$ Banks

- **Citizens Bank** · 201 Spring Garden St
- **PNC** · 6th St & Spring Garden St
- **Third Federal** · 905 N 2nd St
- **Wachovia** · 2 W Girard Ave

🚗 Car Rental

- **Rent-A-Wreck** · 959 N 8th St
- **U-Haul** · 223 W Girard Ave
- **U-Haul** · 501 Callowhill St
- **Wolfson Fred Car Renting** · 8th St & Girard Ave

❋ Community Gardens

⛽ Gas Stations

- **Mobil** · 600 N Columbus Blvd

➕ Hospitals

- **St Joseph's** · 16 W Girard Ave

○ Landmarks

- **Liberty Lands Park** · 3rd & Poplar Sts
- **St John Neumann Shrine** · 1019 N 5th St

📖 Libraries

- **Ramonita de Rodriguez Branch** ·
  600 W Girard Ave

℞ Pharmacies

- **Ellis Pharmacy** · 25 Brown St
- **Get Well Pharmacy** · 708 W Girard Ave
- **Rite-Aid** · 339 Spring Garden St

🚌 Schools

- **Bodine High** · 1101 N 4th St
- **Kearny** · 601 Fairmount Ave

Map 19 · **Northern Liberties**

Map 19

Many Philadelphians assume the Standard Tap is the pure dope, but there are other possibilities, including the 700 Club and the Aqua Lounge. Neighborhood punks will dig The Fire and village idiots can check out Tiki Bob's. Chow is also on grand display here, including Azure, Las Cazuelas, and the amazing Silk City.

Coffee

- **Latte Lounge** • 816 N 4th St
- **Tabula Rasa Café** • 944 N 2nd St

Gyms

- **Iron Works II** • 821 N 2nd St

Liquor Stores

- **State Liquor Store** • 232 W Girard Ave

Nightlife

- **700 Club** • 700 N 2nd St
- **The Abbaye** • 637 N 3rd St
- **Aqua Lounge** • 323 W Girard Ave
- **Egypt** • 520 N Columbus Blvd
- **Electric Factory** • 421 N 7th St
- **Finnigan's Wake** • 537 N 3rd St
- **The Fire** • 412 W Girard Ave
- **McFadden's** • 461 N 3rd St
- **Ministry of Information** • 449 Poplar St
- **N 3rd** • 801 N 3rd St
- **Ortlieb's Jazz House** • 847 N 3rd St
- **Palmer Social Club** • 601 Spring Garden St
- **Shampoo** • 417 N 8th St
- **Standard Tap** • 901 N 2nd St
- **Tiki Bob's** • 461 N 3rd St
- **Transit Nightclub** • 600 Spring Garden St

Restaurants

- **The Abbaye** • 637 N 3rd St
- **Azure** • 931 N 2nd St
- **Il Cantuccio** • 701 N 3rd St
- **Johnny Brenda's** • 1201 Frankford Ave
- **Kind Café** • 724 N 3rd St
- **Las Cazuelas** • 426-28 Girard Ave
- **N 3rd** • 801 N Third St
- **Pigalle** • 702-704 N 2nd St
- **Radicchio** • 314 York Ave
- **Rustica Pizza** • 903 N 2nd St
- **Silk City** • 435 Spring Garden St
- **Standard Tap** • 901 N 2nd St

Shopping

- **A Pea in the Pod** • 456 N 5th St
- **Dot Dash** • 630 N 2nd St
- **Very Bad Horse** • 606 N 2nd St

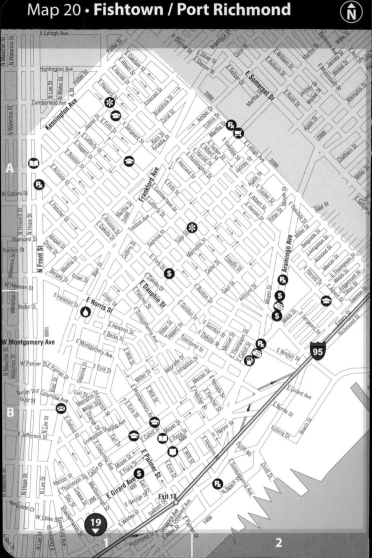
Map 20 · **Fishtown / Port Richmond**

Recently, local press has given this area a lot more exposure. The problem is, only some of it has been positive. While it is yet another burgeoning area, providing relief for suddenly overpriced No-Libs, it is also known for a grisly, shocking killing of a teen—by his supposed best friends and SO. Take your pick.

$ Banks

- **Beneficial Savings** · 2500 Aramingo Ave
- **Citizens Bank** · 2497 Aramingo Ave
- **Fleet** · 423 E Girard Ave
- **Third Federal** · York St & Memphis St

Car Washes

- **New City Car Wash & Detail Center** · 1868 Frankford Ave

Cheesesteaks

- **Grilladelphia** · 2330 Aramingo Ave
- **Slack's Hoagie Shack** · 2499 Aramingo Ave

Community Gardens

Gas Stations

- **Exxon** · 2330 Aramingo Ave

Libraries

- **Fishtown Community Branch** · 1217 E Montgomery Ave
- **Kensington Branch** · 104 W Dauphin St

Rx Pharmacies

- **CVS** · 2400 Aramingo Ave
- **Eckerd** · 2545 Aramingo Ave
- **Friendly Pharmacy** · 2258 N Front St
- **Rite-Aid** · 2132 E Lehigh Ave
- **Wynnebrook Pharmacy** · 54 E Berks St

Police

- **26th Police District** · Girard Ave & Montgomery Ave

Post Offices

- **Kensington Station** · 1602 Frankford Ave

Schools

- **Alexander Adaire** · 1300 E Palmer St
- **H A Brown** · 1946 E Sergeant St
- **Douglas High** · 2700 E Huntingdon St
- **Kensington High** · 2051 E Cumberland St
- **Penn Middle** · 600 E Thompson St

Supermarkets

- **Save-A-Lot** · 2132 E Lehigh Ave

Map 20 · **Fishtown / Port Richmond**

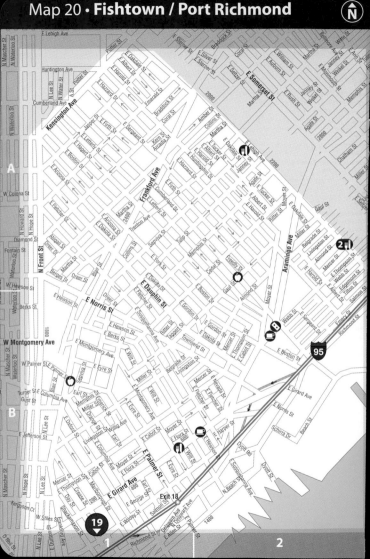

Map 20

Apart from being within shouting distance of (arguably) the best pizza in the city (Tacconelli's), the area is also rife with its own growing culinary scene, including the old breakfast standby, Sulimay's. The expectation remains that this area is about to blow up with hipster goodness, much as No-Libs did several years back.

Coffee

- **Dunkin' Donuts** · 2437 Aramingo Ave
- **Dunkin' Donuts** · 717 E Girard Ave

Farmer's Markets

- **Greensgrow Market Stand** ·
  2501 E Cumberland St
- **Palmer Park** · Frankford Ave & E Palmer St

Restaurants

- **Best Deli II** · 2616 E Lehigh Ave
- **Stefano's Original** · 2200 E Lehigh Ave
- **Stock's Bakery** · 2614 E Lehigh Ave
- **Sulimay's Restaurant** · 632 E Girard Ave

Video Rental

- **Hollywood Video** · 2489 Aramingo Ave

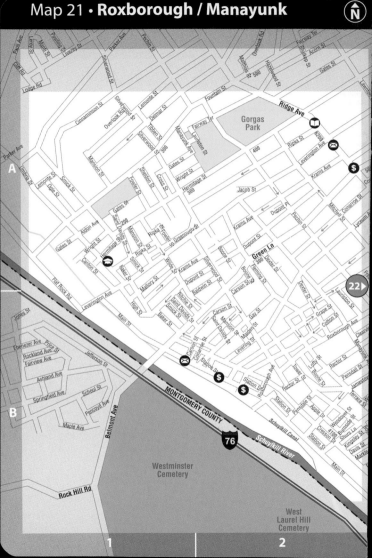

Map 21 · **Roxborough / Manayunk**

The locals might be bitterly divided as to the benefits of Manayunk's glowing nightlife—apart from anything else, the traffic snarl on weekends can be overwhelming—but none would argue about the rise in property values. Perhaps the city's best example of what a few good bars and restaurants can do to a once low-rent area.

Banks

- **Citizens Bank** • 4370 Main St
- **Hudson United** • 4312 Main St
- **Wachovia** • 6128 Ridge Ave

Libraries

- **Roxborough Branch** • 6245 Ridge Ave

Post Offices

- **Manayunk Station** • 4431 Main St
- **Roxborough Postal Store** • 6184 Ridge Ave

Schools

- **Dobson** • 4667 Umbria St

Map 21 · **Roxborough / Manayunk**

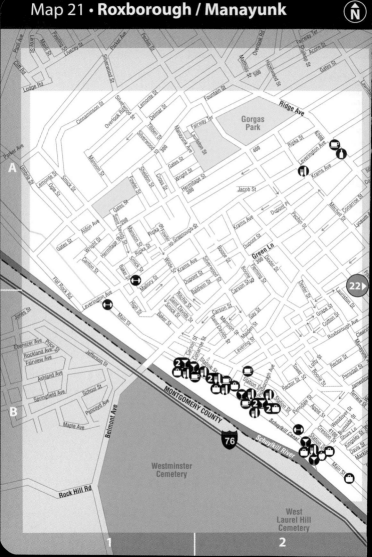

For a certain range of young, eligible yups, the area has it all, from stellar dining (Jake's, Sonoma, Adobe) to balls-out clubs and bars, such as the Grape Street Pub and Bourbon Blue. If you come, be prepared to wait and don't forget the plastic —nothing this splendiferous comes cheap.

Coffee

- **Bucks County Coffee** · 4311 Main St
- **Dunkin' Donuts** · 6191 Ridge Ave
- **Grass Roots Coffee** · 110 Cotton St
- **La Colombe Panini** · 4360 Main St
- **Starbucks** · 4415 Main St

Farmer's Markets

- **Manayunk** · 4120 Main St
- **Roxborough** · Ridge Ave & Leverington Ave

Gyms

- **Curves** · 4590 Main St
- **Dynamite Gym** · 123 Leverington Ave
- **Sweat** · 4151 Main St

Liquor Stores

- **State Liquor Store** · 6174 Ridge Ave

Nightlife

- **Bayou Bar and Grill** · 4245 Main St
- **Bourbon Blue** · 2 Rector St
- **Castle Roxx Café** · 105 Shurs Ln
- **Flatrock Saloon** · 4301 Main St
- **Grape Street** · 4100 Main St
- **Kildare's** · 4417 Main St
- **Manayunk Brewery and Restaurant** · 4120 Main St
- **Sonoma** · 4411 Main St
- **Tonic** · 4421 Main St

Restaurants

- **Adobe Café** · 4550 Mitchell St
- **Ben & Jerry's** · 4356 Main St
- **Bourbon Blue** · 2 Rector St
- **Couch Tomato Café** · 102 Rector St
- **Jake's** · 4365 Main St
- **Kildare's** · 4417 Main St
- **Le Bus** · 4266 Main St
- **Manayunk Brewery & Restaurant** · 4120 Main St
- **Sonoma** · 4411 Main St
- **Zesty's Restaurant** · 4382 Main St

Shopping

- **Chicos** · 4367 Main St
- **Leehe Fai** · 4343 Main St
- **Main St Music** · 4444 Main St
- **Pompanoosuc Mills** · 4120 Main St
- **Pottery Barn** · 4230 Main St
- **Restoration Hardware** · 4130 Main St
- **Somnia** · 4050 Main St
- **Worn Yesterday** · 4235 Main St

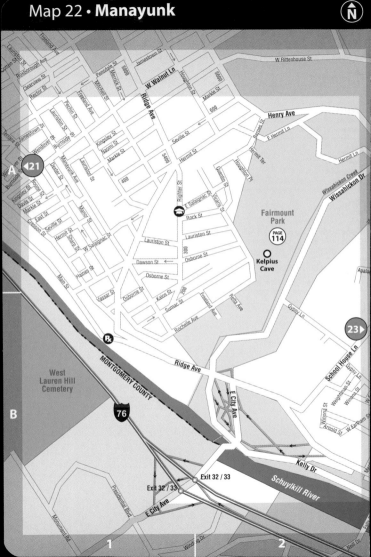

Map 22 • **Manayunk**

The lower section of town has less renown, as most of the nightlife starts north of Walnut Lane, but is that much more livable, accordingly. You also have multiple access points to the gorgeous Wissahickon trail, for both running, biking and sunlit strolls.

Landmarks
• **Kelpius Cave** • Sumac St & Fairmount Park

Pharmacies
• **CVS** • 3780 Main St

Schools
• **Cook-Wissahickon School** • 201 E Salaignac St

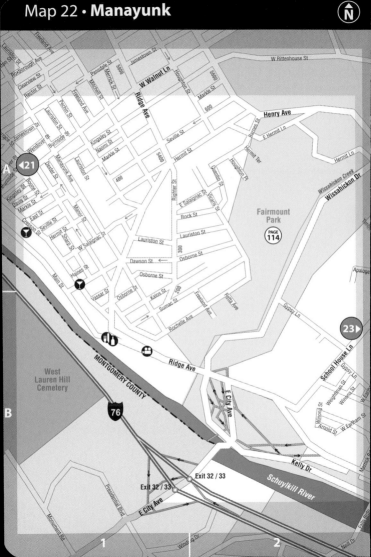

Map 22 • **Manayunk**

A far more mellow section of town than its noisy brethren up slightly to the north, this area still has some choice spots for the nightlife crowd, including the ultra-luxe Chemistry (Map 21) and the decidedly casual Dawson Street Pub. For extra kicks, you can try to locate the Kelpius Cave with your honeybun.

Liquor Stores

· **State Liquor Store** · 3720 Main St

Movie Theaters

· **United Artists Main Street 6** · 3720 Main St

Nightlife

· **Dawson St Pub** · 100 Dawson St
· **Vaccarelli's East End Tavern** · 4001 Cresson St

Restaurants

· **Muldoon's Waterway** · 3720 Main St

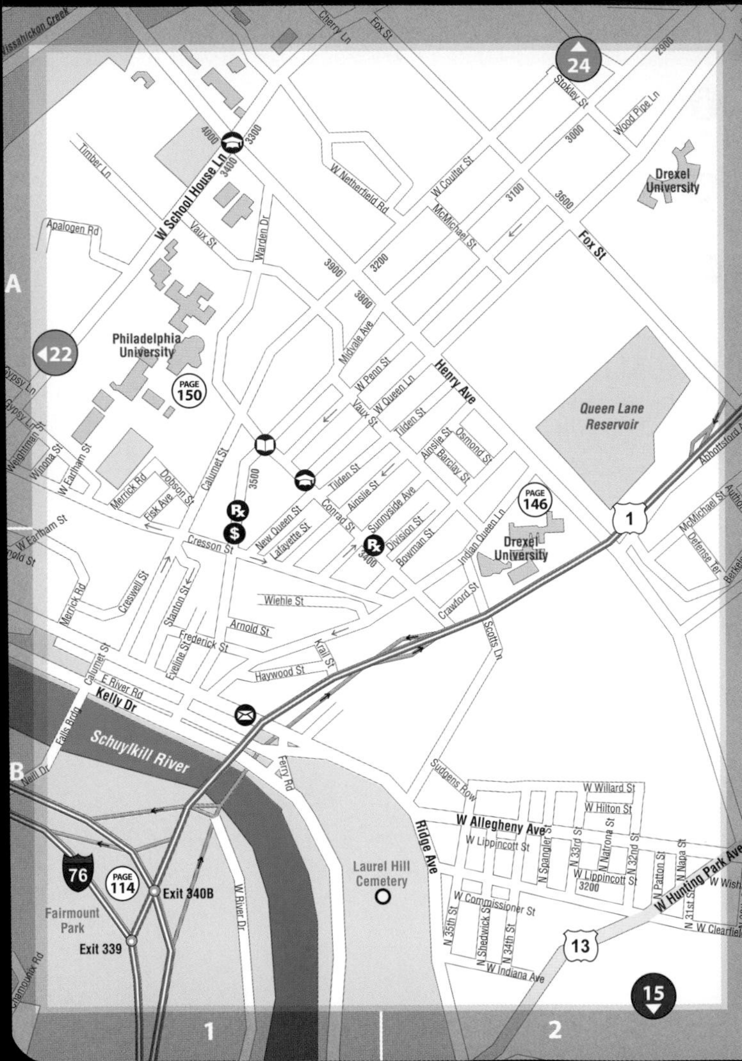

Map 23 • East Falls

N

Wissahickon Creek

Cherry Ln
Fox St

24

Stokley St
Wood Pipe Ln

Timber Ln

W School House Ln

W Netherfield Rd
W Coulter St

McMichael St

Fox St

Drexel University

Apalogen Rd

Vaux St

Warden Dr

A

Gypsy Ln
Gypsy La Rd

Philadelphia University

PAGE 150

Midvale Ave

Henry Ave

W Penn St

Queen Lane Reservoir

122

Wingohocking St
Winona St

W Eatham St

Merrick Rd
Dobson St
Esk Ave
Calumet St

New Queen St
Conrad St

W Queen St
Vaux St
Tilden St

Ainslie St
Ainslie St
Osmond St

Barclay St

3500

Arnold St
Haywood St
Klair St

Rx
$

Cresson St

Merrick Rd
Caswell St

Stanton St

Frederick St
Evoline St

Lafayette St
Sunnyside Ave
Division St
Bowman St

Rx
3400

Indian Queen Ln

Crawford St
Scotts Ln

PAGE 146

Drexel University

1

Abbottsford Ave

McMichael St
Defense Ter

Wiehle St

E River Rd

Kelly Dr

Ridge Ave

Schuylkill River

Manayunk Br

Stokes Row

W Williard St
W Hilton St

W Allegheny Ave

W Lippincott St

Ridge Ave

N Stanger St
N 33rd St
N Natrona St
N 32nd St

W Patton St

W Hunting Park Ave
31st St
N Napa St
W Wish

B

76

PAGE 114
Exit 340B

W River Dr

Fairmount Park
Exit 339

Laurel Hill Cemetery

W Lippincott St
3200

W Commissioner St

W Indiana Ave

N 35th St
N Shedwick St
N 34th St

13

W Clearfiel

15

1   2

At its location, in between the rollicking Manayunk scene and the family-time vibe of Mt Airy and Germantown, this area has the best of both worlds. To the south, the Laurel Hill Cemetery gives you a glimpse of green and the gorgeous folds of the Schuylkill call out to you from Kelly Drive.

$ Banks
· **National Penn Bank** · 3617 Midvale Ave

O Landmarks
· **Laurel Hill Cemetery** · 3822 Ridge Ave

Libraries
· **Falls of Schuylkill Branch** · 3501 Midvale Ave

R Pharmacies
· **East Falls Pharmacy** · 3421 Conrad St
· **Rite-Aid** · 3601 Midvale Ave

Post Offices
· **East Falls Station** · 4130 Ridge Ave

Schools
· **Mifflin** · 3624 Conrad St
· **Philadelphia University** · School House Ln &
  Henry Ave

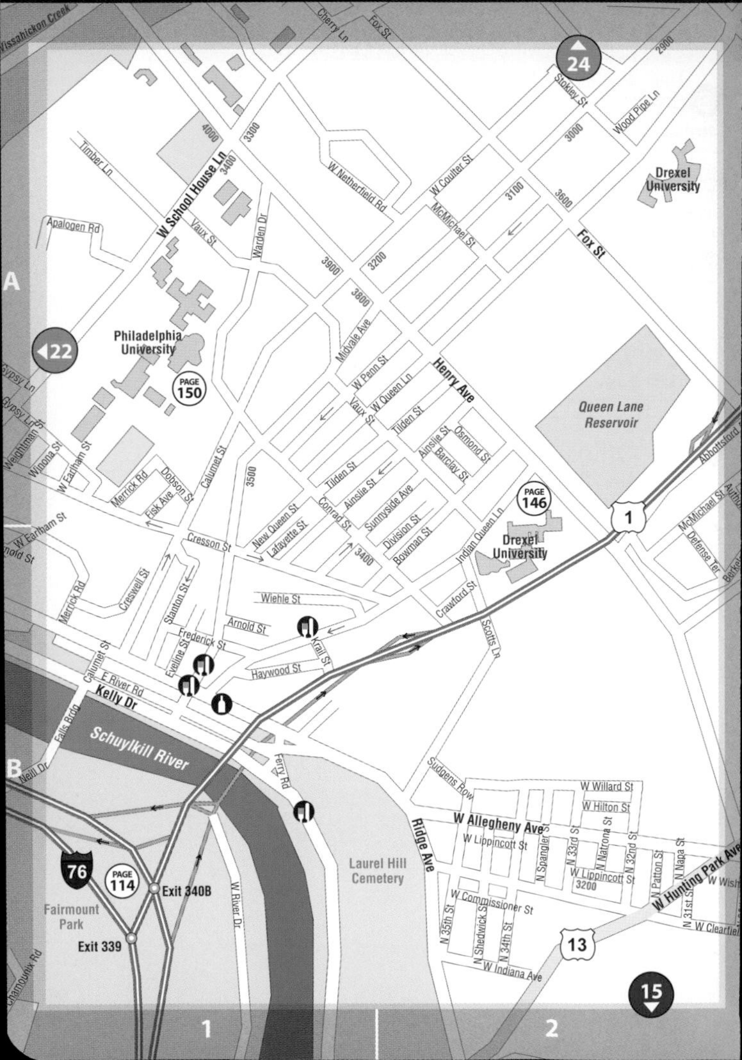

Map 23 · **East Falls** Ⓝ

Wissahickon Creek

Cherry Ln

Fox St

Cherry Ln

2900

▲ 24

Smick St

Wood Pipe Ln

Timber Ln

3800

W Netherfield Rd

W Coulter St

3800

Drexel University

Apalogen Rd

4000

3400

W School House Ln

Vaux St

Warden Dr

3200

McMichael St

3100

3600

Fox St

◀ 122

A

Philadelphia University

Gypsy Ln

Gypsy La Rd

3800

3800

Midvale Ave

Henry Ave

Queen Lane Reservoir

PAGE 150

W Penn St

W Queen Ln

Vaux St

Tilden St

Aurelia St

Ormond St

Abbottsford

Wistanham Rd

Warnington

Wiona St

W Earlham St

Fisk Ave

Dobson St

Merrick Rd

Calumet St

3500

New Queen St

Conrad St

Lafayette St

Ainslie St

Sunnyside Ave

Barclay St

Division St

Bowman St

PAGE 146

Drexel University

McMichael St

Defense Terr

W Earlham St

Cresson St

3400

Indian Queen Ln

1

Arnold St

Rd

Merrick Rd

Craswell St

Stanton St

Wiehle St

Crawford St

Scotts Ln

Calumet St

Epplins St

Frederick St

Arnold St

Krall St

Haywood St

E River Rd

Kelly Dr

B

Schuylkill River

Sudbens Row

W Willard St

W Hilton St

W Allegheny Ave

N Spangler St

N 33rd St

N Natrona St

N 32nd St

W Lippincott St

Neill Dr

Falls Bridge

Ferry Rd

Ridge Ave

W Lippincott St 3200

N Napa St

N Patton St

W Hunting Park Ave

Laurel Hill Cemetery

W Commissioner St

N 35th St

N Sherwood St

N 34th St

N 31st St

N W Clearfield St

76

PAGE 114

Exit 340B

W River Dr

Fairmount Park

Exit 339

13

W Indiana Ave

Rd

N

1

2

▼ 15

Some hot restaurants have opened here in recent years, none more appealing than Sprigs and Verge, both of which are generating a buzz of foodies' accolades. For the more socially conscious, the Hidden River Café offers excellent veggie eats. To satisfy your tequila jones, you could do much, much worse than Johnny Mañana's.

Liquor Stores

- **State Liquor Store** · 4177 Ridge Ave

Restaurants

- **Hidden River Café** · 3572 Indian Queen Ln
- **Johnny Mañana's** · 4201 Ridge Ave
- **Sprigs** · 3749 Midvale Ave
- **Verge** · 4101 Kelly Dr

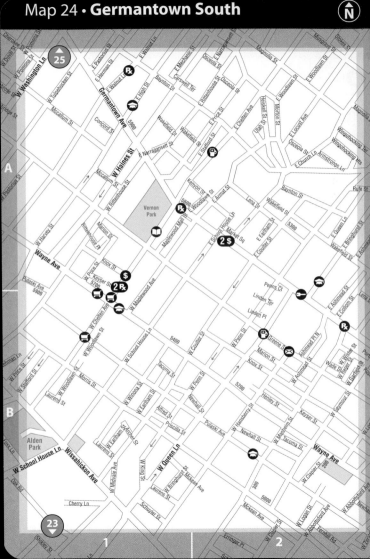

Germantown residents get to live in relative seclusion amidst friendly, tree-lined streets, while still maintaining a close proximity to the big city. For many, this is a winning combo, drawing family-minded folks from all over the area who are tired of the city but don't want to cave in towards the suburbs.

$ Banks

- **Citizens Bank** · 5500 Germantown Ave
- **PNC** · 150 W Chelten Ave
- **Wachovia** · 5458 Germantown Ave

Car Rental

- **U-Haul** · 5240 Germantown Ave

Gas Stations

- **Hess** · 102 E Chelten Ave
- **Sunoco** · 100 W Queen Ln

Libraries

- **Joseph E Coleman Branch** · 68 W Chelten Ave

Rx Pharmacies

- **Germantown Pharmacy** · 5100 Germantown Ave
- **Pathmark** · 176 W Chelten Ave
- **Rite-Aid** · 164 W Chelten Ave
- **Sun Ray Drug** · 52 E Walnut Ln
- **Walgreens** · 5627 Germantown Ave

Post Offices

- **David P Richardson** · 5209 Greene St

Schools

- **Germantown High** · 40 E High St
- **Kelly** · 5116 Pulaski Ave
- **Pickett Middle** · 5700 Wayne Ave
- **Wister** · 67 E Bringhurst St

Supermarkets

- **Pathmark** · 176 W Chelten Ave
- **Save-A-Lot** · 5753 Wayne Ave
- **ShopRite** · 301 W Chelten Ave

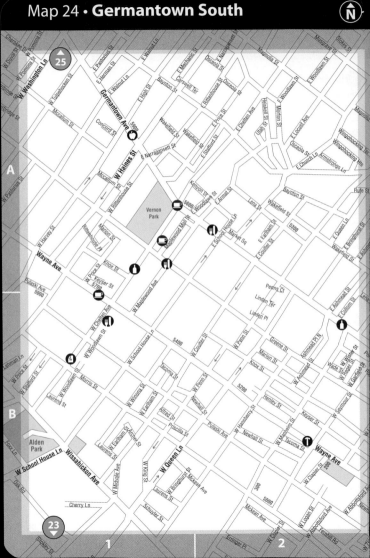

Map 24 • **Germantown South**

While not the eating empire that resides slightly further north, this section of Germantown can still boast of an eclectic mix of possibilities, from the sublime (Dahlak's superb Ethiopian fare) to the fascinating (K&J's Carribean-flavored diner of Americana) and beyond (House of Jin's mix of Asian cooking and jazz).

Coffee

- **Dunkin' Donuts** · 5701 Germantown Ave
- **Dunkin' Donuts** · 5753 Wayne Ave
- **The Flower Café at Linda's** ·
  48 W Maplewood Mall

Copy Shops

- **Cogan Blue Prints** · 326 W Chelten Ave

Farmer's Markets

- **Lancaster County** · 5942 Germantown Ave

Hardware Stores

- **Kane & Brown Hardware** · 5011 Wayne Ave

Liquor Stores

- **State Liquor Store** · 135 W Chelten Ave
- **State Liquor Store** · 5113 Germantown Ave

Restaurants

- **Dahlak** · 5547 Germantown Ave
- **House of Jin** · 234-36 W Chelten Ave
- **K&J Caribbean & American Diner** ·
  5603 Greene St

Map 25 • Germantown North

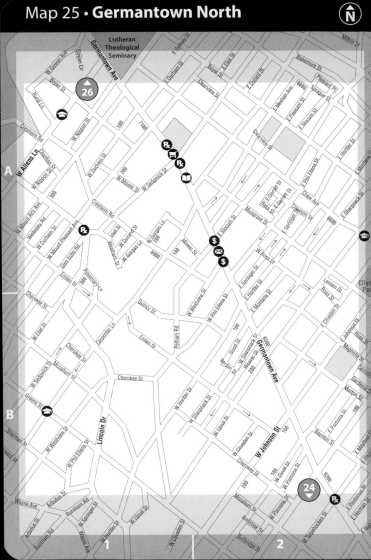

The northern section of Germantown maintains the same genteel friendliness of its neighbors, and is also a bit higher-end as it rises closer to Chestnut Hill. Schools are plentiful, suggesting the family atmosphere that characterizes the area.

$ Banks

· **Philadelphia Federal Credit Union** · 6701 Germantown Ave
· **Sovereign Bank** · 6740 Germantown Ave

Libraries

· **Lovett Branch** · 6945 Germantown Ave

Pharmacies

· **Acme** · 7010 Germantown Ave
· **Cooperman's Pharmacy** · 7060 Germantown Ave
· **CVS** · 7065 Lincoln Dr
· **Rite-Aid** · 6201 Germantown Ave

Post Offices

· **Mount Airy Station** · 6711 Germantown Ave

Schools

· **Emlen** · 6501 Chew Ave
· **Henry** · 601 Carpenter Ln
· **Houston** · 135 W Allens Ln

Supermarkets

· **Acme** · 7010 Germantown Ave

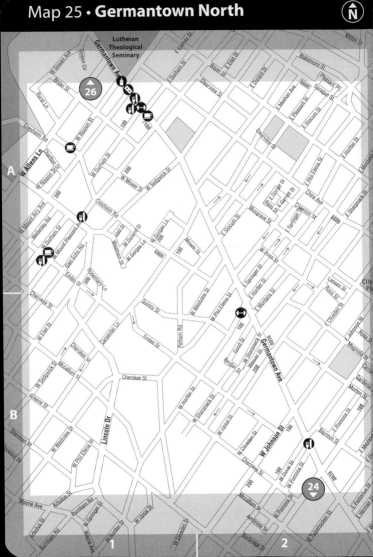

Map 25 · **Germantown North**

A wondrous bounty awaits you, from cozy BYOB's (Umbria) to artfully minded distinction (Rinker Rock Café). For more traditional tastes, you need only travel up Germantown Avenue to find just about whatever your heart may desire, from bars to food to shopping.

Coffee

- **Coffee Junction** · 7210 Cresheim Rd
- **Infusion Coffee & Tea** · 7133 Germantown Ave
- **Rinker Rock Café** · 7105 Fmlen St

Gyms

- **FitLife** · 7140 Germantown Ave
- **Fitness Place** · 18 W Hortter St

Liquor Stores

- **State Liquor Store** · 7204 Germantown Ave

Restaurants

- **Goat Hollow** · 300 W Mt Pleasant Ave
- **Golden Crust Pizza** · 7155 Germantown Ave
- **Rib Crib** · 7777 Germantown Ave
- **Rinker Rock Café** · 7105 Emlen St
- **Umbria** · 7131 Germantown Ave

Video Rental

- **Video Library** · 7157 Germantown Ave

Map 26 • **Mt Airy**

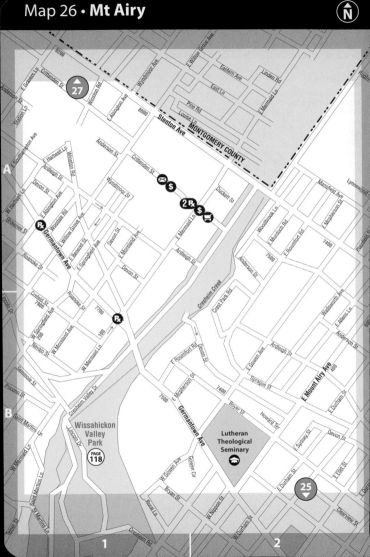

A strange little enclave, but it works beautifully well. There is a large and welcoming gay/lesbian contingency, as well as traditional families and young couples. The wealth of trees and greenery certainly help, but the area has the pleasing vibe of one very in touch with itself. Comfort becomes a huge selling point.

$ Banks

• **Citizens Bank** • 7700 Crittenden St
• **Wachovia** • 7782 Crittenden St

℞ Pharmacies

• **CVS** • 7700 Germantown Ave
• **Eckerd** • 7700 Crittenden St
• **Reese Pharmacy** • 8039 Germantown Ave
• **Super Fresh** • Mermaid Ln & Crittendon

✉ Post Offices

• **Market Square Station** • 7782 Crittenden St

🏫 Schools

• **Luthern Theological Seminary** •
7301 Germantown Ave

🛒 Supermarkets

• **Super Fresh** • Mermaid Ln & Crittendon

Map 26 • **Mt Airy**

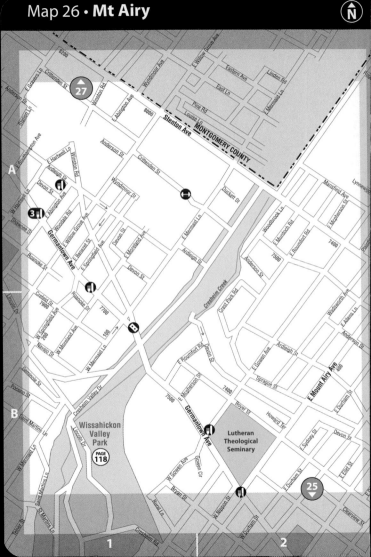

In keeping with the eclectic nature of the population here, you can find all kinds of innovative and delicious cuisine, including CinCin's popular Chinese fare and North by Northwest's winning mix of soul food and jazz. But perhaps the area's most emblematic joint, Cafette, follows its bohemian roots just about wherever they want to go.

Gyms

· **Curves** · 7733 Crittenden St

Restaurants

· **Bredenbeck's Bakery & Ice Cream Parlor** ·
  8126 Germantown Ave
· **Cafette** · 8136 Ardleigh St
· **CinCin** · 7838 Germantown Ave
· **Citrus** · 8136 Germantown Ave
· **Cresheim Cottage Café** · 7402 Germantown Ave
· **Flying Fish** · 8142 Germantown Ave
· **North by Northwest** · 7165 Germantown Ave

Video Rental

· **TLA Video** · 7630 Germantown Ave

Map 27 · **Chestnut Hill**

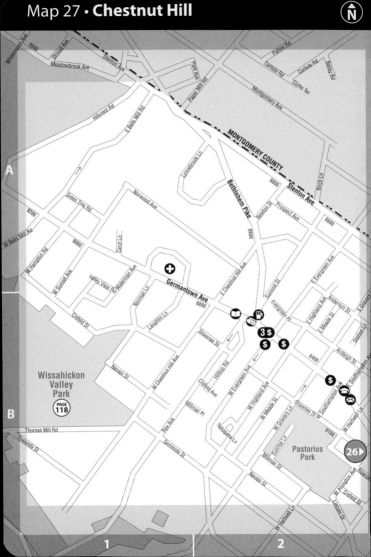

A distant outpost from Rittenhouse Square, but perhaps an apt comparison nonetheless, the populants take pride in the fact that they can enjoy the benefits of city living without all that nasty asphalt and cheesesteak politik. As they say, you get what you pay for.

$ Banks

- **Citizens Bank** · 8616 Germantown Ave
- **Fleet** · 8601 Germantown Ave
- **National Penn Bank** · 9 W Evergreen Ave
- **PNC** · 8340 Germantown Ave
- **Sovereign Bank** · 8623 Germantown Ave
- **Wachovia** · 8527 Germantown Ave

Cheesesteaks

- **McNally's H&J Tavern** · 8634 Germantown Ave

Gas Stations

- **Sunoco** · 10 Bethlehem Pike St

Hospitals

- **Chestnut Hill** · 8835 Germantown Ave

Libraries

- **Chestnut Hill Branch** · 8711 Germantown Ave

Post Offices

- **Chestnut Hill Station** · 8227 Germantown Ave

Schools

- **Jenks** · 8301 Germantown Ave

Map 27 · Chestnut Hill

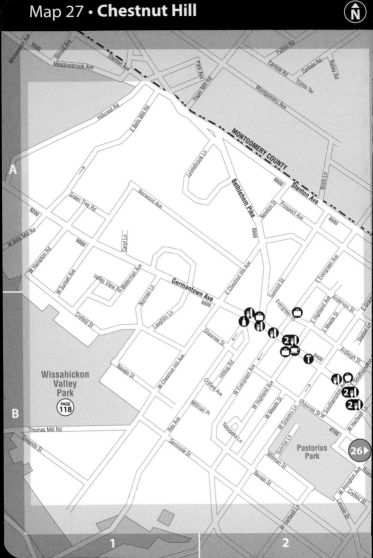

As you would imagine, fine cuisine abounds in this region. Roller's, perhaps the most popular destination, packs them in on a regular basis, but there's still plenty of room for other entrants, including the Stella Notte Trattoria and the Solaris Grille. As long as you have your platinum card, you won't go hungry.

Coffee

- **Starbucks** • 8515 Germantown Ave

Farmer's Markets

- **Chestnut Hill Hotel** • Germantown Ave & Southampton Ave

Hardware Stores

- **Kilian Hardware** • 8450 Germantown Ave

Liquor Stores

- **State Liquor Store** • 8705 Germantown Ave

Restaurants

- **Al Dana II** • 8630 Germantown Ave
- **Best of British** • 8513 Germantown Ave
- **Cake** • 184 E Evergreen Ave
- **Campbell's Place** • 8337 Germantown Ave
- **Chestnut Grille** • 8229 Germantown Ave
- **French Bakery & Cafe** • 8624 Germantown Ave-Rear
- **Melting Pot** • 8229 Germantown Ave
- **Metropolitan Bakery** • 8607 Germantown Ave
- **Pianta** • 8513 Ardleigh St
- **Roller's** • 8705 Germantown Ave
- **Solaris Grille** • 8201 Germantown Ave
- **Stella Notte Trattoria** • 8229 Germantown Ave

Shopping

- **Calve** • 184 E Evergreen Ave
- **Chestnut Hill Cheese Shop** • 8509 Germantown Ave
- **French Bakery & Cafe** • 8624 Germantown Ave

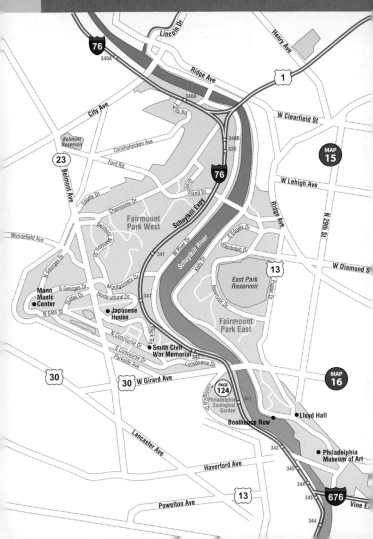

General Information

NFT Maps: 15 & 16
Address: 4231 N Concourse Dr
               Philadelphia, PA 19131
Phone: 215-685-0000
Website: www.phila.gov/fairpark

Overview

Although all three major Philly parks (Fairmount Park, Wissahickon Valley Park, and Pennypack Creek Park) are part of the Fairmount Parks System, when we refer to "Fairmount Park" here, we mean only this particular section, not the entire sprawling Parks System.

Fairmount Park is where the sports fields are located. People usually go there to be active, whether it's playing in a softball league, jogging along Kelly Drive, or rowing on the Schuylkill. It's not the place to go when you want to commune with nature, smoke an apple bong, or gulp home-stilled Kahlua.

Fairmount Park is also home to the Mann Center, the Philadelphia Museum of Art, the Japanese House, and the Smith Civil War Memorial (the place where the Statue of Liberty was supposed to end up).

The Drives

Kelly and West River Drives make up what locals call the "Loop." The paved path that runs along the east and west banks of the Schuylkill River is 8.4 miles if you cross the river at the Falls Bridge and loop back to the beginning. The trail (happily separated from the curvy road, where idiots tend to drive way too fast) is Philly's somewhat misbegotten answer to South Beach: there are lots of expertly fit, hot-assed singles giving each other the long once-over as they pass on bike, blades, or foot.

The Loop is also home to numerous runs, bike races, and regattas. If a few miles of open road are required for a race, you can bet at least some of it will occur here. It's also the host of charity walks like the annual AIDS Walk, the Walk for the Whisper (ovarian cancer), and Philadelphia Cares Day.

Boathouse Row

www.boathouserow.org
Just around the corner from the Art Museum, ten charming and colorful 19th-century Victorian structures comprise Boathouse Row, including the oldest rowing club in the country, Bachelor Barge Club, which was founded in 1853. It's definitely worth seeing the Row at night when the houses are lit like Whoville at Christmas.

Lloyd Hall

1 Boathouse Row, Kelly Dr, 215-685-3934; Hours vary by season
Operated by the Fairmount Park Commission, Lloyd Hall has a multi-purpose gym, lockers, and restrooms, making it a popular meeting place for those heading out on the Loop. Next to Lloyd Hall is a Drive Sports location, commonly called the Hut. It's one of the few places in Philly that rents bicycles, as well as child carriers and rollerblades. Keep in mind that the joint gets busy on nice weekends, with people stuck in the aisles waiting impatiently to be fitted (215-232-7368).

How to Get There—Driving

We can't tell you how to get to every spot in the park. It's over 1,000 acres with countless destinations. In general, if you want to get to the western section, take the West River Drive. If you want to go to the eastern part, take Kelly Drive (formerly East River Drive).

From I-95 to Fairmount Park East, take 676 W to the Ben Franklin Parkway exit. From the parkway, keep the Art Museum on your left, and you will end up on Kelly Drive. From I-95 to Fairmount Park West, do the same except once you're on the parkway, keep the Art Museum on your right (you have to go around Eakins Oval in front of the museum), and you'll end up on West River Drive (unless you goof and end up on the Spring Garden Bridge or back on the Parkway heading towards the city).

From the west, take the Schuylkill/76 E. For Fairmount Park East, get off at Exit 340A Lincoln Drive/Kelly Drive. Stay in the left-hand lane to exit on Kelly Drive. Actually, the exit sign will say East River Drive—the only sign left with the road's old name. For Fairmount Park West, take Exit 341 Montgomery Ave/West River Drive. Go left at the bottom of the ramp, and you'll run into West River Drive.

Parking

Parking depends entirely on where and when you visit the park. There are free parking lots scattered throughout, but on warm and sunny weekends, you'd better arrive early.

How to Get There—Mass Transit

Again, this really depends on where you want to go. Your best bet is to go to www.septa.com and click on the link for the "Plan My Trip" page. Addresses for most points in the Park can be found through the park's website.

General Information

Environmental Center Address:
    8600 Verree Rd
    Philadelphia, PA 19115
Environmental Center Phone:
    215-685-0470
Fairmount Park System Phone:
    215-683-0200

Overview

Once used as hunting and fishing grounds for the Lenni-Lenape Indians, Pennypack Creek Park was established in 1905. Today, the 1,600 acres of woodlands, meadows, wetlands, and fields provide a great habitat for wildlife. More than two hundred species of birds and a variety of native mammals, reptiles, and amphibians call Pennypack home. Somewhat incongruously located in Philly's Northeast section, the park runs roughly from Huntingdon Pike all the way over to I-95 N. Hiking trails and biking trails (both off-road and paved) are filled with people walking their dogs and children.

A new 65-acre stretch called Pennypack on the Delaware was added to the southern end of the park in 1998. New additions include a large recreational complex with soccer and softball fields, a paved path, fishing piers, picnic venues, and extraordinary views of the Delaware River.

Pennypack Environmental Center

8600 Verree Rd, 215-685-0470;
www.nlreep.org/pennypack.htm
Surrounded by a bird sanctuary, the Pennypack Environmental Center on Verree Road is a massive historical and environmental information bank. In addition to the usual animal-centric displays, the center also has an Early America exhibit and a new 300-gallon aquarium. The resource library is open to the general public, but materials are not available for loan. The center is open weekdays from 8 am until 4 pm, and some weekends for special events.

Fox Chase Farm

8500 Pine Rd, 215-728-7900; www.foxchasefarm.org
Fox Chase Farm on Pine Road is the only remaining working farm in Philadelphia and it doubles as a school campus. The farm is open to the general public only for special events and festivals, including the once-a-month Saturday Morning Open House. For a complete schedule of events, check the website or visit the Pennypack Environmental Center. Activities in the past have included tours of the farm and workshops in various crafts, wood working, ice cream churning, and flower pressing. Most of the activities cost $2 per person.

Friends of Pennypack Park

215-934-PARK; http://balford.com/fopp
While the budget for Pennypack Park has remained the same for the past two decades, many of the improvements to the park have been carried out by hundreds of local volunteers. In addition to their invaluable contribution to the park, the FOPP website has information about everything from the best place for wedding photos to why the dams have not been repaired.

How to Get There—Driving

From Center City Philadelphia, take I-95 N about five miles to the Bridge Street exit (Exit 27). Continue on Aramingo Avenue 0.3 miles to Harbison Avenue. Take Harbison for about two miles and turn right on East Roosevelt Avenue. Take East Roosevelt 1.7 miles to the park entrance.

Parking

There is loads of free parking within the park.

How to Get There—Mass Transit

Many buses will take you close or into Pennypack Park, depending on which part of the park you're headed to. For the southeast side of the park, ride bus 10, 20, or 77. To get to the northwest section and the Environmental Center, hop on the 67. For the northernmost tip of the park, take the 88.

By Regional Rail, take the R7 and get off at Holmesburg Junction at the southern end of the park. You can also take the R3 to Bethayres and walk a few minutes south to reach the northern end.

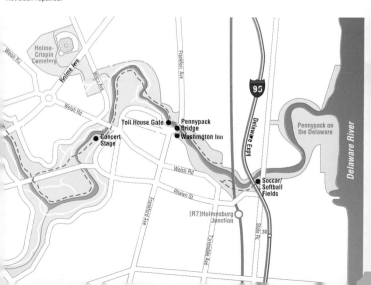

General Information

Environmental Center Address:
300 Northwestern Ave
Philadelphia, PA 19118
Environmental Center Phone:
215-685-9285
Websites: www.fow.org
http://philaparks.org/wv.htm
www.phila.gov/fairpark (Permits & Maps)

Overview

Wissahickon Valley Park is where Philadelphians go when they want to get away from the urban grind without actually leaving the city. Part of the massive Fairmount Parks System, the Wissahickon Valley consists of 1,426 acres of urban forest. While Fairmount Park East/West is known for its ball fields and recreational areas, the Wissahickon Valley offers Philadelphians the opportunity to get back to nature.

The Park is also loaded with Wissahickon schist (that's a type of rock, for you non-geologists) and many varieties of trees, such as Lofty Hemlock, American White Elm, and Native Beech.

The valley is an ideal location for hiking, canoeing and kayaking, rock climbing, mountain biking, picnicking, ice skating, fishing, and horseback riding. (Permits are required to bicycle or ride horseback on all trails except Forbidden [Wissahickon] Drive.) The mountain bike trail is a 30-mile loop that swoops and drags over the terrain—many sections are fine for amateurs, but there are enough technical climbs and downhills to keep even experienced riders entertained.

Trail Highlights

Devil's Pool, once a spiritual area for the Lenape tribes, can be reached on foot from Valley Green by taking the footpath on the eastern bank and walking downstream to the mouth of Cresheim Creek. For a truly stunning view, take a walk to Lover's Leap. Enter the main footpath at the Ridge Avenue entrance and follow the west bank over to Hermit's Lane Bridge. You'll find yourself peering over a giant precipice to the gorge below. Legend has it the daughter of a mighty Indian chief and her lover plunged to their deaths in a desperate attempt to escape the woman's wily marital arrangement to an old chieftain.

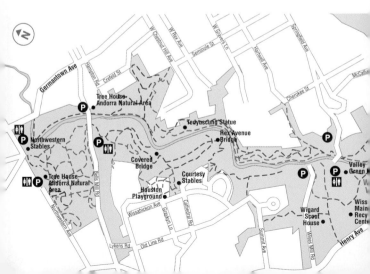

A map of the Wissahickon trails costs $2 on the Fairmount Park website and onsite at the Wissahickon Environmental Center. Also available at the Center is a more detailed map from the Friends of Wissahickon, which costs $6.50.

How to Get There—Driving

Park, big. Roads, many. In other words, it all depends on where you want to go. If you've never been to the Wissahickon Valley before, consider cruising up Lincoln Drive, which takes you right along part of the Wissahickon Creek. To get to Lincoln Drive from the Schuylkill/76, get off at Exit 340A Lincoln Drive/Kelly Drive. From the exit ramp, get in the middle lane and follow the signs for Lincoln Drive.

Henry Avenue is a good way to get to many points as well. From the Schuylkill/76, still get off at Exit 340A, but instead follow the signs for Ridge Avenue E (stay left, left, then left again). At the dead end, go right onto Ridge Avenue S. Drive through three lights, then turn left on Midvale Avenue (go through three lights again, and turn left on Henry Avenue. The Park runs along the right hand side of Henry Avenue.

Parking

It's not hard to find parking in the Wissahickon Valley Park. There are numerous locations throughout the park where parking is free.

How to Get There—Mass Transit

For the southern part of the park, take the R6 to Wissahickon Station or any of the buses that go through the Wissahickon Transit Center (1, 9, 27, 35, 38, 61, 65, 124, 125, R). The R-8 makes regular stops to the east of the park including Chelten Ave, Tulpehocken, Upsal, Carpenter Lane, Allen Lane, St Martins, Highland, and Chestnut Hill West. Using septa.com's "Plan My Trip" feature will help you find your way by public transportation.

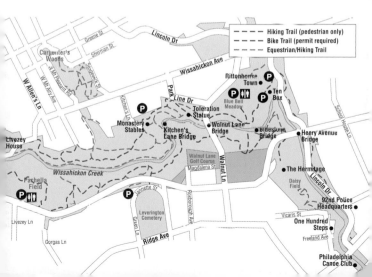

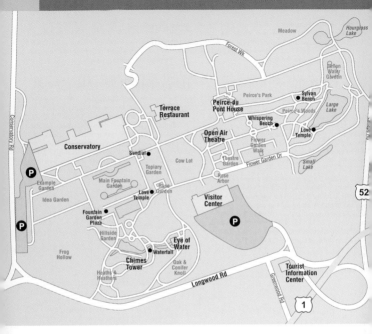

Conservatory

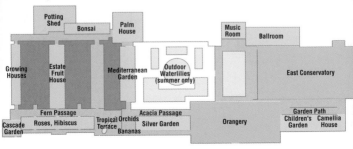

General Information

Address:	1000 Longwood Rd
	Kennett Square, PA 19348
Phone:	610-388-1000
Website:	www.longwoodgardens.org
Hours:	Open daily from 9 am (closing time depends on season)
Admission:	Adults $8-$15 (depends on season), Youths (16-20) $6, Children (6-15) $2

Overview

If you're not into horticulture, you're probably not reading this. If you are, you'll be happy to learn that over 11,000 different types of plants grow at Longwood. We strongly urge you to look at their website, which includes dozens of pages dedicated to the gardens.

Although Longwood is sprawled out over 1,050 acres, most visitors limit themselves to the impressive collection of forty outdoor gardens, indoor gardens, and heated greenhouses located within a 4-acre radius. Because of the wealth of wondrous plants, it's difficult to give all of them individual shout-outs, but we feel compelled to point out the showcase orchid display in the Conservatory. And the Bonsai exhibit. And the various banana trees. And the super-cool insect-catching plants display. And that's just the indoor plants. The fountains are also a huge draw year round, with various water shows playing daily and special holiday presentations come Christmastime.

Eating

If you look in your wallet and exclaim, "There's just way too much money in here!" we recommend the Terrace Restaurant located next to the Conservatory. The cafeteria (in the same building) is a more reasonably priced dining option. If you enjoy a limited budget, you can always pack some food and eat it in the picnic area located outside of the gardens.

Pets

Service dogs are the only animals permitted at Longwood. There are no kennels or other pet-housing facilities, so no chance for Queenie to weigh anchor on the Italian Water Garden.

2005 Calendar of Events

January 15 - March 18 - Welcome Spring
Witness the early blooming stages of bulbs. Expect to see the classic daffodils and tulips as well as their more exotic relatives, like the blue poppy.

March 19 - April 1 - Easter Display
The conservatory is filled with over 1,000 lilies. Outside, bulbs tentatively press upward through the still thawing soil.

April 2 - May 27 - Acres of Spring
Outdoor color-fest with purple phlox, white foam flowers, and azaleas to die for.

May 28 - September 3 - Festival of Fountains
Visit the fountain gardens for concerts and water spectaculars, all while sitting surrounded by roses and water lilies.

September 10 - October 4 - GardenFest
The garden railway takes visitors on a ride through the heritage trail, while experts point out autumn gourds and squash. The Gardens also host talks and demonstrations on the art of gardening.

October 8 - October 28 - Autumn's Colors
Indoor and outdoor gardens alike explode in shades of yellow, red, and gold. Local bands perform during the weekends.

October 29 - November 20 - Chrysanthemum Festival
See chrysanthemums in quantities and shapes that you've never seen before. Weekend performances showcase Asian culture and arts in honor of these flowers from the East.

November 24 - January 2 - Christmas
400,000 tasteful decorative lights transform the gardens into a winter wonderland. Water and light shows set to music are staged in the Open-Air Theater.

How to Get There—Driving

From Philly and vicinity, take I-95 to Route 322 W (Exit 3A), to Route 1 S. Longwood is located just off Route 1 once you cross Route 52. Alternatively, take I-76 to I-476 S, to Route 1 S.

Parking

Free parking is available in the parking lot. On busy days, expect a short trek from your car to the visitor center. Accessible parking is located next to the visitor center but it fills up quickly; passenger drop-off at the visitor center is permitted.

How to Get There—Mass Transit

Take the R2 to Wilmington on Septa Regional Rail. From Center City to Wilmington, Delaware, you'll pay either $4.25 (off-peak) or $5 (peak) one-way. From there, you'll have to take a taxi or rent a car, as there is no regularly scheduled public transit to Longwood. Taxis run about $30 one-way. So, to recap: Septa = $10 round trip. Taxi = $60 round trip. Total = $70 + tip for cab driver. You make the call.

Squares, Circles, and Small Parks

General Information

Websites: www.phila.gov/fairpark/squares
www.ushistory.org/lovepark
www.geocities.com/ccartsfair
www.clarkpark.org

Overview

When William Penn initially imagined the city of Philadelphia back in 1682, he pictured "a green country town" filled with lush trees and garden escapes. One of his visions was multiple city squares in Philly's downtown. Penn envisaged that the squares would provide a welcome retreat from the swirl of city activity—certainly an advanced method of city planning.

Each of the five city squares originally bore the names of their locations: Northeast, Northwest, Center, Southwest, and Southeast. Many decades later, in the nineteenth century, the parks were renamed after important historical figures. Aside from the five central squares, there are other quaint neighborhood parks to wile away the time in.

1. Logan Square

Logan Square, originally Northwest Square, was once the site of burial plots, pasturage, and public executions. In 1919, a French architect remodeled the square to include a large traffic circle with an area for gardens, monuments, and a memorial fountain. The fountain still serves as a memorial, but is most often used by hot children in the summertime as an impromptu public swimming area. Plenty of adult supervision is almost always at hand.

2. Franklin Square

Just outside the Old City's main drag, Franklin Square offers an odd mix of down-and-outs sleeping off benders and Tai Chi practitioners (mostly coming east from nearby Chinatown). Not a particularly well-kept or safe park (especially in the evenings), Franklin Square nevertheless provides a much-needed splash of green in an otherwise concrete and brick area.

3. Penn Square

Center Square is the largest of the original five city parks. It was renamed Penn Square in tribute to William Penn, whose initial desire to see this land

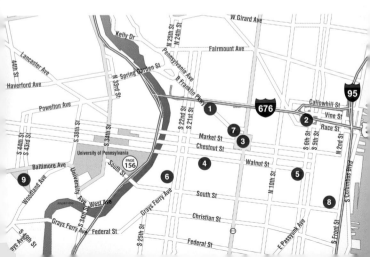

used for public buildings was overruled; instead, early Philadelphians used the space for residential properties. It wasn't until the late-19th century that the square became a location for new public buildings and the mammoth City Hall was built. The square has some of the most intriguing architecture in the city, including the imposing Penn statue, standing high over City Hall.

4. Rittenhouse Square

Southwest or Rittenhouse Square remains the most fashionable residential district in Philly and home of the equivalent of an affluent Victorian aristocracy. You can still see some of the mansions from that period, though most of the homes were turned into apartment buildings after 1913. Of all the squares, Rittenhouse Square is the most neighborly of the parks. Some of the city's best-loved sculptures reside here among the plants, annual flower markets, and outdoor art exhibits. Fancy bars and restaurants circle the area, keeping it chic and elite.

5. Washington Square

Washington Square, the Southeast Square, is known as the final resting place of more Revolutionary soldiers than anywhere else in the United States. It wasn't until 1825 that the city renamed the square and its uppity reputation began to grow. In the first half of the 20th century, this became the heart of Philly's publishing industry, and such popular publications as *The Saturday Evening Post* and *Ladies' Home Journal* were conceived here. Be sure to check out the Bicentennial Moon Tree. This sycamore was planted from a seed carried to the moon by the Apollo Space Mission. There is also a large public fountain in the center that serves as a great place for people and their pooches to chill out during summer months.

6. Fitler Square

Just a few blocks southwest of Rittenhouse Square and five blocks east of the Schuylkill River, Fitler Square is surrounded by a slew of expensive single-family dwellings and an array of fine restaurants, quaint shops, and small businesses. Named for former mayor Edwin H. Fitler, a well-regarded 19th-century mayor of Philadelphia, Fitler Square lies just a stone's throw from Philly's most commercial Center City shopping district, and plays host to a series of annual events like the Spring Fair, Easter Egg Hunt, and Christmas tree lighting. Woe betide you if you walk on the grass or let your dog do same; they are very pricklish about their lawn.

7. Love Park

This little enclave across from City Hall opened in the free loving '60s. The park is famous for Robert Indiana's 20-foot tall LOVE sculpture, the symbol for the "City of Brotherly Love." For years, Love Park was a mecca for skateboarders, who came in droves to test their mettle against the park's ramps, stairs, and fountains. But the mayor has imposed a strict no-skating policy, forcing the young-uns to sneak around like ninjas in order to snag a few blissful runs. The park has also been set up for wireless Internet service.

8. Headhouse Square

This charming, cobblestone-lined street square in Center City is definitely worth strolling. Surrounded by cozy restaurants and picturesque parks, Headhouse Square also houses the nation's oldest firehouse. For twenty-one consecutive weekends during the year, beginning at Memorial Day, check out the Creative Collective Craft and Fine Arts Fair. It's a great way to spend the weekend, meeting with local artists, browsing their wares, and sending the kids off to any one of the free art workshops for an afternoon of t-shirt painting or puppet-making. Saturday fair hours are noon to 11 pm, and Sunday noon to 6 pm. Children's classes are only offered on Sundays.

9. Clark Park

Though West Philly on the whole is still considered somewhat dangerous, many areas are fast becoming safer and more culturally vibrant. Initially established in 1895, Clark Park, located in the University City section at 43rd Street and Chester Avenue, adds to the scene by attracting artists and musicians who showcase their talents throughout the nine acres of greenery. The Clark Park Music and Arts Community plays a huge role in facilitating an array of arts and music festivals in the park. The CPMAC, (entering their 34th year as a non-profit organization) and The Friends of Clark Park (in their 31st year) are two key organizations working to help maintain and promote the park as a safe and culturally diverse public green space. Check out the life-sized Charles Dickens statue, or drop by for a night of Classic Movies in the Park. Shows start at 8:45 pm at 45th Street and Chester.

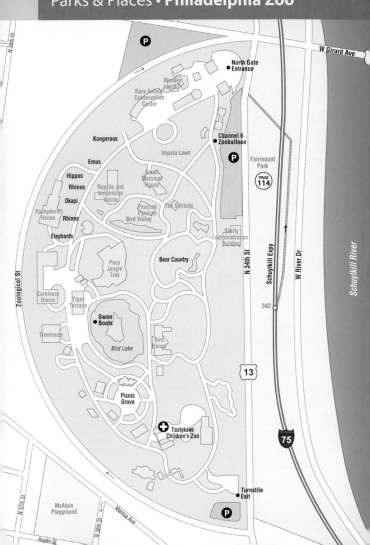

P

North Gate
Entrance

W Girard Ave

Monkey
Junction

Rare Animal
Conservation
Center

Channel 6
Zooballoon

Kangaroos

Impala Lawn

P

Fairmount
Park

PAGE
114

Emus

Small
Mammal
House

Hippos

Rhinos

Reptile
and
Amphibian
House

Okapi

The Solitude

Pachyderm
House

Peacock
Pavilion
Bird Valley

Rhinos

Elephants

Shelly
Administration
Building

Bear Country

Peco
Jungle Trek

N 34th St

Schuylkill Expy

Carnivora
House

W River Dr

Schuylkill River

Tiger
Terrace

342

Swan
Boats

Treehouse

Bird Lake

Bird
House

13

Picnic
Grove

75

Tastykake
Children's Zoo

Turnstile
Exit

Zoological St

N 37th St

N 36th St

McAlpin
Playground

Mantua Ave

P

Aspen St

N 38th St

General Information

Address:	3400 West Girard Ave
	Philadelphia, PA 19104-1196
Phone:	215-243-1100
Website:	www.philadelphiazoo.org
Hours:	In-Season - Feb-Nov 9:30 am-5 pm daily
	Off-Season - Dec-Jan 9:30 am-4 pm daily
Admission:	In-Season - Children $12.95, Adults $15.95
	Off-Season - $9.95

Overview

Pack plenty of food and water in the car. No, not to save money once you're there (though not a bad idea, as you can bring food in), but to keep up your strength while you wait for hours tied up in traffic on the drive. Weekend visitors during the season can count on sitting in their cars and destroying the ozone layer at an alarming rate over an exhausting amount of time.

The good news is that once you get to the zoo, it's worth it. Opened in 1874, the Philadelphia Zoo is the oldest in the country. It's laid out over 42 acres and has 1,600 animals from six continents, a remarkable display of historic architecture, an impressive botanical collection of over 500 plant species, and superior research and veterinary facilities.

But kids today have become more jaded than their predecessors. These days, maybe because of television shows like Animal Planet and the Discover Channel, it seems to take more than a moping hippo hiding in the corner of his cage to excite the kiddies. So, like zoos in most cities, the Philadelphia Zoo has been evolving with the times and placing greater emphasis on its amusement park facilities than on its animals.

In order to fit in these new rides, the play areas, and—but of course— the ubiquitous market places, the zoo has scaled down its number of actual animals. Fewer than ten years ago, the zoo had 1,800 animals; today, the zoo's collection is down to 1,600 and dropping fast. Ironically enough, the Philly Zoo, known as the setting of the first chimpanzee birth in the country (1928), no longer even houses chimps.

Rides and Activities

The new Zooballoon (open April through October), takes visitors 400 feet above the ground to see the giraffes and zebras oddly juxtaposed against the Philadelphia skyline. The quaint Amoroso PZ Express Victorian-era train is another fun attraction for the kids (and adults) who prefer the comfort of feeling ground beneath their feet. The crowds around Bird Valley waiting to ride the Swan Boat (open April through October) are bigger than the ones trying to catch a glimpse of the rhino. Make sure to bring along some extra cash if you're planning on partaking in the fun, as all of these rides cost money on top of the entrance fee.

How to Get There—Driving

From I-76, take Exit 342 to Girard Avenue. Follow signs to the Zoo.

From I-95, take exit 676 W to I-76 W. Get off at Exit 342 to Girard Avenue. Follow signs to the Zoo.

Parking

As you drive toward the zoo, turn right on Girard Avenue or continue straight to the 34th Street parking lot. The cost of parking is $8.

How to Get There—Mass Transit

Ride SEPTA bus 15 to 34th Street and Girard Avenue. Bus 32 stops at 33rd Street and Girard Avenue. Bus 38 stops close by at 34th Street and Mantua Avenue.

Zoo Tours

All tours are lead by volunteer docents and are free! For more information about Zoo Tours, or to make reservations (which are required), call 215-243-5317.

Thematic Tours:
· Conservation Tour
· Endangered Species
· Adaptations
· Fur, Feathers, and Scales
· Up Close and Personal (Adults only)

Geographic Tours:
· Central and South-American Wildlife
· Wildlife Australia
· Asian Wildlife
· African Wildlife
· South America

Seasonal Tours:
· Winter Warm-up
· Beat the Heat

About the Zoo Tours:
· Art and Architecture
· Horticulture
· History of the Zoo
· Reptile and Amphibian House
· Zoo Careers

Children's Tours
· The Five Senses Tour
· My, What Big Teeth You Have
· Fur Feet, Scale Feet, Duck Feet, Pig Feet, How Many Feet Do We Meet?

Spring Garden St ● Finnigan's Wake

Festival Pier

Callowhill St

675

95

Ride the Ducks

Benjamin Franklin Bridge

● Penn's Landing Corporate Office

Race St

N 6th St
N 5th St
N 4th St
N 3rd St
N 2nd St
Front St

Arch St

N Delaware Ave
Point St
Vine St
Elm St

Erie St
York St
State St

PENNSYLVANIA

Linden St

Penn St

Market St

Cooper St

N Front St
N 2nd St

N Columbus Blvd

Independence National Historical Park

PAGE 132

Market St
Market-Frankford Trolley Line

Chestnut St

Market St

22

New Jersey State Aquarium at Camden

Federal St

Walnut St

MAP 8

Dock St

St James Pl

Spruce St

● Independence Seaport Museum

● Columbus Monument

Riverside Dr

City Park

Dr Martin Luther King Jr

S 6th St
S 5th St
S 4th St
S 3rd St

Penn's Landing Visitor and Operations Center

Delancey St

Pine St

Penn's Landing Marina

● International Sculpture Garden

20

S Delaware Ave

Clinton St

Lombard St

S 3rd St
S 2nd St

NEW JERSEY

S 2nd St

South St

S Columbus Blvd

Fitzwater St

Delaware River

Pine St

Catherine St

Division St

Queen St

● Sterling Heliport

Spruce St

Christian St

Carpenter St

Walnut St

Washington Ave

S Front St
S Chest

General Information

NFT Map: 8
Phone: 215-922-2FUN
Website: www.pennslandingcorp.com

Overview

Comprising 13 acres stretching from Spring Garden Street to Washington Avenue along the Delaware, Penn's Landing is gradually becoming more than just the port where all the Jersey kids get off the Camden ferry in order to snort glue and get their asses pierced on South Street. In spite of the improvements, it still houses the regrettable "Jersey Night Out" mix of huge, unbearably lame dance clubs and stripper bars, and many darkened sections of wharf and park where you can get into drunken throw-downs with like-minded barbarians.

Events

Despite all that, Penn's Landing does host many of Philly's biggest events and festivals each year. Many shindigs take place at the Great Plaza (Columbus Blvd & Chestnut St), like WXPN's Singer Songwriter Weekend (www.xpn.org) in July. Others occur at the Festival Pier (Columbus Blvd & Spring Garden St), such as the Sippin' by the River Festival (www.sippinbytheriver.com) in September.

Blue Cross River Rink

During the winter, the Blue Cross River Rink (www.riverrink.com) hosts ice skating fun for everyone (you can even skate with Santa a couple of times in December). During the 2004/05 season, entry cost $6 and skate rental was an additional $3. The rink is open 6 pm–9 pm weeknights (and until 1 am Friday nights), 12:30 pm–9 pm on Saturdays, and 12:30 pm–1 am on Sundays. Check the website or call 215-925-RINK before you go though, because sometimes the rink is closed for private rentals.

Other Attractions

There's the Seaport Museum, which chronicles the history of Penn's Landing—one of American's oldest ports. The aforementioned lame-ass clubs are towards the north, past the BF Bridge. Otherwise, you'll find interesting park space and absolutely filthy-rich yachts if you walk south towards South Street.

If you want to get out on the water—notice we said *on*, not *in*, pollution being what it is—and you don't own one of those expensive yachts, you'll find everything from 12-minute ferry rides to paddle wheel riverboat dining departing from the banks of the Delaware.

How to Get There—Driving

From I-95, take Exit 20 (Washington Ave/Columbus Blvd). Make a left onto Columbus Boulevard and proceed north.

From the Walt Whitman Bridge, take I-95 N to Exit 20. Follow directions above.

From I-76, travel east to I-676 E until you hit I-95. Take I-95 S to Exit 20, and follow the above directions.

Parking

There are loads of parking options around Penn's Landing. Most charge $10-$12 per day:

Festival Pier (Spring Garden & Columbus Blvd) - 300 spaces.
Pier 24 (Columbus Blvd & Cavanaugh's River Deck) - 120 spaces.
Vine St & Columbus Blvd (across from Dave & Buster's) - 280 spaces.
Columbus Blvd & Market St 400 spaces.
Columbus Blvd & Walnut St - 220 spaces.
Lombard Cir & Columbus Blvd - 220 spaces.
South Street Pedestrian Bridge (& Columbus Blvd) - 400 spaces.

Ticketed concert parking at Festival Pier costs $15.

Monthly parking permits are also available the last five days through the first five days of every month. They offer 24-hour parking for permit holders, and can be purchased at the Penn's Landing Operations/Visitor Center at 301 S Columbus Boulevard for first-time buyers.

How to Get There—Mass Transit

Take SEPTA bus 17 to Penn's Landing via 20th Street and Market Street, or bus 48 Tioga.

By subway, ride the Market-Frankford Line east, get off at 2nd Street, and walk south to Penn's Landing.

Eastern State Penitentiary

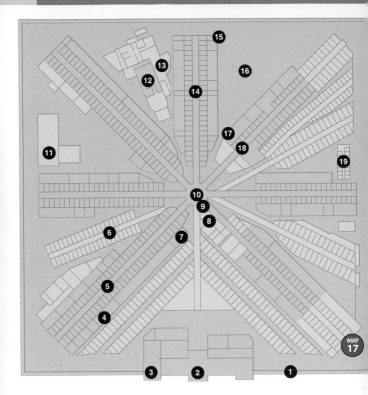

MAP 17

1. Facade
2. Front Tower
3. Administration Building Office
4. Synagogue
5. Cellblock 7
6. Cellblock 12
7. Al Capone's Cell
8. Chaplain's Office
9. Rotunda
10. Central Guard Tower
11. Chapel
12. Kitchen
13. Dining Hall
14. Cellblock 4
15. Exercise Yard
16. Baseball Diamond
17. Hospital
18. Outside the Operating Room
19. Death Row
20. Outside the Cellblocks

General Information

NFT Map:	17
Location:	22nd St & Fairmount Ave
	Philadelphia, PA 19130
Phone:	215-236-3300
Website:	www.easternstate.org
Hours:	Apr-Nov, Wed-Sun: 10 am-5 pm (last entry at 4 pm); Closed Dec-Mar, Easter, Thanksgiving, Mon & Tues
Admission:	Adults $9, Students & Seniors $7; Kids (7-12 years) $4
	Children under the age of 7 not permitted

Overview

Of Philly's tourist traps, Eastern State Penitentiary is probably one of the more interesting. Built in 1829 in what is now the Fairmont section of Philadelphia, ESP was once the largest and most expensive building in America. People flocked from around the globe to marvel at the prison's architecture and penal system. The prison was closed in 1971 and promptly fell into disrepair.

The non-profit preservationist group, Eastern State Penitentiary Historic Site, was formed in 1994, and today organizes tours and educational programs in an effort to restore the crumbling prison. The once-oppressive environment is also used today as an art gallery. Art installations, motivated by the prison's history and created specifically for the space, are featured throughout the complex. Among the many moving works is a piece called *Ghost Cats*; the 39 cat sculptures scattered all around the grounds represent the colony of cats that ran wild in the penitentiary following its desertion in the '70s.

During Halloween, the prison hosts a haunted house event called *Terror Behind The Walls*. Although it's ranked ninth in the country by *HauntWorld Magazine*, the truly creepy environment can be somewhat reduced by gaggles of teenagers talking on their cell phones behind you.

History

Eastern State Penitentiary was created by Quakers who believed that true penitence could come only from a life of solitude and reflection. To prohibit communication between inmates and guards, prisoners were required to wear masks anytime they left their cells. They received meals through small feed doors.

Although the concept of Eastern State Penitentiary was based on ending ill treatment common in prisons of the day, the punishments exacted were far from pleasant. If inmates were caught trying to communicate with other prisoners, they would be denied meals or sentenced to solitary confinement for several days. If the infraction was more serious, an inmate might be chained to an outside wall in the winter months, stripped from the waist up, and doused with water until ice formed on his body. The "iron gag" was another form of punishment involving a five-inch piece of metal clamped onto a tongue. If captives exhibited resistance, the gag would be forced deeper into their mouth. At least one inmate died from the iron gag.

This history of cruelty and twisted sadism was not lost on the good folks at MTV, who featured ESP on a memorable early episode of their *Fear* series.

How to Get There—Driving

From the north or west, take I-76 (Schuylkill Expressway) to Exit 344 (Old Exit 38)/I-676 (Vine Street Expressway). On I-676 take the first exit, Benjamin Franklin Parkway/23 Street, then take the first left onto 22nd Street. Pass the Philadelphia Museum of Art (on your left) and continue five blocks north, to Fairmount Avenue.

Coming from the south or east, take I-95 to Exit 22 (Old Exit 17) and follow I-676 W. Get off at the Art Museum/Benjamin Franklin Parkway exit. At the top of the ramp, turn right onto 22nd Street, pass the Philadelphia Museum of Art (on your left) and continue five blocks north to Fairmount Avenue.

Parking

While there is plenty of un-metered street parking in the area around the penitentiary, some streets have a two- or three-hour limit. If you're planning on taking your time touring the prison, there's a public lot next door where you can park for up to two hours for $4, and $5 anytime after that.

How to Get There—Mass Transit

Take the 7, 32, or 48 SEPTA bus to 22nd Street and Fairmount Avenue then walk east one block to the penitentiary. The 33 bus stops at 20th and Fairmount; walk west one block to the entrance. The 43 bus stops at 21st and Spring Garden Streets. Walk north to Fairmount Avenue, the next major street parallel to Spring Garden Street.

Big Bus (Stop #8) and Philadelphia Trolley Works (Stop #11) both stop right in front of the ESP, a sure sign that you're smack bang in the middle of the tourist route. Be sure to show your ticket stub from the tours and save $1 on admission to the prison. The Phlash has an Eastern State Penitentiary stop at 22nd Street and Benjamin Franklin Parkway. Get off and walk four blocks north on 22nd Street to Fairmount Avenue.

Overview

To Philadelphians, Benjamin Franklin is more than just the picture on the $100 bill or the dude who flew a kite. He's the guy who started, well, just about everything. He's responsible for our first fire company (Union Fire Company, 1736), our first insurance company (Philadelphia Contributionship, 1752), our first university (University of Pennsylvania, 1749), our first hospital (Pennsylvania Hospital, 1751), and our first library (Library Company, 1731). In addition, he was one of our first postmasters (appointed in 1737), and he ran one of our first newspapers, *The Pennsylvania Gazette*, in which he penned the very first political cartoon. Not to mention what he did for the country. (You remember that whole Declaration of Independence thing, right?)

All of this from a man who began his writing career at age fifteen by sending letters to his brother's Boston newspaper, *The New England Courant*, pretending to be an old widow named "Silence Dogood." His brother James was none too happy when he found out and within two years, the 17-year-old Benjamin ran away to Philadelphia with hardly a penny to his name. Lucky us.

Franklin arrived in Philadelphia on October 6, 1723. To show our appreciation for all he brought to our city, we've named just about everything we can after him. From almost any street corner in Philadelphia, you can spot something named after Benjamin Franklin. Here are just a few choice examples.

The Franklin Institute

222 N 20th St, 215-448-1200; www.fi.edu;
Daily 9:30 am-5 pm

It's virtually impossible to go to the Franklin Institute and not be overrun by children. That being said, it's still a good place for adults to go—if you're young at heart and you don't mind wading through school groups.

The Franklin Institute is divided into several parts. The Franklin National Memorial, located in the rotunda and free of charge, is the only national memorial held in private hands. Not one penny of federal funds helped to create it or support its upkeep. Oh, and there's a massive 20+ foot, 100+ ton statue of ol' BF there. After the rotunda, the Franklin Institute would like your money, please. Exhibits change regularly, so every few months you can go back and see something new. Prices vary depending on the exhibit, but expect to pay at least $20 for adults. The awesome 79-foot IMAX dome screen movies cost $8 for adults, $4 for children.

Franklin at Franklin's University (a.k.a. the University of Pennsylvania)

Penn likes to call itself Franklin's University because Ben founded the joint in 1749. Two buildings are named after the big man: Franklin Field and the Franklin Building (we're not counting the meaningless Franklin Building Annex). The Franklin Building, located at 3451 Walnut Street and used for office space, is among the ugliest buildings on the historic campus. Penn's own website has only this to say about it: "Economical and utilitarian office tower that misses most of the important lines of development of the 1960s campus."

When you think of Ben Franklin, athleticism is probably not the first thing that springs to mind. Nevertheless, Franklin Field, located on 33rd Street between South and Walnut Streets, is old (built in 1922), attractive, and has some historical cache. The first televised football game was played there in 1940; it used to be the home of the Eagles and the yearly Army-Navy football game; it's the country's oldest two-tiered stadium; and it seats 52,000 to boot. Those who saw M. Night Shyamalan's *Unbreakable* (2000) will recognize Franklin Field as the nameless sports stadium that David Dunn (Bruce Willis) worked at as a security guard.

In addition to buildings named after the old boy, it's hard to walk around campus without tripping over a statue of Benjamin Franklin:

- In front of **College Hall** sits a well-known plaster statue of a seated Ben that once resided in front of the old Post Office (9th and Chestnut Streets) as a tribute to Franklin, the United States' first Postmaster General.

- Outside **Weightman Hall** is a statue of a youthful Benjamin as he might have looked when he arrived in Philadelphia: seventeen years old, standing with a staff in one hand and a small bundle in the other. The adorning inscription reads: "I have been the more particular in this description of my journey that you may compare such unlikely beginnings with the figure I have since made there."

- At **37th Street and Locust Walk** is a life-sized bronze of Franklin reading one of his own publications: *The Pennsylvania Gazette*.

- On the second floor alcove of **Stiteler Hall** is a middle-aged, six-foot Ben Franklin holding a scroll in his left hand and a three-cornered hat in his right. Originally displaced from the Odd Fellows Cemetery Company and stored in a crate at Franklin Field for more than twenty years, the figure now resides on campus.

Franklin Statues Everywhere

Around the rest of the city, you'll see Ben popping up everywhere. Catch him wearing a firefighter's helmet at the Fire Hall at **4th and Arch Streets**, or at the **City Hall courtyard** looking out above the east entrance. On **Chestnut Street near 23rd**, Ben is featured seated in a huge mural, and check out the lightning sculpture at the base of the—you guessed it—Ben Franklin Bridge at **5th and Vine Streets**.

Benjamin Franklin Bridge

When they consider their bridges, most Philadelphians think of two thoughts, neither of which is pleasant: New Jersey and bridge traffic. However, the BFB is a beauty. A pedestrian footpath (oddly only open on one side at a time and then for set hours) allows you to run, walk, or bike the expanse. The light show it displays at night is mesmerizing when you're getting loaded at Penn's Landing.

The BFB was designed by Paul Cret, who was also involved in designing the Ben Franklin Parkway. Finished in 1926, the bridge connects Center City Philadelphia to Camden and was originally called the Delaware River Port Authority Bridge. In 1956, it was dedicated to Ben Franklin and renamed in his honor. Like all bridges, keep in mind that it's always free to get to New Jersey, but they make you pay to get back out.

Benjamin Franklin Parkway

The view of Ben Franklin Parkway was made famous in the 1976 movie classic, *Rocky*. In it, Rocky Balboa (Sylvester Stallone) runs to the top of the Art Museum stairs, turns around and raises his arms in victory. Before him is the view of the parkway. This magic moment is recreated endlessly by tourists and visitors, who extol their loved ones to take video footage of themselves striding up the steps and holding their arms aloft.

The Parkway was constructed from 1917 to 1926 with the main objective of getting people from the business district to Fairmount Park. The aforementioned Philadelphia Museum of Art, the Rodin Museum, the Franklin Institute, and the Central Library are all along the Franklin Parkway, which has become quite a popular place for parades and other events. Ironically, it is shut down so often that it makes getting out of the city far more exasperating than it would be if the Parkway had never been built. City planning, anyone?

Franklin Square

Somehow Ben Franklin got short-changed on this one. Of the five squares built into William Penn's design for his "Green Countrie Towne," only Franklin Square hasn't been given the royal refurbishment treatment. Part of the problem is the traffic flow—dangerously fast one-way streets with very little parking surround the park. Still, on any given morning you can see dozens of Tai Chi practitioners from nearby Chinatown and a good little collection of the indigent, sleeping off kerosene benders. Franklin Square is located at Race and Franklin Streets, right at the base of the Ben Franklin Bridge.

Franklin Court

316 Market St, 215-597-8974; Daily 9 am- noon
This is the spot where Franklin's house once stood before it was razed in 1812. That's right: razed. Whoops, our bad. In its place now stands a "ghost structure" (essentially the outline of the house done up in steel support beams) built for the 1976 bicentennial. When digging around in the rubble during its construction, some other cool stuff turned up, including Franklin's privy pit.

B. Free Franklin Post Office & Museum

316 Market St, 215-592-1292; Mon-Sat, 9 am-5 pm
Franklin first accepted the role of postmaster of Philadelphia in 1737, mainly to ensure that his newspaper, *The Pennsylvania Gazette*, was distributed properly. As a royal official, Franklin had "franking privileges," and signed his letters B. Free Franklin. Since he was allowed send letters for free, some think that Franklin was alluding to the fact that his letters were being mailed at no charge. Others believe that "B. Free" was Franklin's statement to the colonies.

The B. Free Franklin Post Office and Museum is an actual working post office. Geeky philatelists will be especially happy to get a letter or postcard that has been cancelled with a hand-stamp bearing Franklin's "B. Free Franklin" signature. Also of note is the fact that this post office is the only one in the country *not* to fly the US flag outside. Why? Because there was no US flag in 1775 when the post office first opened.

Franklin's Grave

After Franklin's death on April 17, 1790, Carl Van Doren wrote, "No other town burying its great man, ever buried more of itself than Philadelphia with Franklin." His grave is located in the Christ Church Cemetery and can be seen through an iron gate at the southeast corner of 5th and Arch Streets. Philadelphia tradition claims that throwing a penny onto Franklin's grave will bring good luck.

Independence National Historical Park

Franklin Square
PAGE 122

Race St →

National Constitution Center

US Mint

Betsy Ross House

Independence Park Institute

Benjamin Franklin's Grave

← Arch St

Christ Church Burial Ground

P

P

Independence Visitor Center (Security Screening Facility)

5th St

MAP 4

4th St

3rd St

Christ Church

2nd St

7th St

6th St

Market St

Market Street Houses

Declaration House

Liberty Bell Pavilion

Independence Mall W

Independence Mall

Independence Mall E

Franklin Court

Liberty Bell Center

Chestnut St

Old City Hall

Second Bank of the US

New Hall Military Museum

Pemberton House

National Park Service Center

Independence Hall

Congress Hall

Philosophical Hall

Library Hall

Carpenters' Hall

First Bank of the US

Sansom St

Independence Square (Security Screening Required)

18th Century Garden

Todd House

Bishop White House

Dock St

Philadelphia Exchange

City Tav

Wel

← Walnut St

St Joseph's Church

Thomas Paine Pl

Dock St

Washington Square

PAGE 122

Tomb of the Unknown Soldier of the American Revolution

Rose Garden

Willings Aly

Locust St

Magnolia Garden

General Information

NFT Map: 4
Websites: www.nps.gov/inde
                www.betsyrosshouse.org

Overview

Instead of the namby-pamby "Philadelphia: The Place That Loves You Back" slogan, perhaps the city should consider a new offering, "Philadelphia: Lots of Significant Stuff Happened Here 200 Years Ago." Tourists flock here because the city's history is so interconnected with the creation of the United States itself. Of course, jaded residents saunter right by these historic buildings where our forefathers determined the country's course with nary a glance. In fact, many of us avoid the Historical Park altogether until out of town guests force us to see downtown and see the Liberty Bell. Paris has the Eiffel Tower; we have the Liberty Bell. Hoo-rah.

INHP comprises "America's most historic square mile." Founded in 1956 on (of course) July 4th, INHP oversees eighteen landmark American institutions, but the most popular attraction by a landslide is the Liberty Bell.

We had to include the Betsy Ross House somewhere, and even though it is not part of INHP, it seems to fit in seamlessly (no sewing pun intended) with the INHP landmarks. And after all, the Betsy Ross House is Philadelphia's second-most visited tourist attraction after INHP.

Admission

Inside the "security zone", access to all buildings is free and generally includes a tour guide and/or some sort of schpiel about the history of each building, including Independence Hall (plus its East and West Wings), Old City Hall, Congress Hall, and the Liberty Bell Pavilion. Outside the security zone, the Declaration (Graff) House is also free, as is the Betsy Ross House (although their request for a "donation" feels suspiciously like a requirement). The one place you do have to pay for a ticket is the National Constitution Center (adults $7, children $5).

Between March 1st and December 31st

There's a lot of stuff to see, but it can all be covered in one pretty full day. Hit the Independence Visitor Center at 6th and Market Streets first, so you can score a free ticket for an Independence Hall tour. Your timed entry ticket could be anywhere from 45 minutes to three or four hours later, depending on how busy it is. Once you have your tour time secured, you can plan the rest of your day. One thing to note: the Declaration (Graff) House is only open

9 am–noon, whereas everything else is open throughout the afternoon, so you might want to squeeze it in early.

Audio Tour

The 74-minute, self guided AudioWalk & Tour narration is available for rent at the Independence Visitor Center. The tour visits twenty important historical sites and the CD (player included) has 64 narrated segments. The cost is $10 for one person, $14 for two people, $16 for three people, and $20 for four people.

Independence Visitor Center

NW corner of Market St & 6th St, 215-965-7676; www.independencevisitorcenter.com; 8:30 am–5 pm (extended in summer till 7 pm)
This is the spot where you pick up the free tickets for your Independence Hall tour time. The ticket window is towards the back of the building on the right. It's also got over-priced food and an over-priced gift shop; on the positive side, it does have a bathroom.

Liberty Bell Center Museum

6th St b/w Market St & Chestnut St (security entrance on 5th St); www.nps.gov/inde/liberty-bell.html, 9 am–5 pm
This is it, the fulcrum of Philadelphia history. Used to be that you could touch it, but after some crazy took a hammer to it in 2001, that practice promptly ended. A National Parks Department Ranger will give a little speech, allow a few brief moments for photography, and then shuffle you out towards Independence Hall.

Independence Hall

Chestnut St b/w 5th St & 6th St, 215-965-2305; www.nps.gov/inde/indep-hall.html, 9 am–5 pm
The Independence Hall tour is where you line up and wait for your tour guide like a good school child. Tours run every fifteen minutes and last about half an hour. First stop is the East Wing of Independence Hall, where the ranger will tell you things about the hall and Philadelphia in general. The quality of your experience will depend entirely on the ranger you draw.

Independence Hall is split into two rooms: the Court Room and the Assembly Room. In the Court Room, you'll learn how a trial was held way back when. The good stuff is in the Assembly Room—that's where the Declaration of Independence and the U.S. Constitution were signed.

After you've covered Independence Hall proper, wander into the West Wing. The Declaration of Independence that was read out loud by Colonel John Nixon to the public for the first time on July 8, 1776 in the State House Yard (now Independence Square). You'll also find a second draft of the Articles of Confederation and Perpetual Union, a draft of the Constitution of the United States, and the inkstand that historians believe was used for the signing of the Declaration and the Constitution.

Congress Hall

www.nps.gov/inde/congress-hall.html
A little bit further westward, you'll run into Congress Hall, which once housed the Senate and House of Representatives. Beyond that, it's special for another remarkable reason. During 1797, Philadelphia was the nation's capital (while Washington, DC, was being built), and on March 4th, George Washington transferred the power to run the country to John Adams, our second president. This was the first time in the modern age that power was transferred peaceably between two people who were not related.

Old City Hall

www.nps.gov/inde/old-city-hall.html
To the east of Independence Hall is Old City Hall, which housed the city's government from 1791 to 1854 and was also the first Supreme Court of the United States. Upstairs was the Mayor's Office and Council Chambers and downstairs was the Mayor's Court, shared with the U.S. Supreme Court for nine years. You'll be struck by how small a space it is.

National Constitution Center

525 Arch St; www.constitutioncenter.org
Open daily 9:30 am-5 pm and until 6 pm Saturday; Tickets: $7 adult, $5 child 4-12 or senior, children under 4 free
All things Constitutional. You can see life-sized bronze statues of the signers, get your picture taken behind the presidential seal, and even complain to your congressional representative at the Participation Café. For $7, it's probably worth it.

Betsy Ross House

239 Arch St, 215-686-1252; www.betsyrosshouse.org
Open 10 am-5 pm daily April-Sept; 10 am-5 pm Tues-Sun Oct-Mar
Did Betsy Ross really make the first flag? We do know that her descendents claim that she made and helped design the first flag in 1776, although the flag we consider to be the Betsy Ross flag (with the 13 stars in a circle) did not appear until the 1790s.

Declaration (Graff) House

7th St & Market St; www.nps.gov/inde/declaration-house.html; Open 9 am-12 pm
This building, like many "historical" buildings in Philadelphia, was razed a long, long time ago. Then for the bicentennial, the city decided to rebuild it real quick in order to capitalize on some fat tourist dollars. Thomas Jefferson rented two rooms in this location from Jacob Graff, Jr. to escape the heat of the city.

City Tavern

138 S 2nd St & Walnut St; 215-413-1443; www.citytavern.com; Opens at 11:30 am
Another building rebuilt for the bicentennial. The original burned down in 1834. While other reproductions (Betsy Ross House, Declaration [Graff] House, Franklin Court) are at best guesstimates, City Tavern is supposed to be a faithful reconstruction right down to the menus. Don't look for any low-carb meals here. Apparently 18th-century types required either bread or potatoes (usually both) with their giant slabs of meat. It isn't cheap, but you're dining in the same air space in which Washington, Jefferson, Adams, and Franklin once dined.

Parking

There's no lack of public parking near INHP—just be prepared to pay for it!

Central Parking Auto Park – 6th St b/w Market St & Arch St
Central Parking System – Market St b/w 8th St & 9th St
Parkway Parking - 8th St & Ranstead Street
Five Star Parking – 8th St & Chestnut St
Parking Plaza-Quaker City Auto – 8th St & Filbert St
HC Parking - 7th St & Cherry St
Bourse Parking – 4th St & Ranstead St

How to Get There—Mass Transit

The Market-Frankford line stops along Market Street at 8th, 5th, and 2nd Streets, with the 5th Street stop being the closest to the Independence Mall.

Many other trains stop at the 8th St/Market terminal, including the subway, trolley, and light rail. Take the Broad-Ridge Spur, Patco High Speed, or Septa bus routes 61 and 47 to the Market Street stop. Many, many other buses stop nearby; consult septa.com for all of the routes.

All Septa Regional Rail trains (R1-2-3-5-6-7-8) stop at the Market East Station, which is six blocks from INHP.

Then there's PHLASH. Nothing says, "Look at me, I'm a tourist!" like the big, purple PHLASH bus. But it is cheap and convenient, costing $1 per ride or $4 per day. The purple bus makes many stops along Market Street between Penn's Landing and City Hall, before cutting up Ben Franklin Parkway to the Philadelphia Museum of Art.

mark and we, the shopping public, are the grand beneficiaries. In addition to all the foodstuffs, there are also plenty of cafes, curios, and, in Fante's at 1006 S 9th Street, one of the best kitchen stores in the country, not to mention, somewhat further south, the cheesesteak landmarks, Pat's and Gino's (Ninth St & Passyunk Ave).

We can't leave the Italian Market without mentioning the annual Italian Market Festival held in early June; it features live music and activities. Check out www.9thstreetitalianmarketfestival.com for this year's program schedule. The same organization also provides Christmas cheer through December.

How to Get There— Driving

From points north or south of Philly, take I-95 to the PA-611 N/Broad Street exit (Exit 14) towards Pattison Avenue. Merge onto S Broad Street. Turn right onto E Passyunk Avenue, then right onto Wharton Street.

From the west, take the US-422 E to I-76 E. Get off at the I-676 E/US-30 E exit (Exit 38) and turn left towards Central PA. Merge onto the Vine Street Expressway and exit at Broad Street/Central PA. Turn right onto N 15th Street. Make a left onto S Penn Square, another right on S Broad Street, and a left onto Washington Avenue. At S 10th Street, turn right, then make a left onto Wharton Street.

Parking

There are four lots that charge by the hour (reasonable rates) and three municipal parking lots in nearby streets. There is also free Saturday parking lot between S Darien Street and S Mildred Street, one block above Christian Street.

How to Get There—Mass Transit

Take bus 23 and get off at Christian Street. Turn right and walk one block to the market. By subway, take the Broad Street line and get off at Ellsworth-Federal. Walk east to 9th Street and turn left. Walk six blocks north and you'll arrive at the market.

General Information

NFT Map: 8
Address: 700-1100 S 9th St
Philadelphia, PA 19147
Phone: 215 334 6008
Website: www.phillyitalianmarket.com
Hours: Tue- Sat: 9 am-4 pm, Sun: 9 am-2 pm

Overview

If going to a supermarket and seeing a freezer filled with frozen chickens isn't a personal enough experience for you, you might consider the Market. You can wander around living, breathing chickens, and many, many fresh carcasses (vegans can find all kinds of great stuff there, but they'll have to learn to avert their eyes). Freshness is what the Italian Market is all about, from meat to produce to bread to homemade cheese and spices.

Located in the heart of South Philly's vibrant Italian community, the Italian Market (sometimes referred to as "9th Street") is the country's oldest daily outdoor market—one hundred years and counting. Whereas the Italian Market used to be just that—Italian—other ethnicities (Asian and Latino) have shouldered their way in. Diversity makes it

Arch St

Dienner's Bar-B-Q Chicken

Lancaster County Dairy

Caviar Assouline

Blue Mountain Vineyards & Cellars

Beiler's Bakery

Dutch Eating Place

Golden Fish Market

Metropolitan Bakery

$ PA General Store

Market Operations

The Rib Stand

Esh Egg Farms

Glick's Salads

Fisher's Soft Pretzels and Ice Cream

D&D Produce

Foster's Gourmet Cookware

Demonstration Kitchen

Rick's Philly Steaks

Hatville Farms

12th Street Cantina

Amazulu

Don't Forget Your Pet

Bee Natural

Kauffman's Lancaster County Produce

DeSimone's Salad Express

Cold Storage

Rocco's Hoagies

Olympic Gyro

Natural Connection

Dutch Country Meats

Andro's Fine Prepared Foods

Market Office Upstairs

Golden Bowl

Kamal's Middle Eastern Specialties

Martin's Quality Meats & Sausages

John Yi Fish Market

DiNic's

Sandwich Stand

Spice Terminal

Seating Area

The Shoe Doctor

Bassett's Ice Cream

The Flower Basket

Four Seasons Juice Bar

Shanghai Gourmet

Mezze

Seating Area

❶ Terralyn

Philbert

Seating Area

Braverman's Bakery

Miscellanea Libri

Nomad Trading

Delilah's at the Terminal

Tea Leaf

Harry G Ochs & Son

Spataro's

The Original Turkey

Basic 4 Vegetarian

Tokyo Sushi Bar

Franks-A-Lot

Beer Garden

Seating Area

Pearl's Oyster Bar

Profi's Creperie

Sang Kee Peking Duck

Nanee's Kitchen

OK Lee's Produce

Young Botanicals

De' Village

Godshall's Poultry

Coastal Cave

Seating Area

Old City Coffee

Downtown Cheese

Cookbook Stall

Little Thai Market

Salumeria

Market Blooms

Annie's Irish Gifts

L Halterman Family Country Foods

Famous 4th St Cookie Co

Le Bus Bakery

Amy's Place

Chocolate by Mueller

Wan's Seafood

AA Halterman Poultry & Meat

Parcel Pick-Up

$ Market Information

Chocolate by Mueller

Termini Brothers Bakery

Down Home Diner

Down Home Diner

by george!

Iovine Brothers Produce

MAP 3

Filbert St

❶ Fair Food Farmstand (Fri and Sat Only)
Livengood's Produce (Sat only)

	Groceries		Shops
	Bars/Beverages		Parkings
	Restaurants		Other

12th St

General Information

NFT Map:	3
Address:	12th St & Arch St
	Philadelphia, PA 19107
Phone:	215-922-2317
Website:	www.readingterminalmarket.org
Hours:	Mon-Sat: 8 am-6 pm

Overview

A giant food market, with representative cuisine from all over the area (and then some), Reading offers everything from organic produce to Amish bakeries to fresh seafood.

From 1889 through 1985, the market lived in the train shed beneath the tracks of the station at 12th and Market streets. When the commuter-rail system was rerouted to bypass the station, the tracks were removed and the market remained. Today, many Philadelphians make RTM their destination every Saturday morning for the truly fabulous and unbelievably cheap breakfasts at the Dutch Eating Place. $3-$5 will get you *anything* on the breakfast menu, but be prepared to wait for a stool, and, since nearly all of their dishes come with a stick of butter melting over the top, you might want to book ahead at your local hospital. Other Philadelphians go to RTM for their lunch hour. Still others do their grocery shopping there, drawn by the locally grown fruit and vegetables and excellent meats from local farms and their butchers.

It's impossible to name all the varieties of chow here, but there's a diner, an excellent pizza joint, great vegan food, good Mexican, Gyros, Vietnamese, some of the best local ice cream in the city, a great culinary shop and, believe it or not, regular cooking lessons in a giant open-air kitchen. If you want to impress the snooty foodies who come to visit you (meaning, among others, anyone from NYC) take 'em there, load them up with a Vietnamese hoagie and a giant mint chocolate milkshake, then buy them a copper sauté pan. That'll learn 'em.

How to Get There—Driving

From the Schuylkill/76, take Exit 344/676 E. From 676, take the second exit, Broad Street. From the exit ramp, continue straight on Vine Street and follow the signs that say "PA Convention Center." Turn right onto 12th Street and proceed two blocks to Arch Street. Reading Terminal Market is on the southeast corner of Arch and Market.

From I-95 S/N, take Exit 22/676 W. From 676 take the first exit, Broad Street. Turn right off of exit ramp onto 15th Street. Turn left onto Vine Street (second light) then right onto 12th St and proceed two blocks to Arch Street. Reading Terminal Market is on the southeast corner of Arch and Market.

Parking

"Free" parking is available to market shoppers (as long as you spend big at the market) on the 3rd, 5th, and 7th floors of the Parkway Garage, located across the street from the 12th Street market entrance on Filbert Street between 12th and 13th Streets. The only catch is that you have to be done shopping in two hours and present ten 50¢ parking tokens at the ticket booth upon departure.

To get one 50¢ token, you have to spend $5 at a market vendor. So for $50 worth of purchases, you can park for free. Or you can just pay the $5 parking fee and be done with it. If you park for longer than 2 hours, the regular garage rates apply so check the current rates as you enter (or call 215-922-2317). If you have patience and time to spare, there's a less complicated alternative—nearby metered parking.

How to Get There—Mass Transit

Take any of SEPTA's Regional Rail lines to the Market East Station and follow signs to the PA Convention Center and Reading Terminal Market.

From the Broad Street subway, get off at City Hall and walk east on Market Street. Turn left on 12th Street and walk one block until you hit RTM. From the Market/Frankford line, get off at 13th Street. Walk one block east to 12th Street and RTM is one block along 12th Street.

By trolley, get off at Juniper Station and walk two blocks east to 12th Street. Turn left onto 12th Street and walk one block to RTM.

There are loads of buses that pass close to the market. Routes 9, 17, 23, 33, 38, 44, 61 Express, and 121 all go by 12th and Market Streets.

Pennsylvania Convention Center

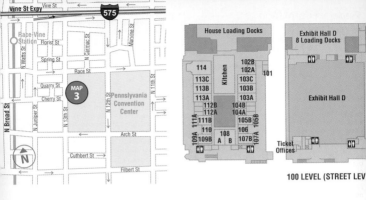

MAP 3

575

House Loading Docks

114	Kitchen	102B
113C		102A
113B		103C
113A		103B
112B		103A
112A		104B
111B		104A
110	108 A B	105B
109B		106
		107B

111A 109A 107A 105B

101

Exhibit Hall D
8 Loading Docks

Exhibit Hall D

Ticket Offices

100 LEVEL (STREET LEV

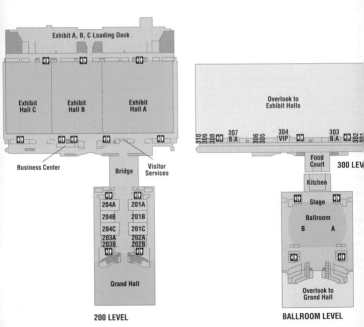

Exhibit A, B, C Loading Dock

Exhibit Hall C

Exhibit Hall B

Exhibit Hall A

Business Center

Bridge

Visitor Services

204A	201A
204B	201B
204C	201C
203A	202A
203B	202B

Grand Hall

200 LEVEL

Overlook to Exhibit Halls

310 309 308 | 307 B A | 306 305 | 304 (VIP) | 303 B A | 302 301

Food Court

Kitchen

Stage

Ballroom
B   A

Overlook to Grand Hall

300 LEV

BALLROOM LEVEL

General Information

NFT Map:	3
Address:	1101 Arch St
	Philadelphia, PA 19107
Phone:	215-418-4700
Website:	www.paconvention.com

Overview

Spanning six downtown city blocks and covering 1.3 million square-feet, the Pennsylvania Convention Center is gigantic: the second largest convention center in the Northeast, as a matter of fact. This would be wonderful indeed if conventioneers packed the place week after week but, because of union squabbles and poor city planning, such has not been the case. After years of bickering, the Convention Center is still not being used anywhere near its capacity, which, if you're of the inclination, can work as an apt metaphor for the bureaucracy of the city at large: the party is ready to roll up in the penthouse suite, but the guests aren't allowed to use the elevator to get up there.

Unless you are attending an event, the Convention Center is not open to the public. Ergo, it's not really a hangout. If you happen to be there for business, however, you will be pleased to note it has state-of-the-art meeting facilities, high-speed Internet access with gigabit LAN connections, and many of the other flashy amenities true-blue bizzers crave.

For the rest of us, it's still worth checking out the calendar of events listed on the Convention Center's website. Cool exhibits and events come along every year, including such faves as Mardi Paw (www.mardipaw.com), the Philadelphia Auto Show (www.phillyautoshow.com), the Philadelphia Furniture and Furnishings Show (www.pffshow.com), and for God's sake, people!—the Philadelphia Flower Show (www.theflowershow.com), to which the entire city kowtows every March.

As far as eating in the area goes, we recommend the **Independence Brew Pub**, located inside the massive Convention Center structure at street level, right above Market East Station (just follow the signs for Market East). It's got pool tables upstairs, lots of seats at the bar downstairs, TVs, video games, etc. It's a bit pricey ($15-$20 for most entrees), so if you're on a budget, venture outside of the Convention Center, and you'll find yourself in **Chinatown** where cheap eats are plentiful. It's also very close to **Reading Terminal Market**, a most-impressive array of restaurants, produce, and Amish farmers. It's an often-chaotic, never-dull glimpse of the different cultures and cuisines that make up the city.

How to Get There—Driving

From the Schuykill/76, take Exit 344/676 E. Once you're on 676 E, take the second exit, Broad Street. From the exit ramp, continue straight on Vine Street and follow all the huge signs that say "PA Convention Center." Turn right onto 12th Street and proceed two blocks to the Convention Center.

From I-95 S or N, take Exit 22/676 W. Once you're on 676 take the first exit, Broad Street. Turn right off of the exit ramp onto 15th Street. Turn left onto Vine Street (second light) then right onto 12th Street and proceed two blocks to the Convention Center.

Parking

There are 42 private lots located within a 7-block radius of the Convention Center. The only street parking in that area is at two-hour meters, with restrictions during rush hours (check the signs).

How to Get There—Mass Transit

All Regional Lines (R1, R2, R3, R5, R6, R7, and R8) connect directly to the Convention Center via the Market East Station. From Market East, follow signs inside the station for the Convention Center. There's no need to go outside to get to the Convention Center, which is perfect on cold or rainy days.

The Market-Frankford line stops at the Pennsylvania Convention Center/11th Street Station for easy access to the center. If you're taking the Broad Street line, make a free transfer at City Hall for the Market-Frankford line.

Trolley routes 10, 11, 13, 34, and 36 go to the Juniper Station. Walk one block north to Arch Street and then one block east (right) to 12th Street.

Bus routes 12, 17, 23, 33, 38, 44, 48, and 121 all stop at the Convention Center.

Essentials

This part of Philadelphia consists of neighborhoods like Bustleton, Pennypack, and Torresdayle in the far northeast and Foxchase, Frankford, Mayfair, and Oxford Circle in the near northeast. Northeast is an authentic area, often overlooked in the cultural landscape of one of America's best cities. Ripe with tradition and loyal denizens, Northeast Philly (to those who reside here) is Philadelphia minus the exorbitant dining fares and posh Old City scenes. The cuisine, the sites, and the people make it great.

Northeast Philadelphia is like the guy who can go anywhere but refuses to wear a tie. Proud of its history and a personality unlike anywhere else in the city, Northeast, though bucolic, is worth the trip down "The Boulevard" (the oldest north- and south-running artery in the country established over fifty years before I-95). Row homes and brick-faced storefronts are the norm in the neighborhoods, while shopping centers, replete with great finds, accent the highways and byways. Locals brag that the pizza, Italian ice, and cheesesteaks are better here than anywhere else in the world.

O Landmarks

- **The Boulevard** • Roosevelt Blvd
- **Burlhome Park** • Cottman & Central Aves
- **Flyer's Skate Zone** • 10990 Decatur Rd
- **Knowlton Mansion** • 8001 Verree Rd
- **Nabisco Factory** • Comly Rd & Roosevelt Ave
- **Northeast Philadelphia Airport (PNE)** • 8000 Essington Ave
- **Pennypack Creek Park** • 8800 Verree Rd

Sundries

 ### Coffee

- **Coffee Connection** • 6441 Frankford Ave
- **The Coffee Tree** • 2226 Cottman Ave
- **Cool Beans Café** • 1466 E Cheltenham Ave
- **Country Club Restaurant & Pastry Shop** • 1717 Cottman Ave
- **Quaker Diner** • 7241 Rising Sun Ave

Nightlife

- **Chickie and Pete's** • 11000 Roosevelt Blvd
- **Jillian's** • 1995 Franklin Mills Cir, Franklin Mills Mall
- **Molly Maguires** • 427 Rhawn St
- **Nutty Irishman** • 8138 Bustleton Ave
- **Sweeney's Station Saloon** • 13639 Philmont Ave
- **Whiskey Tango Tavern** • 14000 Bustleton Ave

Restaurants

- **Benny the Bums** • 9991 Bustleton Ave
- **Blüe Ox Brauhaus** • 7980 Oxford Ave
- **Chink's Steaks** • 6030 Torresdale Ave
- **Dining Car** • 8826 Frankford Ave
- **Guido's Restaurant** • 3545 Welsh Rd
- **LaPadella** • 1619 Grant Ave
- **Macaroni's Restaurant** • 9315 Old Bustleton Ave
- **Mayfair Diner** • 7353 Frankford Ave
- **Nick's Roast Beef** • 2212 Cottman Ave
- **Nifty Fifty's** • 2491 Grant Ave
- **Santucci's Pizza** • 4010 Cottman Ave
- **Steve's Prince of Steaks** • 7200 Bustleton Ave

Shopping

- **Contempo Cuts** • 2218 Cottman Ave
- **Dutch Country Farmers' Market** • 2031 Cottman Ave
- **Harry's Natural Food Store** • 1805 Cottman Ave
- **International Coins Unlimited** • 1825 Cottman Ave
- **Peters Handbags** • 8314 Bustleton Ave
- **Roosevelt Mall** • 2311 Cottman Ave
- **St Jude Shop** • 6902 Castor Ave

General Information

Websites: www.virtualnjshore.com
www.shore-guide.com

Overview

Beginning in Sandy Hook in the north and extending down to Cape May in the south, the 127-mile Jersey Shore is a prime destination for weekenders and summer vacationers. Some of these people may even have been known to you at one time.

There are many communities lining the shore, and each is known for its own distinct attractions, from sandy dunes and lighthouses to gambling and shopping (and a lot of other crap). Whatever their differences, all of the towns are known for their abundance of fresh seafood—by far the Shore's best asset. The Jersey Shore experience is an indispensable part of what it means to be a Philadelphian (and, no, not all memories involve fake IDs, ugly tattoos, and vomit—only most). If you're planning a trip to the shore, check out Virtual New Jersey Shore's calendar of events at www.virtualnjshore.com/events.html.

Towns/Cities

Asbury Park

While efforts are being made to restore this "seaside ghost town", Asbury Park has struggled with its growing decrepitude since the July 4th, 1970 race riots. In its heyday, Asbury Park was one of the most prominent and thriving seaside resorts along the Jersey Shore. The Convention Hall, designed in the 1920s, hosted The Rolling Stones, Jefferson Airplane, The Doors, The Who, and, of course, Bruce Springsteen (who adopted Asbury as his hometown). At one point, Asbury Park drew over half a million visitors to its wide tree-lined streets, swanky hotels, lively restaurants, and packed boardwalks. Today, the beaches are empty, the boardwalks barren, and a sad nostalgia permeates the air. Sing it, Bruce.

Atlantic City

Visitors expecting a Vegas-like wonderland are in for a serious surprise. Sure, Atlantic City features the same gambling and topless dancers as does Sin City, but AC doesn't shield its guests from the more distressing side of the gambling world. The winos, the bums, and the broke grandmothers are inescapable. And while the surrounding population sinks deeper into its own morass, the casinos keep getting glitzier, with additions like the swanky billion-dollar Borgata, which opened a couple of years ago.

Harrah's remains the premiere casino venue, playing host to the 2005 World Series of Poker. Donald Trump himself owns three glittering casinos here, and the Hilton provides a touch of old-school glam. Caesar's is one of the largest casinos in the city, while Bally's Wild Wild West Casino attracts a mixed clientele. When it comes to choosing a casino, you can't really go wrong—until you start dipping into Junior's college fund.

Gambling and strip joints aren't Atlantic City's only attractions. There are golf, sailing, fishing, shopping malls on boardwalks, and slums too! Plans for a new multi-billion-dollar state-of-the-art Convention Center and Grand Boulevard are currently in the works. Stay tuned.

Long Beach Island
www.longbeachisland.com
Perhaps the least-crowded and least-schlocky of all shore destinations, LBI is a family-oriented stretch of small and even smaller towns such as Beach Haven, Surf City, Loveladies, Harvey Cedars, and Barnegat. Each town has its own character (Harvey Cedars = $$$; Beach Haven = mellow) and one or two decent restaurants/attractions. However, without a boardwalk like Seaside Heights, LBI will fortunately never get hordes of teenage retards cruising the main drag and puking in hotel rooms. Courses in sea kayaking, yoga, pottery, and photography are set against a panorama of waves, white sand, blue skies, and brilliant sunsets (thank you, New Jersey pollution!). Albert Music Hall (www.alberthall.org) hosts live country, folk, and bluegrass music year-round on Saturday nights. Broadway fans can take in their favorite song and dance routines at the Surflight Theatre (www.surflight.org).

Ocean City
Ocean City without the Boardwalk is like Paris without the Champs d'Elysees: so much of this Jersey Shore town's gestalt is fashioned down at the boardwalk. One of the last authentic walkways in the area, the Boardwalk is a mixture of classic and contemporary seaside attractions. The timeless 140 foot Ferris Wheel, the requisite rollercoaster, and the ubiquitous boardwalk bumper cars stand next to the newer mini-golf courses, water rides, and waterpark (Li'l Buc's Bay), where adults are admitted only with a child. It's easy to spend a packed day without leaving the ocean front, if you can subsist on a diet of beer and funnel cake. Check out the Ocean City Ghost Tour, a candlelit walking tour which runs every evening between May 28th and September 5th, where guides recount spooky tales of local folklore (www.ghosttour.com).

Ocean Grove
www.oceangrovenj.com
Deemed worthy of historic preservation In 1976 by the National Register of Historic Places, Ocean Grove is as distinguished as it gets at the Jersey Shore. Here you'll find the biggest collection of Victorian houses in the country; the elaborately built pastel-colored homes are on every block and run the gamut of Victorian sensibility from Mansord and Gothic style, to Colonial Revival, Queen Anne, and Italianate-influenced homes. The Mid-Atlantic Center for the Arts offers hourly walking tours explaining the history and significance of these mansions. If you'd rather trek solo, don't miss the Abbey Bed 'n Breakfast on the corner of Gurney Street and Columbia Avenue, and the 15 elaborately decorated period rooms at Emlen Physick Estate, located at 1048 Washington Street.

Point Pleasant
www.pointpleasantbeach.com
Point Pleasant offers up the archetypal beach experience: swimming, surfing, sun bathing, ice cream, Fun House, etc. The south end of the beach is public, but has no lifeguard on duty, while Bradshaw Beach at the north end requires an entry fee. The Sinatra House (on the corner of Water Street and Boardwalk) heats things up at night with Old Blue Eyes' crooning out the window. There's no shortage of bars or dance clubs to choose from.

Sandy Hook

Think pristine white sandy beaches, old wooden boardwalks, surf fishing, historic lighthouses, bird observatories, salt marshes, and you've got a good picture of Sandy Hook. Located at the northern tip of the NJ Shore, Sandy Hook is also known as home of the Ocean Institute— the oldest working lighthouse in America.

Seaside Heights

www.seasideheights.net

This is the spot for the surfing crowd. Seaside Heights touts itself as having "some of the top lifeguards anywhere," and its public beaches are open year-round. Beyond the waves and surf, the bustling boardwalk is another attraction. Local pubs and nightclubs line the vast stretch of wooden planks. All of them are bad. If you're older than 17 ½, this isn't the place for you.

Spring Lake

This 100-year old, quiet family resort town is comprised of tranquil coastline, a non-commercial boardwalk, and sand dune beaches. The main street is full of quaint shops, gourmet restaurants, and cozy B&Bs. If you're looking for privacy, aim for a mid-week getaway, as the four beaches get crowded on the weekends. The area is known for great scuba diving (including an off-shore ship wreck to explore), and fresh- and salt-water fishing. If you're looking for high-energy activity, this may not be your spot, but it remains a romantic getaway for couples.

Wildwood

www.wildwoodsnj.com

Little-known fact: the collection of three resort communities that make up Wildwood—including Wildwood Crest, The City of North Wildwood, and the City of Wildwood—is known as the "Mecca of the Kiting World." Memorial Day weekend sees the place flooded with kite enthusiasts. *Conde Naste Traveler Magazine* also chose Wildwood as the "Best Sports Beach." Activities include golfing, shopping, deep-sea fishing, kayaking, biking, beach aerobics, water-parks, and a large beach Ultimate Frisbee tournament in the summer. Kids can't get enough of the Morey Piers Amusement Park (www.moreyspiers.com), and "House of Shells" has an impressive collection of nautical décor, seashells, and antiques.

Attractions

Barnegat Lighthouse

604-494-2016

Once upon a time, there were actually two lighthouses built in Barnegat. The first, standing at a puny 40 feet, was built in 1835 and crumbled shortly after. The second lighthouse, which soars nearly four times taller than its predecessor, at a majestic 165 feet, was built in 1859, and still stands to this day. Located at the north end of Long Beach Island, the Barnegat Lighthouse has become the symbol of the Jersey Shore. The red and white structure, retired in 1927, is affectionately referred to by the locals as "Old Barney." Barney is open for public viewing 9 am-4:30 pm during the winter and until 9:30 pm in the summer months.

Cape May Lighthouse

609-884-5404; Hours vary: Open daily April- November; $5 adults, $1children; Free Parking

The 157-foot tall lighthouse is actually the third built in Cape May. The first (built in 1823) and the second (built in 1847) were both destroyed by erosion. The one that shines its beacon today, located in Cape May Point State Park's Lower Township, has been standing since 1859 and was built with bricks from the 1847 version. It's worth huffing and puffing up the 199 steps for spectacular panoramic vistas of the Cape May Peninsula. The lighthouse is currently managed by the Mid-Atlantic Center for the Arts (MAC). The non-profit group sponsors cultural and artistic events and offers daily guided tours (www.capemaymac.org).

Cape May Point State Park

609-884-2159; Open sunrise to sunset

Mockingbirds, warblers, and sparrows, oh my! Located just off the southern end of Garden State Parkway, this 253-acre no-fee park is a haven for bird-lovers. Several trails lead to ponds, marshes, dunes, and forest habitats where all sorts of migratory birds can be spotted. Following one of the three main hiking trails, the Red Trail (0.5 mile), the Yellow Trail (1.5 miles), or the Blue Trail (2 miles), is the best way to explore the park. If you're looking to spice up your vacation with education, the park hosts nature clubs and programs for children.

Edwin B. Forsythe National Wildlife Refuge

b/w Brick Township & Brigantine

This refuge encompasses over 43,000 acres and has two divisions (Brigantine and Barnegat). Bird-watching, nature walks, great views of protected wetlands, and learning about migratory bird habitats are the main deal here. For more information, go to http://forsythe.fws.gov.

Island Beach State Park

This majestic barrier island is made up of 3,000 acres of preserved land and over ten miles of pure, untainted white sand. The park is filled with historic buildings, hiking and biking trails, naturalist programs, bathhouses, and pristine bird-watching spots. This natural wonder is a must-see for outdoor enthusiasts, and in complete contrast with the crazed, crowded Seaside Heights just up the road. Highly recommended.

Lucy the Elephant

9200 Atlantic Ave, Margate, NJ, 609-823-6473; www.lucytheelephant.org

The legendary 65-foot wooden elephant, which stands mid-stride overlooking the sea, is one of the Shore's oddest intrigues. Built in 1881, Lucy's stout legs serve as a 350-step stairwell linking the bottom floor with the anterior rooms and howdah. She can be seen without binoculars from up to eight miles away. The 90-ton mammoth pachyderm was added to the National Registry of Historic Places in 1971 and now offers tours for groups of ten or more. Recommended.

Rutgers Unversity Marine Field Station/ Great Bay Boulevard

Great Bay Blvd, Tuckerton, NJ

A completely overlooked gem amidst a morass of mid prole dreams, the drive out to Rutgers University's Marine Field Station along Great Bay Boulevard is absolutely incredible. Low wetlands, small wooden bridges, lots of wildlife, ruined canneries, amazing sunsets, and almost no people make this about as far an experience from Seaside Heights, Wildwood, or "AC" as you can get. You can find cheap-ass boat rentals along the Boulevard, so you can explore, go crabbing or fishing or swimming, or just be cool. The Field Station has tours occasionally, so for more information, go to: http://marine.rutgers.edu/cool/info/directions.html.

Sea Girt Lighthouse

Beach Blvd & Ocean Ave, 732-974-0514; Open one Sunday/month

Sea Girt, once appropriately called "Wreck Pond," earned its menacing name because of the countless shipwrecks in the Manasquan River. With the construction of the lighthouse in 1896, which warned boats of the upcoming shoreline, "Wreck Pond" traded in its ill-omened moniker for the less threatening "Sea Girt." The lighthouse closed after the Second World War, 50 years after its opening, and has been preserved as a historic site. The site has become a popular destination for elementary school fieldtrips, and public tours are given once a month on Sundays.

Twin Lights

732-872-1814; www.twin-lights.org; Memorial Day-Labor Day weekdays 10 am-5 pm, Wed-Sun 10 am-5 pm

Towering 200 feet above sea level in Highlands, New Jersey, the two-towered Navesink Light station has been used as the shore's primary lighthouse since 1828. The lighthouse standing today was built in 1862, and has been open as a museum since it was acquired by the state in 1967. A climb to the top offers an unbeatable ocean-view panorama and the exhibition gallery offers historical background on the site.

Wildwood Boardwalk

16th Ave to Cresse Ave; Open daily Palm Sunday weekend through Columbus Day

Wildwood is filled with more rides than Disneyland, including the East Coast's tallest and fastest wooden coaster, the Great White. There are five amusement piers to visit with a cornucopia of carnival games, souvenir shops, and food stands (rumor has it that there are more pizza joints here per square foot than anywhere else in the world). A tram line makes transportation between venues fast and easy. Dust off your poodle skirt for DooWop '50s Night, or mingle with the other car connoisseurs at Classic Car shows. Check out the *Cape May Times* newspaper for a calendar of events.

How to Get There—Driving

From Center City, cross the Franklin Bridge into New Jersey and follow signs to Cherry Hill (Route 38) and the beaches (stay to your left). Once on Route 38, get into the right hand lane and merge onto I-70. Take I-70 until you hit the I-72 Junction East and keep right around the circle. Follow I-72 for 26 miles and you'll end up at the Jersey Shore. If you leave on a weekday and it's not rush hour, you can make the journey in an hour and a half. At all other times, don't leave without your mixed tapes, as you'll most likely be sitting in traffic.

From the northeast, go over the Tacony-Palmyra Bridge onto Route 73 S. Head to the I-70 intersection and drive east. At the I-72 Circle, take 72 to Long Beach Island (about 26 miles). From the south, take Route 42 E to Route 35 N, which takes you to Route 70 E. Or take the 42 to the NJ Turnpike and get off at Exit 4 (Route 73 S). Follow the directions above.

Colleges & Universities · **Drexel University**

1. Neuropsychology Laboratories
2. Language and Communication Center
3. 3210 Cherry Street
4. Academic Building
5. 3201 Arch Street
6. Campus Security Office
7. Frederic O Hess Engineering Research Lab
8. Nesbitt Hall
9. Leonard Pearlstein Business Learning Center
10. Matheson Hall
11. Korman Center
12. Disque Hall
13. Bossone Research Enterprise Center
14. LeBow Engineering Center
15. Center for Automation Technology
16. Main Building
17. Randell Hall
18. Curtis Hall
19. Alumni Enginering Labs

Center City Campus
20. Myer Feinstein Polyclinic
21. Bobst Building
22. North Tower (Main Hospital Entrance)
23. South Tower
24. New College Building H
26. Franklin Office Center, 1427 Vine Street
27. Stiles Alumni Hall
28. Bellet Building
29. 221 N Broad Street
30. 219 N Broad Street
31. 207 N Broad Street

Center City Hahnemann Campus

Henry Ave/Queen Ln Campu

General Information

NFT Map: 2, 14, 23
Mailing Address: 3141 Chestnut St
Philadelphia, PA 19104
Phone: 215-895-2000
Website: www.drexel.edu

Overview

In what has to be considered something of an amazing development, Drexel U is now considered to be one of the top schools in Pennsylvania, at least according to *US News & World Report*. The *USN&WR* finds the institution excellent in its national doctoral program, its nursing program, and its online graduate program for business, engineering, and library science. Take that, you Penn snobs!

The actual campus is composed of three locations, though most classes are held at the University City Main Campus. Nursing and Health students hang out at the Center City Hahnemann Campus, and students at the Drexel University College of Medicine take their classes at the Queen Lane Medical Campus.

There are many extracurricular activities to keep students occupied, including 140 different student clubs. Athletic types should head over to the John A Daskalakis Athletic Center; an impressive facility housing a swimming pool and indoor basketball/volleyball and squash courts.

When students really crave the campus-escape, they're only minutes from Center City. There are even several classes that offer region-specific courses with field trips into the heart of the city, including the always-popular "Swear, Spit and Battery Throw" seminar held at the Eagles' Lincoln Financial Field.

Tuition

Students choose between enrolling in a four- or five-year undergraduate degree program. The former will set you back $27,100 a year, while the 5-year program costs $21,700 a year. Over 92% of students receive financial aid, and they actually encourage all students to apply regardless of whether they think they're eligible or not. As of yet, there are no financial aid incentives for students who can funnel beer through multiple orifices.

Sports

Calling all jocks! Drexel has over 16 NCAA Division I teams to try out. From basketball and field hockey, to wrestling and tennis, there are over 350 Drexel Dragons huffing and puffing their way between classes. More recently, over $900,000 has been raised to help install new scoreboards, bleachers, and renovate the softball complex and tennis courts. If you're not the ultra-competitive type, there

are more casual activities, like the one-day bench-press or dart competitions. Various intramural sports also run year-round, such as beach volleyball and flag football. For the even less physically inclined, check out the Recreation Sports Office's fall term health and wellness program. Designed specifically to help you cope with the stress of those ruthless calculus assignments or how to manage those unyielding cheesesteak and vodka Ovaltine diets, the seminars are popular ways to help you survive your campus experience.

Culture on Campus

Like so many educational institutions, Drexel has its share of co-curricular and extra-curricular fun stuff. One particular favorite is the free Friday Night Movie Series that often showcases the newly released flicks. The Annual Winter Snowball Dinner and Dance is also another popular student-pleaser. There might not be the level and quality of cultural events at Drexel as you might find at Penn, but the sheer volume of quality engineering students assures there will always be opportunity for Drunken Slide-Rule Olympics.

Departments

Log onto www.drexel.edu/contact for a more complete university directory.

Undergraduate Admission 215-895-2400
Alumni Relations/
    Institutional Advancement 215-895-2600
Athletics 215-895-1999
Bursar, Office of Student Accounts 215-895-1445
Career Management: Steinbright
    Career Development 215-895-2185
Co-operative Education 215-895-2185
Computing Resources (IRT) 215-895-2698
Drexel Directory Assistance 215-895-2000
Facilities Management 215-895-1700
Financial Aid 215-895-2537
International Programs 215-895-1704
Institutional Advancement 215-895-2600
Library-Drexel University City
    Main Campus 215-895-1500
Library-Health Sciences Libraries 215-762-7631
President 215-895-2100
Provost 215-895-2200
Research Administration 215-895-5849
Sports 215-895-1999
Student Life- Drexel University City
    Main Campus 215-895-2506
Student Life- Center City
    Hahnemann Campus 215-762-1400
Student Resource Center (SRC) 215-895-2300
University Relations 215-895-1530

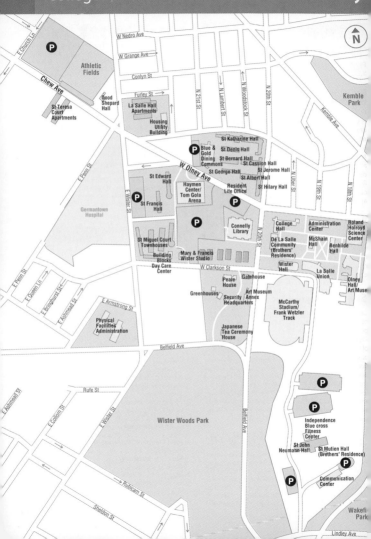

N

W Nedro Ave

W Grange Ave

Conlyn St

Kemble Park

Kemble Ave

E Church Ln

Athletic Fields

Chew Ave

St Teresa Court Apartments

Good Shepard Hall

Furley St

La Salle Hall Apartments

Housing Utility Building

W Olney Ave

N 21st St

N Lambert St

N Woodstock St

N 20th St

N Uber St

N 19th St

N 18th St

St Katharine Hall

Blue & Gold Dining Commons

St Denis Hall

St Bernard Hall

St Cassion Hall

St George Hall

St Jerome Hall

St Albert Hall

St Hilary Hall

St Edward Hall

Haymen Center/ Tom Gola Arena

Resident Life Office

E Penn St

Germantown Hospital

E Wister St

St Francis Hall

Connelly Library

College Hall

Administration Center

Roland Holroyd Science Center

De La Salle Community (Brothers' Residence)

McShain Hall

Benhilde Hall

St Miguel Court Townhouses

Building Blocks Day Care Center

Mary & Francis Wister Studio

Wister Hall

La Salle Union

Olney Hall/ Art Muse

W Clarkson St

Peale House

Gatehouse

E Penn St

E Queen Ln

E Brinyhurst St

E Ashmead St

Greenhouses

Art Museum

Security Headquarters

Annex

McCarthy Stadium/ Frank Wetzler Track

E Armstrong St

Physical Facilities Administration

Japanese Tea Ceremony House

Belfield Ave

E Ashmead St

E Collom St

E Wister St

Rufe St

Wister Woods Park

Belfield Ave

Independence Blue cross Fitness Center

St John Neumann Hall

St Mutien Hall (Brothers' Residence)

Communication Center

Rubicam St

Sheldon St

Wakefi Park

Lindley Ave

General Information

Address: 1900 W Olney Ave
             Philadelphia, PA 19141
Phone: 215-951-1000
Website: www.lasalle.edu

Overview

Founded in 1863 by the De La Salle Christian Brothers, La Salle University is a private Roman Catholic university located on a 100-acre suburban campus not far from Center City. Between its School of Arts & Sciences, School of Nursing, and School of Business Administration, La Salle enrolls over 5,500 students a year in 55 different undergraduate and graduate degree programs. La Salle's ongoing dedication to its Roman Catholic roots is evident in its strong focus on community service and the existence of a theology and ministry graduate school.

Tuition

In the 2003-2004 academic year, tuition and fees were $24,410, while the average room and board costs were $8,430. Of course, these figures do not include books, supplies, lab fees, or personal expenses.

Sports

La Salle's student body is extremely athletic, with more than 500 of its undergraduates participating on one or more of the twenty-three NCAA Division I varsity athletic teams (not to mention the students playing intramural sports). Men's teams include baseball, basketball, crew, cross-country, football, golf, soccer, swimming, tennis, and indoor and outdoor track & field. Women's teams include basketball, crew, cross-country, field hockey, lacrosse, soccer, softball, swimming, tennis, volleyball, and indoor and outdoor track & field. The Explorers basketball teams are also members of the Big Five; Philly's own annual basketball backyard rumble.

Culture on Campus

The La Salle University Art Museum (1900 W Olney Ave, 215-951-1221) proudly touts itself as the only permanent collection of paintings, drawings, and sculpture from the West at any university museum in the Philadelphia region. The permanent collection focuses on European and American landscape, portraiture, still-life, and abstract paintings spanning the Middle Ages to modern times. Smaller collections include Old Master prints and drawings, illustrated rare bibles, ancient Greek terra cotta pottery, African tribal art, and Japanese prints from the 19th- and 20th centuries. The museum is open Tuesday-Friday from 11 am to 4 pm and Sunday from 2 pm to 4 pm, with varying hours during the summer and holidays; call ahead before planning a visit. Access to the museum is free to La Salle University students and staff (though donations are encouraged) and $2.50 for the general public. Group tours are offered by appointment.

Departments

Log onto www.lasalle.edu/contact for a more complete university directory.

Undergraduate Admissions 215-951-1500
Graduate Admissions 215-951-1100
Continuing Studies Admissions...... 215-951-1655
School of Arts & Sciences............ 215-951-1042
School of Business Administration... 215-951-1040
School of Nursing................... 215-951-1430
School of Ministry and Theology..... 215-951-1335
School of Communication........... 215-951-1155
La Salle University Bucks Campus.... 215-579-7335

Wissahickon Creek

Wissahickon Valley Park

PAGE 118

Alumni Field

Hughes Gym

Physical Plant/ Carriage House

Haggar Hall (Learning Center)

Fox St

Townhouses

Archer Hall

Wallenberg Center

Downs Hall

Art Center 1

Student Center

Information Technology

Althouse Hall

Campus Store/ Mailroom

Gutman Library

Independence Plaza

Netherfield Rd

White House

Scholler Hall

Architecture & Design Center

Roxboro House

Design Center

Henry Ave

Hayward Hall

Search Hall

E Netherfield Rd

Fashion Mechandising

White Corners

W Netherfield Rd

Softball Field

Gibbs Hall

Tuttleman Center

Timber Ln

Henry A

Apalogen Rd

President's House

Vaux St

Smith House

W School House Ln

Ronson Hall

MAP 23

Warden Dr

W Coulter St

Architecture/ Interior Design Studios

Chapel

Weber Design Studios

Dining Hall (Ravenhill)

Mott Hall

Partridge Hall

Ravenhill Mansion

Security

Gypsy Ln

Fortress Hall

Ravenhill Athletic Field

Powers St

General Information:

NFT Map: 23
Address: School House Ln & Henry Ave
             Philadelphia, PA 19144
Phone: 215-951-2700
Website: www.philau.edu

Overview

Founded in 1884, the Philadelphia University was finally granted university status by the state of Pennsylvania in 1999 and now operates five schools—Architecture & Design, Business Administration, General Studies, Science & Health, and Textiles & Materials. The university offers more than forty undergraduate and graduate degree programs to its 3,500 full- and part-time students. The school is known for its interdisciplinary approach to higher education, combining a liberal arts base with professional training. The private university is located on a 100-acre suburban campus about twenty minutes away from Center City, and is otherwise outside of the city's consciousness, despite its name.

Tuition

In the 2004-2005 academic year, a full-time undergraduate's tuition and fees will total $20,940, with an additional $7,782 for room and board. For more information about extra fees, alternative board plans, or financial aid packages, call 215-951-2940.

Sports

The Philadelphia University Rams compete at the Division II level in twelve sports: men's and women's basketball and tennis, men's golf and baseball, women's field hockey, lacrosse, softball, soccer, and volleyball. The men's soccer team is another tough competitor at the Division I level. Athletic scholarships are available to students in all varsity sports. Games are free and open to the public. For scores and game highlights, call the Rams Hotline on 215-951-2852.

Philadelphia University also offers club sports and intramural teams, open to all students, staff, and faculty, that allow participants to compete in athletic events on campus at a less rigorous level than that of the varsity sports teams.

Culture on Campus

The Design Center, located in the Goldie-Paley House (4200 Henry Ave, 215-951-2860; www.philau.edu/designcenter), is one of Philadelphia's most underrated exhibition spaces. The Hollywood rancher-style building holds over 200,000 artifacts related to textiles collected by the university over the past 125 years, from ecclesiastical attire and altar pieces to 19th-century haute-couture and a library of 19th- and 20th-century fabric. The center aims to explore the meaning of design in our everyday lives through ever-changing furniture and design exhibitions and remains a definite must-see for anyone with even a latent interest in fashion and design.

Departments

Log onto www.philau.edu/directory.html for a university directory and links to division and department web pages.

Undergraduate Admissions 215-951-2800
Graduate Admissions 215-951-2943
School of General Studies 215-951-2600
School of Architecture & Design . . . 215-951-2096
School of Business Administration 215-951-2810
School of Science & Health 215-951-2870
School of Textiles
   & Materials Technology 215-951-2750

St Joseph's University

1. Lancaster Court
2. Merion Gardens
3. Wynnewood Hall
4. City Avenue Residence Center
5. Ashwood Hall
6. Overbrook Hall
7. Michael J Morris Quad
8. Alumni House
9. St Alphonsus House-Jesuit Residence
10. Tara Hall
11. Sourin Residence Center
12. LaFarge Student Residence
13. Quirk Hall
14. Power Plant
15. Simpson Hall-University Bookstore
16. Chapel of St Joseph
17. Wolfington Hall-Campus Ministry
18. Campion Student Center
19. Science Center
20. Francis A Drexel Library
21. Bellermine Hall
22. Barblin/Lonergan Hall
23. Post Hall
24. Mandeville Hall
25. Barry Annex-Center for International Programs
26. Barry Hall
27. Flanigan Hall
28. ELS Language Center
29. Alumni Memorial Fieldhouse
30. AFROTC Program
31. Claver House-Honors Department
32. St Mary's Hall
33. McShain Hall/Haub Executive Center
34. St Albert's Annex
35. St Albert's Hall
36. Xavier Hall
37. Bronstein Hall-Office of Undergraduate Admissions
38. St Thomas Hall-Office of Financial Assistance
39. Jordan Hall
40. Boland Hall
41. Regis Annex
42. Regis Hall-President's Office
43. Loyola Center and Carriage House-Jesuit Residence
44. Hogan Hall
45. Sullivan Annex
46. Sullivan Hall
47. University Press-Merion
48. Human Resources-University Communications
49. University Press-Bala Cynwyd
50. Office of Development-5th Floor (off map, at 50th St & City Ave)

General Information

Address: 5600 City Ave
             Philadelphia, PA 19131
Phone: 610-660-1000
Website: www.sju.edu

Overview

Founded in 1851, St. Joseph's University is a Catholic college located on a 65-acre campus in western Philadelphia and Montgomery County. The 3,500 full-time undergraduates and 3,000 graduate students are schooled in the Jesuit tradition with a strong liberal arts-focused curriculum that fosters rigorous and open-minded inquiry and maintains high academic standards.

St. Joseph's also counts itself among the 142 schools in the country with a Phi Beta Kappa chapter and AACSB business school accreditation. With forty undergraduate majors, ten special-study options, twenty study abroad programs, and 52 graduate degree possibilities to choose from, students have a variety of academic options. But co-eds at St. Joe's aren't *all* work and no play. Following the men's basketball team's thrilling run to the Elite Eight in last year's NCAA tourney, the school is suddenly garnering national attention. Go Hawks!

Tuition

For the 2004-2005 academic year tuition costs were $25,770; room and board was an additional $9,500. Of course, these prices exclude student fees, books, and other personal expenses.

Sports

"The Hawk Will Never Die!" is a slogan that can be heard echoing from the Alumni Memorial Fieldhouse throughout the school year. In addtion to the championship men's and women's basketball squads, St. Joseph's fields teams in twenty varsity sports including cross-country, lacrosse, rowing, soccer, tennis, and track & field for men and women, men's baseball and golf, and women's softball and field hockey. The teams compete in Division I of the National Collegiate Athletic Association and belong to the Atlantic 10 as well as Philly's own Big Five. SJU athletics, however, extend much further than varsity competition. Hundreds of students participate in intramural and club sports; thousands, including alumni and friends of the university, make the Fieldhouse and adjoining Student/Sports Recreation Center a thriving area on campus year-round. Visit www.sjuhawks.com for news and events on Hawks of all ages.

Culture on Campus

The University Gallery at Boland Hall (5600 City Ave, 610-660 1840) hosts eight art shows from September through May. The first five exhibitions feature professional artists who are mostly, but not exclusively, from the area. (Anyone may submit slides for consideration.) The sixth is the Senior Arts Thesis Exhibtion that highlights the year-long projects of the Senior Arts Majors. Then there's a culminating Student Arts Festival that is an all-day celebration of art, music, and theater. Finally, the year closes with the Overbrook High School displaying their students' work. Open and free to the public throughout the school year, the gallery is closed during the summer months.

The Department of Fine & Performing Arts is also home to the Cap & Bells Dramatic Arts Society, the University Singers, and the Bluett Theatre. For specific event information call 610-660-1840 or visit www.sju.edu/fine_arts.

Departments

Log onto www.sju.edu/sju/contact.html for a university directory and links to division and department web pages.

Undergraduate Admissions 888-BE-A-HAWK
College of Arts & Sciences 610-660-1282
Haub School of Business 610-660-1645
University College
  (Continuing Education) 877-NITE-SJU
Graduate Arts & Sciences............ 610-660-1289
Graduate Admissions 610-660-1101
Registrar's Office 610-660-1011

General Information

Address: 1801 N Broad St
              Philadelphia, PA 19122
Phone: 215-204-7000
Website: www.temple.edu

Overview

Every Philly native's safety school, Temple has risen in national standing and prominence to a point where graduating alumni (besides the Cuz, who has always shown much love for the Owl) can feel very good about the quality of education they received. The school is pretty damn huge: more than 34,000 students in seventeen separate schools and colleges crowd its lecture halls. Education at Temple spans five regional campuses, including the flagship Main Campus, Health Sciences Campus, and Center City Campus in Philadelphia, as well as Temple University at Ambler and a suburban art campus—Tyler School of Arts in Elkins Park. The university also has an education center in Harrisburg as well as international campuses in Tokyo, Japan, Rome, and Italy.

Tuition

For the 2004-2005 academic year, full-time undergraduate tuition and fees for Pennsylvania residents averaged $9,082, while out-of-state residents paid an average of $16,248. Room and board for all undergraduate students averaged $7,500. Books, lab fees, and personal expenses are in addition to these prices. Graduate student tuition, fees, and expenses vary by department.

Sports

Perhaps it's better not to speak of the miserable football team, which is losing its membership in the Big East due to its inability to be competitive within the conference. On the positive side, there are the hugely successful men's and women's basketball teams, who play their games in the sparkling Liacouras Center, a 10,200-seat multi-purpose venue that also hosts a full range of concerts, dramatic presentations, and exhibitions. The Center is located less than two miles from Philadelphia's City Hall. Public bus and subway transportation can take you directly to the center. If you're into driving, parking is no problem— there's a connected parking garage as well as a number of well-lighted surface lots nearby. For more information call 215-204-2424 or visit www.liacourascenter.com.

Culture on Campus

The Boyer College of Music and Dance hosts the Temple University Concert Series– over 200 recitals, concerts, master classes, and lectures presented by faculty, students, and renowned guest artists. Classical music, jazz, and dance are just a taste of the series' fare. Call 215-204-7600 for info on specific events or visit www.temple.edu/boyer.

The Tyler School of Art features public programs in many forms that are offered at various campus locations, in the galleries, and in the community. Tyler Gallery (7725 Penrose Ave, 215-782-2776) in Tyler Hall holds exhibitions each year that exhibit works from emerging area artists as well as Tyler students. Penrose Gallery (Elkins Park, 7725 Penrose Ave, 215-782-2883) in Penrose Hall has student-curated exhibitions (known as "Produce") as well as many other student retrospectives and installations. Other informal spaces within Penrose and Tyler Halls host many more student shows each year. On Main Campus the Architecture Department installs student works regularly throughout the school year in a flexible installation space in its building. Visit www.temple.edu/tyler for more information.

Departments

Visit www.temple.edu/directories.html for a university directory and links to division and department web pages.

College of Health Professions 215-707-4800
Tyler School of Art 215-782-ARTS
Fox School of Business
  and Management 215-204-7676
School of Communications
  and Theater 215-204-8421
School of Dentistry 215-707-2803
College of Education 215-204-8011
College of Engineering 215-204-7800
Beasley School of Law 800-560-1428
College of Liberal Arts 215-204-7743
School of Medicine 215-707-7000
School of Pharmacy 215-707-4990
College of Science and Technology . . 215-204-2888
School of Tourism
  and Hospitality Management 215-204-8701

University of Pennsylvania

1. 3216 Chancellor
2. Pafestra
3. Hutchinson Gym
4. Ringe Squash Courts
5. Rittenhouse Laboratories
6. Dunning Coaches' Center
7. Weightman Hall
8. Moore School Building
9. Skirkanich Hall
10. Levine Hall
11. Towne Building
12. Music Building
13. Music Annex
14. Morgan Building
15. Vegalos Labs of the IAST
16. Meyerson Hall
17. Fisher Fine Arts Library /Duhring Wing
18. Irvine Auditorium
19. Jaffe Building
20. Van Pelt Library
21. College Hall
22. Houston Hall
23. Dietrich Graduate Library
24. Sweeten Alumni House
25. Logan Hall
26. Williams Hall
27. Silverman Hall
28. Roberts Hall
29. Pepper Hall
30. Tanenbaum Hall
31. 3401 Walnut St
32. La Terrasse
33. 133 S 36th St
34. Franklin Building
35. Penn Center for Rehabilitation & Care
36. Sansom Place West
37. Institute of Contemporary Art
38. Iron Gate Theater /Christian Association
39. Greenfield Intercultural Center
40. Newman Center
41. Addams Hall
42. 202 S 36th
43. The ARCH
44. Annenberg School
45. 3615/3619
46. Annenberg Center
48. Stiteler Hall
49. Graduate Education
50. Soloman Labs
51. Caster Building
54. Class of 1920 Commons
55. Clinical Research Building
56. Nursing Education Building
57. Biomedical Research Building
58. Stellar-Chance Laboratories
59. Blockley Hall
60. John Morgan Building
61. Anatomy-Chemistry Building

62. Richards Laboratories/Goddard Labs
63. Leidy Laboratories/Kaplan Wing/ Mudd Laboratory
64. Life Sciences
65. Rosenthal Building
66. Mabel Pew Myrin Pavlion
67. Cupp Pavilion
68. Wright/Saunders Building
69. Scheie Eye Institute
70. Heart Institute/Mutch Building
71. Medical Science Research Laboratory
72. 3910 Building

Wharton Business School
47. Colonial Penn Center/ Locust Ho
52. McNeil Building
53. Lauder Fischer Hall
73. Huntsman Hall
74. Steinberg Conference Center
75. Vance Hall

MAP 14

General Information

NFT Map: 14
Address: 3451 Walnut St
              Philadelphia, PA 19104
Phone: 215-898-5000
Website: www.upenn.edu

Overview

Ladies and gentlemen, this is Pennsylvania's Ivy League school, and don't you forget it. One of the oldest universities in the country and the first to institute a modern liberal arts curriculum, the University of Pennsylvania was established in 1749 by founding father Benjamin Franklin.

Today, with nearly 10,000 undergraduate students and 10,000 grad students enrolled in its schools, UPenn consistently ranks among the top ten universities in the annual *U.S. News & World Report* survey. The Wharton School is considered one of the country's top three business schools, and Penn's graduate programs all rank among the top ten in their fields.

The urban campus spans a substantial 269 acres of West Philadelphia, and includes buildings by notable architects such as Frank Furness, Louis Kahn, Robert Venturi, and Denise Scott Brown.

Tuition

Ahem. In the 2004-2005 academic year, an undergraduate student's tuition and fees will total $30,716, with an additional $8,918 for room and board. These figures do not include books, supplies, lab fees, furriers, therapists, polo attire, or other personal expenses. While the high tuition rate and abundance of business types has earned Penn a reputation as a "rich kids' school," in fact, about sixty percent of the undergraduate student body receives some form of financial aid from the university.

Sports

All twenty-eight of Penn's sports teams, nicknamed "the Quakers," compete in the NCAA Division I Ivy League conference. Men's Division I teams include baseball, basketball, fencing, football, golf, lacrosse, rowing, soccer, squash, swimming, tennis, track, and cross-country. Women's Division I teams include basketball, fencing, field hockey, gymnastics, lacrosse, rowing, soccer, softball, squash, swimming, tennis, track, and cross-country. All intercollegiate athletic events are free and open to the public, with the exception of men's football and basketball games, wrestling matches, and the competitive Penn Relays, which all charge admission. Tickets to these events can be purchased at the Penn Athletic Ticket Office at 215-898-6151. Box office hours are Monday through Friday, 10 am-5 pm. You can check out the full roster of all Penn sports events at www.pennathletics.com.

Culture on Campus

The Annenberg Center is a nationally renowned non-profit multi-disciplinary performance venue that offers 170 music, theater, and dance performances every year through the program *Penn Presents*. The Annenberg Center serves as a resource not only for the immediate university community, but for the entire Delaware Valley region. Check out www.pennpresents.org for more details.

The Institute of Contemporary Art (118 S 36th St) exhibits the work of established and emerging contemporary visual artists. Entrance to the exhibition space is free for ICA members and Penn students, $3 for adults, and $2 for children and senior citizens. For more information, visit www.icaphila.org or call 215-898-7108.

The University of Pennsylvania Museum of Archeology and Anthropology (3260 South St, 215-898-4000) has earned international acclaim as a leading resource for anthropologists and archeologists. The permanent collection includes Egyptian, Greek, Roman, Etruscan, Buddhist, Chinese, African, Native American, and Ancient Israeli art galleries. For information on visiting exhibitions, or to take a look at art galleries online, visit www.museum.upenn.edu.

Departments

Log onto www.upenn.edu/directories for a university directory and links to division and department web pages.

Undergraduate Admissions	215-898-7507
Annenberg School for Communication	215-898-7041
Arts and Sciences, Graduate Division	215-898-5720
Law School	215-898-7483
School of Dental Medicine	215-898-8781
School of Design	215-898-3425
School of Engineering	215-898-7246
School of Medicine	215-662-4000
School of Nursing	215-898-8281
School of Social Work	215-898-5511
School of Veterinary Medicine	215-898-5434
Wharton MBA Program	215-898-6183
Wharton Undergraduate Division	215-898-7507

General Information

The Bicycle Network (City):
www.phila.gov/streets/the_bicycle_network.html
Bicycle Club of Philadelphia: www.phillybikeclub.org
Neighborhood Bike Works:
www.neighborhoodbikeworks.org

Commuting

As part of its "Bicycle Network Plan," the City is currently completing a series of street-safe routes for commuting on two wheels. One hopes that the plan is implemented sooner rather than later; because of Philly's many narrow one-way streets, bikers and drivers are often at odds with one another, and you can imagine who normally wins the little tête-à-têtes. The automobile set treats bikers commuting to and from work with an air of hostility, especially during rush hour. As a result, bikers need to think defensively on Philly's streets.

City bikers have more to worry about than just drivers' road rage—the streets themselves are not always biker-friendly. Metal grooves in the roads are the last remnants of Center City's old trolley system. Today, instead of guiding trolleys through the city, the grooves cause bicycle crashes if they're hit at the wrong angle or when they're wet.

Our best advice it to be weary of irate drivers, avoid the trolley rails at all costs, and, whatever you do, wear a helmet! A detailed map of Philadelphia's commuter bike routes can be found on the City's website at www.phila.gov/streets/Philabik.pdf. Check it out and plan your route before you go whizzing around town.

Recreational Riding

If inhaling exhaust fumes and dodging traffic is not your speed, venture towards Philly's more natural settings. Some of the best off-street stretches of pavement run through, or close to, the city's parks. Kelly Drive meanders through picnic areas and fishing holes along the east side of the Schuylkill River. West River Drive runs along the opposite side of the river, zipping past the zoo, the Mann Music Center, and Memorial Hall. If you feel like testing your fitness level, try Forbidden Drive; this spectacular eight-mile loop circles Wissahickon Valley Park. For off-road bikers, the granddaddy is the wild and woolly Wissahickon loop; the 30-mile trail offers sufficient challenge for even experienced riders. Pennypack Creek Park also offers a diverse array of dirt and paved trails near the Delaware River in the Northeast.

Bikes on Mass Transit

Bikes are allowed on SEPTA buses and subway lines, though only on specific routes and at specific times. Bus routes 1, 8, 12, 24, 28, 35, 37, 53, 71, 77, 103, 107, 115, 116, 122, 305, and J all have a front-mounted rack, which accomodates up to two bikes.

On the Broad Street, Market-Frankford, and Route 100 Lines, passengers may board their wheels on weekdays before 6 am, between 9 am and 3 pm, and after 6 pm. Bikes can be taken on board at all times on weekends and the following holidays: Memorial Day, Independence Day, Labor Day, Thanksgiving, Christmas, and New Year's Day. On Regional Rail, there is a limit of two bikes per carriage during off-peak hours. Up to five bikes are allowed at any time during weekends and major holidays. Bikes are not permitted during peak hours.

Shops	Address	Phone	Website	Map
Bike Rack	1901 S 13th St	215-334-9100	www.bike-rack.net	2
Via Bicycle/Bikeville	606 S 9th St	215-627-3370	www.bikeville.com	3
Village Bikes	792 S 2nd St	215-629-4141		3
Bicycle Therapy	2211 South St	215-735-7849	www.bicycletherapy.com	6
Bike Line	226 S 40th St	215-243-2453	www.bikeline.com	9
Wolff Cycle	4311 Lancaster Ave	215-222-2171		9
Trophy Bikes	3131 Walnut St	215-625-7999	www.trophybikes.com	10
Breakaway Bikes	126 S 18th St	215-568-6002	www.breakawaybikes.com	12
Frankinstien Bike Worx	1529 Spruce St	215-893-0415		12
Drive Sports	2601 Pennsylvania Ave	215-232-7368	www.drivesports.net	13
Bike Line	1028 Arch St	215-923-1310	www.bikeline.com	14
Bike Line	1234 Locust St	215-735-1503	www.bikeline.com	14
Breakaway Bikes	311 Market St	215-568-6002	www.breakawaybikes.com	16
Philadelphia Bicycles	826 N Broad St	215-765-9118		17
Jay's Pedal Power	512 E Girard Ave	215-425-5111	www.jayspedalpower.com	18
Bike Line	4151 Main St	215-487-7433	www.bikeline.com	20
Metropolis Bike & Scooter	4159 Main St	215-509-7668		20
Son's Bicycle Shop	6153 Ridge Ave	215-487-1850		20
Bike Addicts	5548 Ridge Ave	215-487-3006	www.bikeaddicts.com	21
Wissahickon Cyclery	7837 Germantown Ave	215-248-2829	www.wiss-cycles.com	24
Bilenky Cycle Works	5319 N 2nd St	215-329-4744	www.bilenky.com	N/A
Bustleton Bikes	9261 Roosevelt Blvd	215-671-1910	www.bustletonbikes.com	N/A
Chuck's Sports Bikes	13440 Damar Dr	215-464-9675		N/A
Liberty Bell Bicycle	7820 Frankford Ave	215-624-7343	www.libertybellbicycle.com	N/A
Neighborhood Bike Works	5958 Vine St	215-476-4436	www.neighborhoodbikeworks.org	N/A

Golf

Over the last few years, the majority of Philly's public courses have been taken over by Meadowbrook Golf, and the results have been largely positive—by and large, the fairways and greens are vastly improved. In terms of accolades, Cobbs Creek, probably the best known of Philly's courses, was rated "6th Best Public Course" in 2000 by *Golf Week*. If you fear your game is not yet up to speed, try the Karakung Course at Cobbs Creek; it's a little cheaper and much more forgiving than the regular Olde Course. Walnut Lane, tucked neatly into Wissahickon Park, is also a very nice run for your money—watch out for the occasional out-of-control mountain biker from the abutting Wissahickon Trail wiping out on the greens. Check out www.golfphilly.com for more information about Meadowbrook courses.

Golf Courses	Address	Phone
Bala Golf Club	2200 Belmont Ave	215-473-8504
Cobbs Creek Golf Club	72 Lansdowne Ave	215-877-8707
Karakung Golf Course at Cobbs Creek	7200 Landsdowne Ave	215-877-8707
Franklin D Roosevelt Golf Club	S 20th St & Pattison St	215-462-8997
Island Green Country Club	1 Red Lion Rd	215-677-3500
John F Byrne Golf Club	9500 Leon St	215-632-8666
Juniata Golf Club	1391 E Cayuga St	215-743-4060
Phila Quartet Golf Club	1075 Southampton Rd	215-676-3939
Walnut Lane Golf Club	Walnut Ln & Magdalena St	215-482-3370

Driving Ranges	Address	Phone
Burholme Park Golf Center	401 W Cottman Ave	215-742-2380
Fishers Glen Driving Range Inc	4717 Fishers Ln	215-533-9466
Strawberry Mansion Golf Driving Range	1500 N 33 St	215-235-9436

Bowling

Walk into a pawnshop anywhere in the country, and you feel a sense of déjà vu— the same grungy light spills over cramped confines with the same crappy metal kids' drum kit piled in the corner next to a Hondo acoustic and a bunch of flickering small screen TVs. Much the same is true for the majority of bowling alleys in this country—dim lighting, empty arcades, and pseudo-psychedelic carpeting from the '50s. The fun comes when you add beer and league nights to the mix.

Most of Philadelphia's bowling alleys follow in this vein, though a couple of them have developed more distinctive personalities. Thunderbird Lanes, the area's most popular, is the purist of the Philadelphia bowling scene. It doesn't contest its "no-frills bowling" reputation: it doesn't have an arcade or a bar (don't worry, it's BYOB—they understand it would simply be impossible to enjoy bowling without being liquored up). They (along with Center Lanes) will, however, offer private birthday party rooms, with bumpers so the little tykes can avoid gutter balls, and karaoke on Friday nights. Newly resurfaced Arsenal Lanes now hosts "21 and Over" nights on the weekends.

All rates are per person/per game, including shoes and tax.

Bowling Alleys	Address	Phone	Rates day/eve	Map
Arsenal Bowling Lanes	212 44th St	412 683-5992	$5.45, $5.95	9
Hi Spot Lanes	3857 Pechin St	215-483-2120	$3.50, $4.50	21
AMF Boulevard Lanes	8011 Roosevelt Blvd	215-332-9200	$6.50, $7.50	N/A
Brunswick	649 Foulkrod Ave	215-533-1221	$6.80, $7.38	N/A
Brunswick	1300 E Erie Ave	215-535-3500	$7.69, $6.38	N/A
Center Lanes	7550 City Line Ave	215-078-5050	$5.75, $5.75	N/A
Seventy Third St Lanes	7235 Elmwood Ave	215-365-1626	$4.50, $5.25	N/A
Thunderbird Lanes	5830 Castor Ave	215-743-2521	$5, $6	N/A
Thunderbird Lanes	3081 Holme Ave	215-464-7171	$5.50, $6.50	N/A

Benjamin Franklin Hwy

422

Northeastern Ext Pennsylvania Tpke

476

309

611

Pennsylvania Tpke

276

Valley Forge National
Historical Park

309

Ridge Ave

Wissahickon
River Gorge

611

76

Pennsylvania Tpke

Schuylkill Expy

PAGE
118

30

76

1

476

1

Broad St

95

Vine Expy

Ross Brdg

Ridley Creek
State Park

676

Middletown Rd

Gradyville Rd

Franklin Brdg

1

Tyler
Aboretum

76

7

John Heinz National
Wildlife Refuge at Tinicum

Lindbergh Blvd

Industrial Expy

95

Delaware River

295

130

Crown Point Rd

New Jersey Tpke

55

Overview

Like most metropolitan areas, greater Philadelphia offers plenty of potential refuge to those growing weary of buildings and asphalt. Fortunately, many of Philly's best parks are nearby and the tranquility and peace of mind can be achieved on a hike can make life in Philadelphia all the more enjoyable.

Relevant Books:

Hikes Around Philadelphia, by Boyd & Linda Newman
50 Hikes in Eastern Pennsylvania, by Carolyn Hoffman

John Heinz National Wildlife Refuge at Tinicum

http://heinz.fws.gov

This 145-acre refuge just north of the Philadelphia Airport provides homes for birds (over 280 different types) and other animals, including rare endangered species such as the red-bellied turtle and southern leopard frog. Hikers and cyclists can enjoy more than ten miles of trails within the refuge, which is open from 8 am until sunset year-round. And for visual irony, you simply can't beat the view of nearby power converters and petroleum refineries over the tops of the trees.

From I-76 E, stay in the left lane and follow signs for Route 291 W/I-95 S/Airport. At the light, turn right onto Route 291 W. Follow signs to I-95 S. Traveling on I-95 S, take the Route 291/Airport Exit 10. Take the right fork, exiting for Route 291/Lester. At the first light, turn right onto Bartram Avenue. At the second light, turn left onto 84th Street, then at the second light, turn left onto Lindbergh Boulevard. SEPTA's route 37 and 108 buses both stop at 84th Street and Lindbergh Boulevard. Regional Rail stops at Eastwick Station, which is several blocks southeast of the refuge's main entrance at 86th Street and Lindbergh Boulevard.

Ridley Creek State Park

Located 16 miles outside Philadelphia, Ridley Creek State Park has an easy five-mile paved loop that accommodates wheelchairs and baby strollers. Four hiking trails (red, white, blue, yellow) through wooded terrain can be mixed and matched to form hikes of varying lengths and difficulty. The park can be reached from Gradyville Road—about 2.5 miles west of Newton Square—which can he found off either PA-352 or PA-252. Both these roads intersect Gradyville Road. You can also get there directly from PA-3 west of Newton Square.

Valley Forge National Historical Park

The 3,600-acre Valley Forge Park is a well-maintained tribute to the Revolutionary War. The main trail is a paved five-mile loop that visits most of the major historical attractions in the park, attracting hikers, cyclists, and rollerbladers. Trails intended solely for hiking and horseback riding include the Valley Creek Trail, Horse-Shoe Trail, and Schuylkill River Trail. Walnut Hill, an area seldom visited by tourists, also provides excellent hiking.

From Philadelphia, take the Schuylkill/76 W to Exit 327, the last exit before the tollbooth. Turn right at the first traffic light, then right onto N Gulph Road. Go north on N Gulph Road for 1.5 miles and turn left at the traffic light at the top of hill into the park entrance. If you're relying on public transportation, take SEPTA bus route 125 to the Valley Forge Visitor Center.

Wilderness Trail

Adjacent to Ridley Creek State Park, the Wilderness Trail is an 8.5 mile hike through the 260 hectare Tyler Arboretum. The arboretum also contains a few shorter routes—the Dogwood and Pinetum Trails— as well as unblazed trails and old roads. Spring is the best time to visit, when blooming wildflowers overtake the landscape. The $3 entrance fee charged by this private not-for-profit association contributes to the park's upkeep. The Tyler Arboretum is located off PA-352 about four miles north of Media. Or you can take PA-3 to PA-352 and travel south for 5.1 miles. Turn east onto Forge Road, then right onto Painter Road to reach the parking lot.

Wissahickon River Gorge

In the northernmost part of Wissahickon Park lies the steep-sided, six-mile-long Wissahickon River Gorge. Forbidden Drive (the name applies to cars only), which runs mostly on the west side of the Wissahickon, is an old carriage road along the river. "Traffic" is heavy here, as many joggers, dog walkers, bicyclists, horseback riders, and anglers enjoy the trail. The eastern side of the gorge is steeper and has more rugged trails for serious hikers. Once you find Wissahickon Gorge (not the easiest place to get to by car), park in one of the three parking lots: Valley Green Inn, Kitchen's Lane, and Bell's Mill Road. Try to arrive early in the day as the lots fill quickly. The following SEPTA buses stop at the trailhead: 1, 9, 27, 35, 38, 61, 65, 124, 125, and the R6 Regional Rail line.

Rowing

The banks of Philadelphia's Schuylkill River (a.k.a. the "hidden river") posses a long and illustrious history, one that many Philly residents take surprisingly seriously. Since the mid-19th century, rowers have been racing the waters along Boathouse Row. Today this span of river is the practice course for top rowing talent in the United States—boat clubs along the Schuylkill count among their members Olympic gold medalists and World Championship winners. Most recently, at the 2004 Athens Olympic Games, the US Men's 8-oar heavyweight crew took home the gold medal after countless hours training along this very stretch of water.

If the lure of Philadelphia's rowing history doesn't draw your interest, the scenery sure will. There are more than a dozen boat houses to view on Kelly Drive along the sublime Boathouse Row, all visible from I-76.

Boat Houses	Address	Phone
Bachelors Barge Club	#6 Boathouse Row, Kelly Dr	215-769-9335
College Boat Club of Upenn	#11 Boathouse Row, Kelly Dr	215-978-8918
Crescent Boat Club	#5 Boathouse Row, Kelly Dr	215-978-9816
Fairmount Rowing Association	#2 & #3 Boathouse Row, Kelly Dr	215-769-9693
Penn Athletic Club Rowing Association	#12 Boathouse Row, Kelly Dr	215-745-4269
Philadelphia Girls' Rowing Club	#14 Boathouse Row, Kelly Dr	215-978-8824
Undine Barge Club	#13 Boathouse Row, Kelly Dr	215-765-9244
University Barge Club	#7 & #8 Boathouse Row, Kelly Dr	215-232-2293
Vesper Boat Club	#9 & #10 Boathouse Row, Kelly Dr	215-769-9615

Marinas

If boating or sailing is more your speed, the Delaware River is the perfect playground. The Philadelphia Marine Center offers 338 deep-water slips with summer rates that run between $375 for personal watercraft and $5,100 for 70' craft. Winter slip rates are $35 per foot, with a $750 minimum. If you just want to dock your boat for a few days, the daily rate is $2 per foot, with a $50 minimum.

Penn's Landing Marina is another option for boat-docking but they have far fewer slips and you need to reserve one in February for the summer months. Rates depend upon the size of the boat. Up to 45 feet is $1.25 per foot while 45-69 feet is $1.50. Penn's Landing Marina is also where you'll board river services such as the Riverboat Queen and the Spirit of Philadelphia.

The Piers Marina offers boat slips year-round for $70 per foot in the summer, and half that in the winter. Boats can be stored year-round while full-time security staff watch out for your property.

Marinas	Address	Phone	Website	Map
Philadelphia Marine Center	Pier 12 N, Christopher Columbus Blvd & Franklin Bridge	215-931-1000	www.philamarinecenter.com	4
Penn's Landing Marina	S Columbus Blvd & Dock St	215-928-8801	www.pennslandingcorp.com	16
Piers Marina	Pier 3, 31 N Columbus Blvd b/w Market St & Race St	215-351-4101	www.pgwebconsulting.com/piers	16

Skating

Lengthy winters and cold temperatures make ice skating an ideal activity for denizens of the city. In fact, Philly is recognized for launching the first skating club in North America back in 1849—The Skater's Club of the City and County of Philadelphia. There are many beautiful outdoor settings in which to strap on your blades, including parts of the Schuylkill and Delaware Rivers and areas within the lush Fairmount and Pennypack Parks.

For a more controlled environment, check out the Blue Cross River Rink at Festival Pier (www.riverrink.com). It opens from late November to early March and costs $6 to skate and an additional $3 for skate rental. On particularly frigid mid-winter days, indoor ice rinks are infinitely more appealing—try the Rink at Old York Road (www.oyrsc.org).

In the warmer months, inline skating is a fun way to exercise, sightsee, or commute. Skating on all bike paths throughout the city is permitted, providing miles of traffic-free skating surfaces. On rainy days or in cold weather, hit one of Philly's indoor rinks, which also run intramural roller hockey leagues.

Ice Skating Rinks	Address	Phone	Rates	Map
Class of 1923 Ice Rink	3130 Walnut St	215-898-1923	$4-6, $2 rental	10
Blue Cross River Rink	Columbus Blvd & Spring Garden St	215-925-7465	$6, $3 rental	19
Rink at Old York Road	816 Church Rd	215-635-0331	$5, $2 rental	N/A
Wissahickon Ice Skating Rink	550 W Willow Grove Ave	215-247-1907	$6, $2 rental	N/A

Inline Skating Rinks	Address	Phone	Rates	Map
Carman Roller Skating Rink	3226 Germantown Ave	215-223-2200	$7, free rental	N/A
Elmwood Roller Skating Rink	2406 S 71st St	215-492-8543	$6 weeekends, $1 rental	N/A
Franklin Mills Mall	1455 Franklin Mills Cir	215-612-1168	$14/2-hours, no rental	N/A
Palace Roller Skating Center	11586 Roosevelt Blvd	215-698-8000	$3.50-6, $2-3 rental	N/A
WOW of Northeast Philadelphia	7015 Roosevelt Blvd	215-335-3400	$2-10, $2.50-3.50 rental	N/A

Billiards

Despite Philly's richly deserved rep as an old-school, blue-collar city, there is a decided dearth of the kind of venerated pool halls that Fast Eddie Felson prefers. This is especially true in Center City, though the welcome addition of Buffalo Billiards on Chestnut and Front at least gives stick men a place to rack 'em up at an hourly rate. Dave & Busters is fine, as long as you don't mind wading through a sea of screaming, hopped up kids playing Super Mega Assault IV and spilling nacho cheez all over your shoes.

Billiard Halls	Address	Phone	Fee	Hours	Map
Tattooed Mom	530 South St	215-238-9880	$1/game	12 pm-2 am	3
Willie Musconi Golden Cue	2027 W Oregon Ave	215-462-0194	$4.75/hr	10 am-4 am	5
Buffalo Billiards	116 Chestnut St	215-574-7665	$6-$10/hr	5 pm-2 am	16
Vuong Viet Pool Hall	2464 Kensington Ave	215-423-8380	$1/game	12 pm-12 am	18
Dave & Busters	325 N Columbus Blvd	214-413-1951	$8-14/hr	11:30 am-2 am	19
Ministry of Information	449 Poplar St	215-925-0999	75¢/game	5 pm-2 am	19
Ballard's Billiard Center	2004 Cecil B Moore Ave	215-765-8334	$5/hr	10 am-late	N/A
Ballbusters	3265 S 61st St	215-727-2550	$4/hr	11 am-3 pm	N/A
Fillian's	1955 Franklin Mills Cir	215-632-0333	$3/hr	11 am-2 am	N/A
Tacony Paylyra	6201 Keystone St	215-338-4733	$3-5/hr	10 am-2 am	N/A

The best thing about the city's 86 municipal pools is that they are all free. Open daily during the summer from 11 am until 7 pm, the pools are much more relaxing during off-peak times. When school is out for the summer, expect thousands of children to flock to the water like some kind of crazed, freely urinating animal migration.

Pools with deep ends are gradually being filled in so that the maximum depth is five feet rather than 12. All but ten Philadelphia deep ends have already been filled in and only a couple will remain when the process is complete. While the shallower water makes it safer for maniac children to splash around in, diving accidents have increased substantially. In pools with a depth of five feet, no diving or jumping in is permitted—obviously.

All indoor pools, with the exception of Rhodes and University City, are open year-round. The Philadelphia Department of Recreation (PDR) conducts aquatic programs at indoor pool locations throughout the city. The programs, many of which are free of charge, are conducted by certified Water Safety Instructors and Lifeguards. Classes include swimming lessons, team swimming, and life guard instruction. For more information, check the PDR website at www.pdraquatics.com.

* indicates indoor pool

Municipal Pools	Address	Phone	Map
Hawthorne/Ridgeway	13th St & Christian St	N/A	1
Marian Anderson	744 S 17th St	215-685-6594	1
Ford	631 Snyder Ave	215-685-1897	2
Fante-Leone	Montrose St & S Darien St	215-686-1783	3
Sacks	4th St & Washington Ave	215-685-1889	3
Chew	19th St & Washington Ave	215-685-6596	6
Murphy	2600 S 3rd St	215-685-1874	6
O'Connor	2600 South St	215-685-6593	6
Herron	250 Reed St	215-685-1884	8
Stinger	32nd St & Dickinson St	215-685-1882	8
39th & Olive	39th St & Olive St	N/A	9
Lee	4328 Haverford Ave	215-685-7655	9
Athletic	1400 N 26th St	215-685-2709	13
12th & Cambria	29 N 11th St	215-685-9780	14
*University City	37th St & Filbert St	215-685-9099	14
Francisville	1737 Francis St	215-685-2762	15
Mander	33rd St & Diamond St	215-685-3894	15
Cione	Aramingo Ave & E Lehigh Ave	215-685-9880	18
Lederer	Moyer St & E Montgomery Ave	215-685-9885	18
East Poplar	8th St & Poplar St	215-686-1786	19
Northern Liberties	321 Fairmount Ave	215-686-1785	19
Hillside	201 Fountain St	215-685-2595	20
Venice Island	Schuylkill Canal & Cotton St	215-685-2598	21
*Pickett Pool	Wayne Ave & W Chelten Ave	215-685-2196	23
Shuler	3000 Clearfield St	215-685-9750	23
Pleasant	E Pleasant St & Boyer St	215-685-2230	24
48th & Woodland	48th St & Woodland Ave	215-685-2692	N/A
American Legion	Torresdale Ave & Devereaux St	215-685-8733	N/A
Amos	16th St & Berks St	215-685-2708	N/A
Awbury	6101 Ardleigh Ave	215-685-2895	N/A
Baker	5431 Lansdowne Ave	215-685-0261	N/A
Barry	18th St & Bigler St	215-685-1886	N/A
Belfield	21st St & Chew Ave	215-685-2220	N/A
Bridesburg	4601 Richmond St	215-685-1247	N/A
*Carousel House	Belmont Ave & N Concourse Dr	215-685-0163	N/A
Cecil B Moore	22nd St & Huntingdon St	215-685-9755	N/A

Municipal Pools	Address	Phone	Map
Cherashore	851 W Olney Ave	215-685-2897	N/A
Christy	56th St & Christian St	215-685-1997	N/A
Cobbs Creek	250 S 63rd St	215-685-1983	N/A
Cohocksink	2901 Ceder Ave	215-685-9884	N/A
Cruz	6th St & Master St	215-685-2759	N/A
Dendy	10th St & Oxford St	215-685-2763	N/A
Feltonville	Ella St & Meritor St	215-685-9150	N/A
Fox Chase	Rockwell Ave & Ridgeway St	215-685-0575	N/A
Francis Myers	58th St & Kingsessing Ave	215-685-2698	N/A
Franklin	Elkhart St & Helen St	215-685-9899	N/A
Gathers	25th St & Diamond St	215-685-2710	N/A
Hancock	Hancock St & Master St	215-685-9886	N/A
Heitzman	Castor Ave & Amber St	215-685-1244	N/A
Houseman	Summerdale Ave & Godfrey Ave	215-685-1240	N/A
Hunting Park	1101 W Hunting Park Ave	215-685-9153	N/A
Island Road	Island Rd & Saybrook Ave	215-685-4196	N/A
James Finnegan	69th St & Grovers Ave	215-685-4191	N/A
Jacobs	4500 Linden Ave	215-685-8748	N/A
Jardel	1400 Cottman Ave	215-685-0596	N/A
Junod	3301 Mechanicsville Rd	215-685-9396	N/A
Kelly Pool	4231 N Concourse Dr	N/A	N/A
Kendrick	5800 Ridge Ave	215-685-2584	N/A
Kingsessing	49th St & Kingsessing Ave	215-685-2695	N/A
Lackman	Chesworth Rd & Bartlett St	215-685-0370	N/A
Lawncrest	6000 Rising Sun Ave	215-685-0597	N/A
*Lincoln	7600 Rowland Ave	215-685-0751	N/A
Lonnie Young	1100 E Chelten Ave	215-685-2236	N/A
ML King	22nd St & Cecil B Moore Ave	215-685-2733	N/A
*Marcus Foster	1601 W Hunting Park Ave	215-685-9154	N/A
Max Myers	Oakland St & Magee Ave	215-685-1242	N/A
McVeigh	D St & Ontario St	215-685-9896	N/A
Mill Creek	48th St & Brown St	215-685-0260	N/A
Mitchell	3700 Whitehall Ln	215-685-9394	N/A
Monkiewicz	Richmond St & E Allegheny Ave	215-685-9894	N/A
Morris Estate	1535 Chelten Ave	215-685-2891	N/A
Penrose	12th St & Susquehanna Ave	215-685-2711	N/A
Piccoli	Castor St & Cayuga St	215-685-1224	N/A
*Rhodes Pool	29th St & Clearfield St	215-227-4907	N/A
Samuel	3539 Gaul St	215-685-1246	N/A
*Sayre-Morris	5839 Spruce St	215-685-1994	N/A
Scanlon	1099 E Tioga St	215-685-9893	N/A
Schmidt	3400 Howard St	215-685-9895	N/A
Shepard	57th St & Haverford Ave	215-685-1991	N/A
Simpson	1010 Arrott St	215-685-1223	N/A
Smith	25th St & Jackson St	215-685-1898	N/A
Tustin	5901 Columbia Ave	215-685-0258	N/A
Vare	26th St & Morris St	215-685-1876	N/A
Vogt	Cottage St & Unruh Ave	215-685-8753	N/A
Waterloo	2503 N Howard St	215-685-9891	N/A
Waterview	Rittenhouse St & McMahon St	215-685-2229	N/A
Ziehler	B St & Olney Ave	215-685-9145	N/A

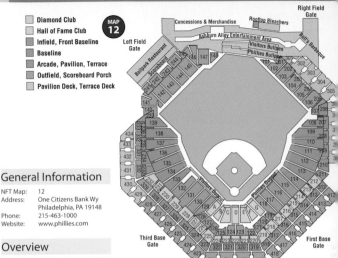

Diamond Club
Hall of Fame Club
Infield, Front Baseline
Baseline
Arcade, Pavilion, Terrace
Outfield, Scoreboard Porch
Pavilion Deck, Terrace Deck

General Information

NFT Map: 12
Address: One Citizens Bank Wy
            Philadelphia, PA 19148
Phone: 215-463-1000
Website: www.phillies.com

Overview

Home to the Phillies, the most-losing team in MLB history, the Cit opened in April 2004. Replacing the reprehensible Veterans Stadium, the venue is an impressive collection of sporting and entertainment facilities including restaurants, stores, interactive baseball, a fine art collection, and even an engagement center. Not that we don't appreciate it, but it feels bit like the city took someone's horrifically ugly sister and draped her in Vera Wang. Still, Phillies fans have to like the new ballpark: unlike the cavernous and malodorous Vet, it has a moderate seating capacity (43,500) and maintains a real grass and dirt playing field.

How to Get There—Driving

The Stadium is conveniently located next to I-95. From the north, take I-95 S to Broad Street/Exit 17 and follow signs into the park. From the south, take I-95 N to Exit 17, turn right and follow signs to the lot.

Parking

Affordable, though inconveniently located, parking is available for $10 per car and $19 per bus in the Sports Complex. Regular cash lots for Phillies games can be found in the Wachovia Center, in the lots located near Packer Avenue and Pattison Avenue (near the Jetro Warehouse). While early birds can snatch up nearby Link Parking, late-comers are relegated to the cramped lots west of 11th Street. Handicapped parking is available for $10 in all Preferred Lots with a valid placard.

How to Get There—Mass Transit

Take the SEPTA Broad Street subway line and get off at the last southbound stop—Pattison Avenue. SEPTA Broad Street trains depart from Pattison Avenue immediately after the game ends. Bus route C also stops at Broad Street.

How to Get Tickets

Ticket prices for Phillies games range from $15 to $40. For season and group sales, call 215-463-5000. For individual game sales, call 215-463-1000. The ticket office is located at the First Base Gate Entrance on Pattison Avenue. For home games, ticket windows also operate at Citizens Bank Way and on Phillies Drive. Tickets can also be purchased on the website.

Lower
Club
Upper

MAP
12

General Information

NFT Map:	12
Address:	11th St & Pattison Ave
	Philadelphia, PA 19148
Phone:	215-339-6700
Website:	www.lincolnfinancialfield.com
Eagles Phone:	215-463-2500
Eagles Website:	www.philadelphiaeagles.com
Ticketmaster Phone:	215-336-2000
Ticketmaster Website:	www.ticketmaster.com

Overview

Fondly referred to as "The Link," this 68,532-seat sports complex is home to the fightin' Philadelphia Eagles, hands-down Philly's most popular team. On game days, tailgate parties are varied and plentiful and often begin before 9 am. It is not advisable to attend a game dressed in enemy garb, but if you must, take ear plugs and a crash helmet. As a study in odd pairings, the Link is also home to the lowly Temple University Owls, soon to be booted out of the Big East Conference for failing to field a competitive team. The Link also plays host to a variety of other sporting and cultural events throughout the year, but the main attraction are those green and silver birds.

How to Get There—Driving

While I-95 is the most direct route, taking Broad Street is a good alternative when traffic is heavy, which it undoubtedly will be if you're heading to a Link event. From the north, take I-95 S to Broad St/Exit 17 and follow signs to stadium parking. From the south, take I-95 N past the airport and Navy Yard, to Broad Street/Exit 17 (formally exit 17). Follow signs to parking.

Parking

Unless you have a parking pass or two club seats to the game you're attending, the closest cash parking is across the street at the Wachovia Center. Additional spots can be found further south in the Triple 7 Lot (b/w Pattison Ave & 7th St). If all else fails, check out the Naval Hospital parking lot. Prices for public lots vary from event to event. Check www.lincolnfinancialfield.com for the most current rates.

How to Get There—Mass Transit

Take the SEPTA Broad Street subway to Pattison Avenue. Once above ground, cross the street, keep your head up, and merge into the stream of event-goers. Broad Street trains are scheduled to depart from Pattison Avenue shortly after events finish. If a game runs past midnight, the reliable shuttle buses on Broad Street replace the closed subway lines. The Route C bus also stops at Broad Street. If you're debating whether to drive or take the subway, you need your head examined.

How to Get Tickets

General events tickets are available through Ticketmaster. To book Eagles tickets, call 215-463-5500. For club seats and group tickets of ten or more, call 1-888-332-CLUB. Box office hours are Monday to Friday, 9 am to 5 pm at Headhouse (the pre-game/post game plaza inside Lincoln Financial Field). On event days, tickets are available at the remote ticket booth located at the 11th Street side of the main Lincoln Financial Field parking lot.

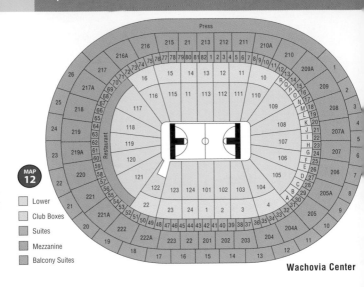

Wachovia Center

- ☐ Lower
- ☐ Club Boxes
- ☐ Suites
- ☐ Mezzanine
- ☐ Balcony Suites

MAP 12

General Information

NFT Map:	12
Address:	3601 S Broad St
	Philadelphia, PA 19148
Phone:	215-389-9587
Websites:	www.comcast-spectacor.com
Flyers:	www.philadelphiaflyers.com
Sixers:	www.sixers.com
Phantoms:	www.phantomshockey.com
Wings:	www.wingslax.com
Kixx:	www.kixxonline.com

Overview

First off, don't get too accustomed to the name. In a few short years, this arena has been named Corestates Center, First Union Center, and its present incarnation Wachovia Complex. Lord help us if Wachovia ever gets bought out by Summer's Eve (inevitably: the Douche Center).

The Wachovia Complex is actually composed of the old-school and much smaller Spectrum (home of the Philadelphia Kixx soccer squad as well as the AHL's Phantoms) and the larger, newer Wachovia Center (home of the NBA's 76ers and the NHL's Flyers). The venue attracts over four million visitors each year, many of whom end up leaving drunk and dissatisfied. (It has been more than twenty years since any of Philly's pro teams has won a &*#*%$# championship.)

The Spectrum was built in 1967. In 1974, the Flyers won their first Stanley Cup on the glistening rink, and in 1976 Elvis Presley shook his hips onstage for the last time in Philadelphia. Today, the new Spectrum is the place to go for circus shows, concerts, and traveling kiddy shows.

The somewhat more elaborate Wachovia Center, meanwhile, offers supreme spectator facilities for sporting events. With five levels and a seating capacity of 21,000, it's a prime venue for large-scale events. Check out the "in-arena" microbrewery for a pint of

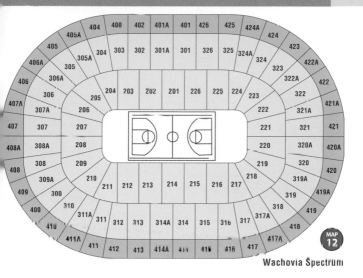

Wachovia Spectrum

six (just be sure to have your credit card relatively free of debt beforehand) before the show.

How to Get There—Driving

Though directions to the Wachovia Complex are simple, the major problem is traffic. From I-95 N/S, take the Broad Street exit and the complex is on the right.

Parking

Eight brightly lit lots with 6,100 spaces are available. You can reserve parking in advance through Ticketmaster or take your chances when you arrive. Patrons with disabilities can park in lots C and D. Rates vary from event to event. Call 215-336-3600 to get the rate for your event.

How to Get There—Mass Transit

Take the Broad Street subway to the last southbound stop—Pattison Avenue. Broad Street trains are scheduled to depart from Pattison Avenue shortly after events finish. If a game runs past midnight, the reliable shuttle buses on Broad Street replace the closed subway lines. The Route C bus also stops at Broad Street. Again, if you have the opportunity to avoid the snarling traffic by going the subway route, you would be wise to do so.

How to Get Tickets

All sports tickets can be obtained from the team's websites. Tickets for special events can be purchased at Ticketmaster. Tickets from the box office are available by calling 216-336-3600 or on location at the Broad Street side of Wachovia Center. Office hours are Monday to Friday 9 am-6 pm and Saturdays 10 am-4:30 pm and Sunday (event day only) 10 am-4:30 pm.

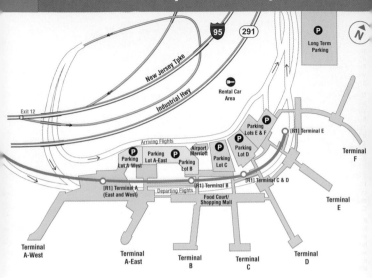

General Information

Address:	8000 Essington Ave Philadelphia, PA 19153
Phone:	215-937-6937
Websites:	www.philadelphia-phl.com www.phl.org
Flight/Gate Information:	800-PHL-GATE
Airport Police:	215-937-6918
Ground Transportation Hotline:	
	215-937-6958
Lost & Found:	215-937-6888
SEPTA (bus and rail):	215-580-7800

Overview

Thanks to the arrival of Southwest Airlines in the Philadelphia area, Philadelphians can finally partake in low-cost airfare. After years of being price-gouged by the major airlines, you can now fly roundtrip from Philly to New England for less than the cost of a night of getting loaded at your local pub. This fortuitous development has grabbed the attention of US Air. The Philly hub-airline recently introduced "Go Fares," in order to remain competitive with Southwest; a big win for frequent flyers.

Philly International has also added many new amenities, like the gleaming new Terminal A-West for international flights, local-cuisine restaurants, a Philly Museum Art Store, and Lamberti's Cucina. Ain't capitalism grand? Just keep in mind, butt heads, last spring PHL announced a 100% smoke-free environment policy.

How to Get There—Driving

Believe it or not, getting to the airport from Center City, the PA/NJ Turnpikes, or Delaware is easiest on I-95. Conveniently situated next to the PHL, this busy interstate is your best option, depending on the part of the city from which you are leaving. From CC, simply take I-95 S to the airport exit.

The other option, when leaving from Center City, is I-76 E (Schuylkill Expressway) to the airport exit. During rush hour, bumper-to-bumper, snail-paced traffic is the norm, so I-76 is not the best route if you're in a hurry. From the Pennsylvania Turnpike, take 476 S to 95. Take 95 N to the airport exit. From the NJ turnpike, take Exit 3 to the Walt Whitman Bridge and be wary of the tricky toll plaza; stay to your far right to merge onto 95 S and keep your eyes peeled for the Philadelphia Airport exit.

How to Get There—Mass Transit

If you're not carrying a lot of luggage, mass transit is the best option. From the airport, take the R1 Regional Rail line, which stops at all terminals except F. The R1 makes many stops along its route to Warminster Station in the northwest, including 30th Street Station, Suburban Station, and Market East Station. The trains operate between 5:25 am and 11:25 pm, and depart every thirty minutes. For the most up-to-date schedules, call 215-580-7800 or visit www.septa.org. One-way fares cost between $3 and $7, depending on your final destination.

Navigating the buses is a little more challenging. Buses 37 and 108 have airport routes, though both are indirect and somewhat "scenic" rides. Bus 37 makes stops at Terminals B (arrivals) and E (arrivals and departures), whereas Bus 108 stops only at Terminal B (arrivals). The bus rides are both lengthy and tiresome—save yourself some pre-flight anxiety and stick with a taxi or the R1.

How to Get There—Really

A drop-off or pick-up buddy is a very handy resource at PHL. If that's not an option, the 24-hour taxi service is a convenient means of fleeing the hordes of travelers. Taxis charge a flat-rate of $20 if you're heading into or out of Center City.

If you've a-hankerin' for some pamperin', door-to-door limousine services are also available. Limousines are an easy and luxurious way to travel, especially during peak hours or if you're with a larger group. A few mainstay services are Dave's Limousine (215-700-1000), which is more "big-red van" than "long-stretch limo," PHLimousine (866-264-5466), or PHL Taxi (610-595-1599).

Parking

PHL has made way for over 6,000 brand new parking spaces in recent years. Though it's now much easier to secure a spot, the daily parking rates can be expensive, depending on where you park. If you're fortunate enough to find a space in one of the terminal garages, parking costs $17 per day. The partial rates here are $3 per 30 minutes, with prices climbing $2 for every additional half hour. The more costly ground level, short-term parking is available at every baggage claim except Terminal F. Hourly rates here are the same as the garage parking, but daily rates

are $38. If you're going to be gone for more than a few hours, drive up to the garages.

If you're leaving for more than a couple of days, economy parking in the remote lot past Terminal F is the best bet. Parking costs $8 per day and blue and white shuttle buses ferry passengers to and from the airport around the clock.

An even more economical parking option, especially for longer stays, is private park-and-shuttle. There are many companies to choose from, including the ever-popular Colonial Airport Parking (610-521-6900). Located just two miles south of PHL, Colonial offers rates as low as $6 a day, including shuttle service. Another reputable service is Winner Airport Valet Parking (800-978-4848), located five minutes northeast of the airport. They chauffeur you in your car to and from the airport and charge around $52 per week.

Car Rentals   *Phone*

Car Rentals	Phone
Alamo:	800-327-9633
Avis:	800-331-1212
Budget:	800-527-0700
Dollar:	800-800-4000
Hertz:	800-654-3131
National:	800-227-7368

Hotel	Address	Phone
Airport Marriot	Airport Arrivals	215-492-9000
Embassy Suites	9000 Bartram Ave	215-365-4500
Extended Stay America	9000 Tinicum Blvd	215-492-6766
Extended Stay Studio Plus	8880 Bartram Ave	215-365-4360
Hampton Inn Philadelphia	8600 Bartram Ave	215-966-1300
Hilton Philadelphia Airport	4509 Island Ave	215-365-4150
Holiday Inn Stadium	10th St & Packer Ave	215-755-9500
Marriott Courtyard	8900 Bartram Ave	215-365-2200
Renaissance	500 Stevens Dr	610-521-5900
Residence Inn	4630 Island Ave	215-492-1611
Sheraton Suites	4101B Island Ave	215-365-6600

Airline	Terminal
Air Canada	D
Air France	A-East
Air France (arrivals)	A-West
Air France	E
Air Jamaica	A-East
AirTran Airways	D
America West Airlines	D
American Airlines/American Eagle	A-East
ATA (American Trans Air)	A-East
British Airways	A East
Charter Airlines	A-East
Charters	A-East
Continental/Continental Express	D
Delta Air Lines/Delta Connection	E

Airline	Terminal
Frontier Airlines	A-West
Lufthansa Airlines	A-East
Midwest Express	E
Northwest Airlines	E
Southwest Airlines	E
United Airlines/United Express	D
US Airways International	A-West
US Airways	B
US Airways	C
US Airways	D
US Airways Express	F
USA 3000	A-East

General Information

E-ZPass Information: 800-333-TOLL
E-ZPass Website: www.ezpass.com
DMV Phone: 800-932-4600
DMV Website: www.dmv.state.pa.us
Radio Traffic Updates: 1060 KYW (every 10 minutes
                          on the 2's)

Real-Time Traffic:
www.traffic.com/Philadelphia-Traffic/Philadelphia-Traffic-Reports.html

Delaware River Crossings

Only you can answer why you want to go to New Jersey in the first place. But if you have to go, you're taking a bridge, which means you're sitting in Bridge Traffic. The Walt Whitman starts close to South Philly, the Ben Franklin takes you from Center City, and the Betsy Ross services most of the Northeast. None of the bridges charge you to go to New Jersey, but they all make you pay $3 to get back. E-ZPass is accepted on all three bridges but, unfortunately, there's no discount.

The I-676 or Vine Street feeds you onto the Ben Franklin, which goes to Camden. The Walt Whitman goes to Camden as well—take 10th Street down to Packer Avenue to get onto the Walt Whitman unless it's 2 am and then I-95 may be (no guarantees) your best option. As for the Betsy Ross (destination: Pennsauken), you're pretty much stuck taking I-95, although you could go from Aramingo to Castor to Richmond. As always, keep in mind that the second you cross over to Jersey, our maps are virtually useless. Get directions beforehand from Mapquest or someone who really knows the area. Otherwise, you're on your own.

Philadelphia's Highways

Highways seem like a good idea until they turn into parking lots; which happens all too often. If you're planning on driving during the evening or on the weekend, check to see if there's a game at one of the stadiums, and devise plans accordingly, i.e. don't go. If you must, do your best to avoid I-95. Unfortunately, there's no good way to get north and south except on I-95, unless you want to go through the city. You can avoid the Schuylkill (I-76) from Center City westward by taking Kelly Drive or, better still, West River Drive. Kelly and West River have very few lights, and the scenery is nice to boot. One thing we can guarantee—the Schuylkill will be a mess on any half-nice weekend as suburbanites drag their packs

of children to the zoo. We should probably mention I-676: it's the little bit of road that connects I-76 to I-95. 'Nuff said.

Driving in Center City

Avoid Broad Street going south and take Juniper, a tiny street between Broad and 13th—it's small and not many people know about it. It has mostly stop signs instead of stop lights, which generally gets you through more quickly. Also, you have the luxury of turning left anytime you like, something you can't do on Broad from City Hall to Pine. We recommend going out to 22nd to go north. If you want to stay on the east side of Center City, take 13th. If you're going east or west, head south a little to do it (take Spruce or Pine Streets), or head north and take Arch Street. If your ultimate destination is West Philly, keep in mind that the bridges are located at South, Walnut, Chestnut, and Market Streets. For the love of God, don't ever drive up Walnut unless you absolutely have no choice. You will inevitably regret every second of the ride.

Driving in Northwest Philadelphia

Take Kelly Drive or West River Drive to East Falls then get on Lincoln Drive to go to Mount Airy or Chestnut Hill. If you're heading to Roxborough, Henry Avenue is a much better road to take than Ridge—get off Kelly and head up Midvale Avenue to get to Henry Avenue. Unfortunately for Manayunk, Main Street is pretty much the street. The good news is that you can completely avoid the Schuylkill to get to Northwest Philly except on some weekends that force the simultaneous closing of West River (closed to automobiles on Saturday and Sunday from April 1 to October 31) and Kelly Drive for regattas (damn boat races). Luckily, boat racing isn't popular enough that this will inconvenience you more than a handful of times each year. Then there are always those people who run or bike for charities that close Kelly Drive, too.

Driving in South Philly

Believe it or not, Broad Street is not the worst route to South Philly. Stay in the middle lane to avoid frequently stopping buses and/or trash trucks. If you actually stick to the speed limit, you'll find that the lights are timed and you can pretty much drive straight through. If you want to avoid Broad Street, try 13th Street going north or 12th Street going south. Buses don't run those roads, however, double parking is a recreational activity in South Philly, and you're likely to spend more time trying to navigate the parking lot than you would toughing it out on Broad.

Driving in West Philadelphia

The lights are timed on Walnut Street (which goes west) and Chestnut Street (which goes east). It's rare that going the speed limit is in your best interest, but, in this case, grit your teeth and stick to about 23 mph. Spruce Street is always a disaster, for reasons unknown, and should be avoided at all costs. If you want to go north and south, you're pretty screwed. 38th Street has four lanes and runs in both directions starting at Lancaster to the north, ultimately becoming University Avenue and feeding into I-76 to the south.

PENNDOT & Exam Centers

To take a driving test and complete the exam, you're going to need to visit one of the following PENNDOT locations. There are other offices in Philadelphia that deal with non-road-testing requirements such as renewals, learner's permits, and photo IDs—visit the Pennsylvania DMV website at www.dmv.state.pa.us and enter your zip code and the service you require to find the PENNDOT location nearest you. Or call 800-932-4600 for customer service.

Columbus • 1530 S Columbus Blvd
Island Avenue • 2320 Island Ave
Lawndale • Oxford Levick Shopping Center, 919 • B Levick St
West Oak Lane • 7121 Ogontz Ave,

DMV Registration

Vehicle safety inspections are performed at official PENNDOT Inspection Stations around the city (usually a repair garage or a service station with a repair shop).

Inspection Station	Address	Phone
Ardsley Auto Tags	2745 Jenkintown Rd, Ardsley	215-572-1409
Best Auto Tags	16 Baltimore Pk, Springfield	610-328-7664
Danny's Auto Sales	89 W Sparks St, Philadelphia	215-927-0730
Danny's Auto Tags	7184 Ogontz Ave, Philadelphia	215-977-0730
Fazio's Tag Service	21 S 12th St, Philadelphia	715-972-5111
Imperial Auto Tags	6400 Frankford Ave, Philadelphia	215-624-5220
Imperial Auto Tags	193 City Line Ave, Bala Cynwyd	610-617-8850
Mid-Atlantic AAA	2040 Market St, Philadelphia	215-864-5155
Mid-Atlantic AAA	394 W Lancaster Ave, Haverford	610-649-9000
Mid-Atlantic AAA	943 W Sproul Rd, Springfield	610-544-3002
Mid-Atlantic AAA	9475 Roosevelt Blvd, Philadelphia	215-289-6100
Nelson's	1501 N Broad St, Philadelphia	715-787-0669
Nelson's	1631 Snyder Ave, Philadelphia	215-463-7000
Nelson's	1632 S Columbus Blvd, Philadelphia	215-755-6600
Nelson's	2501 S 68th St, Philadelphia	215-365-4008
Nelson's	54 Maplewood Mall, Philadelphia	215-849-2886
Nelson's	6137 Ridge Ave, Philadelphia	215-482-1785
Nickens Agency	1550 Wadsworth Ave, Philadelphia	215-242-4090
Nickens Agency	6747 Germantown Ave, Philadelphia	215-848-9633
Pat's Auto Tags	2536 E Allegheny Ave, Philadelphia	215-427-1820
Renuit Now	609 E Girard Ave, Philadelphia	215-423-4563
Renuit Now	7944 Frankford Ave, Philadelphia	215-335-1010
Renuit Now	921 Levick St, Philadelphia	215-831-1147
Sidco Auto Tags	2999 Welsh Rd, Philadelphia	215-464-9950
Success Driving	2704 E Allegheny Ave, Philadelphia	215-739-4711

Transit • **PhillyCarShare**

General Information

Address: 315 S 46th St
                  Philadelphia, PA 19143
Phone: 215-386-0988
Emergency
  24-hour Phone: 267-210-0789
Toll-free
  Reservation Line: 877-744-8775
Website: www.phillycarshare.com
Hours: Mon-Fri: 9 am-6 pm (cars can
                  be reserved and accessed 24
                  hours a day, 7 days a week
                  with on-call staff in case of an
                  emergency)

Overview

PhillyCarShare, the first program of its kind in a major US city, is an environmentally-concerned non-profit organization that makes cars available to members on an as-needed basis. Think of it as time-share car rental that gives you access to a car without the hassle, expense, and responsibility of ownership. PhillyCarShare members don't pay for insurance, gas (a gas card is located in the glove compartment of each car), maintenance, or cleaning—just a low hourly usage fee.

Reserving and Using Cars

You can reserve cars by telephone or online, months or minutes before you plan to pick it up. You can almost always get a car on the spur of the moment, but you probably want to reserve your car at least a day in advance, especially if you want it on a weekend. Once you've reserved a car, pick it up at your requested location, open it with your special electronic key, drive away, and do your thing. An on-board computer tracks your time and mileage and cars must be returned to the location from whence they came.

Most cars in the fleet are hybrid gas-electric Toyota Prius sedans. Some bigger hatchbacks and one pick-up truck are also available, and some cars are even rigged with roof racks.

Becoming a Member

To be eligible for membership, you must be at least 21 years old, have a driving record that is less than atrocious, and possess a driver's license that is at least two years old and legal in the state of Pennsylvania. The organization encourages you to join on the website, where you'll find an online application form. Allow seven to ten days for their driving and credit check. Once approved, you will need to attend a one-hour membership orientation where you will receive the electric key that opens all Philly CarShare vehicles.

Costs

Application fee: $25 (non-refundable)
One-time deposit: $350 (refundable)
Per-hour charge: $3.90
Monthly admin fee: $10
(Plus major late fees for late returns)

Rules

As a courtesy to the next driver, pets are allowed in cars only if they are placed in an enclosed carrier. Smoking is also not allowed in the shared cars, for the same obvious reasons. The most important thing to remember about sharing a car is that it must be returned on time. If you use a vehicle without having made a reservation, you will be charged $50 the first time, and $100 for each subsequent offense. Philly CarShare vehicles cannot be used outside of the extended Philadelphia region, which includes most counties in Pennsylvania, New Jersey, and extends into Delaware and Maryland.

Car Pick-Up Locations

Address	Map
2038 Rittenhouse Sq	1
22nd & Chancellor Sts	1
9th & Locust Sts (Thomas Jefferson University)	3
1314 Spruce St	2
15th & Spruce Sts	2
16th & Cherry Sts	2
1919 Chestnut St @ Ludlow St	2
255 S 6th St (Independence Pl)	4
304 Race St	4
530 S 2nd St	4
1814 South St (Graduate Hospital)	6
1339 S 12th St b/w Reed & Wharton Sts	7
7th & Christian Sts	8
9th & South Sts	8
45th & Pine Sts	13
38th & Walnut Sts	14
22nd St & Fairmount Ave	N/A
22nd & Lombard Sts	N/A
47th St & Baltimore Ave	N/A
Midtown garage at Broad & Sansom Sts	N/A

General Information

Philadelphia Parking Authority
Phone: 215-683-9812
Website: www.philapark.org

Meters

All meters in Philadelphia accept nickels, dimes, quarters, and dollar coins. Smart Cards, which are basically credit cards for parking (buy one online at www.philapark.org) are also accepted at most meters. If parking is prohibited on a specific block at a certain time, you will be ticketed even if you plug your meter full, so make sure to check signs before deserting your car. If a parking meter is missing or broken, parking is still allowed for the maximum time on the posted sign. Vehicles can still receive "Over Time Limit" tickets in spots with broken or missing meters. Say what you will about the Philly Police Department, but their meter-people are the most efficient and ruthless on the force.

Residential Parking Permits

Residential parking permits cost $35 per vehicle for the first year and $20 for annual renewal. Visitor permits are available for $15 for up to fifteen days. Permits can only be used on blocks posted for permit parking, and only within the district for which they are registered. To qualify for a parking permit, a vehicle must possess Pennsylvania license plates and be registered to a home address in Philadelphia. You will also need to provide a proof of residence (and the promise of giving up your first-born child) to apply. To request an application for a residential parking permit, call 215-683-9730.

General Parking Violations

- Vehicles can be ticketed or towed (by the request of the property owner) for blocking a driveway even when there are no signs indicating "No Parking."
- Many streets in Philadelphia are narrow, making it difficult for buses to navigate their way through the city. Vehicles can be ticketed if they are observed blocking the progress of any mass transit vehicle.
- Parking over the line of a marked crosswalk will earn you a $35 ticket.
- Throughout the city, it is illegal to park within fifteen feet of either side of a fire hydrant or within twenty feet of a curb—this ain't New York. Sometimes there will be a sign indicating the end of the legal parking area and sometimes there won't. Even in the case of the latter, you *will* get a ticket, so

walk those twenty paces before leaving your car.
- Parking in a street-cleaning zone during street-cleaning times will result in a $25 ticket. Street cleanings are usually on the first and third Wednesdays and Fridays, or Tuesdays and Thursdays, of every month. Read the signs!
- School zone violations are enforced 7:30 am-3:30 pm on school days.
- Handicapped, Disabled Veteran, and People with Disabilities vehicles are granted an additional hour of parking time after the meter expires.

Vehicle Towing and Impoundment

Lost your car? Find out if it's been towed by calling 215-561-3636. Even if your car has been towed by a private towing company, it will be reported to the Philadelphia Parking Authority, and they can tell you where your vehicle has been taken.

To get your car back after it's been towed, you must pay all outstanding parking tickets and present a valid driver's license, registration, and insurance for your car. Vehicles not claimed within twenty-one days are sold at public auction.

Payment Locations

Parking Violations Branch
Address: 913 Filbert St
                Philadelphia, PA 19107
Phone: 215-561-3636
Hours: Mon-Fri: 8 am-8 pm
                Sat: 9 am-1 pm

Parking Authority Impoundment Lot
Address: 2501 Weccacoe Ave
                Philadelphia, PA 19148
Phone: 215-683-9550
Hours: Mon-Thurs: 8 am-9 pm
                Fri-Sat: 8 am-3 am
                Sun: 4 pm-11 pm

Tow Pounds

- 4200 Wissahickon Ave, 215-683-9518
- 334-375 E Price St, 215-683-9521
- 4701 Bath St, 215-683-9510
- 6801 Essington Ave, 215-683-9880

Hours for all tow pounds:
Mon-Fri: 8 am-8 pm
Sat: 8 am-5 pm
Sun: 4 pm-11 pm

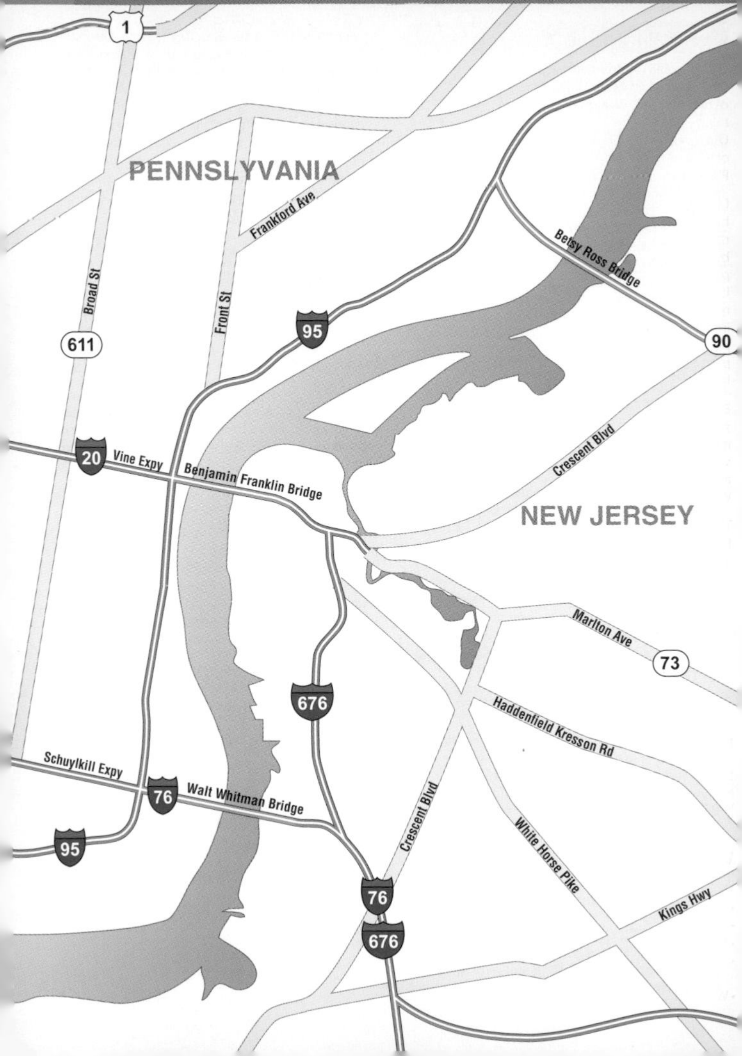
1
PENNSLYVANIA
Frankford Ave
Broad St
Front St
611
95
Betsy Ross Bridge
90
20
Vine Expy
Benjamin Franklin Bridge
Crescent Blvd
NEW JERSEY
Marlton Ave
73
676
Haddenfield Kresson Rd
Schuylkill Expy
76
Walt Whitman Bridge
95
Crescent Blvd
White Horse Pike
76
Kings Hwy
676

Overview

The Benjamin Franklin Bridge (Philly's answer to the Golden Gate) is an essential component to any view of the cityscape. Drive westbound over the bridge at night from Camden, New Jersey into Philadelphia's Olde City and you'll get the most breathtaking sight of Philadelphia's skyline, defined by the bright red PSFS sign (once the largest neon sign in the world).

Driving eastbound on I-676, you'll see the lighted blue BF Bridge looming large on your left, the skyline rising to your right, and you will feel overwhelmed by the technological achievements of mankind. The passing commuter PATCO trains trigger a computerized lighting system in each of the bridge's cables, making it look like an ethereal dancing figure floating above the dark water. Early-risers of the athletic persuasion can walk or jog in the morning on the pedestrian walkway for the longest stretch of traffic-lessness in the city.

Built in 1926, the Ben Franklin Bridge was the largest suspension bridge in the world for three years (today it ranks a less impressive 34th place). The bridge spans the Delaware River, connecting Philadelphia and Camden, a city famous for being home to poet Walt Whitman (in his later life) and Campbell's Soup.

The Walt Whitman Bridge, meanwhile, is the Ben Franklin's Bridge's younger, uglier sibling. Opened in 1957 in order to relieve congestion on the Ben Franklin Bridge, the Walt Whitman carries with it no artistic pretense, serving a wholly utilitarian purpose.

The Walt Whitman Bridge is the best way to bypass Center City, connecting the Schuylkill Expressway (I-76) and the Delaware Expressway (I-95), as well as the North-South Freeway (I-76, I-676, and NJ 42) and US 30. However, the bridge is too far south to be included in any panoramic shots of the city, and is too unattractive for anyone to be sorry about that fact. The 27th longest suspension bridge in the world, the Walt Whitman Bridge spans 6.2 miles total.

The Betsy Ross Bridge, which connects the Bridesburg section of Philadelphia to Pennsauken, New Jersey, carries the distinction of being the first bridge in the country named after a woman. Plans for the Betsy Ross Bridge began almost 20 years before the cantilever bridge opened to traffic in 1976, when officials at the Delaware River Port Authority decided it was past time to replace the Tacony-Palmyra Bridge, whose low suspension level made it an obstacle for passing ships.

The Betsy Ross follows in the footsteps of the Walt Whitman, whose function outshines its art— 45,000 cars cross the Delaware on the back of the Betsy Ross Bridge everyday, making it a valuable asset to both Philadelphia and New Jersey. But the structure looks like it was fashioned out of steel remnants picked up

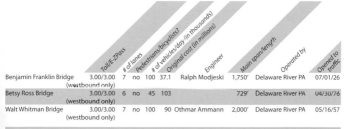

	Toll/E-ZPass	# of lanes	Pedestrians/bicyclists?	# of vehicles/day (in thousands)	Original cost (in millions)	Engineer	Main span/length	Operated by	Opened to traffic
Benjamin Franklin Bridge	3.00/3.00 (westbound only)	7	no	100	37.1	Ralph Modjeski	1,750'	Delaware River PA	07/01/26
Betsy Ross Bridge	3.00/3.00 (westbound only)	6	no	45	103		729'	Delaware River PA	04/30/76
Walt Whitman Bridge	3.00/3.00 (westbound only)	7	no	100	90	Othmar Ammann	2,000'	Delaware River PA	05/16/57

Websites

- Ben Franklin Bridge: www.phillyroads.com/crossings/benjamin-franklin
- Betsy Ross Bridge: www.phillyroads.com/crossings/betsy-ross
- Delaware River Port Authority: www.drpa.org
- E-ZPass: www.e-zpassnj.com; www.paturnpike.com
- Traffic, weather, general transit information:
   www.traffic.com/Philadelphia-Traffic/Philadelphia-Traffic-Reports.html
- Walt Whitman Bridge: www.phillyroads.com/crossings/walt-whitman

SEPTA

Phone: 215-580-7800
Website: www.septa.com

Overview

The SEPTA bus system is the best public transportation the city has to offer. The massive transportation network, with its nearly 170 intercity and suburban bus transit routes, will likely get you everywhere you need to go, if not in style. For the most part, the bus routes revolve around Philadelphia and the surrounding area's main hubs. For transit to major employment centers, entertainment and sporting complexes, shopping centers, and other popular professional and recreational facilities, SEPTA is a decent choice. While the majority of buses operate between the hours of 5 am and 1 am, there are over 20 buses, known as "Owl Buses," that run 24 hours a day on the major transit routes. You just have to keep Philly bus etiquette in mind: if possible, talk loudly about your preferred method of birth control on your cell phone; never give your seat up to anyone, for any reason; and always have a bag of take-out from which you can eat as you burn through your cell minutes.

Fares & Passes

Single Ride: $2 (cash) or one SEPTA token ($1.30 each, packs of 2, 5, or 10).
Day Pass: $5.50
Suburban Weekly TransPass: $18.75
Suburban Monthly TransPass: $70
A Cross County Monthly Pass: $85

All passes and tokens can be purchased online. Exact change is required when paying cash. Like in most large metropolitan cities, having payment ready helps alleviate stressed searches for change and angry glares from impatient bus riders. Simply deposit the cash fare or token into the farebox, or place the transit pass through the electronic reader on top of the farebox. Transfers are available for 60 cents and must be purchased from the driver on the first leg of your ride. Be aware that some suburban routes and some city routes have additional zone charges of 50 cents.

Services

The major SEPTA terminals, where the most facilities and transfer options are available, are the Frankford Transportation Center, Olney Terminal, Wissahickon Transfer Center, 69th Street Terminal, and Norristown Transportation Center. These are also main stops on many of the bus routes. Individual route schedules are available on SEPTA's website, or can be picked up at the aforementioned terminals or other SEPTA locations including Market East Station and Sub-

urban Station. For bike enthusiasts, front-mounted racks that accommodate two bikes are available on routes 1, 8, 12, 24, 28, 53, 71, 77, 103, 107, 116, 122, 305, and J.

Greyhound & Peter Pan

Greyhound Phone: 800-229-9424
Greyhound Website: www.greyhound.com
Greyhound Terminal: 1001 Filbert St
Philadelphia, PA 19107
215-931-4075
Philadelphia Sigler Travel: 1130 W Olney Ave
Philadelphia, PA 19141
215-924-1330
Peter Pan Phone: 800-343-9999
Peter Pan Website: www.peterpanbus.com

Overview

Greyhound and Peter Pan are Philadelphia's main intercity bus services. Both are headquartered at the Greyhound terminal on Filbert Street, mere blocks from Market East Station. The Greyhound terminal and ticketing offices are open 24 hours a day. Greyhound also runs limited bus service out of Philadelphia Sigler Travel between 7:30 am and 9 pm.

Fares & Passes

Fares are comparable between the two bus companies, and booking at least seven days in advance can sometimes halve your fare. Sample fares and tickets are available on either company's website or at the terminal ticketing office. Make sure you check both websites before purchasing a ticket—sometimes they have ridiculous sales like $12 one-way to NYC and $15 to Boston. A variety of student and senior discount fares are also available.

Services

Greyhound services 3,600 locations in North America and Mexico, while Peter Pan travels only to select locations in New Jersey, Connecticut, Massachusetts, Pennsylvania, New York, and New Hampshire. If you're in the mood for some high-falutin' dice-rollin' and chip-throwing, Greyhound runs a direct Philadelphia-Atlantic City Casinos line (800-231-2222). The bus leaves from both Philadelphia Greyhound locations and drops you off at the casino of your choice between 8:30 am and 11 pm daily.

PHLASH Downtown Loop

Website: www.phillyphlash.com

Overview

The flamboyant purple trolley skittering up and down the tracks is not strictly for tourists. Though it does hit many of the city's prime attractions, such as the Philadelphia Museum of Art and Liberty Bell, and runs between major downtown hotels, the PHLASH is a quick and easy connection for locals and visitors alike.

For the affordable price of $1 per ride, the PHLASH hits 18 choice intersections and offers timely service every 12 minutes. Tickets can be purchased on the trolley, at the Independence Visitor Center (6th and Market Streets), or at the Riverlink Ferry at Penn's Landing. You can also make connections to all SEPTA and PATCO rail lines via the PHLASH. The convenient hop-on, hop-off service runs from May 1st to November 30th, between 10 am and 6 pm.

Fares & Passes
The PHLASH costs $1 per ride, $4 per day, or $10 per day for a family of four. Seniors ride free at all times except between 4:30 pm and 5:30 pm.

Services
The PHLASH makes stops near Market East Station and Suburban Station, as well as the PATCO Station at 8th and Market Streets. When driving into Center City, it's a good idea to park in the AutoPark at Independence Mall (5th and Market Streets), the AutoPark at Old City (2nd and Sansom Streets), or the AutoPark at the Gallery (10th and Filbert Streets). Show your PHLASH ticket here for discounted parking rates.

Chinatown Buses

New Century Travel:	55 N 11th St
	Philadelphia, PA 19107
	215-627-2666
	www.2000coach.com
Today's Bus:	121 N 11th St
	212-964-6334
	Philadelphia, PA 19107
	www.todaysbus.com
Apex Bus:	121 N 11th St
	Philadelphia, PA 19107
	888-688-0893
	www.apexbus.com

Overview
Craving some dim sum New York City-style? Hop on any number of buses running directly from Philly's Chinatown to NYC's Chinatown and, in less than two hours, you'll be gorging on pork dumplings and fried taro cakes to your heart's content. Even if 88 East Broadway in NYC isn't your main destination, passengers are conveniently dropped within walking distance of multiple New York City subway lines, the closest of which is the East Broadway F train stop.

Fares & Passes
New Century Travel currently offers a Philadelphia-New York City bus route, and plans to operate a Philadelphia-Washington DC express service in the near future. The first bus departs Philly for New York from 55 N 11th Street at 6:30 am and the last bus leaves at 11 pm. Tickets are $20 roundtrip and can be bought online (bring photo ID), at the bus station, or on the bus. Reservations are recommended and seat selection is made on a first-come, first-served basis. Transfers can be made to Boston-bound buses in New York City.

Today's Bus provides another low-cost service between Philadelphia, New York City, Washington DC, Richmond, and Atlanta. The buses depart every hour on the hour, between 7 am and 11 pm. Passengers are allowed two bags each (including a carry on) and bikes are permitted onboard. A $20 roundtrip ticket can be purchased online at www.todaysbus.com or when boarding the bus, depending on availability. In addition to Chinatown, Today's Bus makes an addition New York City stop for passengers wishing to disembark at 290 Seventh Avenue, between 26th and 27th Streets.

Apex Bus offers a "guaranteed seating" policy on the Philadelphia-New York City routes. The first and last buses leave at 6:50 am and 11:00 pm. New York City-bound bus schedules vary depending on the day, so make sure to contact the Apex office directly at 215-351-9167, or check online at www.apexbus.com. Roundtrip tickets ($20) can be purchased by phone or via the Internet.

New Jersey Transit Buses

Phone:	215-569-3752
Website:	www.NJtransit.com

Overview
New Jersey Transit offers an extensive network of 17 bus services running intrastate routes. It is an excellent travel option, offering subsidized prices for students, families, children, and frequent riders.

Fares & Passes
Monthly passes can be purchased at various New Jersey bus terminals, or at the Greyhound Bus terminal at 1001 Filbert Street. Depending on zones traveled, fares vary between $1.20 (Zone 1) and $14.40 (Zone 14). On many of the bus routes, exact coin or dollar fare is required. Monthly passes or ten-fare packages are also available. Check the website for more details.

30th Street Station

Address:	2955 Market St Philadelphia, PA 19104
Phone:	215-249-3196
Website:	www.30thstreetstation.com
Amtrak:	215-349-2270
SEPTA:	215-580-7800
NJ Transit:	937-491-9400

Overview
Architecturally, it's a marvel. The 70-year-old, eight-story concrete framed building boasts a remarkable interior laden with marble statues and skyscraper-high ceilings.

30th Street Station is a hub for SEPTA, Amtrak, and NJ Transit, accommodating 25,000 commuters each day. Amtrak's intercity trains and NJ Transit's Atlantic City line run through the station's lower level, while SEPTA Regional Rail trains serve the upper level.

Ticket Windows
Tickets for NJ Transit, Amtrak, and SEPTA are sold at the main hall ticket windows, which are accessible through the 30th Street or Market Street entrances. Amtrak's ticket window is open from 5 am to 10 pm, seven days a week, while SEPTA's ticketing office maintains a more restricted schedule: weekdays 6 am-9 pm, Saturday 8 am-8 pm, and Sunday 8 am-7 pm. You can also purchase tickets for the NJ Transit trains at the Amtrak ticket counter. Though the station is open 24 hours a day, if you are passing through during less-active hours (10 pm-5 am), the station assumes a more ominous aura because the shops are closed and the main clientele becomes folks escaping the elements.

Parking
Finding a spot at 30th Street Station is rarely a problem. There are two new parking garages, though prices are far from wallet-friendly. Parking in the new garage or underground lot (both accessible on 30th Street) costs a whopping $10 for two hours. Pricing on Arch Street's surface lot and the 29th and 30th Street surface lots are slightly more affordable. Rates are listed at $1.50 for every 20 minutes. Valet service is available at an expectedly high price of $5 per half hour. For quick pick-ups and drop-offs, the meters are the best bet; scattered around 30th, Market, and Arch Streets, meters cost 25 cents for every 7.5 minutes and $2 per hour. Unreserved monthly garage parking is available for $200 a month. Unfortunately, "unreserved" often means

"unlikely availability"—there is a lengthy waiting list for these in-demand spots. For all parking inquiries, call 215-386-2393.

Services
Most of the shops and restaurants maintain 7 am-7 pm business hours, though a select few stay open 24 hours. Among the many fast food joints and newsstands riddling the station there is a post office, Wachovia bank, FYE music store, National Car Rental (800-328-4567), Budget Rent A Car (800-642-0408), and some delectable eateries such as Delilah's Southern Cuisine (try their scrumptious fried chicken and strawberry lemonade) and Surf City Freeze/East Coast (their smoothies are divine coastal treats).

Transit Connections
All SEPTA Regional Rail lines, the Market-Frankford line, and Trolley routes 10, 11, 13, 34, and 36 stop at 30th Street Station. Due to a recent rise in crime and loitering, the underground passageway to the Frankford line is closed; now when transferring between the stations, you must walk above ground for about a block. The NJ Transit's Atlantic City line runs from 30th Street Station to Atlantic City, while SEPTA's R7 heads to Trenton and connects to the NJ Transit. If you're feeling weary from train travel, switch it up with a bus ride (Bus 30) from 30th Street Station to the 69th Street Terminal.

Suburban Station

Address:	N 16th St & JFK Blvd Philadelphia, PA 19019
Phone:	215-563-5580

Overview
The fabulously ornate Suburban Station was once the shining star of Philadelphia's rail stations. That is, before the ultra-magnificent 30th Street Station came along and snatched the spotlight from its elder counterpart. Its proximity to City Hall, Love Park, and the shops at Liberty Place still make it a popular commuter station.

Built in the 1920s, with the aim of revamping Philadelphia's transportation system, the exterior of Suburban Station still stands as a glowing example of Art Deco architecture, with its gray limestone and elaborate gold and bronze gilded light fixtures. The top of Suburban Station houses an enormous 22-story office structure that spans an entire city block. From the exterior, the station is easily identifiable by the giant clothespin statue outside.

The bleak 1970s interior is disappointing in comparison to the grandiosity of its exterior. During rush hours, the station comes to life with the movement of corporate commuters, but when Friday evening arrives, the building becomes desolate.

Ticket Window

SEPTA's ticket office is on the underground's first level. The hours are Monday through Friday, 6 am-9 pm, and Saturday and Sunday, 8 am-6 pm. Electronic ticket machines are also available on this floor, along with service desks, public telephones, and ATMs.

Parking

Unfortunately, SEPTA provides no parking at Suburban Station, though there is metered street parking in the vicinity for pick-ups and drop-offs.

Services

During peak hours, the usual snack bars, fast food joints, and even a couple of sushi shops are open. There is little choice in terms of sundries on the weekends—you'll be lucky to find a shop or eatery open.

Transit Connections

Dismal weekend atmosphere aside, Suburban Station is truly a connection haven. The Regional Rail lines, the Market-Frankford line, the Broad Street line, and several Trolleys all zip through this major hub. All connections are made via walkways running from Suburban Station to City Hall Station. Buses 17, 27, 31, 32, 33, 38, 44, 121, 124, 125, and C all arrive at City Hall. Bus 30 travels both east and westbound from 30th Street Station to the 69th Street Terminal, making a stop at Suburban Station. The PHLASH also has a pickup spot at 16th Street and Benjamin Franklin Parkway.

Market East Station

Address:	1100 Market St
	Philadelphia, PA 19107
Phone:	215-580-7800

Overview

Though Market East Station has little to offer visually, its location is convenient to many popular destinations including City Hall, Chinatown, Independence National Historic Park, Reading Terminal Market, and the Pennsylvania Convention Center. The station services SEPTA Regional Rail and the Market-Frankford line.

Originally labeled "the handsomest terminal passenger station of its time" after its completion in 1893, the old Reading Railroad Terminal is now the entrance to Pennsylvania's Convention Center. Also located at Market East Station is The Gallery, the first enclosed shopping mall in the US.

Ticket Window

It's best to enter the station on 12th or Filbert Streets, steering clear of The Gallery. The ticket office is open weekdays 6 am-9 am, 8 am-8 pm on Saturday, and 8 am-7pm on Sunday. Ticket machines are also available on the main level near the ticket windows.

Parking

SEPTA provides no parking, but there are some alternative parking options: two parking garages at The Gallery are nearby, as well as one at Reading Terminal Market. Metered street parking is available, but it's often hard to come by in this neighborhood.

Services

The range of food options at Market East Station, The Gallery, and the Reading Terminal Market is endless. Think delis overflowing with fresh produce, cafés brewing freshly roasted coffee, cheesesteak vendors simmering marinated meats, famous Italian bakeries offering fresh baked bread—even the most picky palates will be pleased. The Gallery also houses name brand stores like Gap, K-Mart, CVS, and T-Mobile.

Public Transportation

Beyond Regional Rail and the Market-Frankford line, buses 17, 27, 31, 32, 33, 38, 44, 121, 124, 125, and C stop at City Hall, not far from Market East. If you're looking to hit up some tourist attractions, hop on the purple PHLASH bus. With stops at 12th and Market Streets, it's convenient and cheap. The PATCO from New Jersey also stops nearby, dropping passengers off at the 8th Street Station, just blocks from Market East Station.

General Information

Phone: 215-580-7800
Website: www.septa.com
System Map: NFT Foldout

Overview

Philly's SEPTA subway system is relatively small. It only has two lines—the Broad Street Line and the Market Frankford Line (also fondly named the "Frankford El"). The lines are efficiently integrated into the overall SEPTA system and provide a valuable link in Philly's transit network. The subway system manages a remarkably efficient routing and connecting schedule—a noteworthy distinction from its Regional Rail cousin.

The subway is a popular transit option for commuters traveling to venues where parking is difficult, such as the Wachovia Complex, Citizens Bank Park, or Market East Station.

It's also an efficient way to connect between regional and local rail services. It is, without question, a great alternative to the endless traffic-jams congesting the city's roadways.

Fares & Passes

A one-way subway ticket costs $2 cash or $1.30 token (available in packs of 2, 5, and 10). Transfers to other lines are an additional 60 cents, unless otherwise noted. If you're going to be traveling around for the day, pick up a DayPass for $5.50. If you're a devoted subway user or plan to stick around Philadelphia for more than a couple days, the TransPass is a good investment ($18.75 per week and $70 per month). This card offers unlimited travel on all city transit routes, not just the subway.

The Market-Frankford Line

"You can't get to heaven on the Frankford El, because the Frankford El goes straight to Frankford"
—American Dream (1970)

The Frankford Elevated Line (also known as the "Blue Line") carries many Northeast commuters from the Frankford Transportation Center to the 69th Street Terminal between 5 am and midnight. Anytime after midnight, a reliable bus service replaces the Market-Frankford course, making similar stops along the route. Free transfers are available at 15th and Market Streets (City Hall) to all connecting Broad Street Line buses, which pass every 15 minutes during the morning hours.

In addition to regular trains, the Market-Frankford line is served by A and B trains during peak hours from Monday to Friday, 7:00 am-8:30 am and 3:45 pm-5:15 pm. A and B signs are displayed on the side and front of trains, so make sure you get on a train that's stopping at your destination (see map).

Broad Street Line

Also known as the "Orange Line," the BSL is actually divided into two parts—Broad Street proper, which runs 10.1 miles and the Broad Ridge Spur, which extends 1.9 miles. The former runs mostly underground, from the Fern Rock Transportation Center down to Pattison Avenue (near the sports and entertainment complex). Broad Ridge Spur is an eastern extension line from Fairmount down to 8th/Market (Chinatown).

Seven days a week, local trains operate every few minutes from 5:02 am to 12:30 am. A bus service continues takes over at night, running every 15 minutes and making a connection to all Market-Frankford Line buses at City Hall.

Between 5:50 am and 6:32 pm, express trains make stops every seven minutes (during peak hours) and every 15 minutes (non-peak hours) at Fern Rock, Olney, Girard, Spring Garden, Race-Vine, City Hall, and Walnut-Locust. The Ridge Spur starts its weekday southbound service at 5:25 am and its northbound service at 5:45 am. On weekends, the first train travels south at 6:15 am and heads north at 6:38 am. Bikes are allowed onboard only during non-peak hours—before 6 am (for the early-birds), from 9 am to 3 pm, of after the 6 pm rush.

The Broad Street Line is absolutely your best option for attending sporting events. The local train will get you there from City Hall in 11 minutes, and you won't have to deal with the hassle of parking. **Sports Express** trains make stops at Fern Rock, Olney, Erie, Girard, Race-Vine, City Hall and Walnut-Locust en route to Pattison Station. After events, there are northbound trains standing by to provide local and express service back to City Hall and Fern Rock.

Parking

Parking during the week costs $1 at the Frankford Transportation Center and $2 at Fern Rock and the 69th Street Terminal. There is free parking on weekends in the daily lots, while overnight and permit parking is only available at stations that also operate as Regional Rail stations. Don't forget that the parking fare boxes at SEPTA only accept change.

General Information

Phone:	215-580-7800
Website:	www.septa.com
Lost & Found:	215-580-7800
Parking Information:	215-580-3400
System Map:	NFT Foldout

Overview

The streets of Philadelphia are covered in trolley tracks; some of them are in current use, but many of them are no longer in operation. You'll find yourself cursing the unused portions of rail as your car twists and bumps over the tracks like a 19th-century wagon (and God help you if you are on a bike or skateboard when you hit one), but their ubiquitous remains remind us of the city's past.

At the height of service in 1911, nearly 4,000 streetcars traveled more than 86 routes. After major financial difficulties, including multiple bankruptcies and debts with other transportation companies, SEPTA finally took control of the trolley service in 1968. Today, only a few select routes continue trolley service, also known as "Subway Surface Routes."

Route 10 runs from 13th Street Station to Overbrook in West Philadelphia, while Routes 11, 13, 34, and 36 travel to points in southwest Philadelphia and Delaware County. Trolleys make stops at Suburban Station and 30th Street Station, where transfers to Amtrak, Regional Rail, and other subway lines are available. Routes 100 and 101 connect at the 69th Street Terminal and run to points south in Delaware County. Light rail Route 100 also runs northwest out to Norristown in Montgomery County.

Trolley hours vary depending on the line, but most begin service around 5 am and run until just after 1 am. Bikes are permitted on trolleys and light rail lines only during non-peak hours (before 6 am, 9 am-3 pm, and after 6 pm and anytime on weekends).

Fares & Passes

Trolley fare costs $2 cash or $1.30 with a token. Convenient multi-token packs are available in groups of 2, 5, or 10. All transfers and retransfers cost another 60 cents, unless otherwise posted. Be aware that on Routes 100, 101, and 102 there is an additional charge of 50 cents for crossing suburban zones. A DayPass costs $5.50.

Like on the subways, the TransPass and TrailPass are good options for unlimited and cost-effective travel on a weekly or monthly basis. Tickets for seniors, students, and the disabled are also sold at reduced prices. Up to two children may ride free with any fare-paying adult, as long as they are less than 42 inches tall.

Parking

Finally, a place to park for free! Parking lots are available at many stations on Route 101 and 100. Visit www.septa.com for detailed listings. Other stations charge a meager $1 (in quarters!) for parking, except the 69th Street Terminal, which charges $2.

General Information

Phone: 215-580-7800
Website: www.septa.com
System Map: NFT Foldout

Overview

After coming to terms with the expected SEPTA rail delays and hassles (including the infamous SEPTA strike season), you'll find SEPTA to be an effective, comfortable, and popular means of transportation. The eight-line service extends to the outer corners of Pennsylvania, carrying passengers to the airport and as far as Trenton, Doylestown, and Thorndale. Regional Rail also connects to Amtrak and NJ Transit services, making trip to Washington DC, Chicago, Boston, and New York City very easy.

All SEPTA trains stop at Suburban Station, Market East Station, and 30th Street Station, and all three stations connect to the Market-Frankford Line. A Broad Street Line connection can be made at Suburban Station, and Amtrak train service is available at 30th Street Station. Trolleys connect at Suburban Station and 30th Street Station.

Fares & Passes

Every Regional Rail station has a zone number, which is based on its distance from Center City. Tickets cost between $3 and $7 one-way. Regular riders can save some cash by purchasing 10 Trip Tickets. It's also cheaper to travel some zones off-peak. Keep in mind that there is a $2 surcharge for tickets bought on the train if a ticket window is open or a functioning ticket machine is available at the station where you boarded.

Zone	Peak	Off-Peak	10 Trip Tickets
1	$3.00	$3.00	$28.00
2	$3.75	$3.00	$35.50
3	$4.50	$3.75	$42.50
4	$5.00	$4.25	$47.50
5	$5.50	$4.25	$52.50
6	$7.00	$7.00	$60.00

All fares are one-way

In addition to single-fare rides, fare options such as TransPass, TrailPass, Cross County Pass, and Intermediate Two Zone passes are also available for purchase on SEPTA's website and at various locations throughout the city.

TransPass is a deal that offers unlimited travel on all city transit routes and the first zone of suburban transit routes. The pass costs $18.75 per week and $70 per month.

TrailPass is valid for travel on Regional Rail to destinations within the zone indicated on the pass. Depending on the zones you plan to traverse, pass prices vary between $106 (Zone 2) and $163 (anywhere) per month ($28.25-$45.50 per week).

The **Cross County Pass** offers unlimited travel in three zones or more operating outside Center City, including all suburban bus routes, Routes 100, 101, 102, and Regional Rail. Passes cost $85 per month.

The **Intermediate Two Zone** pass is valid on Regional Rail for travel through one or two zones outside Philadelphia. The past costs $60 per month (single trips are $2.50).

Regional Rail also offers discounts for persons with disabilities, seniors, students, some college students, families, and groups. Check www.septa.com for a detailed listing discounts and ticket purchase locations.

Bikes on SEPTA Regional Rail

There is a limit of two bikes per carriage during off-peak hours, and five bikes per carriage during weekends and major holidays. Bikes are never permitted during peak hours, unless they fold and can be stored out of the way.

Parking

Park-and-Ride is another cheap and efficient way to get into the city. Parking at the Frankford Transportation Center costs $1, while Fern Rock and the 69th Street Terminal each charge $2. Be sure to take lots of loose change with you—the slot boxes only take quarters. Most SEPTA stations have numbered parking spaces next to the platform, but spots fill up quickly, so you should plan to arrive early or arrange for a drop-off buddy for the more bustling hubs like Jenkintown. Parking at smaller stations and connecting to your desired line is another option for avoiding parking congestion.

Overnight parking is also available at many stations *except* Ardmore, Bryn Mawr, Downingtown, Doylestown, Elkins Park, Haverford, Overbrook, Swathmore, and Villanova. You need to reserve your overnight parking slot at least one day in advance and rates vary depending on location. Reservations can be made between 9 am and 4 pm by calling 215-580-3400.

General Information

Phone:	800-USA-RAIL (872-7245)
Website:	www.amtrak.com
30th Street Station (PHL):	2995 Market St
North Philadelphia (PHN):	
	2900 N Broad St (& Glenwood Ave)
System Map:	NFT Foldout

Overview

Two stations provide Amtrak service in Philly. 30th Street Station (PHL), which is the main Amtrak station, is located in the heart of Philadelphia. This massive Art Deco architectural gem is on the National Register of Historic Places and serves as a hub for both Amtrak and SEPTA. To the north is the aptly named North Philadelphia (PHN) station. It's a decrepit stop with such limited service that you're better off catching a train at the 30th Street Station. If you're a Harrison Ford fan, you might experience a little déjà vu at 30th Street Station: It was here that Peter Weir shot the beginning of his film *Witness*.

Acela Express

Traveling at speeds of up to 150 mph, the Acela line serves major cities along the northeastern seaboard. Philadelphia and New York City are two major stops along the Boston to Washington DC route, with several smaller stops in between. Both the Metroliner and the Regional trains run similar routes, with more stops and at a slightly slower pace. Roundtrip tickets from Philadelphia to NYC on the Acela line start at $98; on holidays and at peak travel times, the fare goes up dramatically. It's far from cheap, but if you want the quickest, least-hassle method of getting to New York, Acela is your best bet.

If you're traveling to Boston and back, plan on paying a minimum of $160. And if you haven't maxed out your credit card on Amtrak fares, you can head down to DC and back for a mere $94.

Other Lines

You might be wondering, "Why would I ever pay for an exorbitant ticket on an Amtrak train?" Well let's say you wanted to take a scenic tour of Pennsylvania Dutch country without the hassle of driving—you could hop on the *Keystone* line in Philly and cruise through the Pennsylvania corridor straight to Harrisburg. Or maybe you always wanted to go on a sprawling trip to New Orleans—board a train for a leisurely turn on the *Crescent* line. Or maybe you simply have the desire to waste hundreds of dollars on a drawn-out trip to a destination that could be reached much cheaper and more efficiently by any other mode of public or private transportation. You decide.

Baggage Check & Pet Policies

Each passenger can check up to three pieces of baggage thirty minutes before departure. You're allowed to check up to three more pieces for a $10 fee but, at that point, you'd be wiser renting a U-Haul truck. You can also take two items on board with you. Electronic equipment and plastic or paper bags cannot be checked. All pets are prohibited on Amtrak trains, except for service animals.

How to Get There—Driving

The 30th Street Station is conveniently located off of I-76. Take Exit 345 and follow the signs for the station. The North Philadelphia Station can be reached from US-13.

Parking

There are five parking lots at the 30th Street Station. Two short-term lots charge $25 per 24 hours. Two long-term lots charge $20 per 24 hours. One valet lot is available for $35 per 24 hours.

How to Get There—Mass Transit

SEPTA commuter trains offer frequent service between 30th Street and Center City Philadelphia (Penn Center/Suburban Station and Market East Station). You can ride free on these trains to and from Center City with your Amtrak ticket stub. Visit www.septa.com for more information.

Transit · NJ Transit

● Station
○ Under Contruction Station

Port Jervis Line

Pascack Valley Line

Main Line & Bergen County Line

Montclair-Boonton Line
MidTOWN DIRECT Service to
New York from Montclair Heights
Note: no weekend service

Morris and Essex Lines
MidTOWN DIRECT Service to New York
from Dover and Gladstone

Raritan Valley Line

Northeast Corridor Line

North Jersey Coast Line

PENNSYLVANIA

Otisville
Middletown
Campbell Hall
Salisbury Mills - Cornwall
Port Jervis
Orange
Harriman
Tuxedo
Rockland
Sloatsburg
Suffern
Spring Valley
Nanuet
Mahwah
Pearl River
Ramsey
Montvale
Allendale
Park Ridge
Waldwick
Woodcliff Lake
Ho-Ho-Kus
Hillsdale
Ridgewood
Westwood
Glen Rock-Main Line
Glen Rock-
Emerson
Lincoln
Boro Hall
Oradell
Park
Hawthorne
Radburn-
River Edge
Towaco
Fair Lawn
Essex St
Paterson
Broadway-
North Hackensack
Mtn View-Waynes
Fair Lawn
Anderson St
Little Falls
Plauderville
HACKENSACK
Great Notch
Clifton
Garfield
Teterboro-Williams
Montclair Heights
Passaic
Wood-Ridge
Mountain Ave
Delawanna
Rutherford
Upper Montclair
Watchung Ave
Walnut St
Lyndhurst
Kingsland
Glen Ridge
Bloomfield
Watsessing
Secaucus
Highland Ave
Junction
Mountain Station
New York
South Orange
Penn Sta
Madison
Hoboken
Chatham
Newark Hudson
Murray Hill
Penn Station
Newark Liberty
North Elizabeth
International Airport
Elizabeth

Sussex

Warren

Mt Olive
Lake Hopatcong
Netcong
Dover
Denville
Hackettstown
Morris
Mt Tabor
Mountain Lakes
Boonton
Morris Plains
Morristown
Convent
Basking
Ridge
Gladstone
Bernardsville
New Providence
Peapack
Far Hills
Lyons
High Bridge
Annandale
Lebanon
White House
North Branch
Raritan
Somerville
Bridgewater
Bound Brook
Dunellen
Plainfield
Netherwood
Fanwood
Westfield
Garwood
Cranford
Roselle
Park
Linden
Rahway
Avenel
Woodbridge
Metropark
Metuchen
Edison
Perth Amboy
South Amboy
New Brunswick
Jersey Ave

Essex
Brick Church
East Orange
Orange
Broad St
Newark
Maplewood
Millburn
Short Hills
Summit
Gillette
Stirling
Millington
Berkeley Heights
Union

Hunterdon

Somerset

Middlesex

Princeton
Princeton Junction
Hamilton
Trenton

Mercer

Monmouth

Bucks

NEW JERSEY
PENNSYLVANIA

Burlington

Ocean

Aberdeen-Matawan
Hazlet
Middletown
Red Bank
Little Silver
Monmouth Park
(seasonal service)
Long B
Elberon
Allenhu
Asbury Pa
Bradley Be
Belmar
Spring Lake
Manasquan
Point Pleasant
Bay Head

Atlantic Ocean

Staten
Island

New
York
City

PENNSYLVANIA
NEW JERSEY

NEW YORK
NEW JERSEY

General Information

Address: 1 Penn Plz E
             Newark, NJ 07105
Phone: 973-762-5100 (out of state)
             800-772-2222 (in state)
Website: www.njtransit.com

Overview

New Jersey Transit's buses, rail, and light rail services, while less luxurious than Amtrak trains, provide a far more affordable means of transportation between Philadelphia, Jersey cities, Newark International Airport, and Manhattan. Combined NJ Transit and SEPTA trains can get you to New York for less than half of what it costs to travel Amtrak. Just hop on SEPTA's R7 train from Philadelphia's 30th Street Station to Trenton, NJ, then ride NJ Transit's Northeast Corridor line to New York.

Because of the low-cost fares and reliable schedules, travel during weekends and peak hours gets rather crowded—you could find yourself standing all the way to New York. NJ Transit also provides service between Philadelphia and Atlantic City for $6.60 or less (and the ride takes less than an hour and a half). Just remember to buy your ticket before you get on the train, otherwise you'll be paying a five dollar surcharge (and you don't need to be wasting those five bucks before you even set eyes on the casinos).

With fourteen bus terminals located in and around New Jersey, NJ Transit buses can take you across the river from Philadelphia to Camden, Six Flags Amusement Park, Trenton, or even to Bruce Springsteen's hometown, Asbury Park. Philadelphia's NJ Transit Bus Terminal is located at the Greyhound Bus Terminal, 1001 Filbert Street.

Fares & Passes

Bus passes must be purchased at an NJ Transit bus terminal—otherwise passengers are required to provide the driver with exact change in coins or $1 bills. Frequent riders can purchase ten trip tickets and monthly passes for reduced rates. Single-ride bus fares cost between $1.10 and $15.75, depending on the length of your trip.

Purchasing monthly passes for either the bus or train saves daily commuters about thirty percent of regular ticket costs. Monthly passes are valid for an unlimited number of trips between designated stations during the month for which they are purchased. Weekly passes, also valid for unlimited trips between designated stations, save about fifteen percent of the cost of regular tickets. Check out the Quik-Tik option on the NJ Transit website to purchase passes online.

BusinessPass, offered through employers, can save commuters even more money on monthly rail and bus passes by deducting a portion of the cost from pre-tax salaries. These monthly passes are mailed directly to the work site. **PatronPass** gives businesses an opportunity to buy one-way tickets in bulk for either the bus or train in advance.

NJ Transit also offers special Family SuperSaver Fares, Student Monthly Passes, Children's Fares, and Senior Citizens packages. For more information on fare options, check out www.njtransit.com/sf_tr_fo.shtml. You can also view schedules and fares online at www.njtransit.com, or can pick up a hard copy of schedules at any station.

Parking

Some train and bus stations provide free daily parking. Parking at other stations requires a permit. For parking information for each station, visit www.njtransit.com/rg_pk_station_parking.jsp.

Baggage & Pets

Small pets are permitted on trains, but must be transported in carry-on travel cases. Service animals are always allowed to ride. On buses, each passenger is allowed to store two pieces of "conventional sized" luggage in the under-seat storage area.

Bikes Onboard

Many—but not all—NJ Transit buses carry bike racks attached to the front of the bus. The "Bike Aboard" program allows passengers to carry their bikes on NJ Transit trains for no extra charge. Most train and bus stations also offer parking facilities for up to 1,600 bicycles.

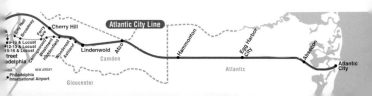

January

Mummer's Parade	Broad St	Men in dresses, drunk off their asses. www.mummers.org
MLK Jr Day of Service	Various locations	Day of action and celebration. www.campusphilly.org/mlkday

February

Philly Auto Show	Convention Center	More than 700 vehicles on show. www.phillyautoshow.com
Mardi Gras	South St	We just do the drinking part. www.south-street.com
Chinese New Year	Chinatown	Day of the firecracker. www.phillychinatown.com
African American History Month	Various locations	City-wide events celebrate African American history. www.aampmuseum.org

March

Philly Flower Show	Convention Center	Biggest annual flower show in the country. www.theflowershow.com
St Patrick's Day Parade	City parade route	All the green beer you can stomach.

April

Penn Relays	UPenn	High-profile track meet. www.thepennrelays.com
Philly Film Festival	Various locations	Fast-growing international cinema orgy. www.phillyfests.com
Philly Antiques Show	UPenn Hospital	Proceeds go to the hospital. www.philaantiques.com

May

Broad Street Run	Broad St	10-mile road race. www.broadstreetrun.com
Police & Fire Memorial	Franklin Square Park	Honors fallen police officers and firefighters. www.phila.gov
Dad Vail Regatta	Schuylkill River	Largest collegiate rowing race in the country. www.dadvail.org
Rittenhouse Row Spring Fest	Rittenhouse Square	Indoor/outdoor street fair. www.rittenhouserow.org
Race for the Cure	Fairmount Park	5K road race to support breast cancer cure. www.komen.org
Jam on the River	Penn's Landing	Musicfest to kick off the summer. www.pennslandingcorp.com

June

FirstGlance Film Festival	Various locations	Bi-coastal indie film fest. www.firstglancefilms.com
Philly Pride Festival	Broad & Pine Sts	LGBT pride extravaganza. www.phillypride.org
Pro Cycling Championship	Ben Franklin Pkwy	Wachovia-sponsored bike race. www.wachoviacycling.com
Bloomsday	Rosenbach Library	Reading of Joyce's *Ulysses* on the day it supposedly took place. www.rosenbach.org

July

Independence Day Ceremony	Independence Hall	Stars 'n stripes forever. www.americasbirthday.com
Gay & Lesbian Film Festival	Various locations	Huge selection of disparate choices. www.phillyfests.com/piglff

August

Unity Day	Ben Franklin Pkwy	Celebration of Brotherly Love. www.wdasfm.com
Philly Folk Festival	Various locations	Props for not spelling "folk with a "ph." www.folkfest.org

September

Philadelphia Distance Run	Schuylkill River	Half-marathon. www.philadistancerun.org
Phashion Phest Philadelphia	Penn's Landing	Industrial Design Fair. www.phashionphest.com
Philly Fringe Festival	Various locations	Indie theater, dance, and art performances. www.pafringe.com
Puerto Rican Festival Parade	City parade route	Puerto Rican pride celebration. www.elconcilio.net

October

Dragon Boat Races	Schuylkill River	Over 100 teams and eight lanes of action. www.philadragonboatfestival.com
Terror Behind the Walls	Eastern State Penitentiary	Jail transforms into a haunted house. http://easternstate.org
OutFest	Various locations	Coming-out block party. www.phillypride.org
Columbus Day Parade	S Broad St	Name says it all. www.phila.gov
Pulaski Day Parade	City parade route	Polish heritage celebration. www.polishamericancenter.org
215 Festival	Free Library	Showcase of established and emerging writers/musicians. www.215festival.com

November

Philadelphia Marathon	City-wide	26.2 grueling miles. www.philadelphiamarathon.com
Thanksgiving Day Parade	Ben Franklin Pkwy	Turkey Day family fun. http://abclocal.go.com/wpvi

December

City Hall Tree Lighting Festival	City Hall	The usual fanfare beginning Dec 1. www.centercityphila.org/holiday
New Year's Eve	Penn's Landing	Fireworks over the Delaware River. www.pennslandingcorp.com

Useful Phone Numbers

Emergencies:	911
General Information:	411
Philadelphia Police Headquarters:	215-686-3388
City Hall:	215-686-2181
Comcast:	888-633-4266
Fire Department:	215-686-1300
Parking Authority:	215-683-9600
Public Defender:	215-568-3190
Free Library of Philadelphia:	215-686-5322
Block Party Permits:	215-686-5560
Bucks County Board of Elections:	215-348-6154
Philadelphia Board of Elections:	215-686-3469

Websites

www.digitalcity.com/philadelphia • AOL's local city guide, with lots of upcoming events coverage and better-than-most dining and club guides.
www.nba.com/sixers • Official website of Philly's favorite basketball team.
www.notfortourists.com • The ultimate website for everything you ever need to know about anything.
www.phila.gov • The city's official home on the web.
http://philadelphia.about.com • So crammed with information it's a bit hard to read, but has everything you need, including hotel information, cheesesteak recipes, Philly culture quizzes, updated radio guide, info on living in Philly and moving to Philly, local news headlines, and more…
www.philadelphiaeagles.com • Official website of Philly's favorite football team.
http://philadelphia.phillies.mlb.com • Official website of Philly's favorite baseball team.
www.philadelphiaflyers.com • This site only matters if there actually is an NHL next year, of course.

www.philadelphiaweekly.com • Online version of Philly's free weekly newspaper that tells you what to do, where to live, and more.
www.philly.com • Local news, sports, jobs, cars, homes, etc.
www.philly1.com • Local news briefs and links to indie Philly-based publications.

Essential Philadelphia Movies

The Philadelphia Story (1940)
1776 (1972)
Rocky (1976)
Blow Out (1981)
Taps (1981)
Tattoo (1981)
Trading Places (1983)
Birdy (1984)
Witness (1985)
Mannequin (1987)
Philadelphia (1993)
Twelve Monkeys (1995)
Fallen (1998)
The Sixth Sense (1999)
Unbreakable (2000)

Essential Philadelphia Books

A House on Fire: The Rise and Fall of Philadelphia Soul (2004) by John A. Jackon
Common Sense (1976) by Thomas Paine
Diary of Independence Hall (1948) by Harold Donaldson Eberlein & Cortland Van Dyke Hubbard.
Shining Cycles of Love (1959) by Anna Coggins Dart.
The Papers of Benjamin Franklin, by Benjamin Franklin – more than 30 volumes edited and published by Yale University Press.
The Neal Pollack Anthology of American Literature (2002) by Neal Pollack

We're Number One!!!

America's first brick house: Penn House, 1682
America's first public school: Fourth & Chestnut Streets, 1698
America's first public fire engine: 1719
America's first botanical gardens: On the banks of the Schuylkill, 1728
America's first public library: Free Library of Philadelphia, 1731
America's first hospital: Philadelphia Hospital, 1732
America's first university: University of Pennsylvania, 1749
America's first anti-slavery society: 1774
America's first flag: Made in Philly by Betsy Ross, 1777
America's first Congressional meeting: Congress Hall, 1789
America's first law school: University of Pennsylvania Law School, 1790

Philadelphia Timeline—*a timeline of significant events in Philly history (by no means complete)*

1681: King Charles II grants charter of Pennsylvania.

1702: William Penn grants charter for city of Philadelphia.

1704: First Presbyterian Church erected.

1723: Benjamin Franklin arrives in Philadelphia.

1731: First Baptist Church erected.

1732: Independence Hall construction finished. Becomes home of the Liberty Bell.

1749: Ben Franklin founds the country's first university, University of Pennsylvania.

1752: Liberty Bell cracks.

1775: First Continental Congress elects Franklin as Postmaster General of colonies.

1776: Signing of the Declaration of Independence.

1777: British invade Philadelphia.

1778: American army spends cold winter in Valley Forge.

1784: Peace with England ratified by Congress.

1790: Ben Franklin dies in Philadelphia.

1803: Northern Liberties incorporated into city of Philadelphia.

1813: Spring Garden district incorporated into city of Philadelphia.

1829: Eastern State Penitentiary opened.

1829: *The Philadelphia Inquirer* founded.

1857: Academy of Music opens.

1865: City mourns Lincoln's assassination, celebrates defeat of Lee's army.

1866: Coldest night in history (18 degrees below zero): Schuylkill and Delaware freeze.

1872: Friends Meeting House (17th & Girard Sts) opened for public worship.

1874: Famous autopsy of first Siamese twins Chang and Eng completed at College of Physicians and Surgeons.

1875: South Street Bridge opened to pedestrians, 194 buildings erected throughout city.

1876: First train departs from Philadelphia to New York City.

1877: Philadelphia Museum of Art opens Memorial Hall.

1881: First African Americans join police force.

1883: Founding of the National League Team, the Phillies.

1885: City businesses closed for funeral of Ulysses S. Grant.

1889: Labor Day instituted as legal holiday in Pennsylvania.

1915: Phillies make it to the World Series with manager Pat Moran.

1922: Construction begins on the Benjamin Franklin Bridge (then the Delaware River Bridge).

1926: Benjamin Franklin Bridge opens for traffic.

1942: Phillies set club record of losing streak with 111 games.

1957: Walt Whitman Bridge opened for traffic.

1963: Philadelphia purchases Syracuse's NBA team which becomes the 76ers.

1972: The Sixers post a 9-73 record, still the worst in NBA history.

1981: The Eagles make it to the Superbowl. Lose to the Raiders.

1985: Infamous MOVE bombing kills 11 and burns 61 houses to the ground.

1991: Old City institutes the tradition of "First Fridays," an art community open house on the first Friday of every month.

1992: Ed Rendell begins first term as mayor of Philadelphia.

1994: Tom Ridge elected Governor of Pennsylvania.

1996: Larry Brown named coach of the 76ers.

1997: Debut of the Philadelphia Fringe Festival.

1998: Wachovia Center opens as new home of the 76ers and the Flyers.

1999: Sixers make it to the play-offs.

2000: John Street takes office as Mayor of Philadelphia.

2000: Republican National Convention held in Philadelphia.

2001: Sixers lose in the NBA finals in five games.

2002: Kimmel Center opens to rave reviews.

2003: Former mayor Ed Rendell becomes Governor of Pennsylvania.

2003: "Ride the Ducks" debuts and annoys all Philadelphians.

2003: With the purchase of "Striped Bass," Stephen Starr reaches ownership of ten restaurants in Philadelphia.

2003: Eagles open their new playing venue, Lincoln Financial Field.

2004: Eagles lose NFC Championship Game—third year in a row.

2004: Citizens Bank Park, new home of the Phillies, opens.

2004: Mayor John Street announces plans for city to become first major wireless Internet city in the country.

(191)

Television

3	KYW (CBS)	www.kyw.com
6	WPVI (ABC)	abclocal.go.com/wpvi
10	WCAU (NBC)	nbc10.com/index.html
11	WPPX (PAX)	www.paxtv.com
17	WPHL (WB)	http://wb17.trb.com
29	WTXF (FOX)	www.fox29.com
35	WYBE	www.wybe.org
51	WTVE	www.wtve.com
52	WPSG (UPN)	www.upn.com

AM Stations

560	WFIL	Religious
610	WIP	Sports
860	WWDB	Business News
900	WURD	News
950	WPEN	Nostalgia
990	WZZD	Christian Contemporary
1060	KYW	All News
1210	WPHT	Talk
1250	WNAR	Drama/Nostalgia
1480	WDAS	Gospel
1540	WNWR	Ethnic

FM Stations

88.1	WPEB	Variety
88.5	WXPN	Adult Contemporary
90.1	WRTI	Public Radio
90.7	WKPS	Variety
90.9	WHYY	Public Radio
91.7	WKDU	Variety
92.5	WXTU	Country
93.3	WMMR	Rock
94.1	WYSP	Rock
95.7	WMWX	Hot Adult Contemporary
96.5	WPTP	'80s Rock
98.1	WOGL	Oldies
98.9	WUSL	Hip Hop
101.1	WBEB	Adult Contemporary
102.1	WIOQ	Top 40
102.9	WMGK	Classic Rock
104.5	WSNI	Oldies
105.3	WDAS	Urban Contemporary
106.1	WJJZ	Smooth Jazz

Print Media

Al Dia	211 N 13th St, Ste 704	215-569-4666	Latino daily.
Daily News	400 N Broad St	215-854-2000	Daily tabloid.
Daily Pennsylvanian	4015 Walnut St	215-898-6585	UPenn independent news.
Jewish Exponent	2100 Arch St	215-832-0700	Jewish weekly.
Penn Gazette	3910 Chestnut St, 3rd fl	215-898-5555	UPenn alumni magazine.
Philadelphia Business Journal	400 Market St, Ste 1200	215-238-1450	Daily business report.
Philadelphia City Paper	123 Chestnut St, 3rd fl	215-735-8444	Weekly arts & entertainment.
Philadelphia Gay News	505 S 4th St	215-625-8501	Weekly news.
Philadelphia Inquirer	400 N Broad St	215-854-2000	Daily broadsheet.
Philadelphia Magazine	1818 Market St, 36th fl	215-564-7700	City mag with "Best Of" list.
Philadelphia New Observer	1520 Locust St, Ste 501	215-545-7500	Weekly African American.
Philadelphia Tribune	520 S 16th St	215-893-4050	Weekly African American news.
Philadelphia Weekly	1500 Sansam St	215-563-7400	Weekly alternative.
Temple Times	302 University Services Bldg	215-204-8963	Daily Temple University news.
The Philadelphia Independent	1026 Arch St	215-351-1666	Monthly independent broadsheet.
The Triangle		215-895-2585	Weekly Drexel University news.

Libraries

Yet another brilliant idea from the ubiquitous Mr. Franklin, the Philly library system is the oldest in the country, though not necessarily the best. Recent budget cuts have interfered greatly with the service offered.

The imposing Free Library at 19th and Vine Streets hosts a terrific *Author Series* where authors read from their most recent works and then answer audience questions. Entry for the *Author Series* is usually free but operates on a first-come, first-served basis; the bigger the name, the earlier you should arrive. Check out http://libwww.library.phila.gov/calendar/authorevents.cfm to see who's reading when. The Free Library also houses more than 100.000 rare books; spanning almost 4000 years of history, the shelves hold everything from Horace to Beatrix Potter. A recently approved $30 million improvement plan for the main branch will go towards a children's library, more Internet browsing rooms, and a teen center.

In addition to the Free Library main branch, Philly has 55 smaller branches, each of which hosts its own events. Visit www.library.phila.gov/upcomevents/speceven.htm and search by neighborhood for events near you.

Library	Address	Phone	Map
Central Library	1901 Vine St	215-686-5322	2
Charles L Durham Branch	3320 Haverford Ave	215-685-7436	14
Charles Santore Branch	932 S 7th St	215-686-1766	8
Chestnut Hill Branch	8711 Germantown Ave	215-248-0977	27
Falls of Schuylkill Branch	3501 Midvale Ave	215-685-2093	23
Fishtown Community Branch	1217 E Montgomery Ave	215-685-9990	20
Fumo Family Branch	2437 S Broad St	215-685-1758	10
Independence Branch	18 S 7th St	215-685-1633	3
Joseph E Coleman Branch	68 W Chelten Ave	215-685-2150	24
Kensington Branch	104 W Dauphin St	215-685-9996	20
Library for Blind and Handicapped	919 Walnut St	215-683-3213	3
Lovett Branch	6945 Germantown Ave	215-685-2095	25
Philadelphia City Institute	1905 Locust St	215-685-6621	2
Queen Memorial Library	1201 S 23rd St	215-685-1899	6
Ramonita de Rodriguez Branch	600 W Girard Ave	215-686-1768	19
Roxborough Branch	6245 Ridge Ave	215-685-2550	21
South Philadelphia Branch	1700 S Broad St	215-685-1866	10
Thomas F Donatucci Sr Branch	1935 Shunk St	215-685-1755	9
Walnut Street Branch	3927 Walnut St	215-685-7671	13
Whitman Branch	200 Snyder Ave	215-685-1754	11

Northwestern Ave
Stenton Ave
Ivy Hill Rd
Cheltenham Ave
Cottman
Rhawn St
Roosevelt Blvd

Henry Ave
Wister St
Wayne St
Roosevelt Blvd
Frankford Creek
G St

City Ave
Broad St
Lehigh Ave
Allegheny Ave
Front St
Lehigh Ave

Montgomery Ave
10th St
Poplar St
Delaware River

52nd St
Market St
676
95

Baltimore St
49th St
Broad St
Lombard St

Cobbs Creek
Moore St
Tasker St
76

NEW JERSEY

95

76

95

Police Stations

	Address	Phone	Map
1st Police District	24th St & Wolf St	215-686-3010	N/A
2nd Police District	2831 N Levick St	215-686-3020	N/A
South Street Detail (3rd District)	420 Bainbridge St	215-922-6706	8
4th Police District	11th St & Wharton St	215-686-3040	7
5th Police District	Ridge St & Cinnaminson St	215-686-3050	N/A
6th Police District	235 N 11th St	215-686-3060	3
7th Police District	9800 Wistaria St	215-686-3070	N/A
8th Police District	Academy Rd & Red Lion Rd	215-686-3080	N/A
15th Police District	Harbison St & Levick St	215-686-3150	N/A
16th Police District	39th St & Lancaster St	215-686-3160	13
17th Police District	20th St & Federal St	215-686-3170	6
19th Police District	61st St & Thompson St	215-686-3190	N/A
22nd Police District	17th St & Montgomery Ave	215-686-3220	N/A
24th Police District	3901 Whitaker Ave	215-686-3240	N/A
26th Police District	Girard Ave & Montgomery Ave	215-686-3260	20
25th Police District	3901 Whitaker Ave	215-686-3250	N/A

Important Phone Numbers

Life-Threatening Emergencies:	911	Domestic Violence Hotline:	215-291-8742
Non-Emergency Police Service:	215-895-2822	Missing Persons Unit:	215-686-3014
Wanted Persons:	888-992-6833	Sex Crimes Report Line:	215-685-1180
Rape Victims Hotline:	215-985-3333	Noise Complaints (NET):	215-563-8787
Crime Victims Hotline:	800-394-2255	Complaints (Internal Affairs):	215-685-5056

Crime Statistics

	2000	2001	2002	2003
Homicide	319	309	288	348
Rape	1,021	1,014	1,035	1,004
Robbery	10,425	9,604	8,869	1,004
Aggravated Assault	11,047	10,477	9,865	9,651
Burglary	12,089	11,629	11,244	10,656
Theft	46,952	45,318	38,789	37,864
Motor Vehicle Theft	16,147	15,527	13,302	13,934

Hospitals

	Address	Phone	Map
Albert Einstein Medical Center	5501 Old York Rd	215-456-7890	N/A
Chestnut Hill Hospital	8835 Germantown Ave	215-248-8200	27
Frankford Hospital	4900 Frankford Ave	215-831-2000	N/A
Graduate Hospital	1800 Lombard St	215-893-2000	2
Hahnemann University Hospital	Broad St & Vine St	215-762-7000	2
Jeanes Hospital	7600 Central Ave	215-728-2000	N/A
Jefferson Hospital	111 S 11th St	215-955-6460	3
Mercy Hospital of Philadelphia	50 S 54th St	215-748-9000	N/A
Methodist Hospital	2301 S Broad St	215-952-9000	10
Nazareth Hospital	2601 Holme Ave	215-335-6000	N/A
Pennsylvania Hospital	S 8th St & Spruce St	215-829-3000	3
Presbyterian Medical Center	39th St & Market St	215-662-8000	13
St Joseph's Hospital	16 W Girard Ave	215-787-9000	19

Part of the appeal or enjoyment of hanging out with kids is rediscovering the fun and frivolity of childhood. We've created a list of great stores, restaurants, and activities that you should enjoy as much as the little 'uns.

Shopping Essentials

Philadelphia is not often touted as one of the fashion capitals of the world. But with the help of these stores, your kids can be as adorably clothed and accessorized as their counterparts in London, Paris, New York, and Milan.

- **babyGap** · 160 North Gulf Rd, King of Prussia. · 610-354-0232 · Timeless baby fashions at moderate prices.
- **Born Yesterday** · 1901 Walnut St · 215-568-6556. · Up-scale kiddie clothes.
- **Burberry** · 1705 Walnut St · 215-557-7400 · The famous raincoats and plaids in miniature.
- **Children's Boutique** · 1702 Walnut St · 215-732-2661 · First floor stocked with European kids' clothes and shoes, second floor devoted to toys.
- **Chique Bebe** · 1837 E Passyunk Ave · 215-468-9930 · Christening clothes for infants.
- **Chris's Corner: Books for Kids & Teens** · 1940 Pine St · 215-790-1727 · Tiny shop with a great selection and friendly staff.
- **Daffy's** · 1700 Chestnut St · 215-963-9996 · Discounted designer kids' clothes.
- **Gymboree** · 326 Mall Blvd, King of Prussia · 610-332-0470 · Clothing store and play center chain geared at children under the age of seven.
- **Happily Ever After** · 1118 Pine St · 215-627-5790 · Old-school toy store.
- **IKEA** · 2206 S Columbus Blvd · 215-551-4532 · Great deals on kids' furniture and accessories. And kids love playing in the showroom.
- **Karl's—Baby & Teenage Furniture & Clothing** · 724 Chestnut St · 215-627-2514 · The name says it all.
- **Little Beth Boutique** · 1540 Packer Ave · 215-468-2229 · Best christening gowns in the city.
- **Mimi Maternity** · 1615 Walnut St · 215-567-1425 · Maternity wear.
- **O'Doodles** · 8335 Germantown Ave · 215-247-7405 · High-quality toys and beautiful children's books.
- **Office Cents** · 1525 Chestnut St · 215-864-3203 · Discounted back-to-school supplies.
- **Raisman's Baby Furniture** · 5524 Germantown Ave · 215-843-0811 · All the baby basics you need, plus accessories you don't need, but want anyway.
- **SimplyCottage** · 8236 Germantown Ave · 610-642-2905 · Unique hand-made baby goods, from linens to bookcases, to wall hangings.
- **Supercuts** · 209 South St · 215-922-2970 · Cheap cuts for kids. No appointment necessary.
- **Toys "R" Us** · 2703 S 3rd St · 215-334-4600 · Toy superstore.
- **Worn Yesterday of Manayunk** · 4235 Main St · 215-482-3316 · Consignment shop for maternity wear, kids and baby outfits.

Outdoor Activities

Kids cooped up are like fish out of water. Here are some outdoor activities they'll love.

- **Amish Village,** (Rte 896, 717-687-8511.) Guided tours through Amish country and great souvenirs.
- **Fairmount Park,** (Fairmount Ave, 215-683-0200.) Historic houses, boathouse row, running and biking paths, picnic grounds.
- **Longwood Gardens,** (Rte 1, Kennett Square, 610-388-1000) Horticultural display garden that hosts all kinds of activities for kids.
- **Lower Perkiomen Valley Park,** (Oaks exit, Rte 422, Oaks, 610-666-5371) Bike trails along the Schuylkill River, playground equipment along the way.
- **Philadelphia Zoo,** (3400 W Girard Ave 215-243-1100.) Oldest zoo in the country with a primate exhibit to write home about. Check out the Zooballoon!
- **Sesame Place,** (100 Sesame Rd, Langhorne, 215-752-7070) Sesame Street-based amusement park.

Websites

www.gocitykids.com
Philadelphia.babyzone.com
Familyfun.go.com

Rainy Day Alternatives

Nothing can really beat baking or watching movies on a rainy day. But if you're motivated to leave the house, these popular destinations never come up short:

- **Academy of Natural Sciences,** (1900 Ben Franklin Pkwy, 215-299-1000.) Four floors of activities and exhibits about the world's most fascinating species and their habitats.
- **American Historical Theater,** (2008 Mt Vernon St, 215-232-9596.) Educational, historical theater for kids and school groups.
- **Arden Children's Theater,** (40 N 2nd St, 215-922-1122.) Resident professional children's theater.
- **Dave & Buster's,** (325 N Columbus Blvd, 215-413-1951.) Arcade games, pinball machines, laser tag, batting cage (and word on the street is that Allen Iverson hangs out here).
- **The Franklin Institute,** (222 N 20th St, 215-448-1200.) Science museum that takes learning to a new level of fun (seriously).
- **Independence Seaport Museum,** (211 S Columbus Blvd, 215-925-5439.) All things Davy Jones, plus ongoing exhibits of other nautical phenomena.
- **Insectarium,** (8046 Frankford Ave, 215-338-3000.) All-bug museum.
- **Mum Puppettheatre,** (115 Arch St, 215-925-7686.) Stages original puppet works geared at adults as well as children.
- **Mütter Museum,** (19 S 22nd St, 215-563-3737.) For the future doctors of the world.
- **Philadelphia Children's Theater,** (1906 S Rittenhouse Sq, 215-451-7806.) Professional theater for the young 'uns.
- **Philadelphia Doll Museum,** (2253 N Broad St, 215-787-0226.) Diverse dolls from around the world, character dolls, talking action figures, and vintage barbies.
- **Philadelphia Museum of Art,** (26th St & Franklin Pkwy, 215-235-7469.) Art classes for kids aged 3-12.
- **Please Touch Museum,** (210 N 21st St, 215-963-0667.) You're supposed to touch everything. That's the point. Fake supermarkets, science rooms, barnyards, and more.

Kid-Friendly Restaurants

They love kids and kids love them:

- **DiNardo's Famous Fastfood,** (312 Race St, 215-238-9595.) Tasty crabs. Bibs are given to everyone, so the kids won't stand out as the messy ones.
- **Fiesta Pizza,** (8339 Germantown Ave, 215-247-4141.) Caters to kids—gives you crowns and fries while you wait for the 'za.
- **Hard Rock Café,** (1113 Market St, 215-238-1000.) Average food tastes better when you're staring at a signed Elvis EP. No matter how tacky you might find it, the fact of the matter is that kids really like this place.
- **Johnny Rockets,** (443 South St, 215-829-9222.) '50s-style chain diner with standard jukebox and kids' menu.
- **More than Just Ice Cream,** (1119 Locust St, 215-574-0586.) Ice cream in one room, vegetarian delights in the other.
- **Nifty Fifty's,** (1356 Passyunk Ave, 215-468-1950.) '50s-style diner.
- **Scoop de Ville,** (107 S 18th St, 215-988-9992.) Desserts and ice cream you can take to the park.

General Information · **LGBT**

The site of some of the earliest gay rights protests in the 1960s, Philadelphia has long been a gay-friendly town. The city cultivates this image, having recently released a commercial specifically encouraging the LGBT tourist community to visit Philadelphia. The "Gayborhood," whose borders stretch roughly from Walnut to Pine Streets between 11th and 13th Streets, is right in the heart of Center City. It's a conglomeration of plenty of gay-owned businesses and residents, as well as the 12th Street Gym (where gay bodybuilders of Philadelphia unite). Sisters is the only full-time lesbian bar; Thursday night is the most popular evening, by far, and they serve a wonderful brunch on Sunday morning.

Health Centers and Support Organizations

- **Attic Youth Center**, 419 S 15th St, 215-545-4331; www.atticyouthcenter.org—The largest GLBT youth center in Philadelphia, the Attic provides a safe social space for queer youth, as well as counseling and psychological services for young adults between the ages of 12-23.
- **Bi-Unity Social Group**, www.biunity.org—Social group for women who identify as bisexual.
- **Center for Civil Rights**, 1211 Chestnut St, Ste 605, 215-731-1447; www.center4civilrights.org—Advocating equality for the LGBT community in PA.
- **City of Brotherly Love Softball League**, 800-GO-CBLSL; www.cblsl.org—Openly gay softball league with men's and women's divisions.
- **Critical Path AIDS Project**, 1233 Chestnut St, 5th fl, 215-985-4448; www.critpath.org—Offers treatment and referral information to HIV-positive individuals. Their website is a resource in itself.
- **Custody Action for Lesbian Mothers (CALM)**, 610-667-7508—Legal advice for lesbians regarding custody issues.
- **Fairmount Park Women's Softball League,** 215-508-3922—Fairmount Park Women's Softball League has been part of the women's sports community in Philadelphia for over 25 years.
- **Fairmount Park Women's Volleyball League,** 610-565-1807—Volleyball competition for women.
- **Frontrunners Philadelphia,** 215-545-6990—Gay and lesbian running club.
- **Gay and Lesbian Lawyers of Philadelphia**, 215-627-9090; www.galloplaw.com. Call if you need a referral for a lawyer.
- **LayOut Ultimate Discs (LOUD),** www.layoutdiscs.org—Gay and lesbian ultimate Frisbee club.
- **Lavender Visions,** www.lavendervisions.com/married.html. Programs for lesbian and bisexual women, with excellent resources for married women who are coming out or seeking individual or group counseling.
- **Mazzoni Center**, 1201 Chestnut St, 3rd Fl, 215-563-0658; www.mazzonicenter.org—Free and anonymous HIV testing and counseling.
- **PA Gay and Lesbian Alliance for Political Action**, 1315 Spruce St, 215-375-0852—The group meets on the second Tuesday of each month at the William Way Center.
- **PFLAG Philadelphia**, P.O. Box 15711, Philadelphia, PA 19103, 215-572-1833; www.pflagphila.org—Parents, Families and Friends of Lesbians and Gays.
- **Philadelphia Family Pride**, 215-844-3360—Social events for gay and lesbian parents and their children.
- **Philadelphia Lesbian and Gay Task Force**, 215-772-2000—Works on political issues and has a hotline for violence directed at gays and lesbians. Makes use of volunteers.
- **Safeguard: A Men's Health Project**, 1211 Chestnut St, 215-496-9560—Non-profit community health organization promoting a healthy lifestyle for gay men through workshops, HIV testing, community programs, and health information.
- **Sisterspace**, 215-476-8856; www.sisterspace.org—Organizes social events for women, a volleyball league, and a women of color forum.
- **William Way Lesbian, Gay, Bisexual Transgender (GLBT) Community Center**, 1315 Spruce St, 215-732-2220; www.waygay.org—Home to a number of community groups and host of many regular events.
- **Women in Transition Hotline**, 215-751-1111—Support for lesbians in abusive relationships.

Bookstores

- **Giovanni's Room**, 345 S 12th St, 215-923-2960; www.giovannisroom.com—One of the oldest gay bookstores in the country, this little nook offers a wide selection of gay, lesbian, and feminist texts. Women's book discussion group meets at 7:00 pm on the first Sunday of each month.

Publications and Media

- **Philadelphia Gay News**— www.philadelphiagaynews.com. One of the oldest gay publications in the country.
- **WXPN 88.5**—www.xpn.org. Hosts two programs targeted to gays and lesbians: "Amazon Country" and "Qline."
- **Visions Today Magazine**— www.visionstoday.com. New gay & lesbian lifestyle magazine.

Annual Events

- **Blue Ball**—A circuit party weekend fundraiser held every January. 215-731-9255; www.blueballphilly.com.
- **LadyFest**—An annual four-day festival in March showcasing women's activism through the arts. www.ladyfestphilly.org
- **Equality Forum**—Formerly PrideFest America, the GLBT conference and festival takes place every April. 215-732-TEST; www.equalityforum.com.
- **LGBT Pride Parade & Festival**—Held in June each year. 215-875-9288; www.phillypride.org.
- **Philadelphia Gay & Lesbian Theater Festival**—Held in June each year. www.phillygaylesbiantheaterfest.org.
- **Philadelphia International Gay & Lesbian Film Festival**—Held every July, it's the biggest gay film festival on the East Coast. www.phillyfests.com/piglff.

Websites

- **Gay and Lesbian Yellow Pages**—www.qlyp.com
- **Greater Philadelphia Tourism Bureau**— www.gophila.com/gay. Information about GLBT events, culture, and community in Philly.
- **Out in Philadelphia**—www.outinphiladelphia.com. Community website with gay and lesbian news, personals, listings, travel information, and health advice.
- **Philadelphia Gay Singles**—http://philadelphiagaysingles.com. Online meeting place for Philly's gay and lesbians.
- **QueerConnections**, www.phillyqueerconnections.com—Queer Connections (QC) is a social group for women in their twenties who are queer (lesbian, bisexual, gay, or transgendered), women who are questioning their sexuality, and friends of queers (who are straight but not narrow).

- **William Way Community Center**— www.waygay.org. Website with information on a number of community groups and gay & lesbian events.
- **Craigslist**—philadelphia.craigslist.org. General community site (for straights, gays, and everyone else) that includes local "women seeking women" and "men seeking men" personal pages.

Venues—Gay

- **12th Air Command** · 254 S 12th St · 215-545-8088 · www.12thair.com
- **Bike Stop** · 206 S Quince St · 215-627-1662 · www.thebikestop.com
- **Bump** · 1234 Locust St · 215-732-1800
- **Glam** · 52 S 2nd St · 267-671-0840 · http://glamphilly.com
- **Key West** · 207 S Juniper St · 215-545-1578 · www.clubphenomenal.com
- **Pure Nightclub** · 1221 St James Pl · 215-735-5772 · www.purephilly.com
- **Shampoo** (Fridays) · 417 N 8th St · 215-922-7500 · www.shampooonline.com
- **Uncle's** · 1220 Locust St · 215-546-6660
- **Westbury** · 261 S 13th St · 215-546-5170 · www.thewestburybar.com
- **Woody's** · 202 S 13th St · 215-545-1893 · www.woodysbar.com

Venues—Lesbian

- **Elevate** (4th Sat) · 207 S Juniper St · 215-545-1578 · www.elevatephilly.com
- **Girl** (3rd Sat) · 200 S 12th St · 215-574-2110 · www.phillygirlparty.com
- **Pure Party Girl** (1st Fri) · 1221 St James Pl · 215-735-5772 · www.ladies2000.com
- **Sisters** · 1320 Chancellor St · 215-735-0735 · www.sistersnightclub.com
- **The Fabric** (2nd Sat) · 1716 Chestnut St · 215-568-6969 · www.thefabric.net

Venues—Mixed

- **Goosebumps Lounge** · 611 S Seventh St · 215-923-4481 · www.goosebumpslounge.com
- **Tavern on Camac** · 243 S Camac St · 215-545-0900 · www.tavernoncamac.com

Hotels

Philly has a tremendous range of options for you, whether you're looking to put up a relative for the weekend or want a luxurious romantic getaway with your SO. For pure opulence, you could do a lot worse than the recently remodeled Ritz-Carlton or the ever-Tory Rittenhouse. For a more budget-minded stay, you might check out the Alexander Inn or the Shippen Way. Sometimes during the spring and summer months, the city offers a special deal where you get one weekend night free if you book for both days.

Hotel	Address	Phone	Price	Rating	Map
Alexander Inn	Spruce St & 12th St	215-923-3535	99	★★★	3
Best Western City Center Hotel	501 N 22nd St	215-568-8300	110	★★	17
Best Western Independence Park Hotel	235 Chestnut St	215-922-4443	179	★★★★	4
Bond House	129 S 2nd St	215-923-8523	135		4
Carlyle Hotel	1425 Poplar St	215-978-9934	50		18
Chestnut Hill Hotel	8229 Germantown Ave	215-242-5905	129		27
Club Quarters	1628 Chestnut St	215-282-5000	by membership or web rate		2
Comfort Inn Downtown/Historic Area	100 N Columbus Blvd	215-627-7900	134	★★★★	4
Crowne Plaza	1800 Market St	215-561-7500	225	★★★★	2
Divine Tracy Hotel	20 S 36th St	215-382-4310	47		14
Doubletree Hotel	237 S Broad St	215-893-1600	164	★★★	2
Embassy Suites	1776 Benjamin Franklin Pkwy	215-561-1776	212	★★★★	2
Four Seasons Hotel	1 Logan Sq	215-963-1500	280	★★★★★	2
Hampton Inn	1301 Race St	215-665-9100	132		3
Hilton Garden Inn	1100 Arch St	215-923-0100	174	★★★	3
Hilton Inn at Penn	3600 Sansom St	215-222-0200	209	★★★★	14
Holiday Inn	10th St & Packer Ave	215-755-9500	129		12
Holiday Inn	400 Arch St	215-923-8660	170	★★★	4
Holiday Inn Express	1305 Walnut St	215-735-9300	132	★★	3
Hotel Windsor	1700 Benjamin Franklin Pkwy	215-981-5678	139	★★★	2
Hyatt Regency	201 S Columbus Blvd	215-928-1234	152	★★★★	4
Latham Hotel	135 S 17th St	215-563-7474	159	★★★	2
Lowes Philadelphia Hotel	1200 Market St	215-627-1200	179	★★★★	3
Marriott Courtyard Philadelphia Downtown	21 Juniper St	215-496-3200	179		2
Omni Hotel at Independence Park	401 Chestnut St	215-925-0000	209	★★★★	4
Park Hyatt Philadelphia at the Bellevue	Broad St & Walnut St	215-893-1234	215	★★★★	2
Parker Spruce Hotel	261 S 13th St	215-735-2300	45		3
Penn's View Hotel	14 N Front St	215-922-7600	208		4
Philadelphia Marriott Downtown	1201 Market St	215-625-2900	254	★★★★	3
Residence Inn Philadelphia City Center	1 E Penn Sq	215-557-0005	209		2
The Rittenhouse Hotel	210 W Rittenhouse Sq	215-546-9000	235	★★★★	2
The Ritz-Carlton Philadelphia	10 Ave of the Arts	215-523-8000	349	★★★★★	2
Sheraton Rittenhouse Square	18th St & Locust St	215-546-9400	175	★★★★	2
Sheraton Society Hill	1 Dock St (2nd St & Walnut St)	215-238-6000	169	★★★★	4

Sheraton University City Hotel	36th St & Chestnut St	215-387-8000	206	★★★	14
Sofitel Philadelphia	120 S 17th St	215-569-8300	194	★★★★	2
Spruce Hill Manor	331 S 46th St	215-472-2213	123		13
Travelodge	1227 Race St	215-564-2888	119		3
Wyndham Philadelphia at Franklin Plaza	17th St & Race St	215-448-2000	159	★★★	2
The Westin Philadelphia	99 S 17th St & Liberty Pl	215-563-1600	239	★★★★	2

Bed & Breakfast	Address	Phone	Price	Rating	Map
Anam Cara Bed & Breakfast	52 Wooddale Ave	215-242-4327	118		26
Antique Row Bed & Breakfast	341 S 12th St	215-592-7802	100		3
Bed & Breakfast Center City	1804 Pine St	215-735-1137	125		2
Cornerstone Bed & Breakfast	3300 Baring St	215-387-6065	115		14
Gaskill House Bed & Breakfast	312 Gaskill St	215-413-0669	175		4
The Morris House	225 S 8th St	215-922-2446	159		3
Rittenhouse Bed & Breakfast	1715 Rittenhouse Sq	215-546-6500	205		2
Silverstone Bed & Breakfast	8840 Stenton Ave	215-242-1471	95		27
Ten Eleven Clinton B&B	1011 Clinton St	215-923-8144	145		3
Tokio Bed & Breakfast	124 Lombard St	215-922-2515	70		4

24-Hour Services

Pharmacies
	Phone	Map
CVS		
1405 S 10th St	215-465-2130	7
1826 Chestnut St	215-972-0909	3
1901 W Oregon Ave	215-551-8265	9
Pathmark		
3021 Grays Ferry Ave	215-551-7284	5
330 E Oregon Ave	215-462-3450	11
Rite-Aid		
2017 S Broad St	215-467-0850	10
2301 Walnut St	215-636-9634	1
Walgreens		
2014 S Broad St	215-551-3818	10

Groceries
	Phone	Map
Pathmark		
3021 Grays Ferry Ave	215-551-7275	5
330 E Oregon Ave	215-462-4750	11

Copying
	Phone	Map
FedEx Kinko's		
1201 Market St	215-923-2520	3
2001 Market St	215-561-5170	1
Taws		
1527 Walnut St	215-563-8742	2

Gyms
	Address	Phone	Map
Pennsport Athletic Club	325 Bainbridge St	215-627-4900	8

Locksmiths
	Phone	Map
Houdini Lock & Safe	215-336-7233	7
Locksmith 24 Hour	215-564-5214	2
Locksmith 24 Hour	215-574-8830	4
Locksmith 24 Hour	215-545-8453	7

Plumbers
	Phone
Garry's Plumbing, Heating & Mechanical	215-546-5501
Garry's Plumbing, Heating & Mechanical	215-546-5573
Goodman Plumbing	215-455-1000
Philadelphia's Local Plumber	215-739-4343
Plumbing	215-545-7330
Plumbing	215-878-8280
Plumbing	215-743-1755
Plumbing	215-333-8780
Plumbing	215-329-8008
Plumbing	215-745-9552
Plumbing	215-612-0500
Plumbing	215-612-0500
Plumbing	215-425-4454
Plumbing (Emergency Service)	215-425-4737
Plumbing Works	215-329-4993
Plumbing Works	215-473-1610
Sam Wexler Plumbing	215-934-7811
Sam Wexler Plumbing	215-474-8442
Sam Wexler Plumbing	215-922-5555
Roto-Rooter Plumbing & Drain Service	215-744-4207
Roto-Rooter Plumbing & Drain Service	215-545-4509
Roto-Rooter Plumbing & Drain Service	215-535-7644
Roto-Rooter Plumbing & Drain Service	215-849-5067
Roto-Rooter Plumbing & Drain Service	215-763-2021
Roto-Rooter Plumbing & Drain Service	215-925-3079
VJC Mechanical	267-467-1676

Philly is essentially a city of landmarks, some obvious, some a little more esoteric. Some of the city's historic moneymakers are located in the recently refurbished **Mall of Independence**, which houses the **Liberty Bell**, the newly opened **National Constitution Center**, and **Independence Hall**, where the Declaration of Independence was first signed. They are all well worth seeing, if only so you can direct friends and family members when they visit.

Whilst in the Old City, you can also check out **Christ Church** (founded in 1695) and **Franklin Court**, which has an interesting museum of the old guy and a frame replica of his original house. With a great view of the city, the **William Penn Statue** sits high atop **City Hall**, which is also a pretty spectacular structure.

In the artistic realm, the oft-endowed **Philadelphia Museum of Art** has an extensive permanent collection. Nearby is the free **Rodin Museum**, where you can do your best to emulate *The Thinker*. If you have children in tow and want to reward them for trekking through art museums, they'll love the **Franklin Institute**, which has both an IMAX theater and planetarium.

Armchair athletes should check out the brand spanking new **Lincoln Financial Field** and **Citizens Bank Park** offering high-end amenities for fans of the Eagles and Phillies.

Map 1 • City Center West

Franklin Institute	222 N 20th St • 215-448-1200	IMAX, Planetarium and lots of kiddie-fare.

Map 2 • Rittenhouse / Logan Circle

Academy of Music	Broad & Locust Sts • 215-893-1940	Scorsese shot the opening to *The Age of Innocence* here.
Allow Me Statue	17th & Locust Sts	Biz-dude holding umbrella is always creepy.
City Hall	Broad St & Market Sts	Perhaps the best-looking building in the city.
Clothespin Sculpture	15th & Market Sts	Obviously, a take on the ills of modern society. Or something.
Friends Center	15th & Cherry Sts	Check out the helicopters landing and taking off.
Grip the Raven	1901 Vine St • 215-567-7710	Inspiration to Poe and Dickens, at the Free Library.
Harriet's Nervous System	15th & Vine Sts	Medical college entrance still displays her—since 1888.
Love Park	15th St & JFK Blvd • 215-636-1666	The skater Mecca of the world, if only it were legal.
Mary Dyer Statue	15th & Cherry Sts	Hanged Quaker martyr makes for moving piece.
The Masonic Temple	1 N Broad St • 215-988-1900	Giant staircases and oak appointments.
Packard Building	15th & Chestnut Sts	Shyamalanadingdong turned it into a train station for *Unbreakable*. Meh.
Rittenhouse Fountain	B/w 18th & 19th and Locust & Walnut Sts	The perfect wade-to-your-pant-cuffs pool to take the edge off the summer.
St Mark's Church	1625 Locust St • 215-735-1416	Scenes from *Fallen* were shot here. Too bad no one saw the movie.
Swann Fountain	Logan Cir	Summertime, kids swim for free.
Wachovia Building	Broad & Sansom Sts	Parts of *Trading Places* were shot here. Wowee.
William Penn Statue	Broad & Market Sts • 215-686-6263	We will never dress him in Flyers' gear again.

Map 3 • City Center East

Antique Row	Pine St b/w 12th & 9th Sts	Furniture, books, knick-knacks of all kinds.
The Gibbet	15 S 7th St • 215-685-4830	Designed to hold an executed criminal for display. Classy.
Kahn Park	Pine St/11 St	Named for revered Philly architect.
Lord & Taylor Building	13th St & Market St • 215-241-9000	Formerly the Wannamaker's empire, also home of *Mannequin* (*1 & 2!*)
Mask & Wig Club	310 S Quince St • 215-923-4229	Penn's all-male musical comedy group.
Mikveh Israel Cemetary	Spruce St b/w 8th & 9th Sts	Oldest Jewish cemetery in Philly, 1738.

General Information · **Landmarks**

Paul Green School of Rock	1320 Race St · 215-988-9338	10-year-olds playing Zeppelin, AC/DC. Rock out!
Pennsylvania Hospital	800 Spruce St · 215-829-3000	Since 1751, the Nation's oldest. How cute.
Reading Terminal Market	12th & Arch Sts · 215-922-2317	More Amish food than you can shake a stick at.
Washington Square Park	Walnut St b/w 6th & 7th Sts	Tomb of the Unknown Soldier of the Revolution.
William Penn Statue	Broad & Market Sts · 215-686-6263	We will never dress him in Flyers' gear again.
Woman in Window Statue	Chestnut St b/w 6th & 7th Sts	Eerie woman-in-white always peers out sadly.

Map 4 · Old City / Society Hill

American Philosophical Society	104 S 5th St	Kant figure out Schopenhaver? That's off the Hook.
Arch Street Drag	Arch & 3rd Sts	Transformed into old-world Cinci for *Beloved*.
Ben Franklin Bust	Arch & 2nd Sts	Made from 80,000 donated pennies. No joke.
Chestnut Mall	Chestnut St & Columbus Blvd	Exploring the well-lived life of William Penn.
Christ Church Grounds	5th & Arch Sts	Where BF is buried—amongst other notables.
Christ Church Park	2nd & Market Sts · 215-922-1695	Dogs, squirrels and OC workers on lunch breaks.
Dream Garden mosaic	601-45 Walnut St	Maxfield Parrish's creation dominates the lobby.
Elfreth's Alley	b/w Front & 2nd Sts and Arch & Race Sts	The oldest residential street in the US, baby.
Empty Lot	B/w Front & Second Sts and South & Lombard Sts	It could be the biggest real-estate waste in the city.
Franklin Court	Market St b/w 3rd and 4th Sts · 215-965-2305	Museum and "ghost" sculpture of Franklin's digs.
The Gazela	Columbus Blvd & Market St	Many masted boat is more than a century old.
Independence Visitor's Center	6th & Market Sts · 215-965-7676	Learn about Philly's rich cultural history—and use the free public pit stop if you are in need.
Independence Hall	Chestnut btn 5th and 6th · 215-965-2305	Where our forefathers gathered to watch porn.
Liberty Bell	Market St btn 5th and 6th · 215-965-2305	The only thing anyone ever visits us.
Lost Highways Archive	307 Market St · 215 925 3569	Museum dedicated to living on the road.
Mall of Independence	From Walnut to Arch Sts b/w 5th and 6th	The motherlode of Philly's historic tourism.
Mikveh Israel	44 N 4th St · 215-922-5446	Oldest Jewish congregation and an impressive set of scrolls.
Mother Bethel AME Church	6th & Pine Sts	Enclosed section of truly creepy-looking grave markers.
National Constitution Center	525 Arch St · 215-409-6600	A Presidential wonderland.
Penn's Landing Marina	Penn's Landing & Columbus Blvd	Gaze at the $30 million yachts and feel crappy about yourself.
Real World House	249 251 Arch St	The very house those brats used to flop in when they weren't getting wasted.
Second Presbyterian Church	3rd & Arch Sts	Sections of the burial grounds reserved for Africans.
St Peter's Episcopal Church	313 Pine St · 215-925-5968	Est. 1761, so you know it's gotta be good.
St Joseph's Catholic Church	321 Willings Aly · 215-923-1733	Stunning stained glass a testament to old-world can-do.
US Mint	151 N Independence Mall E · 215-408-0112	It's surprisingly easy to stand outside and look suspicious.
WYSP	101 S Independence Mall E · 215-625-9460	Crappy rock station often gives out schwag here.

Map 5 · Gray's Ferry West

Warfield Breakfast Express	Warfield & Reed Sts	Failed mob hit on Joey Ciancaglini caught on tape.

Map 7 · Southwark West

CAPA High School	901 S Broad St · 215-952-2462	Where The Roots first met up and started rollin'.
Cous' Little Italy	901 S 11th St	Angelo Bruno, ancient Don, eats his last meal here before getting whacked.
Lady Day Placard	Broad & South Sts	Billie was born in Philly, remember.
Vulpine Athletic Club	12th & Federal Sts	Where James "Jimmy Brooms" Diadorrio met his ugly demise.

(203)

Map 8 · Bella Vista / Queen Village

Emanuel Evangelical Lutheran Church	1001 S 4th St · 215-336-1444	Saving Philly souls since 1868.
Fabric Row	4th St b/w Bainbridge & Catharine Sts	From prom dresses to curtain rods.
Firefighter Statue	Queen St b/w Front & 2nd Sts	Don't miss the weird-looking Dalmatian at his feet.
Fleischer Art Memorial	719 Catharine St · 215-922-3456	Art classes, exhibits, galleries on the DL.
Gum Tree	3rd & South Sts	Nature's own used chewing gum depository.
Hovering Bodies	Corner of 4th & Catharine Sts	School kids' body molds now disintegrated into horror movie.
Italian Market	9th St b/w Bainbridge St & Washington Ave	You kiddin' me? Cheese, meat, bread, pasta.
Jefferson Square Park/ Sacks Rec Center	Washington Ave b/w 4th & 5th Sts	Hoops, soccer and a pool to take a plunge afterward.
Lebanon Cemetary	9th & Passyunk Sts	Early African burial ground, but the bodies have been moved.
Mario Lanza Park	Queen St b/w 2nd & 3rd Sts	Great doggie run and film series.
Mummers Museum	1100 S 2nd St · 215-336-3050	Philly's answer to Mardi Gras krewes.
Pat's & Geno's Showdown	9th St & Passyunk Ave	Stand in the crosswalk and watch humanity degrade itself by the second.
Rizzo Ice Skating Rink	1101 S Front St · 215-685-1593	Proud home of the Rink Rats.
Sarcone's	758 S 9th St · 215-922-0445	Get your bread on and don't pass up the pizza.
Sherlock Holmes Mural	2nd St b/w Christian & Moyamensing Sts	Hidden maze of characters and images abound.
Weccocoe Playground	Catharine St b/w 4th & 5th Sts	Best public tennis court in CC.

Map 9 · Point Breeze / West Passyunk

Melrose Diner Parking Lot	1501 Snyder Ave · 215-467-6644	Site of brutal mob hit of Frank Baldino.

Map 12 · Stadiums

Chickie's Hit	Curtain & Juniper Sts	Frank Narducci shot 10 times after a court date.
Citizens Bank Park	1 Citizens Bank Wy	Home of the ever-fumblin' Phillies.
Lincoln Financial Field	1020 Pattison Ave	Where the Iggles call home.
Rocky Statue	3601 S Broad St	The Stallion shall always remain in triumph here.

Map 13 · West Philly

Pinwheel House	42nd & Wallace Sts	A folk-art explosion of pinwheels and whirligigs.

Map 14 · University City

30th St Station Bathrooms	Market & 30th Sts · 215-349-3196	Re-create *Witness* and pretend you're a little Amish child.
Biopond	3740 Hamilton Wk	A quiet lunch spot replete with benches and fishpond.
Face Fragment	35th & Market Sts	Half a face with Roman nose, no eyes.
Hill Square	34th & Walnut Sts	Great view of the city, and a series of benches upon which to recline.
Self-Immolation Point	34th & Locust Sts	Where artist/activist Kathy Chang burned herself to death.
Split Button	Btwn 34 & 36 Sts & Locust & Spruce Sts	Oldenburg's giant broken button a keeper.

General Information • **Landmarks**

Map 16 • Art Museum West

Art Museum Steps	26th & Benjamin Franklin Pkwy	Recreate Rocky's infamous romp like all the other jackasses.
Giant Slide	33rd & Oxford Sts • 215-765-4325	Smith Playground's single greatest attraction.
Lloyd Hall	Boathouse Row	Scullers and skaters share the space.

Map 17 • Art Museum East

Eastern State Penitentiary	22nd St & Fairmount Ave • 215-236-5111	Take a tour, buy a t-shirt. Get the daylights scared out ot you.
Rodin Museum	22nd & Benjamin Franklin Pkwy 215-763-8100	Get your Thinker on.
The Thinker	22nd St & Benjamin Franklin Pkwy • 215-568-6020	We know, we know. A cliché. But it's still cool.

Map 18 • Lower North Philly

Metropolitan Opera House	Broad St & Fairmount Ave	Former opera house used in fine *12 Monkeys* film.

Map 19 • Northern Liberties

Liberty Lands Park	3rd & Poplar Sts	Recently reclaimed from junkies and winos.
St John Neumann Shrine	1019 N 5th St • 215-627-3080	Shrine of canonized Philly Bishop.

Map 22 • Manayunk

Kelpius Cave	Sumac St & Wissahickon Park	Historic Monk retreat now used for secret bong shelter.

Map 23 • East Falls

Laurel Hill Cemetery	3822 Ridge Ave • 215-228-8200	Ancient, Victorian-style, and oddly beautiful.

The Northeast

The Boulevard	Roosevelt Blvd	Named after Teddy, Roosevelt Boulevard is a bustling bevy of shopping, eating, and sight seeing stop-offs.
Burlhome Park	Cottman & Central Aves • 215-636-1666	Run, jog, or walk through this Northeast beauty.
Flyer's Skate Zone	10990 Decatur Rd • 215-618-0050	Book private parties and skate where the Philadelphia Flyers practice.
Knowlton Mansion	8001 Verree Rd	Designed in 1879, Knowlton Mansion now hosts private events and weddings amidst breathtaking Victorian design.
Nabisco Factory	Comly Rd & Roosevelt Ave	Smell the unmistakable scent of Nilla Wafers from miles away.
Northeast Philadelphia Airport (PNE)	8000 Essington Ave • 215-677-5592	Pennsylvania's third-busiest airport.
Pennypack Creek Park	8600 Verree Rd	The park covers 1,334 acres in Northeast Philadelphia along Pennypack Creek.

19118

27

19150

19138

19126

19111

19119

25

19128

19144

24

19141

19120

19127 21

22

23

19129

19140

19004

19131

15

19132

19133

19134

19137

19124

19121

19122

19149

16

19130

17

18

19123 19

20
19125

19139

13 19104 14

19103

19107

19106

1 2

3

4

19102

19146

6

5

7

19147

8

Delaware River

19143

9

10

11

19142

19145

19148

12

19153

**NEW
JERSEY**

Branch	Address	Zip	Map
30th Street Train	2955 Market St	19104	14
B Free Franklin	316 Market St	19106	4
Castle	1713 S Broad St	19148	10
Chestnut Hill	8227 Germantown Ave	19118	27
Continental	615 Chestnut St	19106	3
David P Richardson	5209 Greene St	19144	24
East Falls	4130 Ridge Ave	19129	23
Fairmount	1939 Fairmount Ave	19130	17
Fairmount	900 N 19th St	19130	17
Girard Avenue	905 N Broad St	19123	18
John Wanamaker	1234 Market St	19107	3
Kensington	1602 Frankford Ave	19125	20
Lancaster Avenue	4123 Lancaster Ave	19104	13
Land Title Bldg	100 S Broad St	19110	2
Manayunk	4431 Main St	19127	21
Market Square	7782 Crittenden St	19118	26
Middle City	2037 Chestnut St	19103	1
Mount Airy	6711 Germantown Ave	19119	25
Penn Center	1500 John F Kennedy Blvd	19102	2
Penn's Landing Retail	622 S 4th St	19147	8
Philadelphia Main Office	2970 Market St	19104	14
Point Breeze Postal Store	2437 S 23 St	19145	9
Roxborough Postal Store	6184 Ridge Ave	19128	21
Schuylkill	2900 Grays Ferry Ave	19146	5
Snyder Avenue	58 Snyder Ave	19148	11
Southwark	925 Dickinson St	19147	8
University City	228 S 40th St	19104	13
William Penn Annex	900 Market St	19107	3

Map 1

	Address	Last pick-up
Drop Box	100 N 20th St	6:00p
Drop Box	2008 Walnut St	4:00p
Drop Box	2037 Chestnut St	7:00p
Drop Box	2133 Arch St	7:00p
Drop Box	222 N 20th St	4:00p
Drop Box	2400 Market St	7:00p
Drop Box	261 S 22nd St	7:00p
FedEx	2001 Market St	7:00p,
Kinko's		3:00p

Map 2

	Address	Last pick-up
Drop Box	1 S Penn Sq	7:00p
Drop Box	100 S Broad St	7:00p
Drop Box	121 S Broad St	5:00p
Drop Box	1429 Walnut St	7:00p
Drop Box	1500 Chestnut St	5:15p,
		3:00p
Drop Box	1500 Market St	5:00p
Drop Box	1505 Race St	4:00p
Drop Box	1515 Arch St	6:00p
Drop Box	1528 Walnut St	7:00p
Drop Box	1600 John F Kennedy Blvd	7:00p
Drop Box	1600 Market St	7:00p
Drop Box	1601 Market St	7:00p
Drop Box	1608 Walnut St	7:00p
Drop Box	1616 Walnut St	7:00p
Drop Box	1617 John F Kennedy Blvd	7:00p
Drop Box	1628 John F Kennedy Blvd	7:00p
Drop Box	1635 Market St	7:00p
Drop Box	1650 Arch St	7:00p
Drop Box	1650 Market St	7:00p
Drop Box	1700 Market St	7:00p
Drop Box	1717 Arch St	7:00p
Drop Box	1735 Market St	7:00p
Drop Box	1760 Market St	7:00p
Drop Box	1800 John F Kennedy Blvd	6:00p
Drop Box	1801 Market St	7:00p
Drop Box	1801 Walnut St	7:00p
Drop Box	1815 John F Kennedy Blvd	7:00p
Drop Box	1818 Market St	7:00p
Drop Box	1845 Walnut St	7:00p
Drop Box	1900 Market St	5:00p
Drop Box	200 S Broad St	7:00p
Drop Box	216 S 15th St	7:00p
Drop Box	222 N 17th St	6:00p
Drop Box	230 N Broad St	6:00p
Drop Box	245 N 15th St	7:00p
Drop Box	260 S Broad St	6:00p
Drop Box	30 S 17th St	7:00p
FedEx	216 S 16th St	7:00p,
Kinko's		3:00p

Map 3

	Address	Last pick-up
Drop Box	1015 Chestnut St	7:00p
Drop Box	1100 Walnut St	6:00p
Drop Box	1234 Market St	7:00p
Drop Box	20 N 8th St	7:00p
Drop Box	210 W Washington Sq	7:00p
Drop Box	211 S 9th St	7:00p
Drop Box	615 Chestnut St	7:00p
Drop Box	700 Arch St	7:00p
Drop Box	701 Market St	7:00p
Drop Box	714 Market St	7:00p
Drop Box	718 Arch St	7:00p
Drop Box	834 Chestnut St	7:00p
Drop Box	900 Market St	7:00p
Drop Box	925 Chestnut St	7:00p
FedEx	1201 Market St	7:00p,
Kinko's		4:00p

Map 4

	Address	Last pick-up
Drop Box	1 New Market Sq	6:00p
Drop Box	100 Chestnut St	7:00p
Drop Box	190 N Independence Mall	7:00p
Drop Box	200 Chestnut St	5:30p
Drop Box	21 S 5th St	7:00p
Drop Box	325 Chestnut St	7:00p
Drop Box	399 Market St	7:00p
Drop Box	437 Chestnut St	7:00p
Drop Box	510 Walnut St	7:00p
Drop Box	600 Arch St	5:30p
Drop Box	600 Chestnut St	6:30p
Drop Box	600 Market St	7:00p
Drop Box	601 Market St	5:30p
Drop Box	605 Walnut St	7:00p
Drop Box	9 N 3rd St	3:30p

Map 8

	Address	Last pick-up
Drop Box	614 8th St	5:00p
Drop Box	629 S 4th St	6:30p

Map 10

	Address	Last pick-up
Drop Box	1713 S Broad St	6:00p

Map 11

	Address	Last pick-up
Drop Box	2000 S Sawson St	6:00p,
		2:00p

Map 13

	Address	Last pick-up
Drop Box	228 S 40th St	7:00p
Drop Box	3900 Delancey St	7:00p
Drop Box	3900 Woodland Ave	7:00p
Drop Box	3907 Walnut St	7:00p
Drop Box	3930 Chestnut st	6:00p
FedEx	3923 Walnut St	7:00p
Kinko's		

Map 14

	Address	Last pick-up
Drop Box	133 S 36th St	6:30p
Drop Box	2955 Market St	7:00p

Drop Box	2970 Market St	7:00p
Drop Box	3001 Market St	7:00p
Drop Box	3149 Chestnut St	6:30p
Drop Box	3340 Walnut St	7:00p
Drop Box	3400 Civic Center Blvd	7:00p
Drop Box	3401 Market St	6:00p
Drop Box	3535 Market St	7:00p
Drop Box	3600 Spruce St	7:00p
Drop Box	3620 Locust Wk	7:00p
Drop Box	3624 Market St	7:00p
Drop Box	3730 Walnut St	7:00p
Drop Box	3731 Walnut St	4:45p,
		3:00p
Drop Box	415 Curie Blvd	7:00p
Drop Box	418 Service Dr	7:00p
Drop Box	421 Curie Blvd	7:00p

Map 17

	Address	Last pick-up
Drop Box	2000 Hamilton St	7:00p
FedEx	1816 Spring Garden St	7:00p,
Kinko's		2:30p

Map 18

	Address	Last pick-up
Drop Box	1600 Callowhill St	4:30p
Drop Box	400 N Broad St	7:00p
Drop Box	401 N Broad St	7:00p

Map 19

	Address	Last pick-up
Drop Box	300 Spring Garden St	7:00p
Drop Box	820 Spring Garden	5:00p

Map 21

	Address	Last pick-up
Drop Box	10 Shurs Ln	6:00p
Drop Box	161 Leverington Ave	6:30p
Drop Box	6180 Ridge Ave	6:30p

Map 22

	Address	Last pick-up
Drop Box	3901 Main St	6:30p

Map 23

	Address	Last pick-up
Drop Box	3300 Henry Ave	6:30p

Map 24

	Address	Last pick-up
Drop Box	100 E Penn Sq	6:00p
Drop Box	11 Penn Ctr	7:00p

Map 26

	Address	Last pick-up
Drop Box	12 W Wilow Grove Ave	5:00p
Drop Box	7782 Crittenden St	5:00p

Map 27

	Address	Last pick-up
Drop Box	8227 Germantown Ave	5:00p
Drop Box	9 W Highland Ave	6:30p

Dog Runs

Websites:
www.philadelphiapawsandclaws.com
www.devbob.com/dogparks
www.mainlinecanine.org
www.phillyfido.net
www.properpaws.com.

Overview

Dog lovers often grumble about the scarcity of dog runs and dog parks in Philly. But the shortage of dog-designated areas may stem from the fact that the city is really one mammoth dog run. Dogs are welcome in many restaurants, cafés, hotels, parks, and even some clothing stores (like Anthropologie and Urban Outfitters). Annual pooch events include the Paws for the Cause Cancer Walk (www.fccc.edu) and the Pet 'n Pal Walk (www.lmsports.com), both held in autumn.

Most dog runs prohibit aggressive dogs, and do not separate the small dogs from the larger dogs, making it a veritable doggie free-for-all. It goes without saying that you need to supervise your dog(s) at all times and pick up after them.

Dog Runs	Address	Comments
Ben Franklin Parkway	Ben Franklin Pkwy & 19th St	Beautiful downtown setting.
Carpenter Woods	Wissahickon & Mt Pleasant Aves	Woody paths, doggy swimming holes.
Dog Park	48th St & Chester St	Constantly in jeopardy due to UPenn expansion.
Eastern State Dog Pen	2124 Fairmount Ave	Designated fenced-in areas.
Horse & Carriage Rides	Market St & 5th St	Well-behaved dogs are welcome aboard the carriages.
Manuyunk Towpath and Canal	Main St b/w Green Ln & Lock St	Two-mile path along the canal.
Mario Lanza Park	Queen St & 2nd St	Nice neighborhood vibe.
Pennypack Park	Algon Ave & Bustleton Ave	1,600 acres for leashed dogs only.
Rittenhouse Square Park	Walnut St & 18th St	Leashed dogs only.
Schuylkill River Dog Run	25th St & Spruce Sts	Benches for you, fences for them.
Seger Dog Park	11th St & Lombard St	Open 6 am-10 pm, daily.
SPOAC Dog Run	Passyunk St & Dickinson St	South Philly dogs unite.
Univeristy City's Clark Park	48th St & Chester St	$50/year membership.
Washington Square Park	Walnut St & 6th St	Leashed dogs only. (Yeah, right.)

Arts & Entertainment • **Bookstores**

Overview

While not overwhelming, the Philly bookstore scene is solid, with purveyors of nearly every genre represented. We certainly have our share of giant, generic behemoth joints, including the ever-amusing one-upmanship battle between **Borders** and **Barnes & Noble** being waged downtown. Fortunately, there are also plenty of independent bookstores vying for your business.

General New/Used

Robin's is a good place to start, especially if you're looking for a new title. They also stage various readings and other activities to whet your literary appetite. **Joseph Fox** is smaller, more intimate, and a bit more high-end. For used books, **Big Jar** is a treasure trove of tomes, from straight literature to giant art books. South Philly's **Mostly Books** offers more of the same, but they also sell furniture and artifacts. PENN students flock to **House of Our Own** to get slightly off-campus.

Specialty

You can get caught up on all of your anarchy manifestos at **Wooden Shoe** and then learn to love one another again at **Garland of Letters**, which also provides a wafting aroma of fine incense. Design mavens can't get enough of **AIA**, which has a giant array of architecture tomes. The gay/lesbian scene is neatly served by **Giovanni's Room**, which also offers a hugely popular reading series. For untranslated Asian authors, **WJ Bookstore** in Chinatown has thousands of titles, primarily in Mandarin. Finally, to find out who really did do it, **Whodunit** has all the requisite answers.

Map 1 • Center City West

Book Corner	311 N 20th St	215-567-0527	New, rare and good used books in all genres.
Fat Jack's	2006 Sansom St	215-963-0788	Comic books.
Philadelphia Book Shop	2038 Locust St	215-546-7323	Antique books.

Map 2 • Rittenhouse / Logan Circle

AIA Book Store	117 S 17th St	215-569-3188	Architecture and design.
Barnes & Noble	1805 Walnut St	215-665-0716	Chain.
Borders	1 S Broad St	215-568-7400	Chain.
Brentanos	1325 Chestnut St	215-557-8443	Chain.
Chris's Corner	1940 Pine St	215-790-1727	Children's books.
Joseph Fox Book Shop	1724 Sansom St	215-563-4184	Independent.
Out of Time	1410 Chestnut St	215-569-3669	Comic books and paperbacks.
Whodunit Used & Rare Books	1931 Chestnut St	215-567-1478	New and used. Mysteries and thrillers.

Map 3 • Center City East

Bauman Rare Books	1215 Locust St	215-546-6466	Rare books.
Chinese Culture & Arts	126 N 10th St	215-928-1616	Chinese books.
Cookbook Stall	12th St & Arch St	215-923-3170	Cookbooks.
Giovanni's Room	345 S 12th St	215-923-2960	Lesbian, gay, bisexual, and transgender.
Hibberd's Books	1306 Walnut St	215-546-8811	General with emphasis on art.
Horizon Books	901 Market St	215-625-7955	African-American.
Jefferson Bookstore	1009 Chestnut St	215-955-7922	Medical and health science.
Robin's Book Store	108 S 13th St	215-735-1795	General, new, and liberal.
Waldenbooks	9th St & Market St	215-922-3647	Chain.
WJ Bookstore	1017 Arch St	215-592-9666	Chinese book store.

Map 4 • Old City / Society Hill

Big Jar	55 N 2nd St	215-574-1650	Used literary fiction, science philosophy and children's books.
The Book Trader	7 N 2nd St	215-925-0511	Discounted used , first editions, and out-of-print books.
Wooden Shoe Books	508 S 5th St	215-413-0999	Political.

Map 8 • Bella Vista / Queen Village

Atomic City Comics	642 South St	215-625-9613	Comics, Japanese animation, cult films and beyond.
Haneef's on South	832 South St	215-629-2665	African-American.
Molly's Cafe & Bookstore	1010 S 9th St	215-923-3367	Used books.
Mostly Books	529 Bainbridge St	215-238-9838	Used.

Map 13 • West Philly

House of Our Own	3920 Spruce St	215-222-1576	Politics, history, sociology, and multi-cultural topics.
Last Word Bookshop	3925 Walnut St	215-386-7750	Second-hand.

Map 14 • University City

Dolbey's Medical Bookstore	3742 Spruce St	215-222-6020	Textbooks, medical, and health and science reference.
Drexel University Bookstore	33rd St & Chestnut St	215-985-2860	College bookstore.
Penn Book Center	130 S 34th St	215-222-7600	University of Pennsylvania bookstore.
Penn Bookstore	3601 Walnut St	215-898-7595	Used and new textbooks.

Map 17 • Art Museum East

Bookhaven	2202 Fairmount Ave	215-235-3226	Used.

Map 18 • Lower North Philly

Community College of Philadelphia Book Store	1700 Spring Garden St	215-751-8152	Textbooks, reference and more.
Spring Garden Book Supply	1537 Spring Garden St	215-977-9411	College book store.

Map 26 • Mt Airy

Walk a Crooked Mile Books	7423 Devon St	215-242-0854	Used.

Map 27 • Chestnut Hill

Borders	8701 Germantown Ave	215-248-1213	Chain.
Gilmore's	43 E Chestnut Hill Ave	215-248-1763	Rare, Philadelphia history, Americana, decorative arts, art and photography.

In Center City, most of your options fall into two categories: 1. The art house Bermuda triangle of **Ritz** Theaters (**Bourse, Five,** and **East**). 2. The insidious, stadium-seating caverns of **The Riverview** multiplex, which we heartily encourage you to avoid, especially on weekends, unless you truly enjoy loud audiences of fifteen-year-olds hurling gummi concessions at your head. For variety, check out the **Roxy** theater, which also shows independent art-house fare in hugely uncomfortable seats.

A welcome addition to the Philly film scene has been **The Bridge** in University City, which, er, "bridges" the gap between the art-house scene and the mainstream theaters. They also allow you to buy your (pricey!) tix in advance and reserve your seat, which is perfect for big summer movie openings, if that's your thing.

Movie Theater	Address	Phone	Map
Adonis Theater	2026 Sansom St	215-557-9319	1
The Bridge: cinema de lux	40th St & Walnut St	215-386-3300	13
Cinemagic 3 at Penn	3925 Walnut St	215-222-5555	13
Roxy Theatre Philadelphia	2023 Sansom St	215-923-6699	1
Tuttleman IMAX Theater-Franklin Institute	222 N 20th St	215-448-1111	1
Ritz 5	214 Walnut St	215-925-7900	4
Ritz at the Bourse	400 Ranstead St	215-440-1181	4
Ritz East	125 S 2nd St	215-925-4535	4
United Artists Main Street 6	3720 Main St	215-482-6230	22
United Artists Riverview Stadium 17	1400 S Columbus Blvd	215-755-2353	8

Museums

The **Philadelphia Museum of Art** stands proudly as one of the five best art museums in the country; allow yourself several days to peruse their permanent collection. While you're in the area, you should definitely hit up the **Rodin Museum**, which is filled with sculpture from one of the 20th-century's most prominent artists. For the more literary-inclined, the **Rosenbach** has the original manuscript of Joyce's *Ulysses*, among other things. The **Mütter Museum** is filled to brimming with biological specimens.

Museum	Address	Phone	Map
The Academy of Natural Sciences Museum	1900 Benjamin Franklin Pkwy	215-299-1000	2
The African American Museum in Philadelphia	701 Arch St	215-574-0380	3
American Philosophical Society	104 S 5th St	215-440-3400	4
Atwater Kent Museum of Philadelphia	15 S 7th St	215-685-4830	3
Civil War Library and Museum	1805 Pine St	215-735-8196	2
Elfreth's Alley	126 Elfreth's Aly	215-574-0560	4
Fabric Workshop and Museum	1315 Cherry St	215-568-1111	3
Fireman's Hall Museum	147 N 2nd St	215-923-1438	4
The Franklin Institute	222 N 20th St	215-448-1200	1
Germantown Historical Society	5501 Germantown Ave	215-844-0514	24
Historic Philadelphia	123 Chestnut St	215-629-5801	4
The Historical Society of Pennsylvania	1300 Locust St	215-732-6200	3
Independence Seaport Museum	211 S Columbus Blvd	215-925-5439	4
The Johnson House Underground Railroad Museum	6306 Germantown Ave	215-438-1768	25
The Mario Lanza Museum	712 Montrose St	215-238-9691	8
Masonic Temple	1 N Broad St	215-988-1900	2
Mummers Museum	1100 S 2nd St	215-336-3050	8
Mütter Museum	19 S 22nd St	215-563-3737 x211	1
National Constitution Center	525 Arch St	215-409-6600	4
National Liberty Museum	321 Chestnut St	215-925-2800	4
National Museum of American Jewish History	Independence Mall E, 55 N 5th St	215-923-3811	4
New Hall Military Museum	320 Chestnut St		4
Philadelphia Jewish Sports Hall of Fame	401 S Broad St	215-446-3036	2
Philadelphia Museum of Art	Benjamin Franklin Pkwy & 26th St	215-763-8100	17
The Philadelphia Ship Preservation Guild	Columbus Blvd & Market St	215-238-0281	4
Please Touch Museum	210 N 21st St	215-963-0667	1
Polish American Cultural Center	308 Walnut St	215-922-1700	4
Rodin Museum	Benjamin Franklin Pkwy & 22nd St	215-763-8100	17
The Romanian Folk Art	1606 Spruce St	215-732-6780	2
The Rosenbach Museum & Library	2008-10 DeLancey Pl	215-732-1600	1
The TUSPM Shoe Museum	N 8th St b/w Race St & Cherry St	215-625-5243	3
United States Mint	151 N Independence Mall E	215-408-0112	4
University of Pennsylvania Museum of Archaeology and Anthropolgy	3260 South St	215-898-4000	14
Woodmere Art Museum	9201 Germantown Ave	215-247-0476	27

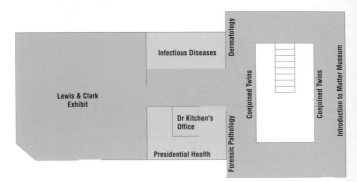

UPPER LEVEL

Dermatology

Infectious Diseases

Lewis & Clark Exhibit

Dr Kitchen's Office

Forensic Pathology

Presidential Health

Conjoined Twins

Conjoined Twins

Introduction to Mütter Museum

MAP 1

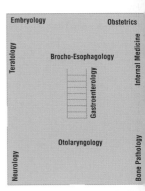

Embryology

Obstetrics

Teratology

Brocho-Esophagology

Internal Medicine

Gastroenterology

Otolaryngology

Neurology

Bone Pathology

LOWER LEVEL

General Information

NFT Map: 1
Address: 19 S 22nd St
Philadelphia, PA 19103
Phone: 215-563-3737
Website: www.collphyphil.org
Hours: Mon-Sun: 10 am-5 pm, every day of the year, except for Thanksgiving, Christmas, and New Year's Day.
Admission: Adults $8, Children & Seniors $5

Overview

Run by the College of Physicians of Philadelphia, the museum, which began as a teaching collection and resource of pathological specimens for doctors, has become a repelling (yet inexplicably appealing) attraction for the ordinary visitor.

In the early 1800s in the US, medical students were lectured for two years then sent out to try their newly acquired knowledge on patients. In Europe at the time, medical students worked with trained physicians and surgeons throughout their education, and Thomas Mütter decided that he wanted to bring European teaching pedagogies to the US. Mütter spent $20,000 of his own money to build a teaching collection of anatomical specimens, medical instruments, and pathological models that were used by generations of medical students as part of their training.

The most popular attraction remains the stomach-churning five-foot long colon, which was removed from a man who lived (and died) around the turn of the century (the colon contained over forty pounds of feces when removed). Other attractions include the cast of Chang and Eng, the original Siamese twins attached at the liver, and a collection of more than 2,000 objects that have been swallowed and removed. Did you ever wonder where Grover Cleveland's secret cheek tumor ended up? It's in a jar on the first floor.

As a warning, you'd be wise to forego that second helping of goulash before you visit, as some of the exhibited collection is definitely not for the weak-stomached. A key goal of the museum is to provide a look at the world of health and medicine as it existed in the 19th century, some of which can be very uncomfortable for contemporary visitors to behold. If you keep an open scientific mind, you'll likely learn a great deal about the modern history of medicine in the US.

How to Get There—Driving

Follow I-76 E (Schuylkill Expressway) to Exit 344 (I-676 E/Central Philadelphia—formerly Exit 38) and the stay in the middle lane in order to get on I-676 E. Merge right and take the first (quick) right hand exit, which is the Benjamin Franklin Parkway/23rd Street exit.

Follow the ramp to the second light and turn right on 21st Street. Stay on 21st Street for about seven blocks and then turn right on Chestnut Street and proceed one block to 22nd Street. The museum is located at 19 S 22nd Street, on the right-hand side of the street.

Parking

Good luck. Trawl the streets and keep your eyes peeled!

How to Get There—Mass Transit

Take the Green Line trolley to 22nd and Market Streets. From the stop, walk down 22nd Street (against the traffic), and the museum will be on your left. Eastbound bus routes 21 and 42 stop at 22nd and Chestnut Streets. Westbound bus routes 21, 42, and 12 stop at 22nd and Walnut Streets.

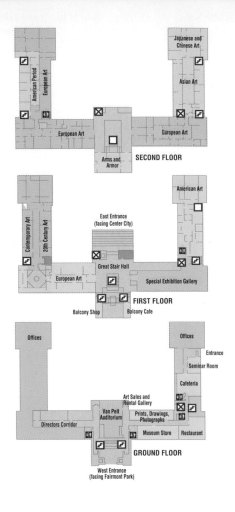

Japanese and Chinese Art

American Period Art

European Art

Asian Art

European Art

European Art

Arms and Armor

SECOND FLOOR

Contemporary Art

20th Century Art

American Art

East Entrance (facing Center City)

Great Stair Hall

European Art

Special Exhibition Gallery

FIRST FLOOR

Balcony Shop

Balcony Cafe

Offices

Offices

Entrance

Seminar Room

Cafeteria

Art Sales and Rental Gallery

Van Pelt Auditorium

Prints, Drawings, Photographs

Directors Corridor

Museum Store

Restaurant

GROUND FLOOR

West Entrance (facing Fairmont Park)

General Information

Address: 26th St & Benjamin Franklin Pkwy
                Philadelphia, PA 19130
Phone: 215-763-8100
Recorded   215-684-7500
 Information:
Website: www.philamuseum.org

Overview

We understand that it's difficult for tourists to resist running up the stairs in front of the Philadelphia Museum of Art and prancing around in a tight circle at the top with their fists raised in the air. Not every city has such a far-reaching pop culture icon. But as a Philly resident, you absolutely CANNOT do it. You lose that privilege the second you move here. Besides, the main purpose of your visit to PMA should be to view the 300,000 splendid art works inside the museum.

The Philly Museum of Art, now in its 125th year, is a world-renowned art institution, recognized for its vast permanent collections of East Asian, American, European, and contemporary art. As with many things in this city, our museum is regularly given short shrift compared to New York's incredible facilities, but the PMA stands on its own. The impressive permanent collections are ably supplemented by the museum's visiting exhibitions in fashion, contemporary art, photography, impressionism, pop art, sculpture, and Old Masters. What's more, just down the parkway sits the fabulous Rodin Sculpture garden, which is free to visit.

Special events take place throughout the week at the PMA. On Friday evenings, the austere Great Stair Hall is transformed into a pseudo-jazz club, with musicians beginning their sets at 5 pm, while visitors enjoy free wine and finger food to ease them into the weekend. The museum also offers lectures, classes, art classes for children, tours of the surrounding historic houses in Fairmount Park, trolley rides, and a guided Schuylkill stroll to picturesque Boathouse Row. Check the PMA website for a calendar of events.

How to Get There—Driving

From the west, take I-76 E and exit at Spring Garden Street. At end of exit ramp go left. Continue past the side of the museum, through the first traffic light and around Eakins Oval, staying in the far left lane. Turn left at the second traffic light and then bear right. Follow the sign for the Art Museum. After the sign, get in the far left lane and turn left at the first traffic light (Art Museum Drive). This will take you to the west entrance of the museum, where limited parking is available.

From the I-676 (Vine Street Expressway), take the Benjamin Franklin Parkway exit on your right. At the end of the exit ramp, turn right onto 22nd Street and get into the far left lane. Turn left onto the outside lanes of the Benjamin Franklin Parkway. Follow the sign for the Art Museum. After the sign, turn left onto Art Museum Drive. This will take you to the west entrance of the museum, where limited parking is available.

Parking

Free museum parking does exist, but in such a limited capacity that you might as well forget about it. Parking at Eakins Oval costs $7 for six hours and $10 for more than six hours, from 7 am until 7 pm daily. Upper terrace parking is available on the weekends from 7 am to 7 pm for $5-$10

How to Get There—Mass Transit

The PHLASH bus (215-925-TOUR) provides direct transportation from Center City and Penn's Landing to the Museum of Art between 10 am and 6 pm, May through November. SEPTA bus routes 7, 32, 38, 43, and 48 all serve the museum area.

General Information

NFT Map:	2
Address:	110 N Broad St (Galleries)
	Philadelphia, PA 19102
	1301 Cherry St (School)
	Philadelphia, PA 19107
Phone:	215-972-7600
Website:	www.pafa.org

Overview

The Pennsylvania Academy of the Fine Arts is an elderly and much-venerated institution: in 2005 it will be celebrating its 200th anniversary. This stunning architectural space is renowned for collecting, exhibiting, teaching, and promoting American fine art. The Academy is made up of a fine arts school, a public programs facility, various art galleries, and the country's oldest museum.

School of Fine Arts

The school has nearly 300 full-time students presently enrolled. The educational program includes a certificate course (painting, sculpture, and printmaking), a Bachelor of Fine Arts program (in conjunction with UPenn), and a one-year post-baccalaureate program (that allows students to work towards the two-year Masters of Fine Arts degree). The 2005-2006 academic year will also include a low-residency MFA, a summer post-BA, and other non-degree art programs. The school is expected to grow to 400 full-time students by 2007. Notable alumni include Philadelphia-born photographer Charles Sheeler, master painter Thomas Eakins, and oddball filmmaker David Lynch—who was so inspired by Philly's blighted glumness in the mid-'70s, he created *Eraserhead* as an homage.

The Galleries

Throughout its history, the gallery has held over 1,000 shows, including artists such as Edgar Degas, Judith Rothschild, and Andy Warhol. The gallery is also renowned for exhibiting the work of new and emerging local talents. Opening hours are Tuesday through Saturday, 10 am-5 pm and Sunday, 11 am-5 pm. September 18-January 8: Entry is free for kids, $5 for adults. January 9-September 17: Kids are free, while adults pay $7.

Museum tours are given at 11:30 am and 12.30 pm during the week, and at 12 pm and 1 pm on weekends. Tours are free with admission.

How to Get There—Driving

From I-95 S, follow signs to I-676. Take I-676 to the Broad Street exit, which will put you on 15th Street. Turn left onto Race Street, then right onto Broad Street. The Academy is one block down on the right.

From I-95 N and I-76 (Schuylkill Expressway), take I-76 W, and exit at I-676/Central Philadelphia. Follow directions above.

Parking

There are three pay lots on Academy grounds. Two are between 16th and Broad Street—one on Cherry Street and one on Race Street. The third is located at the northeast corner of Broad Street and Cherry Street.

How to Get There—Mass Transit

Ride the Market/Frankford Line to the 15th Street Station. Walk one block north to Arch Street, then one block east to Broad Street. Make a left on Broad Street. The Pennsylvania Academy is one block north.

Take the Broad Street line to the Race/Vine stop. Exit the station on Race and Broad Streets. Walk one block south (toward City Hall) on Broad Street. The Museum is at the northeast corner of Broad and Cherry Streets.

By Regional Rail, take any one of the lines to the Market East Train Station. Exit the station on Market Street and walk west (toward City Hall) until you reach Broad Street, then turn right. The Museum is one block along on the left.

When you suffer as much as we do (weather, sports teams, maddening wage tax) you need to be able to take a load off and drink your sorrows away. Have we got some ideas for you.

Beer

Nobody does beer quite as well as the Belgians, which is why **Monk's** remains as popular as ever. For a more Irish perspective, go to **Fergie's**; please be aware that there really is a Fergie there and he is, in fact, quite Irish. **Nodding Head**, Monk's sister location, offers up remarkably good home brews. **Ludwig's Garten** has all kinds of strange German braus that kick your ass. **McGillan's Ale House** packs them in during their ever-popular happy hours. **The Bishop's Collar** is where all the happening folks in the Art Museum area go to tie one on. And the joint that started a revolution in No-Libs is none other than the mighty **Standard Tap**.

Sports

With most of Philly's sports teams performing below par, it helps to suffer with several hundred of your sympathetic friends. **O'Neal's** is a good bet and you can even stay after the game to get your groove going. **Liberties** is pretty hard-core—not the place to take your kids. **12 Steps Down** has cheap beers, decent food, and movie-style projected TV on the wall. **Cheers to You** gives South Street denizens a place to gather, and the **Player's Pub** has a big following of diehards.

Swank

Getting drunk and watching fish is the norm at the **Tank Bar**. **The Happy Rooster** does well with in-town celebs. **The Ritz-Carlton Rotunda** offers the chance to drink martinis like a power-broker. **Zanzibar Blue** is always classy and provides sweet jazz with your cosmo. **Washington Square** gets you rolling right next to the park. **Paradigm**

has 21st-century bathrooms. **The Continental** remains where urban sophisticates like to show off the most, and **Southwark** gives you an opportunity to enjoy fine drinks in a TV-less environ.

Dive

How can you go wrong with a joint called **Doobie's**? The "smokiest bar in the city" award is a toss-up between the **Locust Bar** and **Dirty Frank's**, though their low-key, take-all-comers vibe will keep you representing there. South Passyunk's **Low** has become a hipster haven. **Tattooed Mom's** is a staple of drinking on South Street for natives, and **The Fire** keeps you drunk all day and then puts on bands at night.

Gay/Lesbian

Most the biggest alternative bars are in roughly the same area of Center City (lovingly referred to as the "Gayborhood"). **The 12th Air Command** has multiple floors of dancing fools getting up and getting down. **The Bike Stop** has pool tables and a big dance floor. **Woody's** is the mainstay of the gay community. At **Sisters**, every night is Ladies' Night. For lovers of cabaret, **L'Etage** offers an excellent show every week, and the oft-renamed **Bump** seems to finally have caught hold.

Music Venues

Philly's music scene is as varied and wide-open as you could hope for. For down and dirty indie bands, it doesn't get much better than the legendary **Khyber Pass**. **The Electric Factory** is a larger venue in No-Libs but not as big (or as obnoxious) as the **Wachovia Center**, which gets many of the larger touring bands. For a more gentle vibe, the **North Star** remains a great space to check out up and comers, as does the infamous **TLA**. But perhaps the best place to see a band is the balcony of the **Trocadero**.

Map 1 • Center City West

Cibucan	2025 Sansom St	215-231-9895	Tapas bar keeps you rolling in Latin-style bebidas.
Doobie's	2201 Lombard St	215-546-0316	Smoky and intimate, you'll become friends with everyone in the place.
Irish Pub	2007 Walnut St	215-568-5603	Rowdy student haul unsafe for morally mature.
Roosevelt Pub	2222 Walnut St	215-569-8879	Penn fave and with good reason: best drink deals in the city.
Tank Bar	261 S 21st St	215-546-4232	Giant fish tank highlights this sultry joint.

Map 2 • Rittenhouse / Logan Circle

Bar Noir	112 S 18th St	215-569-9333	Downstairs and uber-hip; look for 'Sixers GM Billy King.
The Black Sheep	247 S 17th St	215-545-9473	Pricey but authentic English pub atmosphere rules.
Bleu	227 S 18th St	215-545-0342	Longtime Rittenhouse standard keeps crankin' along.
Boathouse Row Bar	210 W Rittenhouse Sq	215-546-9000	Swanky Rittenhouse Hotel bar the place to be for power brokers.
Cadence	300 S Broad St	215-670-2388	The resplendent Kimmel Center's house bar. Black tie optional.
Chaucer's Tabard Inn	1946 Lombard St	215-985-9663	Candlelit and small, effectively recreates the Middle Ages.
Copa Too	263 S 15th St	215-735-0848	Strangely intimate sports bar has plain killer fries.
Denim Lounge	1712 Walnut St	215-735-6700	Jeans mogul opens trend-setting lounge/eatery. Acid-washed.
Good Dog	224 S 15th St	215-985-9600	Yumalicious local brews are featured in their draughtpulls.
Happy Rooster	118 S 16th St	215-963-9311	The Passion of the Cristal: Mel's fave bar in Philly.
Library Lounge	1415 Chancellor Ct	215-893-1776	A quiet, respectful art deco bar, replete with the Bellevue great books and roaring fireplace.

Arts & Entertainment · **Nightlife**

Map 2 · Rittenhouse / Logan Circle—*continued*

Loie	128 S 19th St	215-568-0808	French bistro rolls out the DJ and strong drinks after dinner.
Mace's Crossing	1714 Cherry St	215-564-5203	Where Tad and Kitty unwind from grueling regatta-cheering.
McGlinchey's	259 S 15th St	215-735-1259	Brilliantly low-end UArts joint has cheap pints and Ms. Pac Man.
Monk's Café	264 S 16th St	215-545-7005	Possibly the best beer list in the city. Long wait, though.
Nodding Head Brewery	1516 Sansom St	215-569-9525	Monk's much-less-annoying alter ego has good Restaurant home brew.
Paris Bar	10 Ave of the Arts	215-523-8000	The Ritz-Carlton bar has all the graceful amenities you can handle.
Potcheen	1735 Locust St	215-446-5232	The closest approximation of a sports bar in Rittenhouse.
Redhead Lounge	135 S 17th St	215-563-8200	Jazzy piano bar has strong drinks and classy environs.
Ritz-Carlton Rotunda	10 S Broad St	215-523-8000	They say your first million is the hardest. Well worth a toast.
Rouge	205 S 18th St	215-732-6622	Rittenhouse fave is resurrected under Starr's careful guidance.
Tangier Café	1801 Lombard St	215-732-5006	Sparkling little oasis reaches back to North Africa, circa 1932.
Tequila's Bar	1602 Locust St	215-546-0181	When you want to sober up, there's also decent, upscale Mex waiting for you.
Tir Na Nog	1600 Arch St	215-514-1700	Sports-themed Irish bar panders to the City Hall sect.
Tragos	40 S 19th St	215-636-9901	Two floors of rich Euros and wannabes finding their groove.
Tria	123 S 18th St	215-972-8742	Beers from all over this wide world, plus a goodly amount of wine.
Zanzibar Blue	200 S Broad St	215-732-5200	One of the best jazz joints in the city.

Map 3 · Center City East

12th Air Command	254 S 12th St	215-545-8088	Three floors and hot male bods at every stop.
2-4 Club	1221 St James St	215-735-5772	After-hours gay club keeps the action hopping all night long.
Bike Stop Inc.	206 S Quince St	215-627-1662	Play pool; get ogled by gay men. Not that there's anything wrong with that.
Bump	1234 Locust St	215-732-1800	What joint is it this week? Bump? Okay, then, it's bump.
Dirty Frank's	347 S 13th St	215-732-5010	Infamous local haunt always jammed to the gills and smoky as hell.
Doc Watson's Pub	216 S 11th St	215-922-3427	Med students and other mid-town professionals congregate to tie one on.
El Vez	121 S 13th St	215-928-9800	Features fancy, dopey cocktails but many of them still rock.
Fergie's Pub	1214 Sansom St	215-928-8118	Great pulled pints, excellent chow and no TVs of any kind.
Hard Rock Café	1113 Market St	215-238-1000	You've got to be joking.
The Irish Pub	1123 Walnut St	215-925-3311	Simple place with solid pints and great daily specials.
Las Vegas Lounge	704 Chestnut St	215-592-9533	Well, they get the seedy, paying-with-your-last-dollar feel right.
Locust Bar	235 S 10th St	215-925-2191	Not the place to go if you want to quit smoking; otherwise, it's fine.
Ludwig's Garden	1315 Sansom St	215-985-1525	German bar stokes the Bavarian fires & offers some tasty brews.
McGillan's Old Ale House	1310 Drury St	215-735-5562	One of Philly's oldest saloons has historical charm.
Moriarty's Restaurant	1116 Walnut St	215-627-7676	Theater crowd-pleaser has dramatic license to serve.
Polly Esther's	1201 Race St	215-851-0776	Oh, boy, an "ironic" dance joint. Go for the "good times."
Pure	1221 St James St	215-735-8485	Gayborhood destination scene, with massive dance floor.
Sisters	1320 Chancellor St	215-735-0735	Where the sisters go to check out other sisters and grab a bite.
Tellers' Bar at PSFS	1200 Market St	215-627-1200	Posh drinking digs at the Loews Hotel, resistant to irritating conventioneers.
Trocadero	1003 Arch St	215-336-2000	One of the better places to check a show in the city.
Washington Square	210 W Washington Sq	215-592-7787	Go for the champagne on the outdoor patio.
Woody's	202 S 13th St	215-545-1893	For nearly 30 years, a Philly gay institution.

Map 4 · Old City / Society Hill

32 Degrees	16 S 2nd St	215-627-3132	Ice shots and fine champagne attract assorted VIPs.
Bleu Martini	22 S 2nd St	215-940-7900	Yet another trendy OC watering hole. Wear complicated shoes.
Buffalo Billiards	118 Chestnut St	215-574-7665	Poolhall has much to recommend it, including strong drinks.
The Continental	138 Market St	215-923-6069	Lavish drinks & mostly shallow conversation.
Cuba Libre	10 S 2nd St	215-627-0666	Known for its pretty rollicking Mojitos.
Dark Horse	421 S 2nd St	215-928-9307	A rabbit-warren of rooms, bars and mystery alcoves.
Eulogy Belgian Tavern	136 Chestnut St	215-413-1918	Trappist ales have a way of kicking your ass, so be careful.
Five Spot	1 S Bank St	215-574-0070	One-time "swingers" scene now encompasses broad range of dance modes.
Glam	52 S 2nd St	215-671-0840	Drenched in pink, definitely more flash than cash.

Khyber Pass	56 S 2nd St	215-238-5888	Rock institution a rite-of-passage for Indie kids.
LoungeOneTwoFive	125 S 2nd St	215-351-9026	Stationed under a parking garage, the joint has a more intimate feel.
Paradigm	239 Chestnut St	215-238-6900	Overpriced and trying too hard, but the bathrooms are a marvel.
The Plough and the Stars	123 Chestnut St	215-733-0300	Fight through the Jersey crowd to the bar, then expect to wait.
Race Street Café	208 Race St	215-627-6181	Lots of polished wood makes your buzz more noteworthy.
Red Sky	224 Market St	215-925-8080	Let me get this straight: an ultra-trendy bar? In OC? Really?
Rock Lobster	221 N Columbus Blvd	215-627-7625	Nightclub under the BF Bridge appeals to Shore types.
Rotten Ralph's	201 Chestnut St	215-925-2440	Upstairs: chow. Downstairs: rollicking bar with decent prices for the area.
Sassafras	48 S 2nd St	215-925-2317	The place that launched a thousand martinis.
SoMa	33 S 3rd St	215-873-0222	Walk-down joint offers good spins and fab drinks in ultra hip atmosphere.
Sugar Mom's	225 Church St	215-925-8219	Underground grotto bar has pool, video games and a rocking juke.
Swanky Bubbles	10 S Front St	215-928-1200	We can think of at least two things wrong with their name.
Tangerine	232 Market St	215 627-5116	Far-reaching drink selection in this Stephen Starr Mediterranean vehicle.
Warmdaddy's	4 S Front St	215-627-2500	Blues joint offers decent live tunes and stirring drinks.

Map 6 • Gray's Ferry East / Graduate Hospital

L2	2201 South St	215-732-7878	Torchy jazz club has the right feel to it.
Ten Stone Bar & Restaurant	2063 South St	215-735-9939	English pub has darts, billiards, and a stone fireplace.

Map 7 • Southwark West

Bob & Barbara's Lounge	1509 South St	215-545-4511	Perhaps the city's best boozy entertainment center. PBR, ping pong, and drag queens.
Fiso Lounge	1437 South St	215-735-2220	Get your freak on high—check the rooftop deck.
Tritone	1508 South St	215-545-0475	Hip, happening scene and damn fine food.

Map 8 • Bella Vista / Queen Village

12 Steps Down	9th & Christian Sts	215-627-9013	South Philly's esoteric basement booze hall.
Bridget Foy's	200 South St	215-922-1813	South Street people-watching from an upscale environment.
Cheers to You	430 South St	215-923-8780	Unpretentious sports bar has decent beer, many TVs.
Fluid	613 S 4th St	215-629-0565	One of the better DJ spots in the city.
For Pete's Sake	900 S Front St	215-462-2230	Typified eatery, bar has good taps.
Jon's Bar & Grill	606 S 3rd St	215-592-1390	Good outdoor seating area allows you to see South in full regalia.
L'Etage	624 S 6th St	215-592-0656	Classy French-themed lounge. Don't miss Cabaret night.
Low	947 E Passyunk Ave	215-465-5555	Former old man bar repopulated with hipsters
Lyon's Den	848 S 2nd St	215-467-0100	Neighborhood boozeria conveniently across from Wawa.
New Wave Café	782 3rd St	215-922-8484	Rock solid food and a swinging booze crowd. Plus, Quizzo.
O'Neal's	611 S 3rd St	215-574-9495	A sports bar with a DJ? It works, but makes for some strange crossovers.
Player's Pub	615 S 2nd St	215-627-4864	Typical sports haven with TVs aplenty.
Royal Tavern	937 S Passyunk Ave	215-389-6694	Standard Tap South: great menu and beer choice.
Saloon	750 S 7th St	215-627-1811	Reportedly wher Tony Bennett eats when he's in town.
Southwark	701 S 4th St	215-592-4720	Finest potent potions in the city.
Tattooed Mom's	530 South St	215-238-9880	Regulars pack into the one major bar on South that isn't for tourists.
TLA	334 South St	215-922-1011	Indie-band paradise, right down to the crappy bathrooms.
Vesuvio Restaurant & Bar	736 S 8th St	215-922-8380	Rehearsal dinner joint with romance trappings.

Map 9 • Point Breeze / West Passyunk

DeNic's Tavern	1528 Snyder Ave	215-336-2333	Flyers-centric bar has decades of history and dust.

Map 13 • West Philly

Smokey Joe's	210 S 40th St	215-222-0770	Penn's unofficial watering hole has seen many a fine academian fall to ruin.

Map 14 · University City

Mad 4 Mex	3401 Walnut St	215-382-2221	Big college hang-out has decent grub and plenty of booze.
New Deck Tavern	3408 Sansom St	215-386-4600	Sports and students congregate in high volume.
Top Dog Sports Grille	3549 Chestnut St	215-386-5556	Students pack it in on game days, actually watch some of the game.

Map 16 · Art Museum West

North Star Bar	2639 Poplar St	215-684-0808	Cool live music most nights, damn fine drinks every night.

Map 17 · Art Museum East

The Bishop's Collar	2349 Fairmount Ave	215-765-1616	Neighborhood fave. Come for the beer. Stay for the beer.

Map 19 · Northern Liberties

700 Club	700 N 2nd St	215-413-3181	Crowded smoky lower bar, extremely crowded, smoky dance floor upstairs.
Aqua Lounge	323 W Girard Ave	215-769-5114	Hole-in-the-wall DJ-centric joint definitely gets its groove on.
Egypt	520 N Columbus Blvd	215-922-6500	Slightly more reserved than its neighboring brethren, but still.
Electric Factory	421 N 7th St	215-569-9400	Large venue for bigger rock shows: stick to the balcony.
Finnigan's Wake	537 N 3rd St	215-574-9240	Slam a Miller Lite while listening to a cover band jam Puddle of Mudd tunes.
McFadden's	461 N 3rd St	215-928-0630	Great spot to drink shooters with 21-year olds.
Ministry of Information	449 Poplar St	215-925-0999	No-Libs low-key hub of alcohol-drenched hipster revelry.
N 3rd	801 N 3rd St	215-413-3666	A blood-orange margarita, under the right circumstances, can be life-altering.
Ortlieb's Jazz House	847 N 3rd St	215-922-1035	Old school venue has smokey drinks and smokier jazz.
Palmer Social Club	601 Spring Garden St	215-925-500	After-hours joint keeps on pourin' until 3:30 AM.
Shampoo	417 N 8th St	215-922-7500	Where the Real Worlders got down and nasty. And terribly annoying.
Standard Tap	901 N 2nd St	215-238-0630	The legend grows about this trend-setting No-Libs marvel.
The Abbaye	637 N 3rd St	215-627-6711	Belgian bistro uses good beer liberally throughout menu.
The Fire	412 W Girard Ave	215-671-9298	A winning cross of old-man joint and punk dive.
Tiki Bob's	461 N 3rd St	215-928-9200	Polynesian-themed NJ meat-market joint. Whoopee.
Transit Nightclub	600 Spring Garden St	215-925-8878	Enormous danceteria has three floors and six bars.

Map 21 · Roxborough / Manayunk

Bayou Bar and Grill	4245 Main St	215-482-2560	All you can eat crab nights & frat party feel.
Bourbon Blue	2 Rector St	215-508-3360	An upscale rock n' roll joint in the mighty 'Yunk.
Castle Roxx Café	105 Shurs Ln	215-482-9000	Relaxed out-of-the-way joint.
Flatrock Saloon	4301 Main St	215-483-3722	One of the biggest Belgian beer selections in all of Philly.
Grape Street	4100 Main St	215-487-1226	Live music. Located on Main Street.
Manayunk Brewery	4120 Main St	215-482-8220	A multitude of home-brews highlights this popular and Restaurant 'Yunk hangout.
Kildare's	4417 Main St	215-482-3700	The new hot spot in the 'Yunk. Recommended: the Dirty Hoe.
Sonoma	4411 Main St	215-483-9400	Popular (and relatively inexpensive) watering hole in the 'Yunk.
Tonic	4421 Main St	215-509-6005	New martini/cosmo bar. Lounge feel.

Map 22 · Manayunk

Dawson Street Pub	100 Dawson St	215-482-5677	A small escape from the normal Manayunk crowd.
Vaccarelli's East End Tavern	4001 Cresson St	215 482 4944	Cozy neighborhood joint with rocking prices.

The Northeast

Chickie and Pete's	11000 Roosevelt Blvd	215-856-9890	Incredible crab fries inspiring the hilarious "Got Crabs?" T-shirt.
Jillian's	1995 Franklin Mills Cir,	215-632-0333	Dave & Buster's on a budget.
Molly Maguires	427 Rhawn St	215-722-2411	A fun Irish pub.
Nutty Irishman	8138 Bustleton Ave	215-742-6193	A Northeast Philly staple, this Irish bar features solid bands on weekends.
Sweeney's Station Saloon	13639 Philmont Ave	215-677-3177	You might run into a high school friend you haven't seen in a while here.
Whiskey Tango Tavern	14000 Bustleton Ave	215-671-9234	A 3-floor bar with live music, pool tables, and a dance floor.

We know, we know: the only reason you moved here was for the cheesesteaks. But now that you're a resident, we can let you in on a little secret. Philly has a world-class restaurant scene. No, really. We mean it.

Italian

Man, where to begin? **Porcini** provides a more civilized kind of vibe, though the seating is certainly, ah, intimate. **La Viola**, right across the street from the always mega-busy **Monk's**, is a fine example of opportunism, but it also happens to be awfully good. For purists, **Villa di Roma** provides absolutely kick-ass pasta dishes in an atmosphere reminiscent of the house in *All in the Family*. **L'Angolo** is perhaps the best pure Italian joint in the city, and their desserts are absolute bliss. **Mr. Martino's** has the best atmosphere, with its deep wood bar and stairway and **Mezza Luna** is to Italian lovers what the Great Pyramids are to architects.

Asian

Philly is home to an embarrassment of Asian food riches, with the delightful **Susanna Foo** gracing restaurant row and **Joseph Poon** spearheading the team in Chinatown. Non-carnivores can rejoice at the **Kingdom of Vegetarians**. Groups looking to eat dim sum until their belts snap in half can load it up at the **Lakeside Chinese Deli**. Foodies flock to **Morimoto**, where the Iron Chef can produce tempura, the memory of which will stay with you to your dying day. For splendid Malaysian, **Penang** stands tall and you haven't lived until you've had the spring rolls at **Vietnam**.

Pizza

We don't want no trouble, we just want to share some of our favorite slices. To begin at the top of the heap, it doesn't get any better than a fresh, hot slice from **Joe's**, as long as you can stand the wait in line. **Napoli's** has a fine array of pies, but also hits you right in the solar plexus with their sinfully good panzerottis. **Marra's** is a South Philly legend, and you can't get that kind of exalted status unless you know how to twirl some dough. **Lorenzo's** remains the best place to go on South Street when you've had too much to drink and you need to sober up before your ferry ride back to Jersey. **Pietro's** is a fine example of decent wood-fired pie. **Dolce Carini** slings 'em New York style, which is still allowed down here, and **Lombardi's** is a kind of high-falutin' variety of pizza that still packs a wallop.

Breakfast

What better way to sober up than at a solid breakfast joint? **Little Pete's** is, perhaps, the epitome of greasy spoon, but somehow their dry eggs and butter-soaked toast still has the power to refortify you. **Blue in Green** has some of the city's best pancakes, but you'd better not try to special order anything. **Carman's Country Kitchen** remains an iconoclastic culinary wonder. **Sabrina's** was the best ever until they got so popular —now you have to wait even longer for your polenta fries. The nearby **Fitzwater Café** does absolutely sumptuous eggs. The legendary **Melrose Diner** serves up scrapple to spare in South Philly and, for the Rittenhouse sophisticates, **Marathon on the Square** is a fine alternative to sleeping in.

Luxe

Here's where things start to really get interesting. **The Bistro St. Tropez** has carved out quite a niche for itself, though it remains the most difficult restaurant to actually find in Center City. **Le Bec-Fin** remains Philly's most prominent fine dining experience. **Roy's** shakes things up a bit with their Hawaiian-fusion fare. **Bluezette** fills you up right with resplendent soul food. **Brasserie Perrier** provides yet another fine French dining experience. Guests of the Four Seasons enjoy the all-encompassing luxury of **Fountain**. **Rouge** remains a cagey veteran of the Rittenhouse scene, though Stephen Starr had to rescue it. That's okay, because Starr also opened **Barclay Prime** nearby just to show all those Ruth's, Chris's, and Shula's how it's done. Starr also owns **Alma de Cuba**, an excellent place to brush up on your Spanish.

BYOB

One of Philly's most engaging traditions is its affinity for the inexpensive fine dining experience. Stop by a good wine store (say, in Jersey) and head on over to one of these beauties. **Effie's** offers delightful Greek cuisine and plumb outdoor seating. **Lolita** will happily mix you up some killer margaritas, as long as you provide the tequila. OC's **Chloe** continues to be a perennial favorite amongst the foodies of the area, as does the fine French stylings of **Django**. Finally, what would Queen Village life be like without **Dmitri's** loving Mediterranean fare? We shudder to think.

Key: $: Under $10 / $$: $10–$20 / $$$: $20-30 / $$$$: $30+, *: Does not accept credit cards.

Map 1 · Center City West

Amara Café	105 S 22nd St	215-564-6976	$	Tight-squeezed BYOB is fine if you can actually get a table.
Audrey Claire	276 S 20th St	215-731-1222	$$*	Simple, classic dishes done with suitable aplomb.
Bistro St Tropez	2400 Market St, 4th Fl	215-569-9269	$$$$	Way-upscale French bistro has style to spare.
Cibucan	2025 Sansom St	215-231-9895	$$	The tapas-and-bar joint from the future.
Erawan Thai Cuisine	123 S 23rd St	215-567-2542	$	Not a looker, but the dishes (esp. the glass noodles) are solid.
Friday Saturday Sunday	261 S 21st St	215-546-4232	$$	The Tank Bar on the second floor is a great place to get lit.
Fuji Mountain	2030 Chestnut St	215-751-0939	$$	Thoughtful and cozy, belly up to the sushi bar and do a knot of fish.
Mama's Palma's	2229 Spruce St	215-735-7357	$*	Wood-fired, thin-crust pie that'll make you glad to be alive.
Marathon Grill	2001 Market St	215-568-7766		If you're a hungry pig, take note of the MOTS special.
Melograno	2201 Spruce St	215-875-8116	$$	Sophisticated yet unpretentious Italian joint packs 'em in.
Midtown IV	2013 Chestnut St	215-567-3142	$*	Much like their other incarnations: serviceable diner food.
Porcini	2048 Sansom St	215-751-1175	$$	Tiny but amazingly endearing. The ravishing food helps.
Primo Hoagies	2043 Chestnut St	215-496-0540	$	One of the premier hoagie experiences in the city.
Roosevelt Pub	2222 Walnut St	215-569-8879	$	Have some fine pub fare in an FDR-inspired setting.
Salt	253 S 20th St	215-545-1990	$$$$	Please. You can spend $40 on a plate of three asparagus tips at home.
Sushi on the Square	233 S 20th St	215-988-0510	$	All your regular fishy favorites plus Japanese pickles.
Tampopo	104 S 21st St	215-557-9593	$*	Inexpensive and speedy sushi, with lots of veggie options.
Twenty Manning	261 S 20th St	215-731-0900	$$$	Hipster haute with a solid bar scene.
XO Kitchen	106 S 20th St	215-988-9020	$*	Cantonese joint that offers a full breakfast.

Map 2 · Rittenhouse / Logan Circle

Alma de Cuba	1623 Walnut St	215-988-1799	$$	Cuban soul food without all that annoying Communism.
Astral Plane	1708 Lombard St	215-546-6230	$$$	Consistently voted one of Philly's most romantic spots.
Barclay Prime	237 S 18th St	215-732-7560	$$$	Starr's answer to the expense-account steak joints.
Black Sheep Pub	247 S 17th St	215-545-9473	$$	High-end fish & chips in a crowded Irish pub.
Bleu	227 S 18th St	215-545-0342	$$$	Modern French that doesn't blow.
Brasserie Perrier	1619 Walnut St	215-568-3000	$$$$	Pricey fine French food with eclectic accents.
Buca di Beppo	258 S 15th St	215-545-2818	$$	Huge portions help make up for this chain's unmemorable food.
Cadence	300 S Broad St	215-670-2388	$$$$	The Kimmel Center's auspicious fine-dining option.
Capital Grille	1338 Chestnut St	215-545-9588	$$$$	Steakhouse for the Masters of the Expense Account.
Copa Too	263 S 15th St	215-735-0848	$	Great burgers and fries—better than their flagship location.
Davio's	111 S 17th St	215-563-4810	$$$	The calamari, for one, is pretty special.
Denim Lounge	1712 Walnut St	215-735-6700	$$$	Jeans' mogul opens trend-setting lounge/eatery. Acid-washed.
Devon Seafood Grill	225 S 18th St	215-546-5940	$$$	Swanky, but you definitely pay the price.
Dolce Carini	1929 Chestnut St	215-567-8892	$	Unadulterated NY-style pies.
Fountain Restaurant	1 Logan Sq	215-963-1500	$$$$	When money—and expense accounts—are no object.
Genji	1720 Sansom St	215-564-1720	$$	Snack on sublime sushi and hang with the chefs at the bar.
Good Dog	224 S 15th St	215-985-9600	$$	Bark up a good dog burger (presumably still made of cow).
The Grill	10 S Broad St	215-735-7700	$$$	Can you say "expense account"? High-end seafood.
Il Portico	1519 Walnut St	215-587-7000	$$$	Fine Jewish-Italian in the heart of Restaurant Row.
Joe's Pizza	122 S 16th St	215-569-0898	$*	Some of the best 'za in the city. Weird hours.
La Creperie	1722 Sansom St	215-564-6460	$	Pizza crepes? Believe it, pilgrim.
La Viola	253 S 16th St	215-735-8630	$$*	Sweet, cozy BYOB; perfect for when you can't stand waiting in line at Monk's anymore.
Lacroix at the Rittenhouse	210 Rittenhouse Sq	215-546-9000	$$$$	Luxe out at the Rittenhouse hotel. Make a night of it.
Le Bec-Fin	1523 Walnut St	215-567-1000	$$$$	Philly's premier snoot-a-rama. Point your nose up.

Le Castagne	1920 Chestnut St	215-751-9913	$$	Lots of insalatas amidst the rain of pesces, pastas, and carnes.
Le Cigale	113 S 18th St	215-569-1970	$	Provencal French bistro: many things served with baguettes.
Lil' Spot	103 S Juniper St	215-828-6435	$*	Hot doughnuts served in wax paper. That's living, baby.
Little Pete's	1904 Chestnut St	215-563-2303	*	A greasy spoon with no apologies.
Little Pete's	219 S 17th St	215-545-5508	$*	A greasy spoon with no apologies.
Loie	128 S 19th St	215-568-0808	$$	French bistro-cum-rave-on meets the pool hall.
Lombardi's	132 S 18th St	215-564-5000	$*	On the pricey side, but thin-crust pie melts in your mouth.
Los Catrines	1602 Locust St	215-546-0181	$$	Upscale Mex has beautiful, open ceilings and fine offerings.
Marathon Grill	121 S 16th St	215-569-3278	$	If you're a hungry pig, take note of the MOTS special.
Marathon Grill	1339 Chestnut St	215-561-4460	$	If you're a hungry pig, take note of the MOTS special.
Marathon Grill	1617 JFK Blvd	215-564-4745	$	If you're a hungry pig, take note of the MOTS special.
Marathon Grill	1818 Market St	215-561-1818	$	If you're a hungry pig, take note of the MOTS special.
Marathon on the Square	1839 Spruce St	215-731-0800	$	If you're a hungry pig, take note of the MOTS special.
Matyson	37 S 19th St	215-564-2925	$$$	The food is great, but the desserts are sublime.
McCormick & Schmick's	1 S Broad St	215-568-6888	$$$	Enjoy plank-roasted salmon with other dickheads.
Miel Patisserie	204 S 17th St	215-731-9191	$$	Stunning French desserts and fine chocolates. Ooh la la.
Monk's Cafe	264 S 16th St	215-545-7005	$$	Great beer list and monster fries, Belgian-style. Plan to wait.
Morton's	1411 Walnut St	215-557-0724	$$$$	Yet another upscale steakhouse chain begs for your dollars.
Moshi Moshi	108 S 18th St	215-496-9950	$$	Mimamalist setting provides many happytempura memories.
Nodding Head Brewery & Restaurant	1516 Sansom St, 2nd Fl	215-569-9525	$	Almost as good as Monk's and no wait.
Oasis	1709 Walnut St	215-751-0888	$	Eat decent sushi near an actual waterfall.
Paolo's Pizza	1334 Pine St	215-545-2571	$	Salty as a codfish, but a nice hand-tossed crust.
Parkway Diner	1939 Arch St	215-568-4939	$	Retro décor (ugly, in other words) and open all damn night.
Pasion!	211 S 15th St	215-875-9895	$$$	Nuevo Latino in a stately setting.
Pietro's Coal Oven Pizzeria	1714 Walnut St	215-735-8090	$	Delicious thin crust pies and solid salads.
Prime Rib	1701 Locust St	215-772-1701	$$$	Tasteful and elegant steakhouse in the Warwick.
Rouge	205 S 18th St	215-732-6622	$$$	French/Asian foo foo that will not be ignored.
Roy's	124 S 15th St	215 988-1814	$$$$	Rocking the Hawaiian fusion. Surf's up, Kahuna.
Ruth's Chris Steak House	260 S Broad St	215-790-1515	$$$$	The unofficial eating trough of the GOP.
Sansom Street Oyster House.	1516 Sansom St	215-567-7683	$$	Old-school seafood haunt favors the theater crowd
Shiroi Hana	222 S 15th St	215-735-4444	$$	Contemporary sushi house caters to tuna lovers.
Shula's Steak house	201 N 17th St	215-448-2700	$$$$	If you see him there, tell him David Woodley was pitiful.
Smith & Wollensky	210 W Rittenhouse Sq	215-546-9000	$$$	Close your newest merger in grand carnivorous style.
Sotto Varalli	231 S Broad St	215-546-6800	$$$	Soak in the atmosphere—and stick to the wine.
Susanna Foo	1512 Walnut St	215-545-2666	$$$$	Perfection does not come cheap.
Sushi on the Avenue	1431 Spruce St	215-732-5585	$	Volcano Maki an 'explosively' popular favorite.
Swann Lounge	1 Logan Sq	215-963-1500	$$$	Get your blue-blood on and order a crustless water-cress sandwich.
Upstares at Varalli	1345 Locust St	215-546-4200	$$	Grammatically challenged, but fine Italian cuisine.
Valentino	1328 Pine St	215-545-6265	$$	Sumptuous Italian fare in casual setting. The gnocchi is killer.
Vok	1613 Walnut St	215-751-9990	$$	Decent, not-too-pricey, but forget about parking.
Vann	122 S 18th St	215-568-5250	$	Classic French bakery rocks the pastries.
ZanzibarBlue	200 S Broad St	215-732-4500	$$	Jazz club food like long Bird solo.

Key: $: Under $10 / $$: $10–$20 / $$$: $20-$30 / $$$$: $30ı, *: Does not accept credit cards.

Map 3 · Center City East

Angelina	706 Chestnut St	215-925-6889	$$	Fine Italian: Just another outpost in Stephen Starr Row.
Aoi	1210 Walnut St	215-985-1838	$$	Great miso soup and strange décor make it a winner.
Basic Four Vegetarian	1136 Arch St	215-440-0991	$*	Chock full of veggie love in Reading Terminal.
Bassett's Ice Cream	1136 Arch St	215-925-4315	$*	Perfect happy ending to your Redding Terminal experience.
Blue in Green	719 Samsom St	215-923-6883	$*	Great pancakes served by indie rock refugees.
Capogiro Gelateria	119 S 13th St	215-351-0900	$*	Some of the best gelato in the city—pricey, though.
Caribou Café	1126 Walnut St	215-625-9535	$$$	Euroville in CC. Drink in the atmosphere.
Charles Plaza	234 N 10th St	215-829-4383	$	Cool mood lighting sets up a fabulous veggie cornucopia of delights.
Delilah's Southern Café	1136 Arch St	215-574-0929	$	Not that Delilah's, you perv. This soul food joint has got bounce.
Deux Cheminees	1221 Locust St	215-790-0200	$$$$	Huffy-Puffy French food. Bring plenty of plastic.
Down Home Diner	51 N 12th St	215-627-1955	$*	On a clear day, you can see the scrapple.
Effie's	1127 Pine St	215-592-8333	$$*	Simple Greek fare in an adorable setting.
El Azteca II	714 Chestnut St	215-733-0895	$	Food, decent. Salsa & chips, excellent!
El Fuego	723 Walnut St	215-592-1901	$	Fresh, made-to-order burros, but heavy on the rice.
El Vez	121 S 13th St	215-928-9800	$$	Starr's take on Mexican; mixed bag, but it works.
Hard Rock Café	1113 Market St	215-238-1000	$$	Lose all credibility the second you step through the door.
Harmony Vegetarian	135 N 9th St	215-627-4520	$	Mock if you must, but the meat here is unreal.
House of Chen	932 Race St	215-923-9797	$	Perfect if you suddenly need lo mein at 4 am.
Imperial Inn	146 N 10th St	215-627-5588	$	Just chow down on the dim sum. Leave the rest behind.
Jones	700 Chestnut St	215-238-9600	$	Comfort food in a Brady Bunch-like setting.
Joseph Poon	1002 Arch St	215-928-9333	$$	Legendary Poon does not disappoint.
Kingdom of Vegetarians	129 N 11th St	215-413-2290	$	You up for a mock duck that will curl your toes?
La Buca	711 Locust St	215-928-0556	$$$	Get dressed up real nice and enjoy fine Italian cuisine.
Lakeside Chinese Deli	207 N 9th St	215-925-3288	$*	Five hungry people can stuff themselves for $30.
Lee How Fook	219 N 11th St	215-925-7266	$	Low-key and casual, and great hot pots.
Lolita	106 S 13th St	215-546-7100	$$*	Charming and romantic Mex is a BYOT.
Maggiano's Little Italy	1201 Filbert St	215-567-2020	$$	A cute, little "Italian Market" chain? Give us a break.
More Than Just Ice Cream	1119 Locust St	215-574-0586	$	Perhaps the largest slice of apple pie in the world.
Moriarty's	1116 Walnut St	215-627-7676	$	Huge theater crowd enlivens the place.
Morimoto	723 Chestnut St	215-413-9070	$$$	The best shrimp tempura ever. Anywhere.
Nan Zhou	927 Race St	215-923-1550	$*	Home-made noodles go into every bowl of delicious soup.
Penang	117 N 10th St	215-413-2531	$*	Upscale Malaysian in the heart of Chinatown.
Pho Xe Lua	907 Race St	215-627-8883	$*	The fresh mango lassi should be more than enough inducement.
Pine Street Pizza	1138 Pine St	215-922-2526	$*	It'll do—but just barely.
Pompeii Cucina D'Italia	1113 Walnut St	215-735-8400	$$$	Giant antipasto selection and big pasta portions.
Rick's Steaks	1136 Arch St	215-925-4320	$*	Roughing up the Terminal Market crowd.
Salumeria	45 N 12th St	215-592-8150	$*	Load up on huge, fresh hoagies at Reading Terminal.
Samosa	1214 Walnut St	215-545-7776	$*	Stuff yourself silly for seat-cushion change.
Sang Kee Peking Duck House	238 N 9th St	215-925-7532	$$	From obscure to titillating. And back.
Santa Fe Burrito Company	212 S 11th St	215-413-2378	$	Not bad for beans out of a can, but pricier than necessary.
Shiao Lan Kung	930 Race St	215-928-0282	$	South Cantonese joint has good veggie options.
Siam Cuisine	925 Arch St	215-922-7135	$	Local chain of Thai joints toned down for the masses.
Singapore Kosher Vegetarian	1006 Race St	215-922-3288	$	Great for Rabbis with PETA memberships.
Taco House	1218 Pine St	215-735-1880	$	Tiny but flavorful and a favorite of students.
Tai Lake	134 N 10th St	215-922-0698	$$	The place to go when you want live frogs and lobster at 1 am.
Taste of Thai Garden	101 N 11th St	215-629-9939	$	For conventioneers jonesing for Mee Krob.
Vetri	1312 Spruce St	215-732-3478	$$$$	Intimate and romantic, one of Philly's best.
Vietnam	221 N 11th St	215-592-1163	$	One of the best restaurants in Philly. Be prepared to wait.
Vietnam Palace	222 N 11th St	215-592-9596	$	Good, but way outclassed by Vietnam across the street.
Yogi's Eatery	929 Walnut St	215-351-9191	$*	Good sandwiches are like nature's sandwiches.

Arts & Entertainment · **Restaurants**

Map 4 · Old City / Society Hill

Adriatica	217 Chestnut St	215-592-8001	$$$ Mediterranean seafood with Moroccan style.
Anjou	206-08 Market St	215-923-1600	$$$ Global fusion ain't just an economist's dream.
Billy Wong's	50 S 2nd St	215-829-1128	$$ Not just another OC trend-trough. The food is sublime.
Bistro Romano	120 Lombard St	215-925-8880	$$ Eat heavy Italian under dim candlelight.
Bluezette	246 Market St	215-627-3866	$$ Soul food joint that boasts some of the best mac 'n cheese in the world.
Campo's Deli	214 Market St	215-923-1000	$* Over-stuffed sandwiches served by underfed sandwich makers.
Chloe	232 Arch St	215-629-2337	$$$* Bold combinations in an intimate setting.
Cuba Libre	10 S 2nd St	215-627-0666	$$ Fine Mojitos, great atmosphere. Food? Um, we guess.
Dark Horse	421 S 2nd St	215-928-9307	$$ Oy, guv, fancy some bangers 'n mash?
DiNardo's Famous Seafood	312 Race St	215-925-5115	$$ Gulf-coast soft shells are the major draw.
Django	526 S 4th St	215-922-7151	$$ Elegant, Euro-style BYOB has much flava.
Dolce	242 Chestnut St	215-238-6900	$$ Fancy-pants OC-style Italian joint flaunts it nightly.
Eulogy Belgian Tavern	136 Chestnut St	215-413-1918	$$ Great beer selection highlights a so-so menu.
Fork	306 Market St	215-625-9425	$$ Upscale without being obnoxious.
Gianfranco Pizza Rustica	6 N 3rd St	215-592-0048	$* Some think it's the best. It's not, but it ain't bad.
Gianna's Grill	507 S 6th St	215-829-4488	$* Vegan (or standard) pies with homemade soy cheese. Yum.
Karma	114 Chestnut St	215-925-1444	$$ High-end Indian fare but still veggie-friendly.
Konak	228 Vine St	215-592-1212	$$$ Authentic Turkish abounds, and wonderful feta, too.
La Famiglia	8 S Front St	215-922-2803	$$$ Impeccable high-end Italian fare.
La Locanda del Ghiottone	130 N 3rd St	215-829-1465	$$ Gluttonously huge portions. Not that there's anything wrong with that.
Marmont Steakhouse	222 Market St	215-923-1100	$$ Jazzy joint has adequate eats and kind décor.
Marrakesh	517 S Leithgow St	215-925-5929	$$* Sit on circular sofas and stuff your face with phyllo.
Mexican Post	104 Chestnut St	215-923-5233	$ Average chow but solid margaritas.
Moshulu	401 S Columbus Blvd	215-923-2500	$$$$ Elegant food in a century-old sailing vessel. Avast ye matey
Novelty	15 S 3rd St	215-627-7885	$$ Refreshingly adult food in the middle of Flashy Town
Pagoda Noodle Café	125 Sansom St	215-928-2320	$$ Grab a bite on your way to the Ritz East.
Paradigm	239 Chestnut St	215-238-6900	$$ Overpriced and trying too hard, but the bathrooms are a marvel!
Patou	312 Market St	215-928-2987	$$ Masts, sails, and portholes. Oh, and the food is fine, too.
Petit 4 Pastry Studio	160 N 3rd St	215-627-8440	$ Stay away from the chocolate/banana cookies. They're ours.
Philadelphia Fish & Co	207 Chestnut St	215-625-8605	$$$$ Jumping from the sea directly to your plate.
Pizzicato	248 Market St	215-629-5527	$$ Stunning—and that's just the waitstaff.
Plough & the Stars	123 Chestnut St	215-733-0300	$$ If you can fight off the NJ scenesters, the food is fine
Race Street Café	208 Race St	215-627-6181	$$ Decent burgers, great brew selection.
Restorante Panorama	14 N Front St	215-922-7800	$$$ Along with Spasso & Famiglia, the murderer's row of high-end Italian fare.
Sassafras International Cafe	48 S 2nd St	215-925-2317	$$ Snag an ostrich burger and don't spare the cheese.
Sfizzio	237 St James Pl	215-925-1802	$$ The usual suspects, with a focus on fresh seafood.
Sonny's Famous Steaks	216 Market St	215-629-5760	$* Relative cheesesteak newcomer quickly asserting itself.
Spasso	34 S Front St	215-592-7661	$$ Affordable Italian and their clams have earned them a rep.
Swanky Bubbles	10 S Front St	215-928-1200	$$ Score some Dom with your sushi. Come loaded.
Tangerine	232 Market St	215-627-5116	$$$ Moroccan standards meets the Pink Flamingo.

Map 5 · Gray's Ferry West

B&B Restaurant	2629 Christian St	215-732-1430	$* The definition of 'standard fare.'
Bridgit's Deli	1500 S Dover St	215-755-7360	$* When you get a hankering for corned beef that just won't quit.
D'ambrosio's Bakery	1401 S 31st St	215-389-8368	$* Get your rolls on in this South Philly enclave.
Kelly's Deli	1555 S Newkirk St	215-68-5550	$* Stuff your pie-hole with their overstuffed hoagies.
La Rosa Café	1300 S Warfield St	215-339-1740	$* If you ever need a breakfast pizza, this is the joint to hit up.

227

Arts & Entertainment · **Restaurants**

Key: $: Under $10 / $$: $10–$20 / $$$: $20-$30 / $$$$: $30+, *: Does not accept credit cards.

Map 6 · Gray's Ferry East / Graduate Hospital

L2	2201 Snith St	215-732-78/8	$$	Great bar and solid food choices.
My Thai	2200 South St	215-985-1878	$	Cozy and casual, with just the right amount of sass to its cooking.
Phoebe's Bar-B-Q	2214 South St	215-546-4811	$*	Take-out only, but worth the mess.
Ten Stone Bar & Restaurant	2063 South St	215-735-9939	$$	Traditional British pub with American food. Go figure.

Map 7 · Southwark West

August	1247 S 13th St	215-468-5926	$$*	Downtown style across from Passyunk Square.
Bitar's	947 Federal St	215-755-1121	$	Baked—not fried—falafel, plus lots of gyros.
Carman's Country Kitchen	1301 S 11th St	215-339-9613	$	Tiny and quirky, but avant garde food is sublime.
Dante & Luigi's	762 S 10th St	215-922-9501	$$*	Heaping out the gravies since 1899.
Felicia's	1148 S 11th St	215-755-9656	$$	Pasta is king here. Long live the king.
Fiso Lounge	1437 South St	215-735-2220	$$	Fine dining that comes with a whole lot of ass-grinding.
Franco's & Luigi's	1549 S 13th St	215-755-8900	$	Huge-portioned BYOB packs in the locals. Lots of singing.
Govinda's	1408 South St	215-985-9303	$$	Excellent whole-food eats from vegan hypnotherapists.
Isgro Pastries	1009 Christian St	215-923-3092	$	Fattening you up since 1904. Just order cakes in advance.
Jamaican Jerk Hut	1436 South St	215-545-8644	$	Check out their Caribbean-inspired outdoor space.
Lazzaro's Pizza House	1743 South St	215-545-2775	$*	You like slices the size of Bangladesh? This is the joint for you.
Morning Glory Diner	735 S 10th St	215-413-3999	$*	Huge lines, but pancakes will make you weep.
Pico de Gallo	1501 South St	215-772-1119	$	Cozy Mex joint offers fine margarita mixes.
Ricci Bros	1165 S 11th St	215-334-6910	$*	Old-school deli stuffs the hoagies with charm.
Ron's Ribs	1627 South St	215-545-9160	$	In the middle of BBQ row.
Shank's & Evelyn's	932 S 10th St	215-629-1093	$*	The roast beef could be enshrined in the Luncheonette Meat Hall of Fame.
Tre Scalini	1533 S 11th St	215-551-3870	$$$	The food is extraordinary; the décor, horrendous.
Tritone	1508 South St	215-545-0475	$$	Find your groove while supping on mac & cheese.

Map 8 · Bella Vista / Queen Village

Azafran	617 S 3rd St	215-928-4019	$$	South American fare. Don't pass up the yucca.
Beau Monde	624 S 6th St	215-592-0656	$$	Elegant French creperie. Comment charmant!
Bridget Foy's	200 South St	215-922-1813	$$	Strong drinks and a nice spot to survey the crowd.
Café Huong Lan	1037 S 8th St	215-629-9966	$*	Vietnamese hoagies done with flair.
Café Nhuy	802 Christian St	215-925-6544	$*	A Vietnamese veggie hoagie that will slap your ass and call you sonny.
Café Sud	801 E Passyunk Ave	215-592-0499	$$*	Small Moroccan bakery/BYOB has splendid rum cake.
Copabanana	344 South St	215-923-6180	$	Decent Tex-Mex in a busy bar atmosphere.
Cucina Forte	768 S 8th St	215-238-0778	$$	Plump, light gnocchi just one highlight.
Dmitri's	795 S 3rd St	215-625-0556	$-$$*	Popular neighborhood BYOB; be prepared to wait.
El Fuego Del Sol	619 South St	215-629-3786	$	Some of the best burritos in the city, hands down.
Famous 4th Street Deli	700 S 4th St	215-922-3274	$	Great cookies, and the largest order of eggs you have ever seen.
Fitzwater Café	728 S 7th St	215-629-0428	$*	Blissful eggs and great pancakes.
Geno's Steaks	1219 S 9th St	215-389-0659	$*	Free angioplasty with each phoson sandwiches!
Gnocchi	613 E Passyunk Ave	215-592-8300	$$*	Their eponymous dish does them justice.
Golden Empress Garden	610 S 5th St	215-627-7666	$*	Ho-hum Chinese with many veggie options.
Hikaru	607 S 2nd St	215-627-7110	$$	Delicate specialty rolls in keeping with the low-key atmosphere.
Hosteria Da Elio	615 S 3rd St	215-925-0930	$$$	There really is an Elio, and he's a magician with a whisk.
Ishkabibble's Eatery	337 South St	215-923-4337	$*	Fast, late night chow at its finest.
Jim's Steaks	400 South St	215-928-1911	$*	For those who love smelling of onions while standing in line.
Johnny Rockets	443 South St	215-829-9222	$*	If you like your burgers served with '50s-style doo-wop, be our guest.
Judy's Café	627 S 3rd St	215-928-1968	$$	Solid comfort food—just don't step out of line.

La Fourno Trattoria	636 South St	215-627-9000	$	Good pastas, solid wood-fired 'za.
La Lupe	1201 S 9th St	215-551-9920	$*	Traditional Mex in the heart of Cheesesteak Central.
La Viqna	1100 S Front St	215-336-1100	$$	Fine food served by tux-bearing waiters.
Latest Dish	613 S 4th St	215-629-0565	$$	DJ spins tunes as you throw down irresistible chow.
Little Fish	600 Catharine St	215-413-3464	$$*	Intimate seafood bistro. The chef can't hide.
Lorenzo Pizza	900 Christian St	215-922-2540	$*	Very parm-heavy but it definitely sticks to your ribs.
Lorenzo & Son Pizza	305 South St	215-627-4110	$*	Philly's most famous (not necessarily best) pie.
Lovash	236 South St	215-925-3882	$$	Decent Indian with a bit of fire in its loins.
Mezza Luna	763 S 8th St	215-627-4705	$$	Authentic, classic Italian picked just the right neighborhood.
Mustard Greens	622 E 2nd St	215-627-0833	$-$$	You must try the garlic noodles. Trust us.
Napoli Pizzeria	944 E Passyunk Ave	215-336-3833	$	Panzerotti: a pizza, deep fried. This is so good, it's worth the heart attack
New Wave Café	784 S 3rd St	215-922-8484	$$$	Locals pub with elegant chow.
Next	223 South St	215-629-0688	$$*	Trendy BYOB starting to get its feet wet.
Pat's King of Steaks	1237 E Passyunk Ave	215-468-1546	$*	When you've gotta have a cheesesteak at 5 am.
Pif	1009 S 8th St	215-625-2923	$$	BYOB French bistro offers plenty of escargot.
Pink Rose Pastry Shop	630 S 4th St	215-592-0565	$$	Edifying cakes, cookies and pies.
Ralph's	760 S 9th St	215-627-6011	$$*	Serving up pasta for more than a century.
Sabrina's Cafe	910 Christian St	215-574-1599	$	Brunch specials and great décor, plus polenta fries
Saloon	750 S 7th St	215-627-1811	$$$$	Reportedly where Tony Bennett eats when he's in town.
Salsolito Café	602 South St	215-928-0200	$*	Decent burros and very veggie friendly.
Snockey's	1020 S 2nd St	215-339-9578	$$*	Down and dirty oyster house.
Tamarind	117 South St	215-925-2764	$$	Dutiful Thai in casual atmosphere.
Taqueria La Veracruzana	908 Washington Ave	215-465-1440	$*	Not much to look at, but authentic and delicious.
Termini Brothers Bakery	1523 S 8th St	215-334-1816	$	The cannoli is legend. Spoken of in whispers.
Vesuvio	736 S 8th St	215-922-8380	$$	Put it this way: This would be Paulie Walnuts' favorite joint.
Villa di Roma	932 S 9th St	215-592-1295	$*	If loving their ricotta/mozzarella pasta is wrong, then we don't want to be right.

Map 9 · Point Breeze / West Passyunk

Barrel's	1725 Wolf St	215-389-6010	$$	No-frills Italian joint, popular for lunch.
Buon Appetito	1540 Ritner St	215-551-8378	$$*	A fried zucchini blossom that will curl your toes.
L'Angolo	1415 Porter St	215-389-4252	$-$$	Homemade Italian. Ravioli. To. Die. For.
La Stanza	2001 Oregon Ave	215-271-0801	$$$	Standard Italian, but the joint's on stilts.
Matteo Cucina	1900 W Passyunk Ave	215-463-5848	$$	Family-inspired Italian with a cozy atmosphere.
Melrose Diner	1501 Snyder Ave	215-467-6644	$*	A breakfast institution 24 hours a day.
Mio Sogno	2650 S 15th St	215-467-3317	$$*	A hidden-away little bit of Italian bliss.
Royal Villa Café	1700 Jackson St	215-462-4488	$$	Plenty of clams from which to choose.

Map 10 · Moyamensing / East Passyunk

Criniti Pizza & Restaurant	2601 S Broad St	215-465-7750	$*	Unpretentious, inexpensive spaghetti house.
Cucina Pazzo	1000 Wolf St	215-755-5400	$$$	Look no further than their monster crabcakes.
Johnnie's	2240 S 12th St	215-334-8006	$*	Inexpensive BYOB holds its own in the heart of South Philly.
Mamma Maria	1637 E Passyunk Ave	215-463-6884	$$$$	Seven-course prix fixe varies from evening to evening.
Marra's	1734 E Passyunk Ave	215-463-9249	$*	Zounds! The thin crust pie is heavenly.
Mr Martino's Trattoria	1646 E Passyunk Ave	215-755-0663	$$*	Elegant, understated, and the food is bliss.
Scannicchio's	2500 S Broad St	215-468-3900	$$	NJ legend finally opens branch in Philly.

Map 11 · South Philly East

China House	49 Snyder Ave	215-462-9956	$$*	Better-than-average standard Chinese fare.
Chuck E. Cheeses	9 Snyder Ave	215-551-4080	$	Some would find the visage of a giant rat hovering over your food disconcerting.
Langostino	100 Morris St	215-551-7709	$$*	Another yummy crustacean from the folks who brought you stone crabs.
Tony Luke's	39 E Oregon Ave	215-551-5725	$*	No higher honor amongst the various sandwich gods.
Two Street Pizza	1616 S 2nd St	215-468-5551	$	Where the mummers go when they need a slice.

229

Arts & Entertainment · **Restaurants**

Key: $: Under $10 / $$: $10–$20 / $$$: $20–$30 / $$$$: $30+, *: Does not accept credit cards.

Map 12 · Stadiums

Talk of the Town	3020 S Broad St	215-551-7277	$*	Stop by for a breakfast 'wich on your way to the game.

Map 13 · West Philly

Dwight's Southern Bar-B-Q	4345 Lancaster Ave	215-879-2497	$*	Even their mac and cheese is superior.
Kabobeesh	4201 Chestnut St	215-386-8081	$	Tasty kabobs of many varieties.
Koch's Deli	4309 Locust St	215-222-8662	$*	You will have to wait, but the Dagwood-like sandwiches are indeed worth it.
Pattaya Grill	4006 Chestnut St	215-387-8533	$$	Not your father's Thai restaurant: exotic and challenging.
Rx	4443 Spruce St	215-222-9590	$$	Ivy League-style BYOB has the goods.
Thai Singha House	3939 Chestnut St	215-382-8001	$$	Another in the long line of superior Thai joints in the 'hood.

Map 14 · University City

Abner's of University City	3813 Chestnut St	215-662-0100	$	Or you can just have them FedEx you a sandwich.
Lemon Grass Thai	3626 Lancaster Ave	215-222-8042	$$	Charming Thai cuisine. Order extra corn fritters.
Lou's Retaurante	305 N 33rd St	215-386-5687	$$	Small but winningly eclectic Mex gets much student love.
Mad 4 Mex	3401 Walnut St	215-382-2221	$	Student-friendly joint has edible burritos, good beer.
New Deck Tavern	3408 Sansom St	215-386-4600	$$	Bar food of a standard order, but whiskey selection is a plus.
Penne	3611 Walnut St	215-832-6222	$$$	The Hilton's pasta emporium has abundance of wine.
Picnic	3131 Walnut St	215-222-1608	$	Gourmet deli has the goods to go.
Pod	3636 Sansom St	215-387-1803	$$$	If Kubrick had opened a sushi bar...
Rana/Ed's	3513 Lancaster Ave	215-222-7136	$*	Great for those in the mood for both hummus and wings.
White Dog Cafe	3420 Sansom St	215-386-9224	$$$	Eclectic and organic without being annoying.
Zocalo	3600 Lancaster Ave	215-895-0139	$$	Fine Mexican flava. No tacos or chimichangas for miles.

Map 15 · Fairmount

Dominics Fish Market	2842 Cecil B Moore Ave	215-232-7120	$*	All the fresh seafood you might expect—only cheaper.
H&J Pizza Delite	2832 Ridge Ave	215-787-0411	$*	Nothing special, but it still gets the job done.
Norma's Steak & Hoagie Shop	2604 Cecil B Moore Ave	215-236-1010	$*	Cheesesteaks wit' all the trimmin's.
Yuri Deli	1618 N 29th St	215-763-7395	$*	Small spot filled with bunly goodness.

Map 16 · Art Museum West

China Lotus	1301 N 29th St	215-236-4423	$*	Decent, but not exactly greaseless, if you catch our drift.
Eg Zolt Soul Food	2624 Brown St	215-236-9320	$$*	Big portions of happy time comfort chow.
Regional Pizza	873 N 26th St	215-769-0722	$*	Sort of Greek style, with a powdery crust.
Rose's Deli	847 N Stillman St	215-235-8559	$ *	Popular with the Girard College crowd.

Map 17 · Art Museum East

Aspen	747 N 25th St	215-232-7736	$$	Authentic fish & chips don't come any better.
The Bishop's Collar	2349 Fairmount Ave	215-765-1616	$	Sandwiches and good barfood highlight this AM staple.
Bridgid's	726 N 24th St	215-232-3232	$$	Popular neighborhood joint has good chow & great beer.
Figs	2501 Meredith St	215-978-8440	$$*	Mediterranean BYOB hot spot has class to spare.
Gloria's Gourmet	2120 Fairmount Ave	215-235-3081	$$$	Eat fresh crab whilst grooving on smooth jazz.
Illuminare	2321 Fairmount Ave	215-765-0202	$$	Rocking the brick-oven pizzas for all a youse.
Jack's Firehouse	2130 Fairmount Ave	215-232-9000	$$	Former fire station still brings the BBQ heat.
Little Pete's	2401 Pennsylvania Ave	215-232-5001	*	A greasy spoon with no apologies.
London Grill	2301 Fairmount Ave	215-978-4545	$$	Weirdly enough, expect Asian, Latin, AND Mediterranean chow.
Rembrandt's	741 N 23rd St	215-763-2228	$$	Perhaps the best plate of calamari in the city.
Rose Tattoo Cafe	1847 Callowhill St	215-569-8939	$$$	Like being on the set of a Tennessee Williams opus.

Map 18 · Lower North Philly

City View Pizza	1547 Spring Garden St	215-564-1910	$*	Standard-issue pizza joint, big with CCP students.
Siam Lotus	931 Spring Garden St	215-769-2031	$$	Not the most inspiring neighborhood, but the cuisine more than makes up for it.
Warsaw Cafe	306 S 16th St	215-546-0204	$$	Load up on the pierogi and wiener schnitzel, then try to stand up.
Westy's Tavern & Restaurant	1440 Callowhill St	215-563-6134	$*	Old-man joint that reeks of smoke, grease, and greatness.

Map 19 · Northern Liberties

Abbaye	637 N 3rd St	215-627-6711	$	Belgian bistro uses good beer liberally throughout menu.
Azure	931 N 2nd St	215-629-0500	$$	"Vacation cuisine" for the terminally under-whelmed.
Il Cantuccio	701 N 3rd St	215-627-6573	$$*	Small, trend-setting trattoria, simple but effective.
Johnny Brenda's	1201 Frankford Ave	215-739-9684	$*	Just the kind of place your mom (and dietician) warned you about.
Kind Café	724 N 3rd St	215-922-5463	$*	Raw vegan chow served with life-affirming panache by rampant Aquarians.
Las Cazuelas	426-28 Girard Ave	215-351-9144	$$	Mexican Seafood that will knock your calcetines off.
N 3rd	801 N Third St	215-413-3666	$$$	Yummy chalkboard specials abound in this busy bar/bistro.
Pigalle	702-704 N 2nd St	215-627-7772	$$$	Parisian brasserie serves up the escargot-fare.
Radicchio	314 York Ave	215-627-6850	$$	Old City's version of a simple little BYOB with updated Italian cuisine.
Rustica Pizza	903 N 2nd St	215-627-1393	$*	Gianfranco's No-Libs extension: good and salty.
Silk City	435 Spring Garden St	215-592-8838	$*	Hipster mainstay—but don't let that keep you away.
Standard Tap	901 N 2nd St	215-238-0630	$$	Flagship joint with sumptuous dinners & brunches.

Map 20 · Fishtown / Port Richmond

Best Deli II	2616 E Lehigh Ave	215-291-9310	$*	Fine, but perhaps a bit of an inflated self-image.
Stefano's Original	2200 E Lehigh Ave	215-426-7595	$*	Quality pie that sticks to yer ribs a bit.
Stock's Bakery	2614 E Lehigh Ave	215 634-7344	$*	"Stock" up on all your baked goods needs. Forgive us.
Sulimay's Restaurant	632 E Girard Ave	215-423-1773	$*	High-class eggs and wondrous pancakes.

Map 21 · Roxborough / Manayunk

Adobe Café	4550 Mitchell St	215-483-3947	$$	Southwestern-style steakhouse offers seitan options.
Ben & Jerry's	4356 Main St	715-487-9320	$	Ice cream is good, right?
Bourbon Blue	2 Rector St	215 508-3360	$$$	Great Cajun food; blackened everything & a great rustic décor.
Couch Tomato Café	102 Rector St	215 438-2233	$	Worth a slice if you're in the neighborhood.
Jake's	4365 Main St	215-483-0444	$$$$	Pricey Manayunk flagship that got the ball rolling.
Kildare's	4417 Main St	215-482-3700	$$	Fine Irish food. Recommend the Boxtys.
Le Bus	4266 Main St	215-487-2663	$	Continental style with top-shelf baguettes.
Manayunk Brewery & Restaurant	4120 Main St	215-482-8220	$$	Lots of outdoor space and solid sushi.
Sonoma	4411 Main St	215-438-9400	$$	An ever-changing organic menu keeps regulars on their toes.
Zesty's Restaurant	4382 Main St	215-438-6226	$$	Nice Greek spot.

Map 22 · Manayunk

Muldoon's Waterway	3720 Main St	215-483-7500	$$	Typical higher-end seafood joint with its own lobster tank.
Vaccarelli's East End Tavern	4001 Cresson St	215-482-4944		Cozy neighborhood joint with rocking prices.

Map 23 · East Falls

Hidden River Café	3572 Indian Queen Ln	215-843 0955	$*	Eclectic vegetarian eats in a cozy atmosphere.
Johnny Manana's	4201 Ridge Ave	215-843-0499	$$	Unusual Mexican, but forget that and check the tequila shelf.
Sprigs	3749 Midvale Ave	215-849-9248	$$$	Can't pass on the inverted chocolate souffle.
Verge	4101 Kelly Dr	215-689-0050	$$$	No smokes, no cell phones. Just some fine eatin'.

Key: $: Under $10 / $$: $10–$20 / $$$: $20–$30 / $$$$: $30+, *: Does not accept credit cards.

Map 24 · Germantown South

Dahlak	5547 Germantown Ave	215-849-0788	$$	Ethiopian imported from West Philly.
House of Jin	234-36 W Chelten Ave	215-848-7700	$$	Fusing Chinese, Japanese and American Jazz? Whatever.
K&J Caribbean and American Diner	5603 Greene St	215-849-0242	$*	Have some red beans with your french toast.

Map 25 · Germantown North

Goat Hollow	300 W Mt Pleasant Ave	215-242-4710	$$	Restaurant/live music bar offers good vibe & existential eats.
Golden Crust Pizza	7155 Germantown Ave	215-248-2929	$*	Pedestrian, uninspired. Kids love it.
Rib Crib	6333 Germantown Ave	215-438-6793	$*	Meaty joint has cult following.
Rinker Rock Café	7105 Emlen St	215-247-5800	$*	Much art to peruse and a constantly shifting menu to keep you honest.
Umbria	7131 Germantown Ave	215-242-6470	$$*	Cozy little BYOB that remains a hit with locals.

Map 26 · Mt Airy

Bredenbeck's Bakery & Ice Cream Parlor	8126 Germantown Ave	215-247-7374	$	Fight through the line to score sweet ice cream treats.
Cafette	8136 Ardleigh St	215-242-4220	$$*	Bohemian bistro shows off its (mismatched) colors.
CinCin	7838 Germantown Ave	215-242-8800	$$	Highly-rated Chinese in a largely non-Asian community.
Citrus	8136 Germantown Ave	215-247-8188	$$	Vegetarian delights abound, but you best not wear your mink.
Cresheim Cottage Café	7402 Germantown Ave	215-248-4365	$$	Munch seafood quesadillas in cobblestoned historical setting.
Flying Fish	8142 Germantown Ave	215-247-0707	$$	Perfunctory seafood joint with predictable results.
North by Northwest	7165 Germantown Ave	215-248-1000	$$	Soul food and jazz roll off the tongue, Cats.

Map 27 · Chestnut Hill

Al Dana II	8630 Germantown Ave	215-247-3336	$	Popular Middle Eastern joint slams the chickpeas.
Best of British	8513 Germantown Ave	215-242-8848	$$	Jolly good show, wot? Have another cuppa.
Campbell's Place	8337 Germantown Ave	215-242-2066	$$	Pub fare in a busy neighborhood joint.
Chestnut Grill	8229 Germantown Ave	215-247-7570	$$	Cajun-flavored fare with Asian accents.
Melting Pot	8229 Germantown Ave	215-242-3003	$$	You may fondle your date as you enjoy your fondue.
Metropolitan Bakery	8607 Germantown Ave	215-753-9001	$*	Great breads, rolls, soups—and brownies to die for.
Pianta	8513 Germantown Ave	215-248-4557	$	Rounded pizzas and a rocking fresh juice bar.
Roller's	8705 Germantown Ave	215-242-1771	$$*	Gourmet international cuisine, prepared by masters.
Solaris Grille	8201 Germantown Ave	215-242-3400	$$$	Pricey nouveau fare set upon a lovely patio and bar.
Stella Notte Trattoria	8229 Germantown Ave	215-247-2100	$$	Fine Italian (including yummy pizzas) and massively good desserts.

The Northeast

Benny the Bums	9991 Bustleton Ave, Ste 3	215-673-3000	$$	Try the buffalo shrimp.
Blüe Ox Brauhaus	7980 Oxford Ave	215-728-9440	$$$	Authentic German food with great service.
Chink's Steaks	6030 Torresdale Ave	215-535-9405	$	A less than PC name, but a delicious cheesesteak for over fifty years.
Dining Car	8826 Frankford Ave	215-338-5113	$$	As the name indicates, a former working sidecar turned purveyor of above-average diner chow.
Guido's Restaurant	3545 Welsh Rd	215-335-1850	$$	BYOB Red sauce Italian overflowing with portions and flavor.
LaPadella	1619 Grant Ave	215-677-7723	$$$	Delicious seafood and Italian cuisine with a great piano player to serenade you.
Macaroni's Restaurant	9315 Old Bustleton Ave	215-464-3040	$$	Pedestrian name with cooking like Momma used to make.
Mayfair Diner	7353 Frankford Ave	215-624-4455	$$	Philly's answer to the New York Diner ego trip.
Nick's Roast Beef	2212 Cottman Ave	215-745-1292	$	Get your roast beef sandwiches here. Period.
Nifty Fifty's	2491 Grant Ave	215-676-1950	$*	Glorious diner chow and the best milkshakes in the city.
Santucci's Pizza	4010 Cottman Ave	215-332-4333	$	Generations of Santuccis have made these square pie classics since 1960.
Steve's Prince of Steaks	7200 Bustleton Ave	215-338-0985	$	Try their signature steak with melted white American cheese on top.

Times may be tough, but you still have to look good, even if you don't feel so well. After all, nothing brings a spring to your step more than a total makeover. Honey, we're right with you.

Beauty

For sophisticates whose hair is of the utmost importance, **Giovanni & Pileggi** will lovingly apply their brand of follicle therapy. For a totally different experience, hit up the **School of Hard Knox Barber Shop**, only you'd best read up on the Eagles beforehand. For tired and aching muscles, troop over to the **Body Klinic**, where a fine massage awaits. Finally, if you crave an edgy 'do, check out **Julius Scissor** or make your way past the Italian market to **Le Bomb Chelle**, where the owner maintains several rock star heads.

Clothing

You have a platinum card, you might as well use it, right? **Charlie Porter Boutique** will enable you to go a long way towards eventual max-out, but you'll be doing it in style. If

you want a unique wedding band, may we suggest **Halloween**? Ladies like their shoes, and no one understands that better than **Danielle Scott LTD**. After a shoe splurge, those same ladies can hit up **Very Bad Horse** or the **Pleasure Chest** to stock up on seduction-wear. For the men folk, if **Boyd's** is good enough for NBA 'ballers, it's probably okay for you too. And for the sports fan who has (nearly) everything, **Mitchell & Ness** sells the unique throwback jerseys that can't go out of style.

Home

It doesn't get more urbane than **Foster's**, where you can find everything from an ironic dish rack to an ironic ashtray. For the kitchen, **Fante's** offers every conceivable kind of appliance, device, and gadget. For students trying to fill up an empty apartment, fine deals can be had at **Uhuru**. If price is no object, **Lunacy Antiques** has things worth hoarding. Finally, after a long day of hitting the pavement, stop by the **House of Tea** and score a bag of something entirely soothing.

Map 1 • Center City West

Bilt Well Furniture Showroom	2317 Chestnut St	215-568-4600	You hope there merchendize is beter then there speling.
Body Klinic	2012 Walnut St	215-563-8888	Enjoy all their various transdermal services.
Chaos Hair Studio	2032 Chestnut St	215-569-9244	We can only hope that's the family name
Classical Guitar Store	2038 Sansom St	215-567-2972	Dude, where do you keep your Strats?
Dahlia	2003 Walnut St	215-568-6878	Unique jewelry pieces in a refreshingly Israeli atmosphere.
Julius Scissor	2045 Locust St	215-567-7222	A hair artiste, with various hair-crafted sculptures on display.
Pleasure Chest	2039 Walnut St	215-561-7400	Honey, where are my dang nipple clips?
Springboard Media	7212 Walnut St	215-988-7777	Best Mac store in the city.
Wonderland	2037 Walnut St	215-561-1071	Pipes, bongs, hookahs—strangely, all just for tobacco.

Map 2 • Rittenhouse / Logan Circle

Adresse	1600 Pine St	215-985-3161	You know you can't afford it if they only have three items for sale.
AIA Bookstore & Design Center	117 S 17th St	215-569-3188	Architectural specialists have lots of amazing design books and portfolios.
Ann Taylor	1713 Walnut St	215-977-9336	Elegant and WASP-y, just as Ann would have it.
Anthropologie	1801 Walnut St	215-568-7114	UO-owned, but this one's for the ladies and femmes.
Barnes & Noble Books	1805 Walnut St	215-665-0716	Ho-hum, just another behemoth of a bookstore with all the usual trimmings.
Benjamin Lovell Shoes	119 S 18th St	215-564-4655	Tasteful Euro-wear with a conservative bent.
Benton Method Electrolysis	1601 Walnut St	215-563-9917	Get rid of your back, nose, ear, leg, pit, and crotch hair painlessly.
Bon Voyage	1625 Chestnut St	215-567-1677	Luggage and travel gadgets up the yin yang.
Borders Book Shop	1 S Broad St	215-568-7400	Largely generic, but a decent selection of books, CDs and DVDs.
Boyd's	1818 Chestnut St	215-564-9000	Where visiting NBA players score sweet suits.
Bundy	1809 Chestnut St	215-567-2500	Mac specialists have somewhat limited selection but solid service.
Burberry's Limited	1705 Walnut St	215-557-7400	Robert the Bruce is rolling in his grave.
Center City Business Systems	105 S Juniper St	215-732-0566	Solid repair work for computers, plus they will work on old typewriters.
City Sports	1608 Walnut St	215-985-5860	Full-service from sneaks to parkas.
Daffy's	1700 Chestnut St	215-963-9996	Either you'll find a Versace shirt for $8 or nothing at all.
Danielle Scott LTD	1718 Walnut St	215-545-9800	Female footwear that will bring a catch to your throat.
David Michie Violins	1714 Locust St	215-545-5006	Exquisite, tuneful, and strung with cat guts.
Estetica	1726 Chestnut St	215-569-9624	People swear by their colorings. Hair colorings, we mean.
Francis Jerome	124 S 19th St	215-988-0440	One of Philly's fanciest sellers of insanely expensive beauty products.
Frankinstien Bike Worx	1529 Spruce St	215-893-0415	If you're really lucky, one of the Dead Milkmen will stop by.
Gentleman's Retreat	20 S 18th St	215-569-0695	You just know all kinds of twisted stuff happens there.
Giovanni & Pileggi	1701 Walnut St	215-568-3040	Fancy-pants folks love to have their follicle paradigm shifts here.

Map 2 • Rittenhouse / Logan Circle—*continued*

Halloween	1329 Pine St	215-732-7711	Gothic jewelry but really tasteful.
Hangers	1933 Locust St	215-854-0100	Decent service and slightly used designer duds
Hope Chest	200 S Broad St	215-545-4515	Naughty-wear in opulent surroundings.
Jacob's Music Pianos	1718 Chestnut St	215-568-7800	If you ask, they'll play you "Piano Man" on any of their models.
Joseph A Bank Clothiers	1650 Market St	215-563-5990	High-end Toriewear for today's neoconservatives.
Joseph Fox Bookshop	1724 Sansom St	215-563-4184	Strong-minded underground bookstore (literally).
Kenneth Cole	1422 Walnut St	215-790-1690	Mild-mannered designer wear, emphasis on the feet.
Knit Wit	1721 Walnut St	215-564-4760	Despite the awful pun, an evening wear store for 'mature' ladies.
Lucky Jeans	1634 Walnut St	215-732-8933	When $150 feels about right for a pair of miner-pants.
Maron Chocolates	107 S 18th St	215-988-0125	Candy, ice cream, chocolate—what's not to love?
Motherhood Maternity	1625 Chestnut St	215-569-0211	Casual, comfy clothes for moms-to-be.
Nicole Miller	200 S Broad St	215-546-5007	Manayunk's own designer, gone big-time.
Pearl of the East	1615 Walnut St	215-563-1563	Asian-themed furnishings; plenty of kimonos.
Rittenhouse Camera	135 S 18th St	215-568-5006	Specializing in switching your crappy Super 8 stuff to DVD and so on.
Ritz Camera	1330 Walnut St	215-545-7761	Practical camera chainstore.
Robin's Book Store	1837 Chestnut St	215-567-2615	Sweet hardcover selections and lots of live readings.
Sophisticated Seconds	116 S 18th St	215-561-6740	Upscale consignmentorium has wedding dresses.
Stiletto	124 S 18th St	215-972-0920	Be prepared for some serious sticker shock.
TLA	1520 Locust St	215-735-7887	Several locations of city's fave DVD rentals—auteur/foreign haven.
Tower Records	100 S Broad St	215-568-8001	When you just want to spend more money than you need to.
Tweeter	1429 Walnut St	215-636-9290	Men stand outside the window and drool at the giant HD TVs.
Urban Outfitters	1809 Walnut St	215-564-2313	Started right here and still too flashy and over-priced.
Vigant Inc.	200 S Broad St	215-735-5057	More cow-based products than a butcher shop.
Whodunit	1931 Chestnut St	215-567-1478	Mysteries and suspense thrillers, and a few science books thrown in.

Map 3 • Center City East

After Hours Formalwear	1201 Walnut St	215-923-1230	Tuxes from Dick Cheney to Liberace.
Aldo Shoes	901 Market St	215-625-9854	Reasonably priced footwear haven for both genders.
Armand Records	1108 Chestnut St	215-592-7973	Hip-hop DJs do all their significant shopping here.
Beaux Arts Video	1000 Spruce St	215-923-1714	Small, independent video rental store has helpful staff and solid picks.
Bike Line	1028 Arch St	215-923-1310	Decent chain of stores offering fair service.
Buffalo Exchange	1109 Walnut St	215-627-4647	On a good day, some great finds.
Burlington Coat Factory	1001 Market St	215-627-6933	Seven hundred million coats and no one to help you.
Children's Place	901 Market St	215-627-8187	From infants to adolescents, plus kid beauty products.
Claire's Boutique	901 Market St	215-592-8507	Accessorize, accessorize, accessorize. Quite cheaply.
Comet Camera Repair	1209 Walnut St	215-765-6431	They cover a big array of brands, from Polaroid to Nikon.
De Carlo Salon	1211 Walnut St	215-923-5806	Monster assortment of hair products, including 'poos, gels and sprays.
Eighth Street Music Center	1023 1/2 Arch St	215-923-5040	All kinds of instruments, plus rentals and recording service.
Funk O Mart	1106 Market St	215-963-0500	Rap, soul, and R&B rules this pawn-shop-cum-music outlet.
Giovanni's Room	345 S 12th St	215-923-2960	Gay/lesbian themed tomes, plus visiting writers and readings.
Hibberds Books	1306 Walnut St	215-546-8811	Good used and rare sections.
I Goldburg	1300 Chestnut St	215-925-9393	Army/Navy surplus store with plenty of other goodies.
Lord & Taylor	1300 Market St	215-241-9000	Great light show at Christmas time.
Lunacy Antiques	1118 Pine St	215-238-9028	Expensive but vast and varied.
M Finkel & Daughter	936 Pine St	215-627-7797	Daughter is always there to help you out.
Mid-City Camera	1316 Walnut St	215-735-2522	Wide range, from crappy PaS to super-luxe Hasselblads.
Mitchell & Ness	1318 Chestnut St	267-765-0663	Where the whole retro-jersey craze started.
Quaker Photo	1025 Arch St	215-922-4444	Photo processing for pros, as well as digital imaging.
Rustic Music	333 S 13th St	215-732-7805	Sweet little guitar shop also has a collection of CDs and vinyl.
School of Hard Knox Barber	1105 Walnut St	215-925-4405	Way cheaper than a shrink.
Sound of Market Street	15 S 11th St	215-925-3150	The largest independent music store in the city. Huge amounts of jazz.
Spruce Street Video	1201 Spruce St	215-985-2955	The largest selection of gay porn in the country.
Uhuru	1220 Walnut St	215-546-9616	Politically-minded used furniture store.
W J Bookstore	1017 Arch St	215-592-9666	Thousands of Chinese titles: no waiting.

Map 4 • Old City / Society Hill

Big Jar Books	55 N 2nd St	215-574-1650	Used bookstore numero uno for OC. Manageable and well-kept.
Cappelli Hobbies	313 Market St	215-629-1757	Scale models of all kinds of crap: check out the WWI bombers.

Charlie Porter Boutique	212 Market St	215-627-3390	If you have to ask the price, set your face on stun.
Coach	38 N 3rd St	215 751 0772	I surrender, here's the deed to my house.
Digital Ferret	526 S 5th St	215-925-9259	Great selection of indie and ambient.
Foster's Urban Homeware	124 N 3rd St	267-671-0588	Flash funkified accessories for design hipsters.
Friedman Umbrellas	114 S 3rd St	215-922-4877	Big selection and ingratiating sales force.
Kamikaze Kids	527 S 4th St	215-574-9800	Tiny suits and bow-ties add to the 'fun.'
Lele	30 S 2nd St	215-592-8474	Stunning dresses and evening wear. Bring several credit cards.
Pierre's Costumes	211 N 3rd St	215-925-7121	Well over 100,000 costumes.
Red Red Red Hair Salon	222 Church St	215-923-4042	Colorings and much teasing.
Rescue 138	138 N 3rd St	215-873-0214	An eclectic mix of vintage, designer, and retro-cool duds.
Subzero	520 S 5th St	215-925-9376	Thrash on your gnarly boards.
Vagabond	37 N 3rd St	267-671-0737	Seasonal fashions and original designs.
Wooden Shoe Books	508 S 5th St	215-413-0999	Anarchist's playground with numerous political tracts.

Map 6 • Gray's Ferry East / Graduate Hospital

Bicycle Therapy	2211 South St	215-735-7849	The best bike-repair joint in the city.
Sweetwater Swimwear	715 S 18th St #B	215-732-1713	Designer swimwear for God's beautiful people.

Map 7 • Southwark West

Awa's Hair Braiding	1608 South St	215-735-3233	Braids, extensions, colorings, and good, genial conversation.
Sistah's Consignment Shop	1442 Wharton St	215-339-0806	The usual assortment, but with an urban contemporary vibe.

Map 8 • Bella Vista / Queen Village

611 Records	611 S 4th St	215-413-9100	Trance out with big techno, house selections.
Antiquarian's Delight	615 S 6th St	215-592-0256	Converted synagogue houses many treasures.
Bella Boutique	624 S 3rd St	215-923-2880	Pre-worn designer wear ain't cheap, apparently.
Cohen Hardware	615 E Passyunk Ave	215-922-3493	Friendly, slightly odd staff make it worthwhile.
Cue Records	617 S 4th St	215-413-3525	A goldmine for underground hip-hop vinyl.
Essene	719 S 4th St	215-928-3722	Organic, vegan market & cafeteria. Plus lots of vitamins.
Fante's	1006 S 9th St	215-922-5557	Exhaustive inventory of all kitchen goodies.
Game Gallery	505 South St	215 625-0795	Everything from scrabble to GTA.
Garland of Letters	527 South St	215-923-5946	New-age books, trinkets and many, many types of candles.
Goldstein's Boys' & Men's Wear	811 S 6th St	215-468-0564	Italian imports since 1902. Loads of suspenders, too.
Greene Street	700 South St	215-733-9261	Boyfriends/husbands bring a magazine—this will take a while.
Guacamole	422 South St	215-923-6174	Groovy clothes for the female form.
Hand Impressions	759 S 4th St	215-928-9286	Gallery with bizarre ceramics and many bags.
Hats in the Belfry	245 South St	215-922-6770	Grab a cool Gandalf hat and be the envy of your D&D club.
House of Tea	720 S 4th St	215-923-8327	Some varieties more expensive than good hashish.
Kroungold's Better Furniture	710 S 5th St	215-925-2483	No-pressure sales and a range of furniture.
Le Bomb Chele	1134 S 9th St	215-755-5976	Delightfully chaotic joint offers saucy cuts.
Maxie's Daughter	721 S 4th St	215-829-2226	The heart of fabric row.
Mood	531 South St	215-413-1930	When you're in the 'mood' for a giant loaf of cheese.
Mostly Books	529 Bainbridge St	215-238-9838	Books, furniture and "20th Century Artifacts."
Nocturnal Skateshop	610 S 3rd St	215-922-3177	X-Games street champ Kerry Getz is the owner.
Pearl Art Supply	417 South St	215-238-1900	Three floors of inks, paints, papers, and vineballs.
Pearl of Africa	624 South St	215-351-7518	Um, that is burning incense, right?
Philadelphia Bar & Restaurant Supply	620 E Passyunk Ave	215-925-7649	From non-stick ladles to sweet wine keys.
Philadelphia Record Exchange	618 S 5th St	215-922-2752	Excellent jazz and rock stuff, plus tons of vinyl.
Retrospect	534 South St	267-671-0116	Clothes, knick-knacks and furniture—though hardly cheap.
Revelations	711 S 4th St	215-945-4022	Phish Phreaks meet Al Swerengen.
Rode'o Kids	721 S 4th St	215-625-9530	Frilly and whacked-out clothes for disturbed children.
Showcase Comics	640 South St	215-625-9613	Fair collection of new titles, classics, and graphic novels.
South Street Vintage	529 South St	215-925-0668	We thought old, used clothes were meant to be LESS expensive.
Spaceboy Music	409 South St	215-925-3032	Not the friendliest, but decent selection and some hard-to-find stuff.
State of the Art Records	638 South St	215-829-8111	Listen before you buy, and get what you buy cheaply.
Termini Brothers Bakery	1523 S 8th St	215-334-1816	Italian bakery. Cannolis!
Triple Play Sporting Goods	827 S 9th St	215-923-5466	Customized fan-ware and lots of USA pride.
Via Bicycle	606 S 9th St	215-627-3370	Unpretentious and nothing fancy—but cheap.
Zipperhead	407 South St	215-928-1123	Where all today's punks score combat boots and eye shadow.

Map 10 • Moyamensing / East Passyunk

Fabulous Finds	1146 McKean St	215-336-5226	From evening gowns to baby booties.
Interior Concepts	1701 E Passyunk Ave	215-468-6226	Leather furniture, beds, and salesmen.

Map 11 • South Philly East

Forman Mills	22 Wolf St	215-389-5353	Lots of bargains, but be prepared to hunt for them.
IKEA	2206 S Columbus Blvd	215-551-4532	
Lowe's	2106 S Columbus Blvd	215-982-5391	

Map 14 • University City

EMS	130 S 36th St	215-386-1020	Decent selection of camping gear, wait for the sales.

Map 16 • Art Museum West

Drive Sports	2601 Pennsylvania Ave	215-232-7368	Nice fellows, but forget about timely service.

Map 18 • Lower North Philly

Diving Bell Scuba Shop	681 N Broad St	215-763-6868	Just don't watch *Open Water* first.

Map 19 • Northern Liberties

A Pea in the Pod	456 N 5th St	215-873-2200	Funky, urbane duds for preggers.
Dot Dash	630 N 2nd St	215-925-2432	Buy, sell and trade your oddball CDs—plus vintage duds.
Very Bad Horse	606 N 2nd St	215-627-6989	Where Steven Tyler would shop if he were 22 and cool.

Map 21 • Roxborough / Manayunk

Chicos	4367 Main St	215-482-3536	High-end women's clothing.
Leehe Fai	4343 Main St	215-483-4400	Ritzy clothes and cloying service.
Main Street Music	4444 Main St	215-487-7732	Indy music store.
Pompanoosac Mills	4120 Main St	215-508-3263	Great high-end furniture.
Pottery Barn	4230 Main St	215-508-6778	Pottery barn...what can you say.
Restoration Hardware	4130 Main St	215-930-0300	See Pottery Barn.
Somnia	4050 Main St	215-487-1515	Furniture, mattresses, beds, etc...
Worn Yesterday	4235 Main St	215-482-3316	Designer infantwear? They're too young to care, people.

Map 27 • Chestnut Hill

Leehe Fai	4343 Main St	215-483-4400	Ritzy clothes and cloying service.
Worn Yesterday	4235 Main St	215-482-3316	Designer infantwear? They're too young to care, people.
Chestnut Hill Cheese Shop	8509 Germantown Ave	215-242-2211	Family-owned cheese bazaar.
Cake	184C E Evergreen Ave	215-247-6887	Beware of the butter. Deliciously rich, yet simple desserts.
French Bakery & Cafe	8624 Germantown Ave -Rear	215-247-5959	Delectable croissants, soups, and sandwiches.

The Northeast

Contempo Cuts	2218 Cottman Ave	215-742-5156	An all in one salon, spa, hair, and nail boutique.
Dutch Country Farmers' Market	2031 Cottman Ave	215-745-6008	Vendors selling pretzels, produce, and rotisserie meats year round.
Harry's Natural Food Store	1805 Cottman Ave	215-742-3807	After 25 years, Harry still sells herbs, vitamins, and specialty natural foods.
International Coins Unlimited	1825 Cottman Ave	215-745-4900	Rare and new coins for sale or trade.
Peters Handbags	8314 Bustleton Ave	215-728-1624	Stylish handbags for less.
Roosevelt Mall	2311 Cottman Ave	215-331-2000	A shopping bonanza.
St Jude Shop	6902 Castor Ave	215-742-6045	Known for its religious artifacts.

Two things you need to know about Philly's burgeoning art scene: 1. You can buy works from as-yet-unheralded artists for relatively cheap. 2. The scene itself is a whole lot less eviscerating in Philly than with our illustrious neighbors to the north. The three highly-regarded art schools in the area produce an abundance of artists at various stages in their careers.

A great way to become acquainted with some of the galleries, at least in Old City, is to regularly attend Philly's First Friday gatherings. On the first Friday of each month, the OC galleries stay open late, launch lots of new exhibits, and pander to guests with cheap wine and Triskets. Check out the works at **Pentimenti**, **Artists' House**, **Gallery Space 1026**, **Hot Soup**, and **Nexus**, among others. For performance space as well as fine arts exhibits, **Painted Bride** has long been a Philly stalwart.

If you have money to burn for art, you can hit the big leagues at **Locks** or, for considerably less, purchase a world-class piece from **The Clay Studio**.

Map 1 · Center City West

Dolan/Maxwell	2046 Rittenhouse Sq	215-732-7787
The Galleries at Moore College of Art & Design	20th St & Benjamin Franklin Pkwy	215-965-4027
Helen Drutt: Philadelphia	2220 Rittenhouse Sq	215-735-1625
Sande Webster	2006 Walnut St	215-636-9003

Map 2 · Rittenhouse / Logan Circle

Creative Artists Network	237 S 18th St	215-546-7775
Fleisher/Ollman Gallery	1616 Walnut St	215-545-7562
Gross McCleaf	127 S 16th St	215-665-8138
Newman Galleries	1625 Walnut St	215-563-1779
Pennsylvania Academy of the Fine Arts	118 N Broad St	215-972-7600
Philadelphia Art Alliance	251 S 18th St	215-545-4302
The Print Center	1614 Latimer St	215-735-6090
Schmidt/Dean Gallery	1710 Sansom St	215-569-9433

Map 3 · Center City East

African American Museum in Philadelphia	701 Arch St	215-574-0380 ext. 235
Bridgette Mayer Gallery	709 Walnut St	215-431-8893
The Fabric Workshop and Museum	1315 Cherry St	215-568-1111
Gallery Space 1026	1026 Arch St	215-574-7630
Matthew Izzo Gallery	928 Pine St	215-922-2570
The Philadelphia Sketch Club	235 S Camac St	215-545-9298
Seraphin Gallery	1108 Pine St	215-923-7000

Map 4 · Old City / Society Hill

3rd Street Gallery	58 N 2nd St	215-625-0993
Artist's House	57 N 2nd St	215-923-8440
ArtJaz	53 N 2nd St	215-922-4800
The Clay Studio	139 N 2nd St	215-925-3453
Gallery Joe	302 Arch St	215-592-7752
Hot Soup Gallery	26 S Strawberry St	215-922-2332
Indigo	151 N 3rd St	215-922-4041
Larry Becker	43 N 2nd St	215-925-5389
Locks Gallery	600 Washington Sq S	215-629-1000

Muse Gallery	60 N 2nd St	215-627-5310
Nexus	137 N 2nd St	215-629-1103
Painted Bride	230 Vine St	215-925-9914
Peng Gallery	35 S 3rd St	215-629-5889
Pentimenti	145 N 2nd St	215-625-9990
Pringle Gallery	323 Arch St	215-592-7746
Rosenfeld Gallery	113 Arch St	215-922-1376
Wexler Gallery	201 N 3rd St	215-923-7030

Map 8 · Bella Vista / Queen Village

Da Vinci Art Alliance	704 Catherine St	215-829-0466
Fleisher Art Memorial	719 Catherine St	215-922-3456 ext. 318
Spector	510 Bainbridge St	215-238-0840

Map 14 · University City

Arthur Ross Gallery/University of Pennsylvania	220 S 34th St	215-898-2083
Esther M Klein Art Gallery	3600 Market St	215-966-6188
Institute of Contemporary Art/ University of Pennsylvania	118 S 36th St	215-898-5911

Map 17 · Art Museum East

Philadelphia Museum of Art	26th St & Benjamin Franklin Pkwy	215-763-8100
Rodin Museum	22nd St & Benjamin Franklin Pkwy	215-763-8100

Map 18 · Lower North Philly

Rosenwald-Wolf Gallery	320 S Broad St	215-717-6480

Map 19 · Northern Liberties

ADM Gallery	314 Brown St	215-925-6040

Map 21 · Roxborough / Manayunk

Artforms Gallery -Manayunk	106 Levering St	215-483-3030

Map 27 · Chestnut Hill

JMS Gallery	8236 Germantown Ave	215-248-4649
Woodmere Art Musuem	9201 Germantown Ave	215-247-0476

General Information

NFT Map: 2
Address: 1729 Mt Vernon St
                    Philadelphia, PA 19130
Phone: 215-685-0754
Website: www.muralarts.org

Overview

If graffiti-covered buildings and dreary gray walls can look ominous and depressing on the most vibrant blocks, one can only imagine their effect on the psyche of poverty-stricken neighborhoods. But like concealer that hides facial blemishes, the Mural Arts Program covers up blights on the cityscape; more than 2,400 indoor and outdoor murals have been commissioned across the city since 1984. Philadelphia has quickly become the mural capital of the country, and the Mural Arts Program continues to commission up to 100 murals each year in neighborhoods that request their help.

This same public art program now offers bi-weekly trolley tours that guide participants to some of the more obscure mural sites. Often led by mural artists, the tours explore different neighborhoods each week and provide a "behind-the-scenes" look at the making of the intricate paintings.

There's also a free Mural Arts Program map with a walking route and a driving route that you can follow in your own time at your own pace. The walking tour is approximately 3.3 miles long and takes at least an hour and a half to complete. The driving tour also takes about an hour and a half and covers 10.5 miles of territory. Pick up a map at the Independence Visitor Center on 6th and Market Streets.

Regular Tours

Bi-weekly tours (Wednesdays and Saturdays) depart from the Market Visitor Center on the corner of 6th and Market Streets at 11 am from April to October on Saturdays, and May to October on Wednesdays. Tour tickets are $18 for adults, $15 for students and seniors, and $10 for children 5-12. The tour schedule is as follows:

1st Sat and Wed of each month: Center City
2nd Sat and Wed of each month: North Philly
3rd Sat and Wed of each month: South Philly
4th Sat and Wed of each month: West Philly
If there is a 5th Sat or Wed, the tour features Broad Street highlights.

Murals and Meals

"Murals and Meals" is a combined tour/restaurant program that couples mural-viewing with neighborhood dining, so you can chomp down on a greasy cheesesteak from Pat's and/or Geno's in South Philly while gazing at the mural of the infamous Italian mayor Frank Rizzo. You'll definitely need to make reservations (215-685-0754), as tours are limited to just 35 people per trip. Tours are held on different Saturdays and Sundays each month, so check the website for schedules and pricing.

Winter Tours

There are no regularly scheduled winter tours, but the Mural Arts program does offer specific programs and lectures between October and April. Check the website for events.

A little-known fact about Philadelphia: it has a pretty vibrant theater community. Sure, you don't think of us in the same league as Chicago or that rinky-dink city to our Immediate north, but the truth is that theater is huge here. The wonderful **Wilma Theater** on Broad Street produces top-of-the-line works by Stoppard and Shepard. Nearby, the **Adrienne** delivers serious fare, while the **Prince Music Theater** has a little bit of everything, including a robust film series.

History-lovers will know that the venerated **Walnut Street Theater** is, in fact, the oldest in the country. Downtown a wee bit, the **Arden** offers fascinating local productions. For those who enjoy the puppetry arts, there are two main hubs of activity: the **Spiral Q** performs a variety of shows and the **Mum Puppettheater** is more politically minded and serious. Broadway enthusiasts should head to the **Forrest** and the **Merriam**, which both provide plenty of high notes and shoe-tapping.

Theater	Address	Phone	Map
2nd Stage	2030 Sansom St	215-563-4330	1
Academy of Music	S Broad St & Locust St	215-893-1999	2
Adrienne Theatre	2030 Sansom St	215-569-9700	1
Adonis Theater	2026 Sansom St	215-557-9319	1
Arden Theater	40 N 2nd St	215-922-1122	4
Bistro Romano Mystery Dinner Theatre	120 Lombard St	215-925-8880	4
The Bridge: cinema de lux	40th St & Walnut St	215-386-3300	13
Cinemagic 3 at Penn	3925 Walnut St	215-222-5555	13
Forrest Theatre	1114 Walnut St	866-886-7049	3
The Gershman Y	401 S Broad St	215-545-4400	2
The Harold Prince Theatre	3680 Walnut St	215-898-6701	14
International House Theater	3701 Chestnut St	215-895-6546	14
Irvine Auditorium	3401 Spruce St	215-898-6701	14
Kappa Achievement Center	5927 Germantown Ave	215-848-4227	24
Kimmel Center	260 S Broad St	215-790-5800	2
Merriam Theater	250 S Broad St	215-732-5997	2
Mum Puppettheatre	115 Arch St	215-925-7686	4
Philadelphia Arts Bank	601 S Broad St	215-545-0590	7
Philadelphia Theatre Company	1714 Delancey St	215-985-0420	2
Plays & Players	1714 Delancey St	215-735-0630	2
Prince Music Theater	1412 Chestnut St	215-569-9700	2
Ritz 5	214 Walnut St	215-925-7900	4
Ritz at the Bourse	400 Ranstead St	215-440-1181	4
Ritz East	125 S 2nd St	215-925-4535	4
Roxy Theatre Philadelphia	2023 Sansom St	215-923-6699	1
Society Hill Playhouse	507 S 8th St	215-923-0210	3
Spiral Q Puppet Theater	3114 Spring Garden St	215-222-6979	14
Theatre of Living Art	334 South St	215-922-1011	8
Tuttleman IMAX Theater-Franklin Institute	222 N 20th St	215-448-1111	1
The Wilma Theater	265 S Broad St	215-546-7824	2
Arts Drake Dance Theater	1512 Spruce St	215-717-6110	2
United Artists Riverview Stadium 17	1400 S Columbus Blvd	215-755-2353	8
Walnut Street Theatre	825 Walnut St	215-574-3550	3
The Zellerbach Theatre	3680 Walnut St	215-898-6791	14

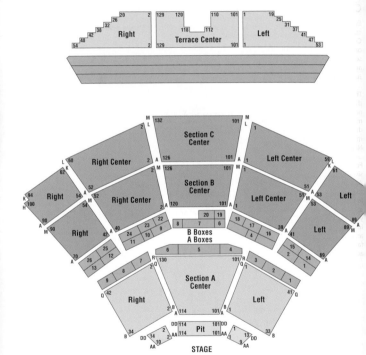

General Information

Address:	52nd St & Parkside Ave
	Philadelphia, PA 19131
Phone:	215-893-1999
Website:	www.manncenter.org

Overview

Every major city in America has a big outdoor concert space on its outskirts; the venerable Mann Center is Philly's. The venue is ideal for picnicking on the grass with family and friends while concerts serve as background music to more pertinent social activity. It's also a great place to watch the Fourth of July fireworks.

The Mann Center was originally built to serve as the summer home of the Philadelphia Orchestra. It now boasts an eclectic concert schedule including mainstream rock bands, operas, stand-up comedians, children's programs, and popular classical music selections, as well as the occasional Christian Night Out.

For most events, lawn tickets are cheap and still in sight of the stage, and pavilion tickets are affordable. All tickets are non-refundable. (IE you'll be expected to plop down on the grass, rain or shine.) You're allowed to take lawn chairs and food with you (you can also buy food there) and, depending on the event, you can also take alcohol (make sure you check before your six-pack is confiscated at the door). There are plans for a big renovation of the confusing eating facilities, but until then we recommend booking in advance if you want a sit-down meal.

How to Get There—Driving

From Center City, take the Benjamin Franklin Parkway to the Art Museum Circle. Follow the signs to West River Drive. Once you're on West River Drive, turn left at the first traffic light (Sweet Briar Cut-Off). Turn right at the stop sign to Lansdowne Drive and proceed on Lansdowne to the parking areas.

Parking

Parking costs $7. Parking areas, as well as the center itself, open two hours before any event, so you can arrive early for dinner before the show.

How to Get There—Mass Transit

SEPTA bus lines 38, 40, and 43 deliver you within walking distance of the Mann Center. The Center City Loop Bus provides service between certain stops in the city and the Mann (one-way fare is $3). Check the bus schedule online at www.manncenter.org/Pages/Transit.html.

How to Get Tickets

You can purchase tickets on the Mann Center website, but be ready to pay a service charge of $5.50 per ticket and $3 per order. Tickets purchased online can only be picked up at the Mann Center box office will-call window at 52nd Street and Parkside Drive. To avoid service charges, you can buy tickets in person from the Mann Center box office, which is open Monday-Saturday from 10 am to 5 pm. You can also purchase tickets from the Center City box office, located at the Kimmel Center (Broad St & Spruce St), for a $2 service charge per order.

General Information

NFT Map:	2
Address:	260 S Broad St
	Philadelphia, PA 19102
Phone:	215-893-1900
Website:	www.kimmelcenter.org
Tele-charge:	215-893-1999
Hours:	Mon-Sun; 10 am-6 pm, and later during
	evening performances.

Overview

The Kimmel Center occupies a full city block on Broad Street's southern side and is considered the crown jewel in the refurbished Avenue of the Arts. Fifteen million dollars of the $265 million project came from philanthropist Sidney Kimmel, the most generous individual donor. Playing home to the Philadelphia Orchestra, the Chamber Orchestra of Philadelphia, PHILADANCO, American Theater Arts for Youth, the Philadelphia Chamber Music Society, the Opera Company of Philadelphia, the Pennsylvania Ballet, and Philly Pops, the place oozes a desperate air of forced renaissance.

The 2,500-seat **Verizon Hall** was custom-built by acoustician Russell Johnson to enhance the orchestral sound of the Philadelphia Orchestra. The architectural design of the hall, with its wood paneling and curves, makes it look like the inside of a violin or cello. Despite pre-construction hoopla about the hall's planned world-class acoustics, classical music connoisseurs have found the sound to be less than exceptional; the average, untrained concert-goer will find little to complain about, though. In 2006, the largest concert hall organ in the US, featuring 6,000 pipes, will be unveiled—stay tuned.

The smaller **Perelman Theater** has 650 seats and is used for chamber music and dance performances. The 2,893-seat **Philadelphia Academy of Music** is owned by The Philadelphia Orchestra Association, managed by the Kimmel Center, and hosts performances by the Opera Company of Philadelphia, the Pennsylvania Ballet, and Philly Pops with Peter Nero.

In addition to a pretty cool eatery and gift shop, the Kimmel Center has a gallery showcasing works from nearby Moore College of Art and Design.

How to Get There—Driving

From the north, follow Broad Street around City Hall and you'll find the Kimmel Center on the southwest corner of Broad and Spruce Streets. The Vine Street Expressway (I-676) will get you to Broad Street, and either I-95 or I-76 will get you to the Vine Street Expressway. From the Ben Franklin Bridge, take the first exit on 8th Street to Spruce Street and continue west to Broad Street. From the Walt Whitman Bridge, take the Broad Street exit and go north.

Parking

Entrance to the Kimmel Center parking garage is south of the Broad Street entrance to the center and can only be accessed by cars traveling south on Broad Street. Garage hours change seasonally, but regular hours are Monday through Thursday 7 am until 10 pm, Friday from 7 am until midnight, and weekends from 8 am until midnight. If you're in by noon and out by 6 pm, you'll pay $10 on weekdays. If you arrive after noon, expect to pay $16. Weekends are a flat rate of $16. If that seems expensive, you can try your luck with street parking or check the rates of the local lots that surround the area.

How to Get There—Mass Transit

Take the subway. The Broad Street line's Walnut-Locust Station is two blocks from the Kimmel Center. Make a free transfer from the Market-Frankford line and the trolleys to the Broad Street Line at the 15th & Market stop. Regional Rail is also an option, with Suburban Station a 15-minute walk away from the Kimmel Center. The PHLASH makes a stop near the Kimmel Center and bus routes C, 27, 32, 12, 9, 21 and 42 all stop at the center.

How to Get Tickets

The only way to avoid the $5 service charge per ticket is by purchasing tickets at the Kimmel Center box office, which is open Monday-Sunday 10 am-6 pm. Tickets are also sold online at www.philorch.org or by phone on 215-893-1999.

If you're on a limited budget, shoot for the $10 tickets to "Kimmel Center Presents" performances. The $10 tickets are up for grabs at the box office starting at 5:30 pm for evening performances and 11:30 am for matinees. "Citizens Bank Broadway" performances offer $25 tickets on a show-to-show basis. Tickets are available two hours before curtain time, must be paid for in cash, and are limited to one per person. Student rush tickets are also available with a student ID.

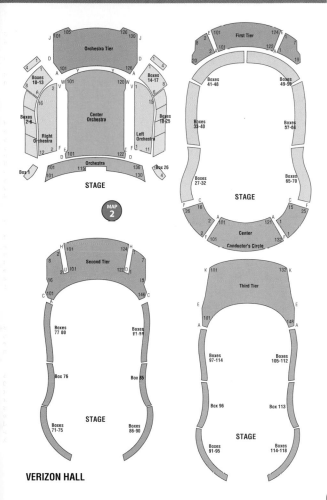

MAP
2

STAGE

Orchestra Tier

Boxes
10-13

Boxes
14-17

Boxes
2-6

Center
Orchestra

Boxes
18-25

Right
Orchestra

Left
Orchestra

Box 1

Orchestra

Box 26

First Tier

Boxes
41-48

Boxes
49-56

Boxes
33-40

Boxes
57-64

Boxes
27-32

Boxes
65-70

STAGE

Center
Conductor's Circle

Second Tier

Boxes
77-80

Boxes
81-84

Box 76

Box 85

Boxes
71-75

Boxes
86-90

STAGE

VERIZON HALL

Third Tier

Boxes
97-114

Boxes
105-112

Box 96

Box 113

STAGE

Boxes
91-95

Boxes
114-118

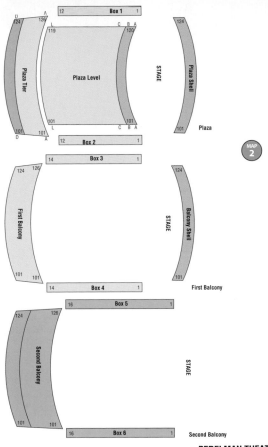

MAP 2

PERELMAN THEATER

BREWERY TOURS
SATURDAYS NOON-3PM

2439 AMBER STREET

PHILADELPHIA

WWW.YARDSBREWING.COM

Your home away from home for news and public affairs.

Fresh Air with Terry Gross, produced at WHYY-FM

WHY**Y** 91 FM

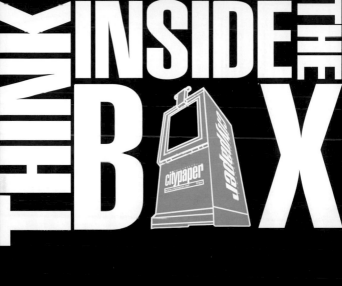

THINK INSIDE THE BOX

citypaper

ROBIN'S

BOOKSTORE

Books & Events for Independent Minds
from Philadelphia's oldest Independent Book Store

RELOAD

BAGGAGE

custom handmade
MESSENGER BAGS
+
ACCESSORIES

+ *rare*
BIKES
PARTS
+
CLOTHING

608 N 2ND STREET
PHILADELPHIA
215. 922. 2018
RELOADBAGS.COM

hiladelphia's premier rock and roll bar.

Street Index

Street	Page	Grid
Main St		
(3700-3999)	22	A1/B1
(4000-4599)	21	A1/B1/B2
Mallory St	21	A1
Manayunk Ave		
(3600-4211)	22	A1/B1
(4212-4799)	21	A1/A2/B2
Mandela Way	13	A1
W Manheim St	24	B2
Manning St		
(400-499)	4	B1
(700-1299)	3	B1/B2
(1300-1949)	2	B1/B2
(1950-2499)	1	B1/B2
Manning Walk	4	B1
Manor St	22	A1
Mansfield Ave	26	A2
Mansion St	21	A1/B2
Manton St		
(100-799)	8	B1/B2
(1500-1749)	7	B1
(1750-2449)	6	B1/B2
(2450-2799)	5	B2
Mantua Ave	14	A1/A2
W Maplewood Ave	24	A2/B1
W Maplewood Mal	24	A2
Marion St	24	A1/B2
Market Sq	24	A2
Market St		
(100-649)	4	A1/A2
(650-1349)	3	A1/A2
(1350-1949)	2	A1/A2
(1950-2400)	1	A1/A2
(2900-3849)	14	B1/B2
(3850-4638)	13	B1/B2
Markle St	22	A1/A2
Marlborough St	20	B1
Marshall Ct	19	B1
N Marshall St		
(300-399)	3	A2
(600-1299)	19	A1/B1
S Marshall St		
(600-1599)	8	A1/B1
(2300-2749)	10	B2
(2750-2899)	12	A2
Marston Ct	16	A2
N Marston St		
(1300-1649)	16	A2
(1650-2999)	15	A2/B2
S Marston St	5	B2
Martha St	20	A1/A2
Martin St	21	A2
S Martin St	6	A2
N Marvine St		
(200-299)	3	A1
(600-699)	18	A2
S Marvine St		
(700-2749)	7	A2
(2750-2899)	12	A1
N Mascher St		
(1-99)	4	A2
(1200-1299)	19	A2
W Master St		
(1-113)	20	B1
(1717-2524)	17	A1/A2
(2524-2999)	16	A1/A2
S Mattis St	4	B2
E Mayland St	25	B2
E Mc Kean St	11	A2
McCallum St		
(5900-6322)	24	A1
(6345-7055)	25	B1/B2
McClellan St		
(100-449)	11	A1
(450-1331)	10	A1/A2
(1700-2399)	9	A1/A2
McKean Ave	24	B1/B2
McKean St		
(1-449)	11	A1/A2
(450-1449)	10	A1/A2
(1450-2399)	9	A1/A2
McMichael St	23	A2/B2
E McPherson St	26	A2/B1
E Meade St	27	B2
W Meade St	27	B2
E Mechanic St	24	A2
Medina St	8	B1
E Meehan Ave	25	A2
Melon Pl	13	A1
Melon St		
(1000-1749)	18	A1/A2
(1750-3749)	14	A1
(3750-3999)	13	A2
Melon Ter	19	A1/B1
Melvale St	19	A2
S Melville St	13	B1
Memphis St	20	A1/A2/B1
Mercer St	20	A2/B1/B2
Mercy St		
(100-449)	11	A1
(450-1299)	10	A1/A2
(2000-2099)	9	A1
Meredith St		
(2400-2499)	17	B1
(2500-2599)	16	B2
Meredith Walk	13	A1
E Mermaid Ln	26	A1/A2/B1
W Mermaid Ln	26	B1
Merrick Rd		
(3600-4400)	23	A1
(4328-4599)	27	B2
Merrick St	22	A1
Midvale Ave		
(2800-2855)	24	B1
(2856-3799)	23	A1/A2/B1
W Midvale Ave	24	B1
Mifflin St		
(1-449)	11	A1/A2
(450-1415)	10	A1/A2
(1411-2399)	9	A1/A2
S Mildred St		
(600-1499)	8	A1/B1
(2000-2699)	10	A2/B2
(2800-2899)	12	A2
Miller St	20	A2/B2
Millman Pl	27	B2
Millman St	27	B2
Mintzer St	19	B1
Mitchell St		
(3800-4149)	22	A1
(4150-4699)	21	A2
N Mole St	2	A2
S Mole St		
(415-426)	2	B2
(700-1649)	7	A1/B1
(1650-2732)	9	A2/B2
Mollbore Ter	12	A1/A2
Monastery Ave	21	A2/B2
Monroe St	8	A1/A2
E Montana St	25	A2/B2
Monterey St	17	B2
E Montgomery Ave	20	B1
W Montgomery Ave		
(100-127)	20	B1
(2512-3299)	15	B1/B2
Montrose St		
(200-935)	8	A1/A2
(926-1749)	7	A1/A2
(1750-2449)	6	A1/A2
(2450-2599)	5	A2
Montrose Way	8	A1
Montrose Way Hall	8	A1
Monument St	15	B1
Moore St		
(1-449)	11	A1/A2
(450-1407)	10	A1/A2
(1408-2399)	9	A1/A2
Moravian St		
(27-1199)	3	B1/B2
(1400-1949)	2	B1/B2
(1950-2099)	1	B2
(3400-3499)	14	B1
(4400-4499)	13	B1
E Moreland Ave	26	A1/B1
W Moreland Ave	26	B1
E Moreland St	26	A1
Morris St		
(1-463)	11	A1/A2
(464-1415)	10	A1/A2
(1415-2399)	9	A1/A2
(4876-5899)	24	B1/B2
E Morris St	11	A2
Morse St	15	B1
Morton St		
(5500-5799)	24	A2
(6300-6499)	25	B2
E Mount Airy Ave	26	B2
W Mount Airy Ave	25	A1
E Mount Pleasant Ave		
(1-124)	25	A1
(120-499)	26	B2
W Mount Pleasant Ave	25	A1/B1
Mount Vernon St		
(900-1749)	18	B1/B2
(1750-2299)	17	B1/B2
(3100-3749)	14	A1
(3750-3999)	13	A2
Mountain St		
(100-299)	11	A1
(500-1099)	10	A1/A2
(1800-2399)	9	A1/A2
Mower St	25	A1/A2
E Moyamensing Ave		
(900-1615)	8	A2/B2
(1601-2099)	11	A1
W Moyamensing Ave		
(500-1415)	10	B1/B2
(1416-1499)	9	B2
Moyer St	20	A2/B1/B2
Murdoch Rd	26	A2
E Murdoch Rd	26	A2
Musgrave St		
(5500-5628)	24	A2/B2
(6400-6899)	25	A2/B2
Myrtle Pl	18	A2

Street Index

Street Index

Street Index

Street	Map	Grid
W Susquehanna Ave		
(100-126)	20	A1
(2550-3299)	15	B1/B2
Swain St		
(1500-2549)	18	A1
(2550-2999)	16	B2
Swain Walk	13	A1
Swanson St	8	A2
(2700-2799)	11	B2
S Swanson St		
(800-999)	8	A2
(1700-2599)	11	A2/B2
N Sydenham St	18	A1
S Sydenham St		
(200-499)	2	B2
(1100-1199)	7	B1
E Sydney St	26	B2
Tacoma St	24	B1/B2
Taggert St	20	B1
Taney Ct	16	A2
N Taney St		
(700-1299)	16	A2/B2
(1700-2999)	15	A2/B2
S Taney St		
(400-560)	1	B1
(561-1699)	5	A2/B2
Tasker St		
(1-949)	8	B1/B2
(950-1763)	7	B1/B2
(1764-2463)	6	B1/B2
(2464-3399)	5	B1/B2
E Tasker St	8	B2
N Taylor St	17	A1/B1
S Taylor St	6	B1
Terminal Ave	12	B1
Terrace St		
(3700-4058)	22	A1
(4059-4399)	21	B2
Thomas Mill Dr	27	B1
Thomas Paine Pl	4	B2
Thompson St	20	A2
E Thompson St	20	A2/B1/B2
W Thompson St		
(1-121)	20	B2
(1700-2535)	17	A1/A2
(2526-3199)	16	A1/A2
Tibben St	21	A1
Tilden St	23	A1/A2
Tilton St	20	B2
Timber Ln	23	A1
Titan St		
(100-599)	8	B1/B2
(1100-1749)	7	B1/B2
(1750-2299)	6	B1/B2
(2600-3099)	5	B1/B2
Tohopeka Ln	27	B2
Towanda St	27	B1
Tower St	21	B2
Townsend St	20	B1
Tree St		
(100-449)	11	B1
(450-1299)	10	B1/B2
(1800-1899)	9	B2
Trenton Ave	20	A1/A2/B1
Trotters Aly	4	A2
Tryon St	1	B2
E Tucker St	20	A2
Tulip St	20	A1/A2/B1
E Tulip St	20	A2
E Tulpehocken St	25	B2
W Tulpehocken St	24	A1
Turner St		
(100-149)	20	B1
(2501-3299)	16	A1/A2
N Uber St	17	A2/B2
S Uber St	2	B1
Umbria St	21	A1
N Union St	13	A2
United States Highway 13	14	B1
S University Ave		
(400-517)	14	B1
(518-698)	5	A1
University Brdg Ave	5	A1
University Mews	5	A1
E Upsal St	25	A2/B2
W Upsal St	25	B1/B2
Utah St	24	A1/A2
Valley View Rd	27	A1
Van Horn St	19	A2
N Van Pelt St	1	A2
S Van Pelt St	1	A2/B2
Vandalia St	11	A2/B2
Vare Ave	5	B1
Vassar St	22	D1
Vaux St	23	A1/A2/B2
E Vernon Rd	25	A2
Vicaris St	22	A2
Vine St		
(1-548)	4	A1/A2
(1099-1299)	3	A1/A2/B2
(1399-1899)	2	A1/A2
(1900-1999)	1	A2
Vine Street Expy		
	3	A2
	19	B1
	17	A2
Vineyard St	17	A2
Vollmer St	10	B2
Wade St	24	B2
Wadsworth Ave	26	A2
Wakefield St	24	A1/A2
Walden St	1	A1
Wallace St		
(400-799)	19	B1
(900-1749)	18	B1/B2
(1750-2399)	17	B1/B2
(3100-3749)	14	A1
(3750-4399)	13	A1/A2
E Walnut Ln	24	A1
W Walnut Ln	24	A1
Walnut St		
(100-649)	4	B1/B2
(650-1312)	3	B1/B2
(1313-1952)	2	B1/B2
(1953-2638)	1	B1/B2
(2639-3849)	14	B1/B2
(3850-4622)	13	B1/B2
Warden Dr	23	A1
Warfield Ave	5	B1
S Warfield St	5	B1
Warnock Pl	18	A2
Warnock St	18	A2
N Warnock St	18	B2
S Warnock St		
(200-299)	3	B1
(700-1399)	7	A2/B2
(1900-2699)	10	A1/B1
(2800-2899)	12	A1
Warren St		
(3400-3798)	14	A1
(3800-4199)	13	A1/A2
Washington Ave		
(2-899)	8	A1/B1/B2
(900-1730)	7	A1/A2
(1762-2398)	6	A1/A2
(2498-2698)	5	A2
E Washington Ln	25	B2
W Washington Ln	24	A1
S Washington Sq	3	B2
N Washington Sq	3	B2
N Water St		
(200-323)	4	A2
(324-499)	19	B2
S Water St		
(900-1649)	8	A2/B2
(1650-2499)	11	A2/B2
Waterman Ave	27	A1
Watkins St		
(100-449)	11	A1
(450-1199)	10	A1/A2
(1700-2399)	9	A1/A2
Watts St	18	A1
N Watts St		
(100-299)	2	A1
(600-1199)	18	A1/B1
S Watts St		
(200-499)	2	B2
(700-1649)	7	A1/B1
(1650-2699)	10	A1/B1
Waverly St		
(698-1379)	3	B1/B2
(1380-1962)	2	B1/B2
(1963-2999)	1	B1/B2
Waverly Walk	3	B1
Wayne Ave	24	A1/B1/B2
Weatham St	25	A1
Weaver St	25	B2
W Weaver St	25	B2
Webb St	20	A2/B2
Webster St		
(600-663)	8	A1
(1100-1749)	7	A1/A2
(1750-2199)	6	A1/A2
(2500-2799)	5	A2
Weccacoe Ave	11	A2/B2
Weightman St	22	B2
Wellesley Rd	25	A1
Wendle Ct	19	B1
Wendover St		
(100-199)	21	B2
(200-299)	22	A1
West River Dr		
	14	A1/A2
	16	B2
Westminster Ave	13	A1
Westmont St	15	B1/B2
W Westmoreland St	23	B2
Westview St	25	B2
W Westview St	25	A2/B1

Street Index

Become Official.

Register online at www.notfortourists.com today.

Official NFT Members receive:

- access to the complete **NFT** online database
- the ability to rate **NFT** listings
- access to our entire guidebook series in PDF form
- event listings
- 10% discount on **NFT** books & apparel purchased on our website
- special promotions
- your very own handy dandy Official **NFT** Member Patch
- and oh, so much more!!

Become an Official **NFT** Member and you'll gain entry to exclusive areas on our website including information about discounts, special promotions, and access to TONS of great new online content available to Official **NFT** Members ONLY.